Essays on Latin Lyric,
Elegy, and Epic

PRINCETON SERIES OF COLLECTED ESSAYS

This series was initiated in response to requests from students and teachers who want the best essays of leading scholars available in a convenient format. Each book in this series serves scholarship by gathering in one place previously published articles representing the valuable contribution of a noted authority to his field. The format allows for the addition of a preface or introduction and an index to enhance the collection's usefulness. Photoreproduction of the essays keeps costs to a minimum and thus makes possible publication in a relatively inexpensive form.

MICHAEL C.J. PUTNAM

Essays
on Latin Lyric,
Elegy, and
Epic

Princeton University Press : Princeton, New Jersey

For
Charles Babcock, Helen North,
and Kenneth Reckford

CONTENTS

PREFACE

The essays gathered in this volume were originally published in various scholarly journals during the past two decades. They are devoted to five of Rome's master poets of the late Republican and early Augustan periods. All are exercises in practical criticism. They attempt to describe and evaluate work of importance and maintain its accessibility to readers of both ancient and modern literature. More often than not my subject is a single poem deserving of renewed interest or a fresh reading, but occasionally the method is comparative, ranging poem against poem or author against author. In one instance, the second essay on Propertius, I have focused specifically on the imaginative structure of a complete book of poems, and the final piece touches on certain themes and ideas that serve to unify Virgil's poetry as a whole.

I have categorized the essays by genres and by authors who, with one exception, are themselves arranged chronologically. The exception is Virgil, the oldest of the Augustan writers. I have placed him after the writers of lyric and elegy to honor the ancient primacy of epic, and in particular to acknowledge the continued vitality of his monumental accomplishment. Within each authorial cluster I have followed the poems' numerical order based on manuscript traditions handed down from antiquity.

The fourth poem of Catullus is my starting point. I presume for it the appearance of autobiography: a boat trip links the coming of spring and the consequent awakening of the poet's desire to return home (poem 46) with the satisfaction of that yearning upon his arrival at Sirmio (poem 31). The style is noteworthy for the brisk immediacy of its narration. But since the skiff is also an emblem for life's leap from birth to senescence, the poem itself is metaphoric for the brilliant tuggings between naiveté and sophistication, the spontaneous and the studied, passion and learning, that so enliven Catullus' poetry. Tension takes a generic turn in poem 11 where lyric verse patterning replaces the iambs usual in invective, and the imagery of Sappho is twisted against her namesake, Lesbia, as complement to her own perversion of the speaker's fragile inner world. A defense of the reading *tritius* at line 13 of Catullus' twenty-second poem leads to a brief look at another main Catullan theme, the need to distinguish between exterior and interior, surface and substance, and the importance of self-distance and self-reflection in this process.

My treatment of the little drinking song, 27, suggests a parallel antinomy, continually at hand in Catullus' poetry, of vulnerable ideal and polluting reality. In the more expanded analysis of poem 64, Catullus' masterpiece, my goal is to illustrate how the *persona* of Catullus as intense spokesman of the lyric "I" equally enriches the detached elaboration of myth. The contrast between happy and wretched love here finds a counterpoint in the transition, incipient with the sailing of the *Argo*, from a visionary communion of gods and mortals in the past to a corrupt present. Finally, poem 66, though a translation of a segment from the fourth book of Callimachus' *Aetia* in which he tells of Berenice and her lock of hair enshrined in the heavens, offers a further instance of Catullus' attraction to the theme of separation and desertion, and bears his imprint throughout, especially in lines 75-88 which seem an original addition to Callimachus' text.

The first essay on Horace studies the figuration of death in love, and love as death, in the famous ode to Pyrrha (1. 5). The reason for Atlas' presence in a poem addressed to his grandson Mercury is the subject of the brief paper on the structure of *Odes* 1. 10. In the critique of *Odes* 1. 20 I watch Horace utilize the metaphor of economics in evaluating his friendship with Maecenas. In the analysis of *Odes* 3. 9 my concern centers on the varied patternings of lovers' rhetoric and with Catullus' distinctive treatment of a similar theme in his poem 45. I see the essential point of *Odes* 3. 15 in Horace's deployment of words as a verbal imagining of human grace or inelegance. The last essay devoted solely to Horace traces his allusions to religion and political power when assaying his own metaphysical accomplishment.

My discussion of Horace's two poems addressed to Tibullus serves as a transition to four articles on the elegists. In *Odes* 1. 33 Horace makes intricate use of the figure of oxymoron to warn his friend against taking love's vicissitudes too seriously, and again in *Epistles* 1. 4 humor and a bemused perspective on one's self is the poem's saving message. The single treatment of Tibullus alone seeks to further the recent revival of interest in that neglected poet through a close look at aspects of his so-called "simple" style. There follow three pieces on his contemporary elegist, Propertius. The first examines 1. 22, the "seal" poem of the first book, watching the poet define himself, literally, by proximity to the destruction of civil war, and generically, by reference to the sepulchral epigram, a still potent force in the heritage of Roman subjective elegy. The second essay, outlining various structures of Propertius' third book, deals especially with the interaction of subjective and objective elements as the poet manifests his deepened distress over Roman amorality. The final essay devoted to Propertius looks in detail at one complex poem from the third book, 22, in which the speaker urges his friend Tullus away from a life of wandering and militaristic adventure toward acceptance of familial and civic responsibilities in Rome itself.

The last group of papers is devoted to Virgil. One is concerned with the first *eclogue*, three with individual books of the *Aeneid*, and a concluding study surveys reasons why we continue to honor his poetry.

My treatment of Virgil's initial *bucolic* seeks to define pastoral space in terms of a rhetoric of literal and figurative enclosure in which vertical, horizontal, and circular elements each play a part. In my analysis of the third book of the *Aeneid* I first evaluate the interplay of impetuosity and learning in Aeneas' progress toward the founding of Rome, and then set this stretch of experience as a crucial element in the first third of the epic. In the next paper I trace the theme of metamorphosis, either downward from man to animal or evolutionary in a negative sense—from pastoral to martial, from golden to more iron times—as basic to the *Aeneid*'s seventh book. Metamorphosis is also an essential motif in my interpretation of *Aeneid* 10 as Aeneas, after killing Lausus, alters from fervid actor to contemplator of *imagines*, living the intricate pattern of physical doing and intellectual pondering that operates in the epic from the second book on. The meaning of the poem's finale, as Aeneas kills his humbled adversary Turnus and Virgil concludes not with praise (or blame) of his titular hero but rather with the soul of Turnus going indignant to the shades, is a recurring theme in all four essays. Discussion of it is central to my overview of the Virgilian achievement, which surveys certain patterns of thought that run throughout his poetic career.

To read one's writing from a twenty-year period is to experience all too clearly the humbling axiom that criticism is an evanescent procedure, one moment's, one person's idiosyncratic view of the permanent excellence of the masterworks with which classicists are privileged to deal. There are details that I would emend and more substantial matters of interpretation that cry out for further examination and elaboration. For instance, much extraordinary work has been done on Catullus 64 since I wrote in 1961, work which apprehends the crucial role of the poem in the evolution of Rome's understanding of the ambiguities of its historical destiny. I feel also that some of my earlier work on Virgil places too much stress on the emotionalism of the *Aeneid* at the expense of the idealism that serves as foil to its negativity. Nevertheless, I cherish the hope that the present collection will be of value in fostering the continued appreciation of Latin poetry, which is to say, of one of the basic documents of our humanistic heritage.

In the two articles reprinted from *Arethusa*, "Propertius' Third Book" and "*Pius* Aeneas and the Metamorphosis of Lausus," references in the notes are given in abbreviated form. For full citations readers are referred to the relevant issues of *Arethusa* (Spring 1980 and Spring 1981), where comprehensive bibliographies appear at the back.

Finally, I must thank my colleagues and students at Brown, whose stimulus and encouragement fostered these essays, and Mrs. Frances Eisenhauer for her loyal help in their improvement.

Providence, Rhode Island   Michael C. J. Putnam

SOURCES AND ACKNOWLEDGMENTS

I wish to thank the following editors, journals, and publishers for gracious permission to reprint these essays:

"Catullus' Journey," *Classical Philology* 57 (1962), 10-19. Reprinted by permission of the University of Chicago Press, copyright 1962 by the University of Chicago.

"Catullus 11: The Ironies of Integrity," *Ramus* 3 (1974), 70-86. Reprinted by permission of Aureal Publications.

"Catullus 22. 13," *Hermes* 96 (1968), 552-58. Reprinted by permission of *Hermes* and Franz Steiner Verlag, GMBH.

"On Catullus 27," *Latomus* 28 (1969), 850-57. Reprinted by permission of *Latomus*.

"The Art of Catullus 64," *Harvard Studies in Classical Philology*, 65 (1961), 165-205. Reprinted by permission of the publishers from *Harvard Studies in Classical Philology*, Volume LXV, Cambridge, Mass.: Harvard University Press, Copyright © 1961 by the President and Fellows of Harvard College.

"Catullus 66. 75-88," *Classical Philology* 55 (1960), 223-28. Reprinted by permission of the University of Chicago Press, copyright 1960 by the University of Chicago.

"Horace *Carm*. 1. 5: Love and Death," *Classical Philology* 65 (1970), 251-54. Reprinted by permission of the University of Chicago Press, copyright 1970 by the University of Chicago.

"Mercuri, facunde nepos Atlantis," *Classical Philology* 69 (1974), 215-17. Reprinted by permission of the University of Chicago Press, copyright 1974 by the University of Chicago.

"Horace *c*. 1. 20," *Classical Journal* 64 (1969), 153-57. Reprinted by permission of *Classical Journal*.

"Horace Odes 3. 9: The Dialectics of Desire," *Ancient and Modern: Essays in Honor of Gerald F. Else* (Ann Arbor, 1977), 139-57. Reprinted by permission of the editors, John H. D'Arms and John W. Eadie, and of the University of Michigan.

"Horace *Odes* 3. 15: The Design of *Decus*," *Classical Philology* 71 (1976), 90-96. Reprinted by permission of the University of Chicago Press, copyright 1976 by the University of Chicago.

"Horace *C*. 3. 30: The Lyricist as Hero," *Ramus* 2 (1973), 1-19. Reprinted by permission of Aureal Publications.

"Horace and Tibullus," *Classical Philology* 67 (1972), 81-88. Reprinted by permission of the University of Chicago Press, copyright 1972 by the University of Chicago.

"Simple Tibullus and the Ruse of Style," *Yale French Studies* 45 (1970), 21-32. Reprinted by permission of *Yale French Studies*.

"Propertius 1. 22: A Poet's Self-Definition," *Quaderni Urbinati di Cultura Classica* 23 (1976), 93-123. Reprinted by permission of *Quaderni Urbinati di Cultura Classica*.

"Propertius' Third Book: Patterns of Cohesion," *Arethusa* 13 (1980), 97-113. Reprinted by permission of *Arethusa*.

"Propertius 3. 22: Tullus' Return," *Illinois Classical Studies* 2 (1977), 240-54. Reprinted by permission of the University of Illinois Press.

"Virgil's First *Eclogue*: Poetics of Enclosure," from A. J. Boyle (ed.), *Ancient Pastoral: Ramus Essays on Greek and Roman Pastoral Poetry* (Berwick, Vic., 1975), 81-104. Reprinted by permission of Aureal Publications.

"The Third Book of the *Aeneid*: From Homer to Rome," *Ramus* 9 (1980), 1-21. Reprinted by permission of Aureal Publications.

"*Aeneid* 7 and the *Aeneid*," *American Journal of Philology* 91 (1970), 408-30. Reprinted by permission of the Johns Hopkins University Press.

"*Pius* Aeneas and the Metamorphosis of Lausus," *Arethusa* 14 (1981), 139-56. Reprinted by permission of *Arethusa*.

"The Virgilian Achievement," *Arethusa* 5 (1972), 53-70. Reprinted by permission of *Arethusa*.

Catullus

CATULLUS' JOURNEY (*Carm.* 4)

MICHAEL C. J. PUTNAM

RARELY has a poem been subjected to exegesis exhibiting more violent contrasts than Catullus' *Phaselus ille* (*Carm.* 4).[1] Critical approaches toward it, almost Protean in their variety, run the gamut from complete empirical belief in the reality of the ship, that is to say, from unquestioned acceptance of the poet's objectivity, to equally strong partisanship of a quite opposite view, wherein the ship becomes a kind of mystic symbol and the poem, literally considered, scarcely referable to Catullus at all.

Even by those who concede the reality of the ship, it has been debated whether it could, not to say did, make such a journey as the poet describes. To those for whom the journey appears partly fact and partly fiction, the vessel becomes merely the ex-voto model through which the poet offers homage to Castor and Pollux for his safe return. Finally, progressing from thorough involvement on the poet's part with the ship to an equally complete lack of personal interest, the *phaselus* takes on, for some, a purely imaginary character and the poem is considered a sudden *jeu d'esprit*, written solely for the amusement of guests at the poet's Garda villa. Many other positions between these two extremes have also been proposed by exegetes of the poem.[2]

The most compelling argument against the last approach, that the poem is a purely illusory and imagined experience, is the fact that Catullus' mind, as opposed to Horace's, say, just does not work that way, that tangible, sensory experience was to him the essence of all poetic production. The "symbolic" theory would have had fewer supporters, and there would have been less learned quarreling about the poem, if, in the early stages of discussion, the first explanation had received due attention; if, that is to say, it had been shown that Catullus could have bought a yacht in Bithynia and sailed with it not only to the mouth of the Po but up the Mincio and into the Lago di Garda, on the shore of which Sirmio, the poet's peninsular home, was situated. Yet it is only recently that this route has been authoritatively demonstrated by Svennung to be possible, even probable.[3] He has shown that ancient techniques of navigation up a small river made such a trip as this up the Mincio by no means unusual. Therefore, if Catullus says that he made such a voyage and if the ancient evidence supports his statement, we should accept it as true.

Yet, since many of the problems the poem poses are of a practical rather than interpretative nature, the poetic qualities have rarely been allowed to shine through the exegetical haze. Assuming Svennung's conclusions, that it *was* Catullus' ship and that it did make the very journey the poem describes, I propose to examine some of the ways by which the poet elaborates and enhances the literal aspects of the journey, both in 4 itself and in other related poems.

I shall begin by stressing the fact that no interpretation of 4 which looks to that poem alone can do it justice. It stands, as we shall see, finely unified by itself. But this unity is enhanced by our knowledge and possession of two other poems of Catullus bound closely to 4. These are 46, written before the poet's departure from the east, and 31, the product of his safe and happy arrival back home. Though its quality of reminiscence clearly suggests that it was composed after the address to Sirmio, our poem forms the geographic and literary bridge between these two. It takes the poet from the heat of Nicaea (the setting of 46) into the waves of Lake Garda, translating the eagerness of the mind into the reality of the voyage, the thought into the physical reaction. At the same time it forms the central piece of a lyric trilogy. All three poems complement one another, and each is necessary for the full understanding of the remaining two. Thus the three form a close-knit cycle, the subject of which is the total sweep of Catullus' journey.[4] Literary form is, as a result, perfectly matched with content which, in turn, reflects the rise and fall of an emotion both in and, at the same time, beyond any reference to time and space.

To realize the tight structure of this design, we must first turn away from an examination of the journey itself to the two poems which precede and follow it, 46 and 31. Only when the close connection between these two poems has been demonstrated can it be shown how crucial the position of 4 is in the chain of which they are the beginning and final links. This is not to say that Catullus, writing in Bithynia on the eve of his departure, knew exactly how his imagination would respond when he had finally arrived at his beloved Sirmio, in the same way as Dante, say, was in general aware of the shape and content of the concluding cantos of *Paradiso* as he began the initial part of his *Commedia*. Yet Catullus has given us clear proof that, at his journey's end, his thoughts returned to the manner in which he had expressed his emotion preparatory to taking leave of Bithynia. Let us observe some of the hints he provides.

Poem 46 opens with the coming of spring and continues with a description of the desire for travel which the newborn world arouses in Catullus. Only when we reach the end of the poem and he addresses his companions as those "longe quos simul a domo profectos / diversae variae viae reportant . . ." (10–11) does it become clear that all the initial thoughts, devoted to spring and to the wish to wander, are products of one central desire, to return home. The poet's mind moves swiftly from one thought to the other, so that the coming of spring, which *refert tepores*, leads, in the end, to the devious routes which bring (*reportant*) the poet and his friends back home.[5] And the thought, once conceived, receives immediate physical response as his feet sympathetically absorb the themes of creativity and wandering which spring proposes. Linked as are these ideas, their unity rests with the image of the *domus*. And the *domus*, as we learn explicitly in 31. 14, is, of course, Sirmio.

The poet makes the connection clear when, with appropriate change of mood, he repeats the imagery of 46. 4–5, "linquantur Phrygii, Catulle, campi / Nicaeaeque ager uber aestuosae," at 31. 5–6, "vix mi ipse credens Thuniam atque Bithunos / liquisse campos et videre te in tuto." The emotion first experienced in Bithynia is similar to that which he experiences upon arrival at Sirmio, the only difference being that 46 portrays the birth of yearning, contemporaneous with the coming of spring, while 31 denotes its fulfilment. The feeling of mind which comes to the poet in his faraway province ("iam mens prae-trepidans avet vagari," 46. 7), the pent-up tension which must arise when a long road stretches ahead at the conclusion of which lies a destination which symbolizes love, ends only in Sirmio "cum mens onus reponit, ac peregrino / labore fessi venimus larem ad nostrum" (31. 8–9). The happy feet of the poet, in 46. 8, eager to begin their way, become the figure of the poet himself as he looks happily on his beloved peninsula after safe arrival (31. 4).

These two poems, therefore, run on two levels which are so interconnected as hardly to be separable. On the one hand there is the actual description of the journey's beginning and end, but this is also equivalent to the emotion of desire, the journey's cause, which is aroused in 46 and attained in 31. For this reason, it is important to observe carefully the imagery through which the poet conjures up his final picture of Sirmio.

In its careful craftsmanship and balanced structure 31 closely resembles 46, but the emotional content is conveyed in a manner much more complex. Partially this arises from an undercurrent of ambiguity which runs throughout the piece. It appears in the opening lines: "Paene insularum, Sir-mio, insularumque / ocelle, . . ." The word *ocelle* produces an inner effect. The commentators tell us that it means "gem" and cite a passage in

which Cicero calls his villas *ocellos Italiae*.[6] But Catullus uses this diminutive elsewhere only when addressing a person dear to him. Thus he adjures Calvus "nunc audax cave sis, precesque nostras, / oramus, cave despuas, ocelle, . . ." (50. 18–19). *Ocelle* in 31, there-fore, is equivocal. It seems to be directed to the gleaming beauty of the peninsula jutting out into the Garda. Yet it could with equal validity be applied to a person. This inherent ambiguity gathers force from line 4, where the personification becomes more explicit: "quam te libenter quamque laetus inviso." In the intensity of his feelings, Catullus begins to treat Sirmio as if it did indeed momentarily appear to him as his little eye of love. The word *inviso* means not only to "visit," as it should if applicable to a place, but also to "see and look at." The lines which follow clarify still further this double meaning:

vix mi ipse credens Thuniam atque Bithunos
liquisse campos et videre te in tuto.
o quid solutis est beatius curis,
cum mens onus reponit, ac peregrino
labore fessi venimus larem ad nostrum,
desideratoque acquiescimus lecto [5–10]?

A comparison with similar thoughts in 9, another poem where the focus of attention is on returning home, offers the best commentary on these verses. Catullus asks Veranius

venistine domum ad tuos penates
fratresque unanimos anumque matrem?
venisti! o mihi nuntii beati!
visam te incolumem audiamque Hiberum
narrantem loca, facta, nationes . . . [9. 3–7].

We should note that the position of Catullus is different in the two poems. In 9 he is at home, welcoming Veranius from abroad, experiencing the same emotions as does Sirmio in 31, upon receiving the poet back after his prolonged absence. But the scope of imagery common to the two poems shows that in each case the poet's emotional pattern is following the same course. To Sirmio he says, picking up the initial idea of "seeing" (*inviso*), how happy he is to return safe and sound (*videre te in tuto*). Likewise he will now look upon Veranius, returned without misfortune (*visam te incolumem*). Veranius had come safely back to family and friends just as Catullus did to Sirmio. Of his own home the poet states *venimus larem ad nostrum*, while, with the requisite change of person, to Veranius he asks "venistine domum ad tuos penates . . . ?" (9. 3). And the interrogative is changed to the positive *venisti!* in line 5, as if the poet had suddenly become sure that the news was true. Examples could be multiplied.

The point here is that Catullus depicts his own feelings upon seeing Sirmio in the same manner as he does when speaking to the newly returned Veranius. The *domus*, the symbol upon which the strongest of Catullus' emotions always centered, in the long poems as well as short, becomes here not only the old home but its personification, whom Catullus addresses in terms of deep emotion.[7] And so the desire, born in 46, finds its fulfilment, as journey, in the sight of the lake and of the familiar *lar*, as emotion, in line 10 where Catullus asks "desideratoque acquiescimus lecto ?" The cycle has been completed.[8]

This brings us to the final lines of the poem, another direct address which balances the opening invocation:

salve, o venusta Sirmio, atque ero gaude:
gaudete vosque, o Lydiae lacus undae:
ridete, quidquid est domi cachinnorum.

The implications of the word *venusta* are not now unexpected. Though such an adjective might well be applied to a geographical spot, it only takes on its full significance if applied to a woman, whose beauty manifests inner charm. Likewise, the *cachinni* suggest the roar which waves make lapping against one another when wind strikes the water (so also in 64. 273), but it may also be the raucous noise of joyous laughter. Both meanings are possible here, both, no doubt, intentional, for the wit which *venusta* assumes may also manifest itself in the *cachinni*. When Fabullus is invited to the poet's for dinner, it is expected that he will bring with him wine, salt, and laughter ("et vino et sale et omnibus cachinnis," 13. 5). And we note the manner in which Catullus addresses Fabullus as he immediately adds "haec si, inquam, attuleris, *venuste noster*, / cenabis bene; . . ." (13. 6–7). And how important the sound of loud laughter is on occasions such as this the poet shows when he begs Sirmio to ring out with shouts of glee. Likewise the intimations of personal beauty which the word *venusta* carries[9] are intensified and further realized in the phrase *ero gaude*, and both reinforce the idea of personification.[10] The power of the poet's emotions finds its ultimate expression in the request he makes of Sirmio to share his feelings of joy.

This heightened emotional diction comes in part from poem 4, to which we now turn. We will assume, at the start, that the poet did indeed make the journey he describes through the world of the Aegean. One main critical objection, however, remains to be countered before this hypothesis can be completely acceptable. It is often assumed, from what the poet says in 46, that he was planning a land journey at least as far as the *claras Asiae urbes* and that, therefore, only some of the places named in 4. 6–9 could have been visited by Catullus, at least on this particular trip. And so, the argument continues, if some of the stops on the itinerary of 4 can be thus called in question, why is not the rest of the catalogue placed in jeopardy, why, in short, is it not easier to call the poem purely imaginative? It is best here to look at the metaphors themselves on which this assumption of a land journey is based. In 46. 8, for example, Catullus states "iam laeti studio pedes vigescunt." Now if the word *pedes* be taken, as it is even by Svennung, as proof of a trip by land, then we may equally well assume that Catullus was going to walk his way down the coast of Asia Minor! But this is a poem describing the coming of spring and what effect this event has on the poet personally. He himself is *laetus*, but his happiness arises from the newly reborn desire for home. And so, understandably enough, he transfers the rebirth of nature and of his own longing to his feet because it is through them, metaphorically, that the desire finds its first impulse to be up and going.[11]

There is one other word, again used metaphorically, which strongly suggests that this interpretation is correct, *volemus*. This, too, has no connection with a land journey. Rather, the tense quality of the poet's emotion leads to a wish for speed, for the speed of flying, in fact, and it is this which the poet, crucially enough, transfers to or, better, concentrates on the *phaselus*, which claims to be the swiftest ever fashioned, a ship which none could surpass "sive palmulis / opus foret volare sive linteo."[12] The transition is now easy to the itinerary of the voyage:

et hoc negat minacis Hadriatici
negare litus insulasve Cycladas
Rhodumque nobilem horridamque Thraciam
Propontida trucemve Ponticum sinum, . . .
　[6–9].

Thus the poem is in a sense the log of a very special and exciting journey. But the boat does more than merely carry its master (*erum*, 19) home, it *is* his emotion.[13] It is just this sudden wish for speed on his part that the boat can supply. Only through speed will the *quies* for which he yearns be attained. At the moment when the poem was composed, clearly some little time after the return home, the poet relives his past feelings which placed more emphasis on the vessel's speed than on the actual geography of the trip. Indeed, when he does turn to a mention of place names, in line 6, it is only to show that no spot they passed could deny such unusual ability on the vessel's part.

The stress on speed is not the only way in which Catullus betrays his emotional involvement. The description of the journey's excitement is heightened, also, by the personification of the yacht, a device we have seen the poet utilize to great effect in 31. Just as Sirmio seems to be deliberately portrayed for a moment as a person of flesh and blood, so also it is only right that the *phaselus*, which symbolizes the speed of desire, should be treated in the same manner as the end of longing. The boat carries its *erus* to Sirmio; now Sirmio must, in turn, rejoice at his arrival. Indeed, the *hospites* are expected to listen with understanding as the yacht tells its own tale (and to suspend disbelief of such a possibility in order to become willingly involved in the strength of the poet's emotion) and to visualize it not as the poet's pawn but as the possessor, through the poet, of a life all its own.[14]

We begin to sense this in the opening lines. The geographical catalogue adds to the impression. Instead of merely giving a straightforward enumeration of his stopping places, beginning in Bithynia and ending in his beloved Garda, the poet reverses the order, and takes the reader backward, through Adriatic, Aegean, and Black Sea, through the transition from forest to boat, to the crest of Mount Cytorus "ubi iste post phaselus antea fuit / comata silva." Even then the wood whistled and spoke, a clue to its future function as a storyteller. The lines which describe Mount Cytorus (10–16) form the center of the poem (and, in a sense, of the whole cycle from 46 to 31). Since there is a deliberate balance of language and thought on either side of this middle section, the poem manifests what is usually called the ὀμφαλός technique, so common in Alexandrian poetry.[15] Here, as in the poem on Attis, structure and content are unified through the symbol of the mountain which forms not only the rhetorical apex of the poem but the turning point of its emotion as well (and, in the case of 63, the emotional focus toward which desire is heightened only to fall away into despair).

In 4, however, the mountain top is not the goal of sensation but only its beginning. The desire, described in 46, found its start in Bithynia; and, logically enough, if the boat is the personification of desire, Catullus must establish the origin of his emotion at the actual birth of the boat itself. And this he does as he takes the reader back through the turmoil of the seas to the top of Mount Cytorus, to what was and still is most clearly related (cognitissima) to the vessel as it began its progress through the world.

This special use of the symbol of the mountain is not unique in Catullus. The initial section of 64 furnishes another example of the close connection in Catullus' mind between mountain top, journey by ship, and the birth of desire:

Peliaco quondam prognatae vertice pinus
dicuntur liquidas Neptuni nasse per undas
Phasidos ad fluctus . . .

Except that Pelion replaces Cytorus, and that the mountain-top scene forms the beginning and not the center of the poem, the geographical and emotional situations are closely parallel.[16] The newborn ships each ride with rushing speed toward their destinations. This, in the case of the Argo, changes smoothly from the seamen's search for the golden fleece to Peleus' love for Thetis. Once these two have met, there is no further need for sea journey or ship, and the poem's action, by means of a subtle reference to Tethys and Oceanus, gradually switches from water to land to the wedding itself, where desire, born of the ocean journey and, ultimately, of the mountain top itself, is fulfilled.

From this center in 4 Catullus now reverses direction and, balancing the geographical exposition, gives what might be called a meteorological guide homeward as he puts the emphasis not on the particular place names but on the more universal wind, tide, and shore, until the arrival at Garda. Then in the end, with a temporal change of which Catullus is especially fond,[17] we come out of the violence of the past journey to the calm lake which comprises the *quies* (26) of the present.

It is, of course, in part to this very *quies* that Catullus alludes during the course of poem 31, for the *limpidum lacum* of 4. 24 is surely formed of no other waves than the *Lydiae lacus undae* which the poet asks to rejoice at the end of 31 and which gain by comparison with all the other *liquentibus stagnis* (31. 2) through which the poet has passed on his return journey. The poem's opening lines, in which Sirmio stands pre-eminent among all isles "quascumque in liquentibus stagnis / marique vasto fert uterque Neptunus," are but a comprehensive summary of 4, taking the reader along with the yacht "a mari / novissimo hunc ad usque limpidum lacum" (23–24). During the course from Cytorus to Garda, whether through water fresh or salt, nothing equaled Sirmio for beauty, in the poet's estimation. And since the boat is also a reflection of the poet and his yearning for home, nothing equaled the little yacht for speed and intensity as it made its way back to *venusta Sirmio*.

It is not only geographical exposition, however, which joins one poem with the other. The emotional schema, begun in 46 and continued in 4, reaches its conclusion, as we have seen, in 31, a poem which, tightly unified in its own structure, looks to the other poems for completion just as one book of the *Aeneid* looks to another for commentary on its own place in the epic as a whole. The ambiguity of the phrase *solutis curis*, in 31. 7, is a case in point. If *cura* be taken in its usual erotic sense of "longing,"[18] then the words form part of the strand of sensual imagery woven around the figure of Sirmio and hence are to be restricted specifically to the organic aspects of 31. If, on the other hand, the *curae* are "trials" or "cares," in the word's more general sense, then they are synonymous with one aspect of the *onus* of 31. 8 which the poet's mind can now put behind it, namely the *peregrino labore* of lines 8–9. Looking back at 4, the *labor* of journeying embraces the *impotentia freta* through which the poet traveled in such safety (and this fact, too, is reiterated in 31. 6)

that no vows whatsoever had to be made to deities of the shores. Thus there seems to be almost a deliberate analogy between the *quies* of the boat (4. 26) and the joy which the phrase *desideratoque acquiescimus lecto* (31. 10) makes manifest. They are one and the same, since rest at the journey's end postulates fulfilment of the poet's desire.

Likewise the word *vix* in "vix mi ipse credens Thuniam atque Bithunos / liquisse campos et videre te in tuto" (31. 5–6) stresses again the two spheres in which 31 should be interpreted. If the poet is expressing his pleasure at the accomplishment of a journey with a safety for which he had dared not hope—and recalling the yearning for home from which he suffered in Bithynia—then these lines become strictly limited to the context of 31. Yet they can with equal aptness be taken as a reference to the sudden and swift completion of the passage. And this brings the reader's thoughts back not only to 46 but to the whole of 4.

In short, the *phaselus* of 4 is both real and symbolic at the same time. It is real because it accomplished a journey of some difficulty over the Mediterranean Sea, and it is symbolic because it stands for Catullus himself and his desire. Like the poet's yearning for home which the newly reborn spring activates, it grows green with its *comata silva*, is heightened in the *impotentia freta* of the separating sea, and reaching fruition becomes calm as the poet gains the *quies* of Sirmio.

If we consider 4 by itself, it is the sea which is the basic unifying force of the poem, for it is against the background of the sea that the journey of the *phaselus* takes place and against which the scale of its accomplishment is measured. In this respect the poem

9

bears a close resemblance to 63. Attis also is sailing on the swift ship (*celeri rate*) of his desire through the deep floods which part him from his beloved goddess. In his case the change from sea to the place of emasculation is so rapid that no mention of the shore is even made. When once the basic urge has been accomplished, it remains for him only to climb the mountain to the *domus* of fulfilment on its top. The sea does return for a brief moment in Attis' speech of exhortation to his companions: "rapidum salum tulistis truculentaque pelagi," he says (1. 16).[19] The *truculenta . . . pelagi* correspond to the *impotentia freta* through which the yacht steered an unerring course. But the chief difference between the two poems cannot be observed until Attis reaches the top of the mountain and learns that the *domus* for which he yearned, contrary to the poet's own, has turned out utterly false. From then on the sea becomes one of the crucial images of the poem, not as a symbol of the voyage of desire, as in 4, but rather of eternal separation from true home and true love. At this moment, as at many others, Attis and Ariadne, similarly helpless on the shore, are one and the same. It is only by deliberate and direct comparison with their plight that all the vividness and excitement of Catullus' own journey can be realized and the intensity of their suffering understood.

The image of the *impotentia freta* leads to yet another level of interpretation. The ship now becomes more than an object of special reference to the poet and, if only for a moment, seems to stand as a paradigm for the life of mankind, for the journey of existence,. freed from exact reference to the present and looking beyond that to a more universal archetype. From

birth (*origine*, 15) to old age (*senet quiete*, 26) with the roaring floods between, this is the course of the poet's emotion; but it also suggests something apart from and beyond his own particular factual and emotional voyage, namely, the journey of life itself.

In this sense, the course of the *phaselus* is ideal rather than actual, at least in relation to Catullus' own life. In 68 he compares himself, love-sick for Lesbia, to sailors on a storm-tossed sea, for whom a gentle and benign breeze is as welcome as the aid of Manlius to him:[20]

hic, velut in nigro iactatis turbine nautis
    lenius aspirans aura secunda venit
iam prece Pollucis, iam Castoris implorata,
    tale fuit nobis Manlius auxilium [68. 63–66].

On the other hand, the yacht dedicates itself, in its old age, to the Dioscuri, perhaps because it never had to offer them homage during the stress of life. The poet himself has been less fortunate but, with all brevity and within the emotional context delimited by this journey alone, he may have turned his eyes away from any sorrow, past or possibly to come, to look at the untarnished happiness of the present.[21]

To overemphasize any such profound implications in Catullus' lyric is to do its special lightness and charm an injustice. Though the poem runs on many levels, any allegorical interpretation must remain secondary to the pressing emotion which the particular journey presents.[22] The literary tradition, from which this poem evolves, springs from many sources. Catullus certainly must have known, from his Hellenistic background, poems in which ships were offered *ex voto* after a life of service, or poems where the object dedicated tells its own tale.[23] Yet

10

knowledge of a great poet's tradition is of vital service not to offer proof that he borrowed literary motifs but to show how he transposed and changed them in the light of his own creative personality. Much of the poem's power is gained, as we have seen, from the manner in which actual description is enriched by an emotion which symbolizes Catullus' own feelings as well as describing the actual experiences from which they spring. It remains only to stress once more the importance to Catùllus of the reality of the ship and its adventures, for, however rich the poem by implication, this alone occasioned the composition of *Phaselus ille.*

BROWN UNIVERSITY
THE CENTER FOR HELLENIC STUDIES

NOTES

1. On the spelling of *phaselus* I follow the edition of R. A. B. Mynors (Oxford, 1958). See also W. V. Clausen, *A. Persi Flacci saturarum liber* (Oxford, 1956) on 5. 136.

2. A brief bibliography of the major writings on this poem since 1900 is offered by M. Schuster in *RE*, VIIA2 (1948), 2372. This may be supplemented by reference to K. P. Schulze, "Bericht über die Literatur zu Catullus für die Jahre 1905–20," *JAW*, CLXXXIII (1920), 1–72 (esp. 3–4, 39, 43); H. Rubenbauer, "Bericht über die Literatur zu Catullus für die Jahre 1920–26," *JAW*, CCXII (1927), 196–97; and H. J. Leon, "A Quarter Century of Catullan Scholarship (1934–59) II," *CW*, LIII (1960), 142–43. See also C. L. Smith (*HSCP*, III [1892], 75–89); C. Cichorius (in *Festschrift O. Hirschfeld* [Berlin, 1903], pp. 467–83); L. A. MacKay (*CP*, XXV [1930], 77–78); L. Herrmann (*RBPh*, XXXIII [1955], 493); and F. O. Copley (*TAPA*, LXXXIX [1958], 9–13).

3. J. Svennung, "Phaselus ille. Zum 4. Gedicht Catulls," *Opuscula Romana*, I (1954), 109–24. The questions which he discusses are: Where did Catullus get the money for such a venture? Was it possible for a private person to buy or rent such a ship? Could a vessel of this sort be sailed all the way up into the Lago di Garda? Only the problem of where the trip began, which is treated below, does he leave unsatisfactorily resolved. Svennung owes much, at least in spirit, to A. L. Wheeler, *Catullus and the Traditions of Ancient Poetry* (Berkeley, 1934), pp. 98–102.

4. Closely connected as these poems are to a single happening, this pattern was not necessarily deliberately planned by the poet. It is not a "cycle" in the sense applied to the writings of the post-Homeric bards or to a group of interconnected shorter poems such as the sonnets of Swinburne or even the "Roman" odes of Horace (on the unity of which see F. Solmsen, "Horace's First Roman Ode," *AJP*, LXVIII [1947], 337 ff.). We might better compare the Oedipus plays of Sophocles or the complex emotional and symbolic unity which exists between Yeats's *Sailing to Byzantium* and *Byzantium*, whose composition is separated by a period of four years. Whether or not Catullus arranged the collection of his poetry as we now have it remains a moot question (see K. Quinn, *The Catullan Revolution* [Melbourne, 1959], p. 106, n. 11), but it is hardly an argument against the type of unity proposed here.

5. The structure of this poem is worked out with extreme care. See J. P. Elder, "Notes on some Conscious and Subconscious Elements in Catullus' Poetry," *HSCP*, LX (1951), 103–4, 121.

6. See, e. g., R. Ellis, *A Commentary on Catullus* (Oxford, 1889), p. 110.

7. The importance in poetry of this metaphorical elaboration of the inanimate in personal terms need not be stressed. It is at the core of the mythmaking process (see the interesting chapter on "Elements of Mythopoesis" in J. Huizinga, *Homo Ludens: A Study of the Play-Element in Culture* [Boston, 1955], pp. 136–45). The tendency to personify is also typical of Catullus' intensity of feeling—he uses the device elsewhere, c. g., in 44—and the combination of life as actuality with life as myth is what gives poem 4 its special power.

8. The sensual imagery is anticipated not only by the word *curis* but in the phrase *labore fessi*, which manifestly refers to the trials of the journey, yet also contains sensual undertones. Thus does Catullus describe his limbs *defessa labore* (50. 14), worn out with desire for Calvus, limbs which, significantly enough for a comparison with 31, *lectulo iacebant*. So also the Gallae and their master are described in 63. 35–36 as *lassulae/nimio e labore*, where *labor*, as in 31, can be ambiguously related either to the actual journey (in 63, over the seas and up the mountain) or to their misdirected passion for Cybele.

9. On the importance of the adjective *venustus* in the vocabulary of Catullus see B. Axelson, *Unpoetische Wörter* (Lund, 1945), p. 61. In *De or.* 3. 180 Cicero speaks of the *venustas* of a ship, a reference important for 4 as well as 31.

10. Outwardly meaning "rejoice upon the return of your master" (which is the obvious sense of *erus* also in 4. 19), the phrase may bear more sensual connotations. *Erus*, or rather *era*, in Catullan usage, is applied to one's mistress, whether she seem true, as in 68. 136 (at least momentarily!), or perversely false, as in 63. 18. (On the poet's use of *erus*, -*a*, and their connection with *dominus*, -*a*, see H. Heusch, *Das Archaische in de: Sprache Catulls* [Bonn, 1954], pp. 42–44). These lines in 31 might well be compared to the description, in 61. 116–19, of the manifold joys which the husband will experience in his marriage to such a bride. The double repetition of *gaudia* and *gaudeat* (as in 31. 12–13, *gaude* and *gaudete*), coupled with the mutual use of *erus*, makes one more than suspect that the poet wished the sensual impressions to carry over to the phrase *ero gaude* of 31.

11. Following the Greek commonplace, Catullus constantly associates the foot with some eagerly awaited occasion. Lesbia appears *molli pede* in 68. 70, and Hymen comes to the nuptial ceremony *niveo pede* (61. 9–10). And how often is the eager desire of Attis manifested in his *citato pede*! Hence the constant association of dancing with a happy occasion, be it marriage, or the coming of spring, as, for example, in Horace *Carm.* 1. 4. 7 or 4. 7. 6 (the last a poem in which Horace was recalling Catullus 46; Horace's *frigora mitescunt Zephyris* [4. 7. 9] is a clear echo of *Zephyri silescit* in 46. 3).

12. The iterative form, *volito*, is also thus used in 64. 9.

13. How very personal is Catullus' emotional involvement may be seen by comparing his treatment of the

phaselus with Ovid's imitation of it in *Trist.* 1. 10 (cf. H. A. J. Munro, *Criticisms and Elucidations of Catullus*[2] [London, 1905], pp. 10–21).

14. The personification begins in 1. 2 with the word *ait.* It is a most unusual vessel that can tell its own tale (the same thought is carried further by *loquente*, 12, *ait*, 15, *dicit*, 16). Moreover, though it never had to resort to such measures, the inference of 22–23 is that it was capable of making vows to the gods of the shore, should the need have arisen. Other ambiguities, such as *stetisse* (16) or *imbuisse palmulas* (17)—hands or oars?—should be cited. Likewise the course from birth (*origo*) to old age (*senet quiete*) is strange if applied to an inanimate object only.

15. In this regard see O. Friess, *Beobachtungen über die Darstellungskunst Catulls* (Würzburg, 1929), p. 29, and H. Bardon, *L'Art de la Composition chez Catulle* (Paris, 1943), pp. 13–14. A detailed examination of the use of sound values in this poem shows a clear attempt to balance the first half against the second.

16. The similarity of situation is emphasized by the verbal parallels (e. g., *nasse*, 64. 2, and *natantis*, 4. 3; *palmis*, 64. 7, and *palmulis*, 4. 17). See also n. 12, above.

17. Here the change is from *prius* to *nunc*. Usually as in 8. 3–9 or 72. 1–5, it is *quondam* to *nunc.*

18. Cf., for example, the use of *cura* in 2. 10. For a definition of the word which embraces both the facets proposed here see O. Skutsch in *Rh. Mus.*, XCIX (1956), 198–99.

19. Cf. the use of *trux* in 4. 9 and of *truculentus* in 64. 179. Many of the words which give 4 its dramatic power (e. g., *celer*, *impetus*, *minax*) recur in 63 but are rarely used elsewhere by C.

20. The imagery of love as storm is, of course, basic to the whole poem. On the simile, see J. Svennung, *Catulls Bildersprache I* (Uppsala, 1945), 81f., and the more general discussion of J. Kahlmeyer, *Seesturm und Schiff-*bruch als Bild im antiken Schrifttum (Diss., Greifswald; Hildesheim, 1934), pp. 22–26. E. de Saint-Denis (*Le rôle de la mer dans la poésie latine* [Lyon, 1935]) devotes pages 137–58 to Catullus.

21. For further references to the equation of life and sea journey in ancient literature, see Kahlmeyer, *op. cit.* (n. 20 above), pp. 26–39. The metaphor of life's journey as an ocean voyage is one of the most common imagistic strands in Greek tragedy (it is basic to the structure of the *Suppliants* and the *Antigone*, for example), and, in a form which is almost crystallizing into allegory, offers the background for Odysseus' return home through the world of experience. The analogy between physical movement and any spiritual development outside of space is easily drawn, and Catullus utilizes two of the most common shapes this movement takes—here, the sea voyage, and in 63 the mountain to be climbed, the most well-known literary instance of the latter being Dante's ascent of the hill of Purgatory to the earthly paradise on its top and heaven yet further beyond. It, too, must be taken, in a spiritual sense, as the journey from childhood to age. (This point is finely illustrated by F. Fergusson in *Dante's Drama of the Mind* [Princeton, 1953], pp. 8–10.)

22. For a moment Catullus dips his oars into the main stream of classical Greek poetics wherein life as myth gradually evolved out of life as actuality, as the lyric forms were succeeded by those of tragedy. It was back to this tradition primarily that Horace returned for his inspiration and models, maintaining an aloofness from his Catullan heritage which seemingly borders on disdain. But even without a direct admission of indebtedness, the influence of *Phaselus ille* on Horace is clear beyond a doubt (see C. W. Mendell, *CP*, XXX [1935], 298–99; J. Ferguson, *AJP*, LXXVII [1956], 15–16).

23. On the relation of the tradition of epigram to poem 4 see T. Birt, "Zu Catull's Carmina Minora," *Philol.*, LXIII (1904), 453–58 and O. Hezel, *Catull und das griechische Epigramm* (Stuttgart, 1932), pp. 9–14.

CATULLUS 11: THE IRONIES OF INTEGRITY

Michael C. J. Putnam

Furi et Aureli, comites Catulli,
sive in extremos penetrabit Indos,
litus ut longe resonante Eoa
   tunditur unda,

sive in Hyrcanos Arabasve molles,   5
seu Sagas sagittiferosve Parthos,
sive quae septemgeminus colorat
   aequora Nilus,

sive trans altas gradietur Alpes,
Caesaris visens monimenta magni,   10
Gallicum Rhenum horribile aequor ulti-
   mosque Britannos,

omnia haec, quaecumque feret voluntas
caelitum, temptare simul parati,
pauca nuntiate meae puellae   15
   non bona dicta.

cum suis vivat valeatque moechis,
quos simul complexa tenet trecentos,
nullum amans vere, sed identidem omnium
   ilia rumpens;   20

nec meum respectet, ut ante, amorem,
qui illius culpa cecidit velut prati
ultimi flos, praetereunte postquam
   tactus aratro est.

(Furius and Aurelius, companions of Catullus, whether he will make his way into the farthest Indi, where the shore is beaten by the far-resounding eastern wave, or into the Hyrcani or the soft Arabians, whether to the Sagae or arrow-bearing Parthians, whether into the waters which sevenfold Nile dyes, whether he will cross over the lofty Alps, viewing the memorials of mighty Caesar, the Gallic Rhine, bristling water and remotest Britons — all these things, prepared to test together whatever the will of the gods shall bring: announce a few words to my girl, words not pleasant. Let her live and flourish with her adulterers, whom three hundred at once she holds in her embrace, loving no one of them truly, but again and again breaking the strength of all. And let her not look for my love, as before, which by her fault has fallen like a flower of the remotest meadow after it has been touched by a passing plough.)

A first encounter with Catullus' great lyric of dismissal often raises the question of internal unity. What elements besides meter assure continuity to an apparently tripartite poem that begins with its author posing as explorer of the farthest Indi and concludes with a comparison of himself to a flower in the remotest meadow? And in between we have a brisk vignette of his mistress' open degradation.

The intention of the initial apostrophe is itself open to doubt. Elsewhere in his verse Catullus treats Furius and Aurelius with patent scorn. Here they are apparently envisioned, at the start, as dutiful friends, willing to join the poet in experiencing the varied reaches of the universe — east and west, rivers and mountains, peoples luxurious and bellicose, the accomplishments of a Caesar. The stance is one of power and the epic richness of the language complements the subject. Catullus had himself once been a *comes* (46.9) on the staff of Gaius Memmius and he sympathizes with his friends Veranius and Fabullus for their misfortunes as *Pisonis comites* (28.1). This role, as 'governor' of his world, Catullus now plays for a moment, securing the allegiance of his supposed friends and giving them commands. He is to be an enterprising observer of varied reality, absorbing an existence noteworthy for spatial vividness and sensual breadth.

The tone of these opening stanzas is very Roman, a rich clustering of realms to be explored, named and conquered by a Caesar or described and chronicled by a Nepos in his labored pages, of energies to be channelled, of tribes and places to be turned into *monimenta* — 'warnings' to the memory of an imposing presence. Figures of speech liberally enrich this catalogue and metrical niceties abound. The onomatopoeic *tunditur unda* caught Tibullus' ear (*cautes . . . / naufraga quam vasti tunderet unda maris,* 'the rock . . . on which beats the ship-wrecking wave of the immense sea', 2.4.9-10).[1] The t' sounds are linked with the beginning of the phrase *(litus ut)* while assonance reverberates through *longe resonante Eoa* (resonance echoes, both literally and figuratively, through the

14

ordered reiteration of the vowels from *resonante* to *Eoa*). Brisk dentals conspire with deeper nasal sounds to plot the sea in sound, striking and echoing.

Twice (lines 2 and 9) the principal caesura comes before verbs of importance — *penetrabit* and *gradietur* — which by their parallelism seem to divide the catalogue as a whole into two parts. In each instance the verbs separate adjectives from their nouns to offer a precis of novelty's impact — exciting attribute, verb as effort, noun as result. Twice (lines 6 and 7) lack of principal caesura accents epic vocabulary, a metrical feature which links these verses with line 23, for reasons apparent only then. At line 9 the hypnotic repetition of *sive* in anaphora comes to a stop as we turn from eastern diversity to concentrate specifically on Caesar whose accomplishments lines 11 and 12 rush to exhibit. (Asyndeton and division of a word between lines enhance the poet's purpose. But — to anticipate again — only after making an association with the hypermetric lines 19 and 22 will this purpose be fully apparent.)

The break in the catalogue is marked by a change from *penetrabit* to *gradietur,* the first verb marked by commitment and energy, the second forthright but less colorful. Emotional focus in fact shifts from the adventuring poet and his *comites* to Caesar. The same diversions into peoples and bodies of water are still operative. *Indi* and the Eoan wave, *Hyrcani* and the Nile find their counterparts in Rhine, bristling channel and *Britanni*. Only mountains, the lofty Alps measuring vertical as well as horizontal distance, are new, crossed by Caesar whose deed the poet mimics. Perhaps something of a soldier's dull duty is to be sensed in *gradietur,* a word which notably lacks the sexual overtones of *penetrabit*. In any case the poem is now dominated by mighty Caesar whose capsulated performance depersonalizes, turning rivers and peoples into *monimenta,* symbols of a dictator's special feats of boldness.[2] Geography's variety is reduced to the status of token of public achievement.

The epic flavor of these opening lines, beginning when *longe resonante* echoes the Homeric *poluphloisbos,* was sensed and recaptured by Virgil in two passages outlining the vast extent of Roman domination under Augustus. The first, looking directly to the newer Caesar, speaks of a golden age of might extended over Garamantes and Indi (*Aen.* 6.798-800):

> huius in adventum iam nunc et Caspia regna
> responsis horrent divum et Maeotia tellus,
> et septemgemini turbant trepida ostia Nili.[3]

> (. . . Against whose arrival even now both the Caspian
> realms and Maeotian land shudder from the oracles of

the gods, and the trembling mouths of sevenfold Nile
are in turmoil.)

Other humbled tribes Vulcan engraves into Augustus' Roman triumph
(*Aen.* 8.724-28):

> hic Nomadum genus et discinctos Mulciber Afros,
> his Lelegas Carasque sagittiferosque Gelonos
> finxerat; Euphrates ibat iam mollior undis
> extremique hominum Morini, Rhenusque bicornis
> indomitique Dahae, et pontem indignatus Araxes.

> (Here Mulciber had fashioned the race of Nomads and
> Afri with flowing garments, here the Lelegae and Carae
> and arrow-bearing Geloni; now the Euphrates went
> more softened with its waves, and the Morini, farthest
> of men, and two-horned Rhine, unconquered Dahae,
> and the Araxes chafing at its bridge.)

For Catullus as well as Virgil epic diction enriches epic description of
Roman Catullus' putative or Augustus' more tangible accomplishments.
Yet all the time running counter to the grander swell is the lyric limitation of Sappho's meter. This tells us always, by inner beat if not exterior sense, that we must be prepared for a series of reversals, that we
are concerned with an emotion both personal and private whose piercing clarity will ultimately help condense the expansive and superficial
notes of this opening boast into the simplicity of despair. The surprising
progress whereby Catullus, assured explorer of geography's known
bounds, becomes a fallen flower, is instructive.[4]

Hence, viewing the opening stanzas in retrospect, what at first seems
epic power now appears mere ostentation, while the exaggerated description suggests rather a parody than an imitation of epic — a step in fact
beyond Sappho's undoubtedly honorific use of Homer.[5] And the very
Romanness of these lines smacks of irony coming from the imagination
of a poet who regularly satirizes parallel pretensions in a Caesar or a
Pompey.[6] After we survey what intervenes between vocative (*Furi et
Aureli*) and verb (*nuntiate*), the language, for its context, parades too
heroically, suggesting through hyperbole that the commitment offered
by the addressees was itself too excessive. Even if we examine his verbal
usage alone Catullus seems to call in question the false epic *fides* of his
putative *comites*. It is perhaps the very insouciant brazenness of their
presumption, the hypocrisy of one huge 'preparedness' (*omnia temptare
— a nice *cohors!*), that Catullus wishes to emphasize as he orders them

into a very different campaign. *Pauca* will be hard enough for them to accomplish, let alone *omnia*.

The metamorphosis of *omnia* into *pauca* begins in the magnificent limiting stanza of lines 13-16, as their assertion of unconfined loyalty, to experience life with mutual fidelity, suffers narrowing to a role as message bearer (with further diminution of their implied *fides*). The decisive test of daring given to Furius and Aurelius is to approach not a distant place or exotic tribe but one person, a woman whom the poet never names (by contrast to the previous hyperbolic nominalizing), whom he calls 'mine' but cannot even face himself, as the beauty of past possession is perversely twisted into the most negative rejection. Verbal action literally halts in another way. Furius and Aurelius were to be *comites*. If we may follow the thrust of etymology, they were prepared to be joint voyagers, pursuing adventure in this world of action — ranging, observing, crossing, testing. But their first exploit is not to be mutually shared *(simul)*[7] with the poet but a labor undertaken by the *comites* alone, and to consist of an announcement only, of words not deeds, of words not handsomely descriptive but evil. They are the bearers of a curse.

But once again through an ironic incongruity of meter our expectations are wrongly aroused. The meters which Catullus uses for invective vary. Two of the three poems in virtually straight iambic verse are vituperative (poems 29 and 52), but when he says of Caesar (54.6-7),

> irascere iterum meis iambis
> immerentibus, unice imperator . . .

(You will be angry again at my innocent iambs, you one and only general),

or wonders why Ravidus hurled himself so unwisely *in meos iambos* (40.2), he is probably thinking of hendecasyllabics as well.[8] These words which follow in poem 11 then, in quite a different lyric meter, are the most polished curse, using an exacting rhythm named for one of the perfectionists of ancient poetry — and a woman — against another woman whose name now, were it to be uttered, could be seen as the wryest form of jest. Lesbia's nomenclature should be familiarly at ease with the stanza of Sappho whose scrupulous style is characterized by clarity, limpidity and grace. Sappho's gift was the ability to transform the intense, personal moment into permanence through the brief, quintessential verbal gesture. The true curse lies not so much in explicit revelation as in using Lesbia against herself. It illustrates, as the preceding epic diction had hinted and the subsequent portrait would prove, that far

17

from being a brilliant combination of poetess and lover, able to transmute intense emotion into rigorous word — to combine felicitously elegance of mind and body — she is in reality one of the most notoriously vulgar and degraded women of Roman history. More like Caesar than Sappho, her interests are only in the physical, in sex as conquest and commerce. And the power of lyric limitation remains through to the end, as Catullus himself replaces Sappho, surviving both his own imagined heroic pretensions and his vivid revelation of Lesbia's accomplished promiscuity to conclude with one final, careful poetic bow.

The epic deed, the courage to face this monster more terrifying than Parthians or Britains, who holds three hundred adulterers at once in her grasp, is suggested to Furius and Aurelius, not to Catullus himself. All that could have been said and done 'well', *benefacta priora*, the poet has already performed (76.7-8):

> nam quaecumque homines bene cuiquam aut dicere possunt
> aut facere, haec a te dictaque factaque sunt.

> (For whatever people can either say or do in kindly
> fashion toward anyone, this has been said and done
> by you.)

Catullus is reduced to words only, evil words. The deed of delivery is left to *comites* who are to expose her actions — embracing, holding, bursting. *Omnia haec*, the experiences the gods propose, center now on the *omnium ilia* that her avidity ruptures; mutual agreement to make trial of the world together *(simul)* is transformed into Lesbia's undoubted ability to clasp at once, time and again, a multitude of lovers *(simul)*. And it is not so far, factually or linguistically, from *temptare* to *tenet*. Reasons for wishing the occasion and its possible results on his 'friends' can be any reader's guess, but Catullus washes his hands both of Lesbia and of any such restored intimacy on his part — even of one final confrontation — by the bitter change from *meae puellae* (though it is now a time when his possession is utterly impossible) to *suis moechis*. And the associated image of holding and embracing makes her present possession of others provocatively clear.

In the poem's ordering *omnia* first gives place to *pauca*, the few words that are the last sign of involvement. But for Lesbia life, like epic adventure, is a matter of extremes, of *omnium* or *nullum*.[9] There is no real truth to her affections but her physical lust is overpowering. The actual words of farewell bring to the surface the disparity in Lesbia between appearance and reality, the failure to combine physical beauty and spiritual perfection whose union was, to Catullus, a necessity for true *amor*. In another poem addressed to Lesbia where he can cry *vale, puella* (8.12), impermanent adieu still lacks the full ambiguity of *valeat* in exposing Lesbia's continued thriving which ironically destroys others. Catullus could then describe his girl as (8.5):

> amata nobis quantum amabitur nulla.

> (. . . Loved by me as much as no one will be loved.)

And in another poem where the formulation grows more complex, there is a common emphasis on the truth of the poet's affection (87.1-2):

> nulla potest mulier tantum se dicere amatam
> vere, quantum a me Lesbia amata mea est.

> (No woman can say that she was truly loved as much as my Lesbia by me.)

True *amor* (what Lesbia, *nullum amans vere*, 'loving none of them truly', blatantly lacks) consists not only of legal abstractions such as *fides* and *foedus* but of a certain unanalyzable purity and *castitas*, the emotional bond that links a father with sons-in-law as well as sons, where even blood ties, not to speak of any sexual longing, are absent.

The height of the adventure, then, surpassing the wildest explorations, is to imagine watching the extensive domination of this monster — monster physically, who embraces three hundred lovers at once, monster psychically, who has no truth to her affections. It is a spectacular moment, focussing the previous detachment and bringing the initial mental vagaries to a sudden central standstill. We are brought unexpectedly out of any freeing thoughts of exotic escape into the present reality of a creature who grips and rends. As the mood of the opening stanzas collapses, the hyperbole switches from Catullus to *puella* and leads, with further irony, to disappointment, not accomplishment, to Lesbia's degradation, not the poet's fulfillment.

Catullus curses with exact figuration a woman whose thousands of kisses he once hesitated to count lest he draw on them both the evil eye. That was in a poem which began with an exortation (5.1) —

> vivamus, mea Lesbia, atque amemus

> (Let us live, my Lesbia, and let us love) —

uttered at a moment (imagined or otherwise) when a wish for unity was feasible, by a poet who still supposed that living and loving were synonymous. The realities of Lesbia's present amatory life preclude such a hope.

Catullus probably means us to compare another lyric, poem 51, also addressed to Lesbia in Sapphic meter (perhaps earlier, but chronology is unimportant). Attention is usually called to the verbal parallels (the repetition of *identidem* is the most striking) as if the two poems, though the (apparent) temporal order is reversed in the manuscripts, signalled the beginning and the end of the affair (51.1-7):

> ille mi par esse deo videtur,
> ille, si fas est, superare divos,
> qui sedens adversus identidem te
> spectat et audit
>
> dulce ridentem, misero quod omnis
> eripit sensus mihi: nam simul te,
> Lesbia, aspexi, nihil est super mi . . .

> (That man seems to me equal to a god, that man (if it is right to say) seems to surpass the gods who, sitting opposite, looks at you again and again and hears you laughing sweetly — which takes all sensation from me in my suffering: for as soon as I have gazed at you, Lesbia, I have nothing left . . .)

The poet imagines his physical reaction to sitting in Lesbia's presence, as he hears and above all sees her *(spectat, aspexi)*. In poem 51 Catullus continually watches Lesbia; in 11 Lesbia, in a world apart from the poet, ruptures her lovers. There is no physical contact whatsoever here; not even the act of looking is possible for Catullus. This has been transferred to the exotic catalogue of possible places to be visited, an apparently non-sexual existence away from Lesbia but leading hyperbolically toward her, in which the last action, conveyed through the participle *visens,* is one of viewing. Yet to Catullus remains one possession which Lesbia lacks (and we now know can never again possess), *meum amorem,* the poet's true love, an abstraction to which Catullus, with assured brilliance, attaches a verb of 'seeing,' itself become abstract, *respectet,* for to see is to know. Lesbia cannot again look for his love as she had before. For him physically to behold and for her truly to see are alike impossible.

The habitual 'action' of the past on Lesbia's part would seem to be infidelity leading to forgiveness from Catullus. She could look back to find Catullus and *amor* steadfast, to a time when *meum amorem* meant Lesbia and mutual concord instead of simply the poet's own awareness of his love's meaning. But with a careful stroke of distancing by grammar, *meum amorem* succumbs to *illius culpa*, the fault of that person never named. This leads directly into the topographical remoteness of the simile: his love is like a flower of the remotest meadow which her aggression, like a plough, still manages to pass by and 'touch,' to clip and kill. Before *(ante)* there was forgiveness; now after *(postquam)* her final metamorphosis, forgiveness is impossible.

The simile is remarkable, helping us escape past the monster into a paradigm of nature destroyed. It is in a literary tradition which begins with Homer and Sappho (and reasons for Catullus' special involvement will be given shortly). Virgil knew it well. He imitates it openly when describing the moment of Euryalus' dying (*Aen.* 9.433-37):

> volvitur Euryalus leto, pulchrosque per artus
> it cruor inque umeros cervix conlapsa recumbit:
> purpureus veluti cum flos succisus aratro
> languescit moriens, lassove papavera collo
> demisere caput pluvia cum forte gravantur.

> (Euryalus rolls over in death, blood flows along his beautiful limbs and his neck leans fallen on his shoulders: as when a purple flower cut by a plough withers as it dies, or poppies have drooped their head on weary neck, when weighed down by a chance shower.)

Pallas on his bier is also compared to a wilting flower (*Aen.* 11.68-69):

> qualem virgineo demessum pollice florem
> seu mollis violae seu languentis hyacinthi.[10]

> (Like a flower culled by a girl's finger, the flower of a soft violet or drooping hyacinth.)

In the first simile Virgil arouses our special sympathy by stressing the flower's beauty at the actual moment of death. But Catullus is dealing with an abstraction, not a person, and puts his emphasis more starkly and finally on the setting (the farthest meadow) and on the action of the plough, passing by and touching.[11]

First, the setting. The correspondence between *prati ultimi* and the beginning and end of the exotic catalogue which opened the poem — *extremos Indos* and *ultimos Britannos* — is remarkable. Yet now we are in a world beyond names, beholding an object both generic and universal, though fragile and far-removed. And the poet, instead of initiating and executing this vibrant journey to the extremes of the known world, becomes himself an 'extreme' to be seen, incapable of motion, not a strange tribe but something less noteworthy, perhaps, yet infinitely more precious.

The reader is now forced to redefine still further the character of the initial catalogue from an iterated, even exalted pronouncement of power to a prayer for escape from the inescapable. It was a dream of submission to observed sensory immediacies, a dream in which hearing, touch and sight played their part. The stark reality is a flower which neither receives nor needs a descriptive attribute.

It is logical to compare the simile in Catullus' second *epithalamium* where the unmarried girl is likewise associated with a flower (62.39-40)—

> ut flos in saeptis secretus nascitur hortis,
> ignotus pecori, nullo convolsus aratro . . .

> (Like a flower that grows up apart in a garden hedged
> about, unknown to the flock, torn up by no plough . . .) —

beloved by boys and girls alike until it is culled (*tenui carptus defloruit ungui,* 43). But Catullus, paradoxically, places the flower that is his love in a meadow, not in a cultivated garden or a ploughed field. The image is pastoral. In the *Eclogues,* for instance, meadows *(prata)* 'drink in' the shepherd-singers' songs (3. 111); form a locale for a magic ram to change his colors (4.43); offer soft enticement for Lycoris to join Gallus, momentarily masquerading as a pastoral bard (10.42).[12]

Virgil, of course, also regularly associates ploughs with *arva,* ploughlands, not *prata.* Save for superficial connection through the 'natural' world, plough and meadow have nothing in common. Their meeting here brings into collision the intellectual spheres of pastoral and georgic, often antonymous. Other lesser oppositions — metal and plant, inanimate and alive, motion and stillness, hard and soft, heavy and light — enhance the distinction between the two objects. The plough (and we imagine an object going coldly about its utilitarian task with heedless unconcern) comes into passing contact with a living object, immovable, feeble and vulnerable. Seclusion is no defense against vulgarity while, paradoxically, experience for the poet brings a realization of past innocence.

Where plough and flower do meet, however, is on the level of poetic symbolism. In ancient literature, at least as early as Pindar, the plough is a sign for the male, and there is no more universal symbol than a flower for a woman, especially unmarried.[13] We have noted above an example from poem 62. From Catullus' first *epithalamium* alone there are four instances where *flos* or *floridus* are applied to the bride.

Ariadne, while still a *virgo*, is associated with myrtle or spring flowers (64.89-90):

> quales Eurotae praecingunt flumina myrtus
> aurave distinctos educit verna colores.

> (Like myrtles which gird about the streams of the
> Eurotas, or the many-colored flowers which the spring
> breeze draws out.)

Any reader following the continuity of poem 11 against the background of Catullus' total body of verse would certainly think of the figure of Attis, exhorting his *comites* toward the frenzied devotion of Cybele, yet emasculating himself *Veneris nimio odio* ('from too great a hatred of Love', 63.17). In the past, before robbing himself of his virility, he also was a 'flower' (63.64-66):

> ego gymnasi fui flos, ego eram decus olei:
> mihi ianuae frequentes, mihi limina tepida,
> mihi floridis corollis redimita domus erat . . .

> (I was the flower of the gymnasium, I was the glory
> of the palaestra: my doorways were thronged, my
> threshold warm, my house was crowned by garlands of
> flowers . . .)

Masculine Cybele deflowers and gelds, inspiring a double madness. Similar energies are imputed to Lesbia who causes loins to burst and 'touches' flowers.[14] It is Lesbia to whom all force is imputed at the poem's conclusion.[15] In the adventurous dream that opened the lyric the power of 'going' is allotted to *comites* who with their patron are prepared to 'try' *(temptare)* this brave world. Now it is given to Lesbia, the plough *praetereunte*. And though it is not so far etymologically from *temptare* to *tenet* and *tactus est*, their very similarity points up the revolutionary course the poem has taken, imputing the momentum Catullus would wish for himself to Lesbia, twisting verbal force, outlined in the courage needed to view the farthest Britons, into nominal passivity.[16] The ultimate in projected experience suffers metamorphosis into the finality of assured innocence.

Epic poetry surveys an heroic progress through extent of time. Lyric verse inclines to gaze intently and analytically on the vital, immediate moment. In terms of poem 11, the literal level of temporal action befits a Caesar and a Lesbia. The symbolic time structure the poet rears for himself leads away from any hypothetical, grandiloquent deeds to a stable emblem of fragility, almost out of time. The dialectic turns inward, away from explicit epic fact to analogical, lyric symbol.[17]

It is in such an intellectual context that the verb *tactus est* gains its special strength. A plough need only graze to kill. Lesbia's touch far from being tantalizing, is lethal. But erotic irony does not stop there Masculine prowess is imputed to Lesbia to whom Catullus grants a verb which has associations with sexual intercourse of varied character. Catullus threatens Aurelius *tangam te irrumatione* (21.8) and Horace's Sallustius can claim *matronam nullam ego tango* (*Sat.* 1.2.54).[18] But the context at the end of poem 11 leaves little doubt that Catullus is imagining himself in the role of a girl still *intacta* (62.45 and 56) or *integra* (61.36), to appeal once again to the language of the *epithalamia*. But this act of deflowering which Lesbia performs is applied to an abstraction not a person. It is seen by the poet primarily as a mental, not a physical notion. It has only the slightest connection with the emasculating effect Lesbia has on her lovers, however intensely the elegiacs lead in that direction or however closely runs the parallel with Attis. In the elegiacs, as Catullus agonizes over the tension between loving and hating in his life with Lesbia, he gradually frames and expands a distinction between mere sex and a deeper metaphysical relationship in which love and respect form a necessary combination. Sometimes the search for terminology alone was impressive, as at the end of 72 when the poet imagines Lesbia asking how Catullus can both burn with love for her and yet consider her cheap (72.1-8):

> qui potis est, inquis? quod amantem iniuria talis
>   cogit amare magis, sed bene velle minus.

> (How can that be, you say? Because such an injury
> compels a lover to love more but to respect less.)

Though on the one hand *amare* balances and contrasts with *bene velle,* Catullus, *amantem,* suffers and expounds both feelings.

This is the *amor* at the end of poem 11 which draws to itself the virginal image of the flower. It is virginal not because their relationship lacked passion (at 75.4 Catullus observes that her ability to attract continues no matter what she does, *omnia si facias*) but because now, in what is perhaps his final lyric portrait of their intimacy, he can symbolize his love as transcending previous categorization to become in its essence chaste and pure, beautiful in its fineness, nearly abstracted from reality. And yet on another level of irony the flower is tangible and can be touched no matter how remote. Lesbia's action affects the vulnerable

24

flower in a physical manner. But this masculine potency does not create a marriage or foster the personal *fides* and *foedus* with which Catullus, in his union with Lesbia, sought to replace the usual Roman legal nuptial bonds. This plough does not prepare for planting but for devastation, as it invades for a minute a world it cannot comprehend and should not share.[19]

And the ultimate thought — this is a poem of ultimates — returns appropriately to Sappho as with final irony Catullus acknowledges her *epithalamia* to conclude, not commence, his connection with Lesbia. A virgin bride to Sappho may be an apple on a lofty branch or a hyacinth trampled under foot by shepherds. Sung by a chorus of girls who feign sadness over their companion's fate, the image hides joy beneath a veneer of grief. For Catullus only the opposite can be said.

At three moments in poem 64, Catullus' most influential and intellectual poem, he addresses himself to similar concerns which may serve as commentary on poem 11. One analogy is straightforward, the others are more complex.

At the very end of the poem, after the Fates have sung the exploits of Achilles, redoubtable product of Peleus and Thetis whose marriage the poem celebrates, he contrasts the age of heroes when houses were chaste, *pietas* was still cultivated, and the gods appeared before men, with the present day.[20] One instance of contemporary decadence which the poet counterpoises finds a father desirous of his son's death in order freely to possess his unwed daughter-in-law (64.401-2):

> optavit genitor primaevi funera nati,
> liber ut innuptae poteretur flore novercae.[21]

> (A father desired the death of his young son that he might enjoy in freedom the love of his unwed stepdaughter.)

But matters were not unambiguous in his version of the heroic era and Catullus earlier in the poem eases us more subtly from this realm to the present deterioration of morality, leaving some doubt on the former's idealism.[22] I refer first to a still puzzling moment in the wedding ceremony after the human guests have left and while the gods are assembling before the Fates sing. Five divinities are mentioned: Chiron, Peneios, Prometheus, Apollo and Diana. I suspect that Catullus ordered both them and their gifts with the greatest care. For three of this quintet a connection with Achilles has been found, but since the presence of

25

Peneios and Diana leaves learned commentators still guessing, a new suggestion may be offered.[23] Chiron comes from the top of Pelion (*e vertice Pelei*, 278), bringing flowers (280-84):

> nam quoscumque ferunt campi, quos Thessala magnis
> montibus ora creat, quos propter fluminis undas
> aura parit flores tepidi fecunda Favoni,
> hos indistinctis plexos tulit ipse corollis,
> quo permulsa domus iucundo risit odore.

> (For whichever flowers the plains bear, which the region of Thessaly creates on its mighty mountains, which the fecund breath of warming Favonius begets near the stream's waves, these he brought himself woven in a mass of garlands. The house smiles, soothed by the sweet smell.)

The picture mirrors other moments of perfection in Catullus — the laughter of Sirmio's waves (31.14), the garlands adorning Attis' doorposts (63.66), the warming spring breezes that signal the poet's departure for home (46.1-3). But flowers — they need not be named — especially engage the senses to convey the essence of innocent loveliness. The river god Peneios, on the other hand, dwelling in the valley of Tempe, brings the festal green of trees, decorative like flowers but this time named and analyzed — lofty beeches, straight laurels, bending plane and supple alder (called purposefully sister of Phaethon, the ambitious over-reacher). The explicit scrutiny is upsetting because, in the context of the poem, what was once growth on the summit of Pelion became the Argo, symbol of progress but also decline, the ship made of pine, its oars of fir, its crew like heart of oak.[24] We have moved from innocence to experience, from pastoral to a georgic/heroic existence when woods are cut for lumber and, if we may follow Virgil, alders prove useful in ship-building (*Geo.* 1.136), cypresses for construction of houses (*Geo.* 2.443), beeches for a plough's handle (*Geo.* 2.173).[25]

Next arrives Prometheus carrying not cheering gifts but wounds as evidence that further help to mankind on the road of progress does not pay. Finally we learn that Apollo and his sister do not come at all. If we may work back from the evidence Horace and Tibullus supply some thirty years later, Apollo and Diana were the chief divinities celebrated during the secular games, on the occasion when the ages come full circle and are renewed. Virgil, writing a few years earlier than Horace's *carmen saeculare* of 17 B.C., claims for Augustus Caesar that he will refound the golden age (*aurea condet saecula*, *Aen.* 6.792-93). Catullus

26

felt far otherwise toward the latter's great uncle whose accomplishments, in poem 11, anticipate those of Lesbia and her plough.

Certainly there is no golden age for Apollo and Diana to foresee in Catullus 64. The symbol of heroism's final degradation into vulgarity is Achilles whose conduct elicits from the poet another explicit instance where georgic challenges and overwhelms pastoral as innocence and purity succumb to brutality. Achilles' outstanding courage and famous deeds mothers confess at the funeral of their sons. He is like a reaper (64.353-55):

> namque velut densas praecerpens messor aristas
> sole sub ardenti flaventia demetit arva,
> Troiugenum infesto prosternet corpora ferro.

> (For just as a reaper, cutting the thick ears of grain,
> mows down the tawny fields under a burning sun, so
> he will lay low the bodies of the Trojans with his
> hostile sword.)

And, with portrait and metaphor expanding together, the wave of the Scamander bears witness to his prowess as its channel is narrowed by slaughtered heaps of corpses (*caesis corporum acervis*, 359), making the natural unnatural.[26] The final triumph is Achilles' heaped-up funeral pyre, *coacervatum bustum* (363), which receives the snowy limbs of the virginal Polyxena whom the dead Achilles demands as symbolic bride-victim.

We may indulge a parallel between Achilles, the hero as reaper who, though not even physically present, demands chaste beauty as the ultimate sacrifice, and Lesbia whose valor consists in holding three hundred lovers in one embrace, the non-human plough that automatically fells flowers. Each is an extension through symbol of a coarseness the exacting poet loathed, whether it be discovered in the property-devouring politician or the versifier who overwrites. It may be seen in the inelegant thief who mistakes the superficial value of a piece of linen for its inner worth to the poet as a symbol of friendship, or in the swarthy Spaniard who believes that a dark beard and teeth brushed in urine somehow make one *bonus*. But it is Lesbia whose inability to merge sex with spiritual feeling, superficial charm with a sense of deeper values most hurt the poet's devotion to integrity. Anticipating Mozart's vision of Tamino and Pamina, Catullus would have hoped to combine the sensual-carnal with perfected allegiance to an interior humaneness based on truth and fidelity. Poem 11 expands the ironies of his failure.[27]

Brown University

1. *Cf.* the alliteration and onomatopoeia (if such is the correct term) at 32.11 and 59.5. The phrase also charmed Horace. At *C.* 2.6.4, a poem in Sapphics which also begins with a similar theme, he has the phrase *aestuat unda*, paralleling Catullus in metrical position and, partially, in sound and sense. For an interpretation of the echo see C. P. Segal, 'Horace, Odes 2. 6: Poetic Landscape and Poetic Imagination' *Philologus* 113 (1969), 246.

2. A Roman of the 50s B.C. would have associated the adjective *magnus* automatically with Pompey, not Caesar (as we see from 55.6, Cic. *ad Att.* 33 [=II.13]). See Shackleton Bailey on *ad Att* 161B (= VIII. 11B) and *cf.* Calvus' epigram beginning *Magnus quem metuunt omnes* (frag. 18 *FPL* Morel). For the history and further examples of the attribute see Ellis on Cat. 55.6. It is not out of the question to see in Catullus' usage an attempt to undercut the pretensions of 'great' Caesar which, in the present view, the context fully complements. The problem of Catullus' relationship with Caesar has recently been reconsidered by T. P. Wiseman (*Catullan Questions* [Leicester, 1969] 35ff.) who feels that the reference in poem 11 implies a reconciliation.

3. Catullus seems to have initiated in Latin the association of seven with the mouths of the Nile. Ovid varies a similar designation (*septemfluus*: M. 1. 422, 15.753; *septemplex*: M. 5.187). *Cf.* Moschus 2. 51.

4. In an important but different reading S. Commager ('Notes on some Poems of Catullus', *HSCP* 70 [1965], 83-110) stresses the romantic coloring of these opening stanzas ('a mood of splendid and exotic romance', 100; '...the romantic possibilities of Catullus' and Lesbia's love', 101; 'the romantic journey that Catullus repudiates', *ibid.*; and, of the final stanza, 'Like 58, it conjures up a romantic ideal only to shatter it', *ibid.*).

For another interpretation of the poem that treats both the beginning and the end as essentially light and, in part, humorous, see T. E. Kinsey, 'Catullus 11', *Latomus* 24 (1965), 537-44. Specific reasons for the presence of Furius and Aurelius are offered by L. Richardson, 'Furi et Aureli, comites Catulli', *CP* 58 (1963), 93-106.

There is yet another possibility, suggested to me by Professor Christopher Dawson: the presence of irony is so intense and pervasive that the poem should be viewed primarily as a *jeu d'artifice*. The point is well taken, but we also need no longer treat the union of poetic craft and emotional impulse in Catullus as an unholy alliance. Rather poem 11 is a notable example of their power when joined.

5. The relationship is discussed among many others, by D. Page, *Sappho and Alcaeus* (Oxford, 1955), 65ff., 72ff.; A. E. Harvey, 'Homeric epithets in the Greek lyric', *CQ* 7 (1957), 206-23.

6. One need only refer to poem 29 for Catullus' commentary on the interrelationship of politics and erotic behavior. For Catullus' linking of 'motion' and sexuality see 29.7 (*perambulabit*) and 6.11 (*inambulatio*). This is perhaps a secondary reason why, given the context at 55.6, the portico of Pompey's theatre is called *Magni ambulatio*.

7. But does *simul*, by hinting that the thoughts of joint enterprise occurred only once, also prepare for the supposedly sudden reversal of the next line?

8. See also 36.5 and frag. 3, quoted from Porphyrion on Hor. *C.* 1.16.22: 'denique et Catullus, cum maledicta minaretur, sic ait "at non effugies meos iambos".'

9. This tension, as well as others, is pointed out by Commager, *op. cit.*, 102.

10. The irony here, of course, is that the flower, which ordinarily stands for the maiden, falls victim to her finger.

11. It is also possible that Catullus means *flos ultimus*, by hypallage, or even a series of meadows, one spoiled after another. In each case the effect of distancing is important.

12. See also Vir. *Geo.* 1.289, 3.521; *Aen.* 6.707. The 'pastoral' (as opposed to

'georgic') sense of *prata* is well illustrated by Lucretius at 5.785 (*florida . . . viridanti prata colore*).

13. Pindar *P.* 4.254. *Cf.* Theognis 582; Aes. *Sept.* 753; Soph *O. T.*; Plautus *Asin.* 874; Lucr. 4.1107 (and *cf* 4.1272-3). For Catullus himself as a 'flower' in his youth, see 68.16.

14. The very difference between *convolsus* (62.40), *carptus* (62. 43) and *tactus est* points up the distinctiveness of the latter's use.

15. On Catullus' fascination with this creature, 'his simultaneous alienation and involvement', see the important article by R. Bagg, 'Some Versions of lyric impasse in Shakespeare and Catullus', *Arion* 4 (1965), 64-95, esp. 63ff.

16. At the same time the erotic implications of *temptare* also play their part, even at line 14. For further uses of the verb in a sexual sense see Tib. 1. 2.17, 1.3.73.

17. An examination of the poem's course specifically in terms of its verbs shows a parallel mutation from future to past via present reality. *Penetrabit* and *gradietur* (hypothetic future, the imagined desire of Catullus mocked by Furius and Aurelius) are summarized in *feret* (hyperbolic, mock epic cause). *Nuntiate*, the lyric present, absorbs all from the start and leads to *vivat* and *valeat*, which deflect the command of *nuntiate* into optative and distance the reader by changing from a Furius and Aurelius near at hand to a Lesbia apart. *Feret* maintains the absolute present while *respectet* turns toward the lyric impulse as it had arisen in the past (*ut ante*). *Cecidit* and *tactus* are the present now frozen with finality into the past definite. The future is impossible, the present equally so. Only the past held love and yet, again ironically, only past tenses can now signal love's demise.

18. See also 89.5, Hor. *C.* 3.11.10 etc. At 15. 4 Catullus asks Aurelius to preserve Iuventius *castum et integellum*.

19. For Catullus' tendency to take upon himself feminine roles, see M. C. J. Putnam, 'The Art of Catullus 64', *HSCP* 65 (1961), 167ff.; R. Bagg, *op. cit.* 78ff.; J. Van Sickle, 'About Form and Feeling in Catullus 65', *TAPA* 99 (1968), 499. Of more general bearing is G. Devereux, 'The Nature of Sappho's seizure in fr. 31 LP as evidence of her inversion', *CQ* 20 (1970), 17-31.

20. *Cf.* Catullus' allusions to his own *pietas* at 76.26.

21. Both text and interpretation of this passage are still much in doubt. See Fordyce and Quinn *ad loc.*

22. For more detailed treatment of the negative aspects of the wedding ceremony see L. Curran, 'Catullus 64 and the Heroic Age', *YCS* 21 (1969), 171-92, esp. 186ff. See also E. W. Leach, '*Eclogue* 4: Symbolism and Sources', *Arethusa* 4 (1971), 167-84, esp. 173ff.

23. One simple connection of the Peneios and Achilles is to be found in the territory of Thessaly through which the river flowed and over which Peleus ruled.

24. The wood of the Argo is also specified at 64.10. Catullus makes the transition from trees in a mountain's crest to the manufacturing of the *phasellus* of some importance in poem 4, and we remember that Diana, who does not attend the wedding, is styled *cultricem montibus Idri* (300). For a more detailed discussion of the reasons behind the presence (or absence) of the divinities mentioned, see now J. C. Bramble, 'Structure and Ambiguity in Catullus LXIV', *PCPS* 16 (1970), 22-41, esp. 29ff.

25. Wood was of course used for the construction of the Argo. *Cf.* Virgil's verses devoted to the heroic age at *Ecl.* 4. 31ff. (*pauca tamen suberunt priscae vestigia fraudis / quae temptare Thetim ratibus*, 'yet a few traces of the primal error will remain, prompting to try the sea with ships').

26. *Cf.* the contexts of *flumen* at 89 and 281.

27. I owe thanks to Professors J. P. Elder and J. Van Sickle for their careful criticisms.

CATULLUS 22, 13

hoc quid putemus esse? qui modo scurra
aut si quid hac re tritius videbatur,
idem infaceto est infacetior rure, . . .

(Catullus 22, 12—14, ed. SCHUSTER-EISENHUT)

For the corrupt *tristius* of the manuscripts at line 13, MYNORS, in his Oxford text of 1958, adopts L. MÜLLER's suggestion *scitius*. It is espoused by C. J. FORDYCE, the most recent commentator (»MÜLLER's *scitius* suits the context better [than other conjectures] and *scitius* is a word of common speech . . .«). PONTANUS's conjecture *tritius*, palaeographically the most appropriate of the various readings proposed, is accepted by SCHUSTER into the Teubner text and cogently defended in his »Marginalien zu einer neuen Ausgabe Catulls« (WS 64, 1949, 87). His arguments are worth recollection and may be augmented. They are an answer to the objections of KROLL (»Die Änderung des überlieferten *tristius* in *tritius* ergibt nicht den erforderten Sinn, auch *tersius* nicht, da es hauptsächlich von Stil gesagt wird; so genügt *scitius* am ehesten.«) and anticipate those of FORDYCE (»Both the old correction *tritius* and Munro's *tersius* . . .

30

are palaeographically plausible but neither seems appropriate here. *tersus* when used metaphorically elsewhere refers to neatness of style or nicety of judgment; *tritus* means either 'commonplace' or 'practised' [*tritae aures* Cic. Fam. IX, 16. 4, *tritae manus* Vitr. II. 1. 6]«)[1].

SCHUSTER acknowledges these meanings for *tritus* and their deprecatory side (»viel gebraucht, abgenutzt, . . .«). Yet he stresses a more positive definition for *tero*: »Aber da *terere* auch häufig in der Bedeutung 'glatt reiben, polieren, drechseln' vorkommt (vgl. z. B. Verg. Georg. II 444, Plin. Nat. H. XXXVI 193 p. 376 M), so liegt kein Grund vor, warum *tritus* hier nicht in gleichem Sinne gebraucht werden konnte. Suffenus erscheint eben als ein Mann von 'höchster (städtisch-feiner) Glättung', d. h. als ein Herr von 'feinstem Schliff', wie wir sagen würden, als ein homo perpolitus.«

SCHUSTER's argument becomes more cogent from a closer examination of the appropriateness of one further metaphorical use of *tero* here. We must first turn briefly to the poem itself. Its chief point, a characterization of the poetaster Suffenus, is established in the opening lines:

> *Suffenus iste, Vare, quem probe nosti,*
> *homo est venustus et dicax et urbanus*
> *idemque longe plurimos facit versus.*

Suffenus is charming, witty, urbane. At the same time he writes a great many verses. Anyone aware of Catullus' *credo* in poem 1 or his denunciation of wordy Hortensius or 'swollen' Antimachus in 95 (the opposite of careful Cinna) would realize that, for him at least, these two aspects of Suffenus — charming 'wit' and the production of reams of poetry — are contradictory and mutually exclusive. The contradition carries over into the book or books themselves in which these ten thousand or more lines were scribbled.

Apparently, like Suffenus himself, they are quite attractive (lines 6—8):

> *. . . cartae regiae, novi libri,*
> *novi umbilici, lora rubra membranae,*
> *derecta plumbo et pumice omnia aequata.*

At first this handsome appearance might seem to parallel Catullus' own gift to Cornelius (1, 1—2):

> *Cui dono lepidum novum libellum*
> *arida modo pumice expolitum?*

It, too, is *novum*, just as Suffenus' *libri* and *umbilici* are *novi*. It, too, is *arida . . . pumice expolitum*, just as Suffenus' productions are *pumice omnia*

---

[1] To these we can add HOUSMAN's emendation, *trita manu*, at Ovid A. A. 1, 518 (see CR 4, 1890, 341—2). I am grateful to Professor G. P. GOOLD for this reference.

aequata. But there the resemblances abruptly end. Suffenus' output is ambitious enough to demand *libri* to contain it. Catullus offers only a *libellus* to his friend. It is small, and purposely so, but it has one trait which Suffenus' volumes lack. Superficial elegance they possess in abundance (we need only catalogue the adjectives: *regiae, novi, rubra, derecta, aequata*), yet they are not *lepida*, the first, most important attribute of Catullus' booklet. They lack that *lepos* which is a quality not only of external charm but of that imperative, though rare, inner grace and sensitivity which moves a reader to appreciate poetic worth. Catullus' book is an image of himself — charming and intrinsically valuable as well. Here is where Suffenus fails. At first he seems like his book, he witty and urbane, his book of impeccable and elegant dress. But once one begins to read, once one takes the crucial step from appreciating external charm to evaluating depth and meaning, that person who had appeared *bellus . . . et urbanus* reveals himself, at heart, only a goat-milker and a ditch-digger.

It is my thesis that the same equation between man and book, appearance and reality, continues into the lines quoted at the start of this note, and that the reading *tritius*, least open to doubt palaeographically, introduces a metaphor more suitable for this interplay.

What one seeks under the corrupt *tristius* is a word which is not only synonymous with *venustius, dicacius, urbanius* and *bellius* but can also parallel *infacetior* (14) in tone and meaning. At pro Quinct. 3, 11 Cicero speaks of a *parum facetus scurra*. My contention is that Catullus might well have written the comparative of *tritus* to be understood in a sense akin to *facetus*. The usage would be unique. *Tritus* is nowhere else in Latin applied to a man as a whole being, as it must in this instance, since it is allied to *scurra* and *hac re* as well. But Catullus did not boggle elsewhere at such linguistic singularities nor need we.

According to the Thesaurus Linguae Latinae, the verb *tero* is never actually used of the 'polishing' of a book, as we might expect if the initial link of Suffenus and his book is strengthened by the word *tritius*. Yet once by itself (Ovid A. A. 1, 506) and once in compound (Juv. 8, 16: *attero*), the verb is used literally of 'smoothing' parts of the body with pumice stone.

The Juvenal passage is of some bearing on Catullus 22. The satirist is speaking of an effeminate creature, *tenerum attritus Catinensi pumice lumbum*, who shames his *squalentis avos*, his shaggy-haired ancestors, by rubbing all the hair off his loins[1]. At sat. 11, 80, he speaks of a *squalidus fossor*, a long-haired digger. If you are a *scurra*, a citified wit like Suffenus seems to be, you are

[1] See s. 9, 95 (*nam res mortifera est inimicus pumice levis*) and cf. also Martial 5, 41, 6 (*et pumicata pauperes manu monstras*) and 14, 205, 1 (*sit nobis aetate puer, non pumice, levis*). Pliny (ep. 2, 11, 23) speaks of a *homo pumicatus*. Further references to depilation may be found in MARQUARDT, Privatleben 787, 9 (II 453).

'polished', rubbed down like a good-looking manuscript and a handsome man-about-town. But — at least in the case of Suffenus — touch poetry and you become a *fossor* (22, 10), a man *infacetus*, ill-made, as lacking in external grace as inner charm[1].

Persius 5, 115 ff. offers an analogue. The man who is *fronte politus* (116), with brow smoothed, who nevertheless keeps to his old skin and harbors a crafty fox in his heart, is a contradiction in terms. Persius concludes his indictment of such a character thus (122—3):

> *. . . nec, cum sis cetera fossor,*
> *tris tantum ad numeros Satyrum moveare Bathylli*[2].

Politus here is virtually synonymous with *pumicatus* and *tritus*, when used in the sense of 'smoothed', i. e. nicely rubbed down, physically, polished, intellectually.

Another occurrence of *attero*, relevant to Catullus 22, occurs in a letter of Pliny the younger to Suetonius (5, 10, 3): »*Perfectum opus absolutumque est, nec iam splendescit lima sed atteritur.*« The metaphor has been changed from smoothing with pumice to polishing — or over-polishing so as to wear away — with a file[3]. Nevertheless the use of a compound of *tero* in connection with a metaphor of literary criticism bears on *tritius* as used by Catullus. Suffenus appears to be polished, as his book is. But we are deceived in both regards. The metaphor, whether it comes from polishing with pumice or with a file, is equally applicable to person, book and style. *Tritius*, at 22, 13, has meaning in all three regards.

Dealing with style alone[4], *tero* and its compounds have, of course, the deprecatory sense of 'trite', 'overused', as SCHUSTER and the commentators on Catullus 22, 13 point out. Yet *detero* especially is used of »smoothing away« excess verbiage. We may note Quintilian (2, 4, 7) commenting on a young speaker's early abundance, later pared down (»*Multum inde decoquent anni, multum ratio limabit, aliquid velut usu ipso deteretur, sit modo unde excidi*

---

[1] The pun is intentional, dependent on the common ancient etymology of *infacetus* (see ERNOUT-MEILLET ad v.). It is a motif of the poem, beginning with the phrase *facit versus* (3) and continuing through *poemata* (15) and *poema* (16). That Catullus was also fully aware of the connection between *poema* and ποιεῖν = *facere* is illustrated by 50, 16 (*poema feci*). When Suffenus makes, touches or writes verses he becomes 'un-made'.

There is also a probable pun on the etymology of *palimpseston* (5) in relation to the use of *tritius* in 13.

[2] On *fronte politus* CONINGTON comments »This does not seem to belong to the metaphor.« NEMETHY is more appreciative.

[3] The literal connection between *lima* and a compound of *tero* (in this instance *praetero*) first appears in Plautus (Men. 9).

[4] For *detero* simply in the sense of »smooth«, »give an edge to«, see Pliny N. H. 27, 2, 10.

possit et quod exsculpi; . . .«) or Horace's arraignment of Lucilius (s. 1, 10, 68—70):

> *si foret hoc nostrum fato delapsus in aevum*
> *deteret sibi multa, recideret omne quod ultra*
> *perfectum traheretur, . . .*

The advice might well have been taken to heart by Suffenus. It is Lucilius' verbosity more than anything else which Horace criticizes (s. 1, 4, 9—10):

> . . . *in hora saepe ducentos,*
> *ut magnum, versus dictabat stans pede in uno*[1].

Tero in this sense is closely synonymous with the more familiar *limo*. Since the word is a commonplace in critical vocabulary, only a few salient instances, illustrating the variety of the metaphorical usages of it and its cognates, need be mentioned. In reference to a book and its style we may note Cicero de fin. 5, 5. (»*duo genera librorum, unum populariter scriptum, alterum limatius*«)[2]; to style alone, Horace s. 1, 10, 65 (in conjunction with *urbanus*)[3]; Cicero ad fam. 7, 33, 2 (on Volumnius' judgment about matters of style — *limatulo et polito tuo iudicio*); Pliny ep. 1, 20 (to Tacitus, on a *limatius ingenium*, the wit that creates a good style by confining its thoughts, in partial contrast to the *maius ingenium* of the orator who speaks too much); Cicero de or. 1, 25, 115 (on the polish that *ars* can bring to some orators)[4]; Cicero de n. d. 2, 29 (on personal 'polish' — *vir . . . nostrorum hominum urbanitate limatus* — where *limatus* appears to have virtually the same meaning as *tritus* in Catullus 22, 13).

Instances in Catullus of this contrast between external polish and spiritual or even physical vulgarity are not limited to poem 22. We may take the case of Egnatius who thinks he is *bonus*[5] because he has a dark beard (37, 20):

> *et dens Hibera defricatus urina.*

He is supposedly handsome. His teeth are quite polished and rubbed down. Yet the cause of their glow, ugly enough in itself, is merely symptomatic of a worse social vice. He grins all the time. As poem 39 amusingly illustrates, smiling is to Egnatius what writing verses is to Suffenus. He thinks his habit makes him *elegans* and *urbanus* (39, 8, comparable to 22, 2 and 9). In reality (39, 16)

> . . . *risu inepto res ineptior nulla est . . .*

---

[1] These famous lines are two of many where Horace's sentiments regarding over-writing echo those of Catullus and Callimachus (see, e.g., s. 1, 9, 23; 1, 10, 60—61).

[2] See also Brutus 24, 93; Ac. 1, 1, 3.

[3] See Hor. a. p. 291 (*limae labor et mora*) or Cicero on the diction of Scaevola (de or. 1, 39, 190: *oratione maxime limatus atque subtilis*).

[4] See de or. 3, 49, 190.

[5] Cf. 39, 9, *bone Egnati*.

34

The revelation is as much in order for Egnatius as Catullus' characterization of Suffenus who, once he starts to write, becomes *infaceto . . . infacetior rure* (22, 14)[1].

The point is brought home at the end of poem 39, once more through a metaphor of 'polishing' (39, 17—21):

> *nunc Celtiber ⟨es⟩: Celtiberia in terra,*
> *quod quisque minxit, hoc sibi solet mane*
> *dentem atque russam defricare gingivam,*
> *ut quo iste vester expolitior dens est,*
> *hoc te amplius bibisse praedicet loti.*

We have seen the use of *defricare* at 37, 20. Its appearance at 39, 19 is glossed by Apuleius' misquotation of the line (Apol. 6): »*ut ait Catullus . . . 'dentem atque russam pumicare gingivam'.*«[2] It is not only the extreme polish the *candidi dentes* receive which is noteworthy. Egnatius imagines the 'beauty' of his appearance to be enhanced by the contrast — a favorite of Catullus and of antiquity in general[3] — between his white teeth and the red gums in which they are set and which receive the same treatment. Yet none of this counteracts either the uncouthness of the means whereby the 'polish' is achieved or the 'disease' which is its cause, any more than Suffenus' supposed charm or the exterior polish of his volume makes amends for its essential uncouthness. Suffenus appears to be *tritus*, 'rubbed down' and 'polished' like his book. In reality he is not.

The question could well be asked whether *scurra* itself is capable of receiving an attribute like *tritus*, at least with the meaning suggested for it in Catullus 22, 13. According to WALDE-HOFMANN, the pejorative cognates of *scurra* are Ciceronian or post-Cicero. *Scurrilis* and *scurrilitas* do not appear before Cicero. *Scurror* is unexampled before Horace and *scurrula* before Apuleius. *Scurra* here, however, does not have the meaning of jester or parasite which it usually bears in Cicero[4] and regularly possesses in Horace. Its sense is strictly in the Plautine tradition — an elegant, sometimes over-elegant, man-about-town. Mostellaria 15 (*tu urbanus vero scurra, deliciae popli*) and Trinummus 202

---

[1] At the start of 39, there is as much a tension between Egnatius' white teeth and his constant smiling (*renidet usque quaque*) as there is between Suffenus' 'urbanity' and the production of innumerable verses.

[2] *Defricare* is used by Pliny (N. H. 26, 4, 10) for polishing with pumice. For a metaphorical use, see Horace s. 1, 10, 4.

[3] In Catullus see, for instance, 61, 9—10 (and FORDYCE's note thereto) or 64, 48—49 where, curiously, the words *dente politum* are prominent in the description.

[4] It is too strong to state (as WILKINS on de or. 2, 60, 244) that *scurra* in Cicero »always carries a notion of blame with it.« Cf. in Verr. 2, 3, 146; PEASE on de nat. d. 1, 93; TYRRELL and PURSER on ad Fam. 9, 20, 1—2.

(*urbani adsidui cives quos scurras vocant*) are the standard definitions[1]. There is no reason why *scurra*, in the complimentary sense that the Catullian context demands, should not have such an attribute as *tritus*. The exaggeration makes the denouement all the more amusing when it comes. Far from being himself a *scurra*, much less a *tritus scurra*, or a polished poet capable of writing polished verses decked out in a suitable setting, he is only a ditch-digger, as soon as he sets to work.

In conclusion, to return specifically to the critical metaphor involved in the verb *tero*, we may note that Callimachus adopts a cognate of the verb *tero*, the adjective τορός, to express his displeasure at the bloated contents of the Lyde of Antimachus, which, as mentioned above, is singled out for Catullus' satire in poem 95. I quote fragment 398 Pf.:

Λύδη καὶ παχὺ γράμμα καὶ οὐ τορόν[2].

In his comment thereto, Pfeiffer calls attention to the clash between πάχιστον and λεπταλέην[3] in the famous opening fragment of the Aitia (fr. 1 Pf., 23 ff.) and translates τορόν as σαφές. But in regard to both τορόν and λεπταλέην it is not only clarity which, according to Callimachus, Antimachus lacks — Callimachus himself is not one to disavow the learned reference — but the precision, the thin lightness of style, that comes from the ability to polish. We may join Catullus in classing Suffenus in much the same category.

Brown University   Michael C. J. Putnam

---

[1] See Duckworth on Epidicus 15 for a careful discussion of the seven uses of *scurra* by Plautus. See also Enk on Truculentus 491; Lindsay CQ 14, 1920, 52; Schuster, op. cit.

[2] τορός is cognate with *tero* (see Ernout-Meillet[4], 687; Pokorny, Indogermanisches etymologisches Wörterbuch, 1071; Walde-Hofmann[3], 672). It is also kindred to *tornus*, another word used regularly in critical vocabulary. *Tero* and *tornus* are juxtaposed in one of the two instances Schuster cites (op. cit.) of *tero* as 'polish' — Pliny N. H. 36, 193: *aliud torno teritur*.

Roughly a century after Callimachus, Antipater of Sidon, spiritual member of the opposition, in an epigram honoring Antimachus (A. P. 7, 409, 3), praises the τορὸν οὖας of anyone keen enough to appreciate the epic poet's originality. It is a parallel phrase, *tritae aures*, in a letter of Cicero to L. Papirius Paetus (ad. Fam. 9, 16, 4) that is one of the two examples regularly cited by the commentators on Catullus 22, 13 for the metaphorical meaning 'skilful' applied to the past participle of *tero* (see Fordyce, op. cit.). The context is instructive because the allusion is to a cousin of Paetus who was adept at distinguishing true Plautine lines from false. Other instances of τορός in connection with both style and personality are given in L.-S.

[3] On the etymological connection between λεπτός, λεπταλέος and *lepos, lepidus*, interesting for a study of the influence of Callimachean procedure on Catullian practise, see Walde-Hofmann, 50—51; Pokorny, 678. As metaphors of literary criticism, λεπτός (from λέπω, »peel off«, hence, metaphorically speaking, »dispose of excess«) and τορός serve virtually the same purpose.

On Catullus 27

Minister uetuli puer Falerni
inger mi calices amariores,
ut lex Postumiae iubet magistrae
ebrioso acino ebriosioris.
At uos quo lubet hinc abite, lymphae,
uini pernicies, et ad seueros
migrate. Hic merus est Thyonianus.

The central thought of Catullus' little scolion — Away with water ! Mix me purer, stronger draughts ! — is not new. Its ancestry has been traced to Anacreon and, with clearer direction, to Diphilus (¹). But a literary pedigree, however unsullied, should not mislead us into dismissing the poem as "little more than an expansion of some verses of Diphilus" (Ellis) or as "Ein stilisierter Trinkspruch" (Kroll). Pedigree need not obscure matter and manner essentially Catullian.

The surface structure is masterful. The two sentences set off the primary division, lines 1-4 and 5-7. Catullus is fond of such near symmetries. Poems 47 and 56 parallel 27 exactly. Poem 46 offers a ratio of 6 lines against 5 and other examples could be adduced. But lines 1-4 of 27 fall themselves into two parts. *Minister* (beginning of line 1) anticipates *magistrae*, ending line 3, while the genitives in the lines also complement one another. This balance puts special stress on the imperative *inger* in line 2.

We find a similar correspondence between lines 5 and 7. Each contains an imperative (*abite ... migrate*). *Hic* (7) looks clearly back to *hinc* (5).

The resulting symmetrical arrangement of lines 1-3 and 5-7 leaves line 4 standing alone. Its own particular structure is thus put into relief. *Ebrioso* is carefully repeated in *ebriosioris* so as to surround *acino*, which stands alone. This takes its proper place

---

(1) For the references, see ELLIS, KROLL and FORDYCE. I follow the text of Mynors in reading *ebrioso* at line 4.

at the poem's typographical and intellectual center. We would
have neither inspiration nor song without the grape (¹).

A more subtle, chiastic balance serves the same purpose of emphasizing line 4. This arrangement depends as much on sound as
on meaning. It can be shown best by taking the lines in three sets
of pairs :

> I. 1. *mi*nister *uetu*li puer Falerni
> 7. *mi*grate hic m*eru*s est Thyonianus

Though the quantity in each case is different, the syllable *mi* is
repeated at the beginning of each line. The vowels "e" and "u"
occur at the same metrical position in *uetuli* and *merus*. The proper
names *Falerni* and *Thyonianus*, which end each line, have lesser
echoes.

> II. 2. *in*ger mi cal*ices* am*ariores*
> 6. u*ini* perni*cies* et *a*d seu*eros*

The vowel "i" is in the first syllable of each line, followed by "n".
The letter groups "ices" and "cies", "ores" and "eros", appear
at parallel metrical spots. The second "a" of *amariores* (2) is revived
in *ad* (6).

> III. 3. u*t* lex P*o*stumiae i*u*bet magistr*ae*
> 5. a*t* uos qu*o* *lu*bet hinc abite lymph*ae*

Each line commences with two monosyllables and ends with the
same diphthong ("ae"). The "o" and "u" of *Postumiae* are sounded
again in *quo* and *lubet*. All the letters of *abite* (5) are found in *iubet
ma* ... which holds the same metrical position in line 3.

But sound and structure are ancillary to sense and meaning.
The *minister puer*, on first reading, is the "pourer" of the mellowing
Falernian wine (²). He seems like the *puer* in Horace *c.* 1. 38. 1,
who wears a myrtle crown befitting both servant as he pours (*minis-*

---

(1) Another division is offered by H. Bardon, *L'art de la composition chez Catulle*, 15 :
"Avec plus de simplicité [than in poem 4], les 7 vers de c. 27 s'ordonnent sur le thème
vin-eau-vin, mais sans rechercher un équilibre numérique entre les trois parties".

(2) On the quality of Falernian itself, see Smith on Tib., 2.1.27. Virgil implies that
it has no peers (*g.* 2.96). Pliny (*n.h.*, 14.8.62-3) says that it is the only wine that can
be ignited with a flame !

trum, 6) and drinking poet (*bibentem*, 8). We think also of the slave in *c*. 2. 11. 18-20 :

> ... *quis puer ocius*
> *restinguet ardentis Falerni*
> *pocula praetereunte lympha ?*

Catullus makes a different point. His *puer* is not the poet's servant specifically but the *minister uetuli Falerni*. He is the "slave" of the "old man" Falernus. He does his will while poet and slave alike are subject to the dictates of *Postumia magistra*. It is the old man's banquet, but she calls the shots. The poet instructs the *puer* who fulfills their combined wishes. The hierarchy of rank in the opening three lines runs, structurally as well as logically, from *minister* to *magistrae*. The poet may command the slave of Falernus. Yet both in turn must obey a higher *lex* which does the real ordering.

The personification of Falernus (as opposed to mere *uinum Falernum*) is intensified by two points. The first is the antonymous juxtaposition of *uetuli* and *puer*. The distinction between youth and age would lose some of its sharpness if we were merely dealing with animate versus inanimate, a slave-boy on the one hand, a jug of wine on the other. The second is the attribution of a *minister* to him. Pourer he must be, on one level. But this would be to allow *uetuli Falerni* to signify merely some older vintage from the *ager Falernus*. Rather he is entitled to an attendant who assists him and carries out his requests ([1]). He is a privileged mortal, perhaps even a god.

Catullus' irrespressible penchant for personification has already made its second appearance in the poem by line 3. It is not *Postumia magistra* who does the ordering, but her law. And, since the poet himself has just given the slave instructions, the ruling *lex* is on a par with him in other respects as well.

And along with the *lex*, even *acino* of line 4 is personified. It, too, is drunken, only less so than mistress Postumia. Yet it is at the center of the poem. Without the tipsy grape we would not have Falernus himself.

Postumia magistra has a special role in this banquet. Catullian prosopographers have defended several candidates for her real identity ([2]). The *lex Postumia*, however, has a past which can be

---

(1) *Minister* and *magistra* are used with these meanings first in Latin by Catullus here (*T.L.L.*, 8, *s.v.* : 87.41 ff. [and cf. 78.69 ff.] and 1002.36).

(2) See KROLL, *ad loc.* ; MÜNZER, *P.-W.*, 22.1. c. 949-50, *s.v.* Postumia.

exactly traced (¹). It dates from the reign of king Numa. Thanks to Pliny the elder we know two of its provisions (²). The first Pliny quotes in full : *Vino rogum ne respargito*. The second he paraphrases ; "eadem lege ex imputata vite libari vina dis nefas statuit ". The reason Pliny gives for the latter statute is the necessity to keep those engaged in viticulture carefully attentive to their task. This was only one corollary of a larger contemporary problem — *inopiam rei*, in Pliny's words, an unfortunate scarcity of the product itself.

Catullus's *lex Postumia*, if we may so style it, is far different — a humorous look back at a happily vanished age. His imperative, which her *lex* bolsters, is for more wine, not less, stronger drink, not half-hearted ventures. At a dinner given by Falernus, with the authoress of a refurbished *lex Postumia* as symposiarch, we should except nothing less.

But Catullus has a new command, creatively negative — Away with water ! His first imperative, *inger*, was a colloquial, clipped form, addressed familiarly to the slave. It supports the poet's sense of urgent need for the brisk advent of a necessary commodity. *Abite* and *migrate* demand an equivalent departure. His words are a curse in a form which particularly delighted him (³). We find it twice linked with bad verse. The end of poem 14, for instance, outlaws the work of some trashy poetasters Calvus has sent him. There is the same mock-serious wit (14. 21-23) :

> *uos hinc interea ualete abite*
> *illuc, unde malum pedem attulistis,*
> *saecli incommoda, pessimi poetae.*

The double imperative with asyndeton reveals the same quickness of need as the syncopated *inger* of 27. 2. The triple pun on *pedem* would need no elaboration for a Calvus.

The end of poem 36 (lines 18-20) furnishes a similar instance, this time addressed to Volusius' unfortunate efforts :

> *at uos interea uenite in ignem*
> *pleni ruris et inficetiarum*
> *annales Volusi, cacata carta.*

---

(1) ELLIS, *ad loc.*, mentions the *lex Postumia* but disclaims any connection. We expect *lex Postumia* instead of *lex Postumiae*.

(2) PLINY, *n.h.*, 14.14.88.

(3) As KROLL notes, line 5 echoes closely a moment in *Miles Gloriosus* when the slave Palaestrio orders Pyrgopolyneices to get rid of the unwanted concubine (*M.G.*, 974).

They must make their way but not into a very refreshing spot !

Sometimes the thought is restricted to a curse alone — *at uobis male sit*, to the shades of Orcus who have devoured the sparrow (3. 13) ; *at uobis mala multa di deaeque | dent* to the *nobiles amicos* who take advantage of him and his friends (28. 14-15). Command without curse can be seen, also with a careful pun, in Catullus' words to the bath thief and his son (33. 5-6) : *cur non exilium malasque in oras | itis?*

Here in poem 27 the personification receives special stress from the apostrophe. The Lymphae deserve an initial capital. Paulus-Festus (107L) tells us that "Lymphae dictae sunt a nymphis". But they were a special form of nymph. Varro (*r.r.* 1. 6) mentions *Lympha*, the goddess of moisture. Horace tells how the town of Gnatia was built under the wrath of these water-spirits (*Lymphis iratis* : *s.* 1. 5. 97-8). Vitruvius (1. 2. 5) notes a temple to the *Lymphae* and Augustine twice gives them the same relation to water as Bacchus has to wine (*c.d.* 4. 22 ; 6. 1) (¹).

They are unwelcome guests at a dinner presented by *uetulus Falernus*. They would be the death of him and the collapse of the party. Catullus commands them into immediate exile. They are to make their way, the whole tribe of them (*migrate*), to the *seueri* (²). From the way Catullus refers to *seueri* elsewhere, this means to those who lack love (and hence life). It is the gossip of *senum seueriorum* that Catullus and Lesbia are to ignore, as they go about their thousands of kisses (5. 2).

One line of the *Aeneid* suggests that the direction might be still more specific. A large number of peoples from the Sabine territory flocked to the banner of Turnus, according to Virgil's magnificent description of the hosts marshalling. Among the tribes were the folk who managed to dwell on *Tetricae horrentis rupes montemque Seuerum* (7. 713). Servius glosses the first part of the line in terms applicable to the second as well : "Tetricus mons in Sabinis asperrimus, unde tristes homines tetricos dicimus". Conington rightly approves a comment of de la Cerda which he paraphrases : "... both names are used as adjectives and applied as such to describe the

---

(1) See also Nigidius Figulus, p. 89, line 1 (Swoboda), and Martianus Capella, 1.46.

(2) Commentators on *ecl.*, 9.4 offer other examples.

traits belonging to the Sabine character." Elsewhere Catullus takes as a personal insult the application of the epithet Sabine to his (he claims) Tiburtine villa (44. 1-5). As far as poem 27 is concerned, water is for sober Sabines to imbibe. Let the *Lymphae* go to them as fitting patron divinities. His habits call for sterner stuff.

Their departure leaves the world of straight alcohol without any menace — *hic merus est Thyonianus*. To whom *hic* ("this man here") refers has been debated. It clearly is not the *puer*. Catullus himself has rightly been proposed (the change of person, after *mi* of line 2, is no drawback) (¹). There is another possibility. Kroll suggested that a missing οἶνος should be supplied. This is needless. *Vetulus Falernus* has already been personified in the opening lines. He remains untainted (*merus*) now that the *Lymphae* are on their way. Being wine itself, no one could lay better claim to the title "unpolluted Bacchus". He is a true devoted offspring and partisan of Thyone. His madness can have nothing to do with the *s*(*S*)*everi* nor their sobriety with him.

But the ambiguity remains and is at the core of the poem's wit. *Hic* can be Catullus or Falernus. The poet and his bibulous host share and acknowledge a common ancestor.

The attribution *Thyonianus* completes the circle of the poem. *Hic* at first suggests a specific spot — the dinner party, certainly, the *ager Falernus* from which the old wine comes, perhaps. But *Thyonianus* proves that this is no mere mortal with which we are dealing. It is a god himself. The slave is his *minister*. His "rites" would be profaned by the presence of the *Lymphae* who must be off, one and all. The poet styles himself a different Numa, propounding a new, improved *Lex Postumia*, protecting the cult of a deity much cherished by poets (²).

The many-sided wit of the poem should not hide a very Catullian core. It is like the hymn to Diana in this respect. The apparent uniqueness deceives. One essential point is purity. We may look

---

(1) See J. D. P. Bolton, *Merus Thyonianus* in *C.R.*, n.s. 17 (1967), 12.
(2) Horace briskly makes the connection between wine and wit by asking (*e.*, 1.5.19).

    facundi calices quem non fecere disertum?

The metonomy of *calices* is anticipated at Cat., 27.2. Horace too contrasts the man who is *parcus* and *seuerus* with the wise toper (13 ff.).

at individual words, *merus*, for instance. In poem 13 Catullus claims he cannot offer his friend Fabullus a good dinner, or even wine or "salt". He can present instead something more valuable — *meros amores*, love that is untainted and unstinted (13. 9). Or there is the expression *pernicies uini*. Elsewhere, in totally different circumstances, Catullus can appeal to the gods against the corruption of his love (76. 19-20) :

> *me miserum aspicite et, si uitam puriter egi,*
> *eripite hanc pestem perniciemque mihi.*

In spite of its stringent organization, poem 27 is no simple sententious "away with water, in with wine" such as an Anacreon or a Trimalchio might utter ([1]). It is a superb example of Catullus' easy control, his light, economic craftsmanship. It is also a miniature reaffirmation of an important tenet in the credo of Catullus — precision, directness and sincere expression in poetry ; a strategic unity of surface magnetism with inner value. It is not far from this to the demanding kinship of the sensual and the metaphysical, which the love poems crave.

Catullus' ordinary stance is reversed in one respect. There is no tension between *uetuli* and *puer*, only contrast. This is no lifeless old man ([2]). Nor is it the aged fool attempting to play the young blade, whom Plautus characterizes so nicely in the *Mercator* and Catullus elsewhere styles a *seni recocto* ([3]). Catullus' old man grows stronger instead of weaker with age. Wine is associated by Catullus with good eating, laughter, wit, love, and the writing of verses (in no sense mutually exlusive) ([4]). *Vetulus Falernus* is for the young. The older he gets, the more appealing. The elderly, in time or spirit, prefer water or diluted wine. The thoughts of the old at heart (*seueri*) are a calamity (*pernicies*) for the young. Like water at other times, this wine is creative.

There is a complementary irony in the use of *amariores* to describe the draughts Catullus desires. The sweet is what is ordinarily

---

(1) Cf. SAT., 52. At SAT., 55 Trimalchio's verses contain the following command :
> *quare da nobis uina Falerna, puer.*

(2) CATULLUS is fond of the figure (17.24 ; 25.3, *et al.*).

(3) *Merc.*, 290 ff. and CAT., 54.5. See also PLAUTUS, *Trin.*, 43 and CAT., 108. 1 ff.

(4) 12.2 ff. ; 13.3-4 ; 50.6.

43

beautiful. Five times the poet calls love *dulcis* ([1]). Yet he is no stranger to the eccentricities of Venus (68. 17-18) :

> *multa satis lusi: non est dea nescia nostri,*
> *quae dulcem curis miscet amaritiem.*

Falernus provides only the sternest stuff. Yet, "bitter" as he is, there is no doubt about his acceptibility and importance.

Brown University.   Michael C. J. PUTNAM.

---

(1) 64.120 ; 66.6 ; 68.24 = 68.96 ; 78.3.

THE ART OF CATULLUS *64*

By Michael C. J. Putnam

FAVORABLE criticism devoted to the longer poems of Catullus is
still comparatively rare. Recent signs manifest a worthy trend away
from the hitherto frequent attempt to divide Catullus into two parts, one
supposedly *doctus* and consequently an admirer of Alexandrian models
and disciplines, the other by contrast witty and clever, the recipient of
μανία, in fact the spirit whose lyric fancies offer such endless delight.
Yet this heresy persists in a different guise, more damaging to an appreciation of Catullus, in the tendency to disown the long poems as ob-
scurely motivated, foreign to the more successful aspects of his genius.
We are allowed to admire Catullus, author of the short, brilliant essays in
individualism, while his longer works (though sometimes, especially in
the case of *63*, interesting in themselves) seemingly impersonal and
built on the shaky foundations of tradition and imitation, are relegated
to a secondary position and scorned as abnormal or at least exceptional.

Yet to ignore almost half his production can scarcely result in a
unified picture either of a poet's mind at work or of his personality. If an
examination of Catullus' long poems were only to result in shedding light
on the imagination which poured forth the lyrics, it would serve not only
a useful but an instructive purpose. But such a goal remains here only a
corollary to a search for the unique beauties which one of these, poem *64*,
possesses in its own right. In other words, we offer here, for one work of
Catullus, an analysis comparable to that recently accomplished for the
poetry of William Blake, showing, in fact, that his longer works, far from
being dull asides or at best lengthy footnotes mirroring the taste of the
time, are the offspring of a poet whose special powers can be traced
throughout everything he produced.[1]

The result is a twofold plea for unity, unity first of *64* within itself,
and unity between it and the shorter poems.[2] If *64* is, as has been maintained, a series of narrative sections strung loosely together by means of
the most tenuous and superficial bonds, then we should certainly without
further ado dismiss the poem as a piece of made-to-order Alexandrian
work, a demonstration, as it were, on the part of Catullus that he too
could write in a genre popular with his fellow *neoteroi*. Poem *64* ,we are
often told, is written in a form (though even this fact is subject to doubt)

which may have been prevalent during the so-called "Alexandrian" period, and therefore it goes without saying that it exhibits the worst side of the poetry we associate with Callimachus' contemporaries, wherein subject is molded to fit genre and imagination corrupted to the uses of virtuosity. The opposite is in fact the case. There is no meaningless artificiality here. Rather the whole is consciously calculated and specifically pointed, with Catullus' own directness, toward a grand design.

The long poems, and especially *64*, contain in the elaborate design which epic allows the same situations and emotions from which the lyrics grew. Catullus' genius is personality.[3] Inspiration for him is always drawn immediately out of confrontation with the events of life. Unlike Milton, Catullus was a poet who could never divorce himself from his themes. The end of *63* offers a case in point when the poet prays:

> dea magna, dea Cybele, dea domina Dindymei,
> procul a mea tuus sit furor omnis, era, domo:
> alios age incitatos, alios age rabidos.

In spite of his seeming protest to the contrary, the strength of imagery here repeated from the body of the poem proves beyond a doubt Catullus' own deep participation in this work. The writing of both *63* and *64* appears detached because the stories center upon remote mythology. But in fact they are the heightened imaginative efforts of a poet who left his mark on every line and who, though deliberately disavowing actual participation in the story, tells his reader by no less obvious means than in the lyrics that these are writings of the most personal sort. The longer poems change names, places, and dates; they do not alter either poetic or personal intensity. Catullus speaks through characters, but very much for himself. As John Livingstone Lowes found of Coleridge, we seek to discover Catullus' mind at work even in his longer poems and at the same time find Catullus as a person around every corner. Briefly, these poems are a very important part of Catullus' production, and no general interpretation which omits an examination of them can be completely successful.

Unity of emotion finds its twin, of course, in unity of imaginative expression. Thus we will have frequent recourse to other poems to observe the imagination which created *64* at work elsewhere on similar topics and in a similar manner.

We assume also at the start that *64* is no Hellenistic poem in the deprecatory sense of the word, meaning a superficial exercise containing little or no meaning beyond its form. It manifests only a few structural techniques in common with the poets of Alexandria, such as use of the ὀμφαλός pattern for digressions (and even this is as old as Homer).[4] Rather the language of *64* is simple, straightforward, and intense, only rarely redundant or overelaborate. In a sense *64* gives an even truer portrait of Catullus than do some of the polymetric and elegiac poems, especially those which attempt to falsify and reverse the true situation (a common Catullan habit).[5] In *64*, because the poet is writing epic, he can give his thoughts a freer rein than usual just because he is writing under the mask of symbolic poetry.

During the course of *64* certain almost prose-like statements about love which the elegiacs offer are elaborated into long descriptive parallels which embody in epic story the skeleton of their tortured utterances. Though *72* is a poem to which further references will be made below, it deserves quotation in full here since, in brief compass, it displays many of the tensions which form the core of the subsequent discussion of *64*:

> Dicebas quondam solum te nosse Catullum,
> > Lesbia, nec prae me velle tenere Iovem.
> dilexi tum te non tantum ut vulgus amicam,
> > sed pater ut gnatos diligit et generos.
> nunc te cognovi: quare etsi impensius uror,
> > multo mi tamen es vilior et levior.
> qui potis est? inquis. quod amantem iniuria talis
> > cogit amare magis, sed bene velle minus.

Like *72*, *64* exhibits, par excellence, the opposition of past and present, ideal and real, ever at hand in Catullus and here spread out in narrative detail. This leads to the belief that Lesbia and the poet's brother are also very much involved in the story as it unfolds. In a word, poem *64* shows Catullus writing of himself in the figures of Ariadne and Aegeus, and of the way he had hoped his relationship with Lesbia would evolve in the story of Peleus and Thetis.[6] With the present disguised under symbolic forms, it is true autobiography and consequently it says more than any other of his poems because it can do so with impunity.

I. Divisions; Scene on the Shore and First Flashback

The poem divides essentially into two parts. It opens with the first meeting of Peleus and Thetis, leading the reader to believe that the tale of their love and marriage forms the bulk of the poem. Yet in the midst of the opening description, only fifty lines after the poem begins, Catullus digresses, by describing the coverlet on the marriage bed, into the tale of Ariadne's desertion by Theseus. This, with its various ramifications, takes up more than half the poem. Thereafter the happy wedding description returns, to balance the sadness of the previous episode. Even now all does not remain serene, for the song of the Fates follows, singing bliss to the happy pair, bliss enhanced and yet impaired by their son, the warlike death-dealing Achilles. Once more happy allusions to the *concordia* of the newly founded home surround the bitter lines, but the poet's point is clear. The ideal is never reached, even in the union between Peleus and Thetis, which to ancient authors was above all others the most perfect.[7] The story and the song now over, the work concludes with a few lines of moralizing wherein the virtues of the past are contrasted with present vices, lines which stand as commentary to the two diverse episodes which preceded.

Leaving the opening verses to be discussed along with those which follow the digression, we shall begin with the tale of Ariadne. We find her first in line 52 as she looks out from the sounding shore and beholds Theseus sailing away, unloving and oblivious. She, on the other hand, is in the grip of love for Theseus which even then she cannot suppress.[8] So sudden is her disillusionment that her mind refuses to acknowledge what her eyes admit as fact. She is aroused from a sleep which is *fallax*, because it lulled her into a confidence as false as her lover:

> immemor at iuvenis fugiens pellit vada remis
> irrita ventosae linquens promissa procellae.

The sound of *iuvenis* seems to be reiterated in *ventosae*, just as *linquens* picks up the sense of *fugiens*.

The picture of departure haunted Catullus, meaning to him on most occasions little short of desertion, and in the opening lines Catullus finds the opportunity to enhance this theme. He exploits the situation of Ariadne to the fullest. The winds which bear the youth away are the very ones which waft his promises into the air. As she repeats later in her speech, Theseus gave her *promissa* with *blanda voce*, in alluring and seductive tones but signifying nothing more than mere words. They were (according to lines 59 and 142, both of which utilize the metaphor of winds) *irrita*, a deadly accusation in Catullus' mind.[9] Like his oaths, Theseus' promises were only meant to gain the sensual satisfaction of the moment, remaining invalid for the future (line 148). To adapt the words of Catullus to Lesbia, he was indeed *nullam amans vere*.

Likewise the shore, which finds her deserted on its lonely waste, is a reflection in nature of the situation of her pitiful heart. She has cut herself off from love and home and family only to be surrounded by the girdling sea. The island is *sola* as she is and deserted.

It is not difficult to find other instances of Catullus' commenting on a similar fate. Attis, the victim of the madness of Cybele, is foreign to anything in 64, but the Attis who awakens to find his madness fled, and with it all that was true and human, is a figure who has much in common with Ariadne. The mere parallels in the way the poet represents their external situations are interesting. We would expect the descriptions of each to begin coinciding at the moment of Attis' awakening, and so they do. In 63.42 Catullus relates that

> ibi *Somnus excitam* Attin fugiens citus abiit; . . .

much as he pictures Ariadne (64.56):

> utpote fallaci quae tum primum *excita somno* . . .

The lines which follow find Attis gradually becoming aware of the full implications of his recent deeds (63.45–47):

> simul ipsa pectore Attis sua facta recoluit,
> liquidaque mente vidit sine quis ubique foret,
> animo aestuante rusum reditum ad vada tetulit . . . ,

yet in much the same manner Ariadne yearns for Theseus. *Vidit* of 63.46 (with *visens* of 48) recalls 64.55. The verses which precede Attis' speech (63.48–49):

> ibi maria vasta visens lacrimantibus oculis,
> patriam allocuta maestast ita voce miseriter . . . ,

offer a situation not far different from 64.60:

> quem procul ex alga maestis Minois ocellis,

or from the recurrence of this very same description shortly before Ariadne begins to speak. Each is *miser* and each gives vent to suffering in words which reveal its full extent.

But verbal reminiscences alone — and many more could be adduced — do not tell us why the poet offers so much common ground between Attis and Ariadne, why two such supposedly disparate figures should be depicted in such a similar way. The answer can lie nowhere but in the realization that the circumstances and thoughts of each are very much a part of Catullus himself, and therefore are to be conveyed in like fashion. Each wakes from sleep to bitter truth. Each betakes himself to the shore, which becomes not a symbol for arrival (in the opening lines of *63* the shore is not even mentioned), but of separation from true love. Attis laments the loss of home and family through the excessive *furor* of devotion; Ariadne, while manifestly blaming Theseus, bewails almost exactly the same fate, since she herself has been the victim of mad passion to the detriment of all that remains true and steadfast.

Moreover the phraseology in these lines devoted to Ariadne bears a marked resemblance to the totality of poem *30*. Alfenus, after promising much to the poet, had betrayed and deserted him. He stands to Catullus as Theseus to Ariadne. The numerous parallels between the two poems,[10] many of which may be no more than clichés of situation, come suddenly to life with the reflection of 30.5,

> quae tu neglegis ac me miserum deseris in malis . . . ,

in 64.57, where Ariadne

> desertam in sola miseram se cernat harena.

In malis becomes *in sola harena* because of the epic setting. Otherwise the situations are noticeably similar. Only the emotions aroused in the reader by the pitiful case of Ariadne are heightened by the beauty of the shore scene, as the horror of her desertion is magnified by her loneliness.

It is not, however, to any stray example, such as *30*, that we turn in search of a completely parallel episode in Catullus' life which might have aroused in him the feelings of Ariadne. We look not to the Alfenuses, numerous as they may have been, but to Lesbia, to whom, alone of those mentioned in his poetry, he could ascribe the actions and feelings of a Theseus. This was the great emotion of his life. He describes in *64* Lesbia's desertion of him in epic terms. Lesbia is the one who has fled his embraces only to leave him *miser* with lovesickness.[11] The similarity between this event and the situation described in 64.58ff. is too close to be mere coincidence. Catullus is very much a part of Ariadne.

The irony of circumstance in these lines is thoroughly apparent. When Theseus sails away *celeri cum classe*, we think on Attis' arrival in Phrygia *celeri rate* and ponder the fact that Theseus' desertion is like the madness which drove Attis away from home. Likewise, Ariadne should arise happy on her wedding day. Instead she wakens to find no love at all.[12] These verses contrast in particularly effective fashion with the very opening section of the poem. Line 35 tells how

> deseritur Cieros, linquunt Pthiotica Tempe . . .

The same words used here to describe the home at Pharsalus, crowded with a throng joyously assembled for the marriage rites, recur in the picture of the abandoned Ariadne.[13] The result is direct and deliberate verbal irony to emphasize the distinction between true and false.

We meet another theme from the contrasts within the lines themselves, namely the difference between external and internal value. We had previously read of the waves of care on which Ariadne was tossed. Her sensations are depicted more explicitly in lines 68–70:

> sed neque tum mitrae neque tum fluitantis amictus
> illa vicem curans toto ex te pectore, Theseu,
> toto animo, tota pendebat perdita mente . . . ,

and the imagery is expanded in the lines which follow. She is passionately in love with Theseus with a desire which stems from her whole being, *toto ex pectore*.[14] By contrast, the heart of Theseus is labeled in the course of the poem both *immemor* (line 123) and *immite* (line 138).[15] He is bent on reaping the sexual rewards of the moment while she suffers the true feelings of love. The result is that lines 63 to 67, where her disheveled appearance is described, because they are framed by the similarity of thought in lines 62 and 68–70, bring out the contrast created by the juxtaposition. Ariadne cares nothing for her physical state. Externally all is disorder. Yet she seems what she is, as her heart yearns truly for Theseus.

This contrast between exterior and interior, a familiar one appearing in many guises throughout the poetry of Catullus, makes no more vivid appearances than in 64. Ariadne cries in lines 175–76 (and the words pick up her previous thoughts at lines 136–37):

> nec malus hic celans dulci crudelia forma
> consilia in nostris requiesset sedibus hospes!

The cruel counsels lurk beneath an exterior which tempts toward love. She was carried away by outward charm to hope for inner spiritual values where in fact there were none. The revelation about Lesbia came gradually to Catullus as the elegiacs show, and the tone of *8* clearly suggests that he wanted to postpone acceptance of it until denial was impossible. But Ariadne is the Catullus to whom all is clear. Recognition to her is instant on all levels. It takes place in the seconds which separate sleep from waking. The speech which Ariadne then delivers is the epitome of Catullus' own disillusionment.

In the first twenty lines devoted to the story of Ariadne, then, Catullus prepares the reader for much that is to follow and reveals at the same time his own personal feelings.[16] The very first adjective applied to any aspect of her plight, *fluentisono*, is an apparent coinage of the poet's. But he soon associates both the floods and the sounds with Ariadne in a way which makes the word a precursor of the description which follows. The ebb and flow, as part of the wave imagery, also become internal (line 62); yet we have seen how the turmoil of the sea affects her externally as well (lines 67–68). Again a few lines later the metaphorical usage reappears when the poet in his own person adds the aside (lines 97 -98):

> qualibus incensam iactastis mente puellam
> fluctibus, in flavo saepe hospite suspirantem!

The roar of the beating waves resounds for one last time in the shrill cries of Ariadne bewailing her fate and telling how she began (line 125)

> clarisonas imo fudisse e pectore voces.[17]

With line 73 Catullus commences to tell the story from the start. From here to line 121, where we return to Ariadne on the shore, we are treated to a long flashback, beginning with Theseus' departure from Athens to kill the Minotaur and ending with Ariadne's relinquishment of family and home to take flight with Theseus. As always in Catullus, the voyage means more than geographical wandering. It symbolizes change through departure, the leaving of one kind of life for another. Here it gives scope to what may have been to Catullus merely the agony caused by Lesbia's infidelity. Perhaps we may find the source of the poet's continual return to this picture in his brother's death-journey to Troy. Whatever the case may be, *64* rises and falls on the theme of the journey, which is itself a reflection of the happiness and pain of love.

Here the focus of events upon the earlier stages of Ariadne's love adds to the poignancy of her plight while at the same time preparing the way for the speech in which she concentrates all her bitterness. The figure of Theseus is sketched with a few strokes.[18] His arrival in Crete found him only the *flavus hospes* (line 98), the hero whose boldness, coupled with her brave assistance, overcame the Minotaur. It is rather to her love for Theseus that Catullus primarily devotes himself, showing her as the lover capable of supreme devotion. The imagery of lines 86–90, when compared to like passages in *61*, proves her ripeness for marriage. But in *61* both the husband and wife are at some point called *cupidus*.[19] In *64* not a word is uttered of such a desire on the part of Theseus. It is Ariadne who views her lover *cupido lumine* (line 86), and who later implies that any eagerness Theseus may have had was but the moment's fancy.

Once again Ariadne is the mouthpiece of the poet himself, for rarely does Catullus speak of a desire on Lesbia's part for him.[20] Mention of his for her forms part of *70* and is the core of *107*, where Catullus applies the word *cupidus* to himself three times in the course of five lines. Any such yearning, first suggested in poems like *107*, finds its complete expression in the speech of Ariadne in *64*. In *107* Lesbia returned to the poet, who was beginning to despair of her devotion. In *64*, Theseus has departed for good.

From the word *cupidus* we may turn to other means by which the poet pictures Ariadne's love. As usual for Catullus, the senses play a role of great importance, especially the eyes. Through her eyes Ariadne first conceives (line 92) the flame of love which burns her to the very marrow. After this brief description couched in highly erotic imagery (especially lines 91–93), the poet has so fallen under the spell of, nay, become part of Ariadne's situation, that he suddenly turns and speaks to Cupid and Venus, addressing them in the second person as he had Theseus in line 69, where he was also thinking quite personally of Ariadne's suffering (lines 94–96):

> heu misere exagitans immiti corde furores
> sancte puer, curis hominum qui gaudia misces,
> quaeque regis Golgos quaeque Idalium frondosum. . . .

Line 95 reflects the sentiment of 68.17–18, where Catullus, looking wistfully at his own past, boasts:

> multa satis lusi: non est dea nescia nostri,
> quae dulcem curis miscet amaritiem.

In fact the whole surrounding passage in *68* is a variation on this situation in *64*. When Catullus was, like Ariadne, in the spring of life, 68.16 says, he was much under the power of Venus; yet now, he goes on, all joys are taken from him. The superficial source of the waves of fortune, on which he complains to Manlius he is tossed, is soon revealed as the death of his brother. Yet we know from the second part of *68* that he has also been meditating on Lesbia's infidelity, since he tries desperately to make light of it. Even though he makes no mention at all of Lesbia in *68a*, the *fluctus fortunae* may find a secondary application to Lesbia's faithlessness. So young Ariadne also experienced the *gaudia* of love with Theseus, only to find herself betrayed.

Epic description returns once more in line 105, this time devoted to the battle with the Minotaur. Little more need be said, Catullus hints in line 116, to fill the gap between this heroic achievement and the desertion on Dia. Yet he adds four interesting lines (117–120) narrating

> . . . ut linquens genitoris filia vultum
> ut consanguineae complexum, ut denique matris,
> quae misera in gnata deperdita laeta (batur),
> omnibus his Thesei dulcem praeoptarit amorem. . .

This is a familiar Catullan situation, but it deserves mention here. Ariadne left father, sister, mother, in fact home and family love on account of her passion for Theseus. Such also is the situation in which Attis finds himself when he says

> patria o mei creatrix, patria o mea genetrix
> ego quam miser relinquens. . . .

Each has given way to the violence of a passion which in its joy is fleeting while lasting with pain. Each has renounced the steadfast, lasting *pietas* of home, the love which exists between parents and children, between brother and brother. This is the spiritual side of the love which Catullus bore Lesbia, as he defines it in 72. It is also the way he felt, as we shall later see, toward his own brother. The perfect love would have been ideally a union between this spiritual *pietas* and sexual passion. As it was, he learned that the combination could never be achieved, since the love he felt toward his brother could not be found in Lesbia, lacking as she did the *fides* and *pietas* which formed its very foundation.

Line 121 returns to where line 72 had left off. The description now leads directly into the beginning of Ariadne's lament,[21] and the imagery of these ten lines merely recapitulates and enhances the description at the beginning of her story. She rages. She is *tristis* and *maesta*, words applicable to love as well as grief. And the imagery utilized to depict her sorrow before she speaks recurs at her speech's end (line 202), thereby framing the whole. Once more the sad voice and the suffering of violent revelation recall Attis. Ariadne's words are, or at least so she thinks, her last complaints, *extremae querellae* (line 130).[22] She assumes she is in the very throes of death — and for purposes of this particular moment in the action she is indeed dying. When Bacchus arrives the mood changes completely, to be sure, but it is the story of Theseus' desertion which is the real subject of this section of the poem, not the arrival of the new lover. It is no coincidence that she later describes her complaints as those (lines 196–97)

> quas ego, vae misera, extremis proferre medullis
> cogor inops, ardens, amenti caeca furore.

Catullus is able to make the external situation justify and fit the internal feelings. What might even be called her *Liebestod* from love for Theseus is one with the tragic end she thinks she will have, left alone on a deserted island, a prey to birds and beasts. Her lips are already beginning to grow numb with cold as she begins.

II. ARIADNE'S LAMENT

> sicine me patriis avectam, perfide, ab aris,
> perfide, deserto liquisti in litore, Theseu?
> sicine discedens neglecto numine divum,
> immemor a! devota domum periuria portas?

From these initial questions, the reader learns of her seduction from home and why it is now quite clear to Ariadne that Theseus is carrying *devota domum periuria*, harbingers of the curse which she puts on him at the end. The repetition of *perfide*, with which the indictment opens, is, by standards Catullus sets elsewhere, overwhelming.[23] Theseus has no *fides*, cares not a whit for his promises (as line 144 reaffirms). The *deserto litore* of the first question seems to lead to the *neglecto numine* of the second. Theseus has lost all respect for the *numen divum*, the very accusation Catullus hurls against Lesbia in 76.3–4 when he asserts that he

> nec sanctam violasse fidem, nec foedere nullo
> divum ad fallendos numine abusum homines, . . .

Ariadne's curse is, however, to be fulfilled (line 204):

> annuit invicto caelestum numine rector; . . .

What was *neglecto* is in reality *invicto*, and any failure to worship the divinity of the gods will be punished by an all-too-vivid presentation of their power. Ariadne's accusation takes the reader from Crete to Dia and from Dia to Athens. As Theseus carried Ariadne from home and proved perfidious,[24] so now the results of the crime will be visited on his own father.

Ariadne's tone changes in the next two questions (lines 136–38). They are in the nature of pleas, no longer threatening. Will nothing bend his cruel purpose, she asks (as she does later in 175–76)? Will he offer her no clemency from his pitiless heart? The difference between what might have been and what actually is, a difference inherent in her questions, becomes now explicit as she sets off the *quondam* of the past (line 139) against the *nunc* of the present (line 143).[25] We recall the same distinction in 72. Even in 70 the thrice repeated *dicit* emphasizes the fact that Lesbia *said* she preferred to marry Catullus more than anyone else. But her *dicta* were likewise of little import.

This contrast of time present with time past leads the poet, as Ariadne, into six lines (143–48) of meditation on the infidelity of man:

> nunc iam nulla viro iuranti femina credat,
> nulla viri speret sermones esse fideles;

quis dum aliquid cupiens animus praegestit apisci,
nil metuunt iurare, nihil promittere parcunt:
sed simul ac cupidae mentis satiata libido est,
dicta nihil metuere, nihil periuria curant.

We will later draw in more detail comparisons between the Ariadne-Theseus episode and the description of the present ill times with which the poem concludes. Suffice to quote here lines 398 and 405–6, where Catullus inveighs against the lack of justice in the modern world, saying that men

iustitiamque omnes cupida de mente fugarunt, . .
omnia fanda nefanda malo permixta furore
iustificam nobis mentem avertere deorum . . .

The phrase *cupidae mentis* of line 147 is echoed in *cupida de mente* of 398. The reader cannot but recall the situation of Ariadne in the later line. She is the image which corresponds to the generalizations with which the poem ends.

The next nine lines divide into two sections, 149–53 and 154–57. The first group returns to narration and to a direct address of Theseus. Ariadne's love for him triumphed over all other forms of affection. In order to save him, she even killed her own brother, and in return she is offered to beasts of prey and will lie unburied. Ariadne digresses at line 154 to speculate upon the origin of Theseus, who, she thinks, must be the offspring of a lioness or a Scylla to perform such actions against her.

The chief commentary on these thoughts is poem 60, where the poet also addresses some unknown person (it may or may not be Lesbia) who has failed him in his hour of need. I quote the entire poem:

Num te leaena montibus Libystinis
aut Scylla latrans infima inguinum parte
tam mente dura procreavit ac taetra,
ut supplicis vocem in novissimo casu
contemptam haberes, a nimis fero corde ?

The parallels between the first three lines of this poem and 64.154–56 are both numerous and vivid. There is a close connection between Catullus' thoughts on his own *novissimo casu* and Ariadne's meditation on her supposedly imminent death (*extremo tempore*, line 169, contrasts with *tempore primo* two lines later). Ariadne considers herself about to be *dilaceranda feris*, with the result that her mind (or the poet's) immediately turns to the image of Theseus and the *leaena*. Reality has become metaphor. She is to be torn apart by wild animals, but Theseus is the spiritual beast who in leaving her caused her death. The lioness gives him birth, but it is of the deserter's mind (*mente*, 60.3) and heart (*corde*, 60.5) that the poet is speaking. It is his soul which is animal-like while his form is fair. The adjectives attached to the two nouns are also important. The mind is called *dura*. Its hard and unbending quality is reflected in the phrase *sola sub rupe* (64.154). The heart, in its turn, remains *fero*, an epithet which serves as commentary on the ambiguity latent in the whole section.[26]

Though there may be some connection between the *novissimo casu* of Catullus in *60* and the *casu acerbo* from which Manlius suffers in 68.1, the Laudamia-Protesilaus episode later in *68*, to which we shall return in greater detail, offers an even closer parallel. In 68.105–7, for example, Catullus, very much involved in the feelings of Laudamia, mentions the Trojan war which drew Protesilaus away from her:

> quo tibi tum casu, pulcerrima Laudamia,
>   ereptum est vita dulcius atque anima
> coniugium: . . .

This situation is not at all unlike that proposed by 64.157 when Ariadne asks Theseus if he is the kind of person

> talia qui reddis pro dulci praemia vita ?

Ariadne gave sweet life (*dulci vita*) to Theseus and he leaves her. Protesilaus leaves Laudamia even though he is *vita dulcius* to her. The *casus* is the same. Moreover the reversal pattern we have seen above is illustrated by the verb *eripui* in 64.150. She snatched Theseus from the jaws of death only to have him desert her in the same manner as Protesilaus departed from Laudamia (*ereptum est*, 68.106).[27]

Ariadne in her pain now cries out that even if it had not been in Theseus' heart to marry her because he feared the hard commands of a stern father (lines 160–63),

> attamen in vestras potuisti ducere sedes,
> quae tibi iucundo famularer serva labore,
> candida permulcens liquidis vestigia lymphis,
> purpureave tuum consternens veste cubile.

Ariadne would have come home to Theseus at least as servant if not as wife. The phraseology is quite unusual, displaying in Ariadne incredible devotion and the utmost submission to a stronger force, the weakest feminine impulse yielding to the adamant masculine. The thought here briefly expressed forms one of the basic ideas of *63*, which seems to represent certain salient aspects of the temperament of Catullus. The servitude demanded of Attis in *63* is even greater than that which Ariadne offers here, since it involves renouncing masculinity for abject slavery, whereas Ariadne need only be reduced to the lowest position for one of her own sex. Nevertheless the Catullus who, disguised in the form of Ariadne, proposes herself as servant for Theseus, is the same Catullus who, transformed imaginatively into Attis, will be the perpetual devotee of the Magna Mater. In other words the mistress/servant feeling, here experienced by Ariadne, finds its heightened and extreme expression in the emasculation of Attis.[28]

A complete change of thought occurs as Ariadne says (lines 164–66):

> sed quid ego ignaris nequiquam conquerar auris
> externata malo, quae nullis sensibus auctae
> nec missas audire queunt nec reddere voces ?

This passage is important, and typically Catullan, in two ways: first, it shows the dependence of his intense feelings on the senses, especially seeing and hearing; and second, it specifically draws attention to the need, in such a situation as Ariadne's, of the consolation of speaking and replying. There is no hope, she later cries (lines 186–87):

> nulla fugae ratio, nulla spes: omnia muta,
> omnia sunt deserta, ostentant omnia letum.

Desertion is a motif naturally present, but the key Catullan phrase is *omnia muta*. This imagery is particularly linked with death, as we may see for example in 96.1 and 101.4, especially the latter, where, thinking on his brother, Catullus cries,

> et mutam nequiquam alloquerer cinerem.

Likewise the world around Ariadne is dead. The pointedly repeated *nequiquam* in 101.4 and in 64.164 adds further poignancy to the vain uselessness of her cries, just as *mutam* coupled with *alloquerer* in *101* tells the reader that the poet for his part will speak, but will hear no reply from his beloved brother, for whom sympathy is now fruitless.

Merely the fact that his brother cannot reply to him in *101* and *65* makes it all the more important that he answer the *dicta* of Ortalus in the latter poem. Whatever they were, they deserve reply. Just as Ariadne must complain in vain to the unknowing breezes, so Catullus insists to Ortalus that (65.17):

> . . . tua dicta vagis nequiquam credita ventis.

Very similar imagery, but this time the crucial *nequiquam* will not be true. The poet can and must make answer. When, however, at the end of her speech Ariadne cries to the Eumenides, *meas audite querellas* (line 195), we realize that literally no one can hear and give help and sympathy, except the unseen furies whose help is vengeance for the dead, not life for the suffering.[29]

She is, in fact, *externata* with evil (the same word associated with the ardor of love in line 71). There is no person present to convey the active and manifest sympathy necessary in such a time of trial. In one poem of great suffering, *38*, Catullus had asked Cornificius for a brief *allocutio*. No matter how sad, anything would be comforting. Even such solace was denied Ariadne.[30]

The feelings which overcome Ariadne at this point form the heart of the remainder of her speech. In lines 171–76 she prays to Jupiter, wondering why all this has come upon her. Lines 177-81 return to the interrogative technique used earlier:

> nam quo me referam ? quali spe perdita nitor ?
> Idaeosne petam montes ? at gurgite lato
> discernens ponti truculentum dividit aequor.
> an patris auxilium sperem ? quemne ipsa reliqui
> respersum iuvenem fraterna caede secuta ?

This time she addresses herself instead of Theseus and asks whither she can turn now for help and consolation since the island offers none. She might return to Crete (though in truth she knows that the crime of her brother's death irrevocably bars such a recourse). In fact, as also for Attis, the sea is the great dividing line between true home and false, between lasting happiness and happiness for the moment leading to greater sorrow. The shore is the closest both characters can come to renewing what each now realizes is the only steadfast type of love.

The only thing she can do now is to call on the invisible furies to avenge her wrongs. The curse which comprises the final lines of her speech is important for the episode which follows.[31] In no other version of the legend is the curse of Ariadne connected with the death of Aegeus. Superficially this is the poet's way of linking two seemingly disparate events. More important, however, it helps to show the reactions of two people to one figure who betrays them both, of lover to lover separated by infidelity, and of father and son separated (as Aegeus thinks) by death. Catullus is no little part of both characters.

It will be seen that, taken as a whole, Ariadne's lament centers primarily around her own reactions to the departure of Theseus. But the beauty of the piece lies not in any over-reaching concepts which unify the whole, even though we retain the picture of the deserted Ariadne forever before our mind. Rather it is the series of approaches which she takes to her position which interests us. Around the idea of desertion (in which the loss of *fides* and *iustitia* was of equal importance with the loss of *amor*) the poet has written short elegiac and lyric comments, some four lines, some ten, none of them exactly like any other, but all looking back to the same initial situation and viewing it from various emotional angles. And the descriptions, which interweave among these thoughts, he has taken away from any prosaic setting in Rome or Verona or anywhere else, and placed where they will have the most imaginative effect upon the reader.

In brief, the portrayal of Ariadne, beautifully as it is crafted, is distinctive because of her special relationship with Catullus. Let others find in her speech the latent influence of writers from Homer to Lucretius. Every poet is born to tradition and conversant with his predecessors and contemporaries. Yet the source hunter should go no further. Ariadne expresses in the veiled terms which epic invites the struggles and aspirations which were Catullus' own.

III. Theseus and Aegeus

The curse of Ariadne ends at line 201, as she calls down punishment upon Theseus. And Jupiter, by making the universe tremble, acknowledges that the prayer will be fulfilled. To accomplish this and have the lover's forgetfulness redound to his own suffering, the poet once more turns back the clock to the time when Aegeus gave his final speech of farewell to his son departing for Crete. As the curse of Ariadne depended on the mind of Theseus (the word *mens* appears twice in lines 200–1), so also does its accomplishment (lines 207–9):

> ipse autem caeca mentem caligine Theseus
> consitus oblito dimisit pectore cuncta,
> quae mandata prius constanti mente tenebat, . .

The last line is all but repeated in line 238 at the end of Aegeus' speech. Yet the emphatic stress on Theseus' remembering and then forgetful mind in lines 210 and 238 serves to return the reader's thoughts to Theseus' treatment of Ariadne and to help forge a connecting link between the two episodes.

After a brief mention of the crucial *dulcia signa*, which Theseus forgets to raise upon return as he had been ordered, the digression begins. It presents at the outset the familiar Catullan picture of departure:

> namque ferunt olim, classi cum moenia divae
> linquentem gnatum ventis concrederet Aegeus,
> talia complexum iuveni mandata dedisse: . . .

Here the relationship is between father and son, the son leaving to go off on an adventure (this part of the story parallels the departure of Protesilaus in *68*, and of Ptolemy in *66*). We should recall here that in Catullus' own life there were two departures of paramount importance, different in outward detail, yet on the spiritual side, judging from the poet's reaction to them, interwoven and complicated. The first was the departure (such it must have been) of the brother and his subsequent death in the East. The second was the unfaithfulness of Lesbia. The Protesilaus-Laudamia episode in *68* combines these so intimately that it is sometimes hard to distinguish to whom the poet is applying his feelings, to the dead brother or the deserting Lesbia. Both themes are one in *68*. In *64* they are dealt with in separate sections. In the Ariadne episode it was Catullus' relationship with Lesbia which we saw was of paramount importance. The next event, shorter though it is, remains no less crucial. This time death is the outcome. I suggest that in it the poet is reflecting on his lost brother and, with himself as Aegeus, is speaking words not of hope for return, but of sadness looking to eternal separation.

Even before the speech begins these feelings are conveyed. If we turn to the imagery of the lines quoted above, *linquo* is a verb around which the thoughts of Catullus are much centered. It appears in line 117 when Ariadne is also leaving her parents. And since the word *complexum* (though a noun in one case, a participle in the other) appears in the lines subsequent to each, the poet was probably thinking back to the first passage. It could even be said that the whole emotional cast of the Theseus-Aegeus episode results from an enlargement of the thoughts contained in those lines devoted to Ariadne. Nor, when we think on Theseus' previous conduct and the imagery the poet attaches to it, does the phrase *ventis concrederet* leave much doubt as to the ultimate outcome of the story.

Let us take Aegeus' speech essentially line by line. The opening apostrophe —

> gnate mihi longa iucundior unice vita —

maintains a clear likeness to Catullus' frequent claim that he considered Lesbia dearer than life. Yet such an equation utilizes a comparative adjective only twice elsewhere. The first instance occurs in 68.106 where Laudamia realizes that the *coniugium* torn from her was *vita dulcius*.[32] The other passage is 65.10-11, where the poet is talking of his brother:

> numquam ego te, vita frater amabilior,
> aspiciam posthac ? . . .

This is the first of a series of comparisons we will make with *65* in elucidating the Aegeus passage, and the first where the brother is specifically mentioned.

With line 216,

> gnate, ego quem in dubios cogor dimittere casus,

the imagery begins to border on the sensual. Nor should we forget the simile of 68.119–24 when discussing line 217:

> reddite in extrema nuper mihi fine senectae, . . .

In *68*, Catullus is attempting to describe the extreme passion of love in terms of a relationship which has nothing at all to do with sex. And, even though in the first instance an aged sire has been reunited with his son while in the second a newborn grandson relieves his grandsire of the "vulture," the feeling which the grandfather experiences through contemplation of his daughter's late-born child is exactly that which Aegeus undergoes when he beholds his son returned to him in his late old age.[33]

Aegeus continues in line 218:

> quandoquidem fortuna mea ac tua fervida virtus
> eripit invito mihi te, cui languida nondum
> lumina sunt gnati cara saturata figura, . . .

Though *fortuna* is one of the key words in *68*,[34] it also appears in one other crucial spot, 101.5–6:

> quandoquidem fortuna mihi tete abstulit ipsum,
> heu miser indigne frater adempte mihi, . . .

The word *abstulit* (and also perhaps *adempte*) may find its parallel with the lines from *64* in the word *eripit*, but the surrounding words are more than chance occurrences, i.e., the phrase *quandoquidem fortuna* is repeated in the same metrical position in each passage, and the personal pronouns *mihi tete* of *101*, though linked with *mea ac tua*, are even closer to *mihi te* of 64.219.

The lines which follow are highly ambiguous, and without doubt consciously so. Especially words like *languida*,[35] *cara*, and *saturasset*, in terms of Catullan usage, can be applied to either mad passion or old age and death. *Luctus* is capable of a kindred double meaning. When, in line 226, Aegeus mentions *nostros . . . luctus nostraeque incendia mentis*, he is not only describing grief at parting but also the very pangs of love.[36] To define further the depth and quality of Aegeus' emotions, Catullus emphasizes, as he does in every other similar situation, the yearning eyes of the lover. Even here, then, in a basically spiritual relationship, the depth of the love the father bears his son is denoted in sensual as well as spiritual terms. The repetitions we have adduced from *101* and *65* show that the poet probably had his brother in mind. It remains only to say that Catullus considered himself almost in the place of father toward his brother. The death of his brother, as several passages in *68* reveal, marks the end of their *domus*.[37] Just as his brother's death for Catullus, so also now the death of Theseus would mean that Aegeus' family no longer exists: *domus* symbolizes continuity of tradition as well as personal affection.

Omitting lines 221–22 for the moment, let us continue with lines 223–24, where Aegeus cries in sorrow:

> sed primum multas *expromam mente* querellas
> canitiem terra atque infuso pulvere foedans, . . .

Though the objects involved are different — one refers to Aegeus' cries of woe, the other to poetic production cut off in sorrow and then continued by it — the situation is extraordinarily close to that of *65*, in the opening lines of which Catullus states that, because of his brother's death

> nec potis est dulcis Musarum *expromere* fetus
> *mens* animi, . . .

He can no longer produce the *dulcis fetus* of the Muses, verses of love and happiness,[38] but rather he must sing *maesta carmina* (65.12) while he mourns in the midst of his great sadness (*maeroribus*, 65.15). These plaints for the dead brother are surely akin, as the repeated imagery suggests, to the lament which Aegeus utters in his grief (*maesto*, line 210).

The community between the two poems would stop there were it not for the simile which follows. The songs Catullus sings in mourning are (65.13–14)

> qualia sub densis ramorum concinit umbris
> Daulias, absumpti fata gemens Ityli . . . ,

like those which Philomela sang for her son Itylus, torn from her. By thus depicting in *65* the relationship with his brother in parental terms,

Catullus reveals clearly the psychological impetus behind the whole Aegeus-Theseus episode. The poet is experiencing over again the death of his brother. Aegeus utters the cries of woe and performs the acts of a funeral even before anyone has died. Instead of giving Theseus a joyous sendoff, wishing him the best of fortune, he clothes him with the blackness of death, for he, as poet, knows beforehand what the real outcome of the journey will be.

Hence it is not unexpected that throughout this episode Catullus exhibits his habitual intensity about going and returning. Its most vivid manifestation occurs in lines 236–37 as Aegeus bids his son, upon safe return, to raise a white sail

> quam primum cernens ut laeta gaudia mente
> agnoscam cum te reducem aetas prospera sistet.

The poet means that upon his son's return the life of the old man will again become prosperous and livable.[39] For this reason when, in the lines which follow, Aegeus thinks that Theseus no longer lives, he takes his own life.

Catullus' feelings for his brother, as exhibited in *68*, are all but the same. He realizes that true *gaudia* have gone out of his life since his brother's death. And, along with all *commoda*, he has lost his ability to create poetry. And in each case, as we have said, Catullus focuses his strongest emotions upon a journey. To describe the departure (and at least hoped-for return) of Theseus, Catullus uses imagery which recurs frequently in such lyrics as *9* and *31* to express the pleasure of arrival and the joy of seeing someone else come back after an absence.[40] Aegeus offers the first hint of this theme in line 221 as he cries,

> non ego gaudens laetanti pectore mittam, . . .[41]

The emotions which Catullus centers on words such as *laetus*, *gaudium*, and their cognates can also be illustrated elsewhere within *64* itself by appealing to lines 33–34, where the poet describes the royal home and its guests as follows:

> . . . oppletur laetanti regia coetu:
> dona ferunt prae se, declarant gaudia vultu.

There happiness is the order of the day. And the context is not only that of marriage, but specifically the arrival of the invited to throng the house. And though the wedding guests are not returning home, as is Theseus, the emotions caused by arrival are in each case evoked in similar fashion.

Through such vocabulary, the poet describes his own sensations aroused by the phrase *te reducem*. Catullus feels strongly about the return of Veranius in *9* and of himself in *31*. Where return could never be achieved, the loss was irretrievable, as in the case of his brother, whom he now subconsciously (or even consciously) involves in the figure of the forgetful Theseus.

The lines which follow Aegeus' speech are most crucial because they unify the two sections of the digression.[42] It is the similarity between the actual situations of Aegeus and Ariadne which first strikes the reader. Aegeus stands at the topmost bastion of his citadel looking out over the sea (lines 241–42):

> at pater, ut summa prospectum ex arce petebat,
> anxia in assiduos absumens lumina fletus, . . .

This very kind of prospect confronted Ariadne, as she gazed seaward in longing for her beloved.[43] To show Aegeus catching sight of the ship, the poet employs the very same word he had utilized when describing Ariadne's first glimpse of Theseus (*conspexit*, lines 86 and 243), and many other words, such as *anxius*, *luctus*, and *assiduus*, recur in both passages.[44] But there is no need to elaborate connections of this sort, for the similarity of situation is undeniable: two people are both standing on eminences looking out to sea and losing, or about to lose, someone beloved.

The most obvious connecting link between the two episodes is the curse of Ariadne and its effects. The words which Theseus had once uttered to Ariadne and the *mandata* of Aegeus to Theseus are essentially parallel. Both depend on memory. In the first part emphasis lies on the *promissa* (line 59) of the *immemor iuvenis* (line 58). Line 123 renews this same stress on the *immemor pectus* of Theseus, and of course Ariadne picks up the idea again in her speech (lines 134–35).[45] But the hero's fallibility is exhibited most pointedly in lines 207–9:

> ipse autem caeca mentem caligine Theseus
> consitus oblito dimisit pectore cuncta,
> quae mandata prius constanti mente tenebat,

while his father repeats like words, urging (lines 231–32):

> tum vero facito ut memori tibi condita corde
> haec vigeant mandata, nec ulla oblitteret aetas; . . .

Catullus makes the forgetful mind the explicit link between the two passages when he says of Theseus in lines 247–48:

> . . . qualem Minoidi luctum
> obtulerat mente immemori, talem ipse recepit.

It is surely now clear that in the figure of Theseus, whose *mens immemor* caused both Ariadne's trials and Aegeus' death, Catullus manifests the double suffering caused him by Lesbia and by his brother. The very words of Ariadne, in her final appeal to the Furies, reflect concisely this twofold result of Theseus' actions:

> vos nolite pati nostrum vanescere luctum,
> sed quali solam Theseus me mente reliquit,
> tali mente, deae, funestet seque suosque.

It takes the same kind of character, she observes, to kill one's parent as it does to depart from her. *Reliquit* and *funestet* are to her nearly one and the same. Likewise the same grief as she receives from his departure he will suffer from his father's death. In other words, Ariadne knows that the quality which Theseus most lacks is *pietas*, which he has shown neither in his love for her nor in his devotion to his father.

The phrase *seque suosque* has a pronounced Catullan ring (the contexts of 58.3 and 79.2 show varying uses of it). The genuine, more enduring relationship is that of father to son. Theseus' feelings for Ariadne were merely passing, even though Ariadne's passion was intense and strong. As we have seen from *68*, Catullus hoped ideally to combine the physical with the spiritual in love. It was not only by forgetfulness but also by his unusual impiety that Theseus could, at one and the same time, destroy both Ariadne and his own father, both lover and parent.

The much discussed lines in *72*:

> dilexi tum te non tantum ut vulgus amicam,
> sed pater ut gnatos diligit et generos . . . ,

find their archetype in epic form in the affection shown for Theseus by Aegeus. It is the same as that which the poet felt for his brother, and accounts for the superficially odd comparison in *72*. It was possible that Lesbia might be able to realize for him the combination which formed his ideal love, and apparently she did so, but only for a time. It is certainly true that in his happiness the poet could not, or rather did not need to, formulate the twofold aspect of what he sought in love. Only the suffering brought about by Lesbia's infidelity could make this clear, even to him.[46]

To those who urge that *64* contains nothing of the true Catullus because he was not one to veil his feelings in such a manner, we could reply with many arguments. The most interesting for our present purposes is to appeal to the Laudamia-Protesilaus simile in *68* (lines 73–130), to which occasional references have already been made. This simile is a little epic like *64*, though a good deal shorter. Yet we know that there the poet *is* telling his own story, and it is easy to trace his mind at work during its progress. Suffice to say that Protesilaus is the connecting link in *68* as Theseus is in *64*, for he not only leaves (deserts, Catullus would say) Laudamia as Lesbia did the poet, but he also dies in Troy like Catullus' brother. *68* therefore offers Protesilaus as an example of the same combination of double suffering which Theseus caused, and fuses in the character of Laudamia Catullus' own intense and individual love for Lesbia and for his brother. It thus merges in one episode that to which in *64* Catullus devotes two separate sections, unified in the end by similarity of conception and exposition.

The numerous connections, then, between the two sections of the digression are both external and internal. The poet deliberately emphasizes the external by means of plot and crucial imagistic repetition. We may find the true bond, however, only within the mind of the poet, in his ideas about love and in the aspects of his own feelings which he elaborates through his characters. Ariadne, disappointed of her ideal lover, looks back as Attis looked back, to the true home of the past. Also, in Aegeus' love for Theseus, we find epitomized Catullus' quest for *pietas*, for the true love between human beings, the deeply felt devotion which is only remotely connected with the sensual. But this quest fails. Aegeus' love for his son and Theseus' subsequent forgetfulness, her mother's love for Ariadne and the daughter's flight, are similar disasters. As Catullus says often of Lesbia, it was she

> . . . quam Catullus unam
> plus quam se atque suos amavit omnes, . .

The phrase gains all the more meaning when compared with Ariadne's and Aegeus' plight.

Lines 249–50 return to the opening picture of Ariadne. The digression has gone full circle and, with outward picture and inner metaphor, the poet returns to the initial emotion. Then the spell is broken. A mood bordering almost on death is replaced by life. Bacchus comes with his rowdy throng, seeking the love of Ariadne. Once more all is young, vigorous, full of joy. Perhaps this is the scene which the poet meant originally to have depicted on the coverlet. He does, after all, compare Ariadne to a Bacchant in line 60, and there is not much difference in sound from her *heu* to the *euhoe* shouted by Bacchus' followers. We have

7+C.P.

shown why it would not be difficult for Catullus to be carried away by the picture of the deserted heroine to the point of telling a tale which he had not otherwise planned to include in his narrative. But this is mere speculation. The arrival of Bacchus changes our mood entirely and prepares us for a return to the initial picture of the poem, the happy circumstances attending the wedding of Peleus and Thetis.

IV. PELEUS AND THETIS

The sections of the poem which surround the Ariadne digression deal with Peleus and Thetis. The song of the Fates begins with line 303, and everything up to that point, save the long interlude, consists of a description of the marriage, the circumstances under which Peleus and Thetis first met, when and how the ceremony took place. The narrative divides into two almost equal sections, lines 1–49 and 265–302. The mood of each is the same, and forms such a complete contrast with that of the digression that we cannot but seek the reason for it. For Ariadne all is empty, dark, and above everything else *muta*, yet for the happy pair throngs of people, including the gods themselves, mob the house, filling it with sounds of joy. The black silence of utter despair which surrounds the deserted Ariadne is juxtaposed with the bright shining happiness of the ideal wedding.[47]

Ostensibly, then, the common bond between the two tales is marriage, the one happy in its consummation, the other ill-fated in its sad conclusion. But there is more than this. Let us first examine the atmosphere in which the poet evolves the tale of Peleus and Thetis.

It begins, characteristically enough, on a mountain top. Like the *phaselus* of *4*, whose voyage covers both Catullus' own special journey and the universal course of human life, the Argo was born once long ago on the crest of Mr. Pelion. Thence the Argonauts set out on their journey to capture the Golden Fleece. The ship is fleet and Athena lends her aid with a favorable breeze. It ploughs the sea, which grows hoary (*incanuit*, line 13) with the churning, and out of the whitening deep the Nereids peep to look at the strange sight.[48] It was on this occasion that Peleus saw Thetis (lines 16–18):

> illa, atque (haud) alia, viderunt luce marinas
> mortales oculis nudato corpore Nymphas
> nutricum tenus exstantes e gurgite cano.

Images of whiteness and shimmer are connected by Catullus above all others with happiness, and these of the sea are the first of many instances in *64*.[49] A setting similar to this recurs during the epilogue of the poem. In the opening lines Catullus depicts the specific occasion when men saw the nymphs of the sea rising nude from the water, resulting in the union between mortal and divine which this section of the poem stresses as a prime consideration of the heroic age. At the poem's conclusion, he generalizes from the particular to describe the times in broader terms (lines 384–86):

> praesentes namque ante domos invisere castas
> heroum, et sese mortali ostendere coetu,
> caelicolae nondum spreta pietate solebant.

There is no doubt that Catullus has here in mind the opening part of the poem, the joyous meeting of Peleus and Thetis in that ideal age when men were righteous and the gods consequently did not hesitate to show themselves to the sight of mortals.

The atmosphere of the voyage, carried on as far as need be, is dropped after line 18. The desired result has been achieved. Peleus is *incensus amore* for Thetis (like Bacchus for Ariadne in line 253, a brief inroad of the gods in an otherwise quite mortal story). Thetis does not disdain *humanos hymenaeos*, and above all the *pater ipse*, Jupiter himself, blesses the match. The idea is important for Catullus, and he reiterates it in lines 26–27. There is no hint of jealousy on the part of Jupiter as the legend usually has it. Rather he sanctions the union, thereby throwing into greater relief the love between the happy couple.

For this reason it is important to compare lines 21 and 26–27 with the sentiments of 70.2 (Lesbia had said that she would prefer to marry the poet even more than Jupiter) and 72.2, where Lesbia protests that she would love Catullus even if Jupiter himself sought her.[50] When Catullus addresses the hero in lines 26–27 as

> Thessaliae columen Peleu, cui Iuppiter ipse,
> ipse suos divum genitor concessit amores . . . ,

he surely means to portray Peleus as surpassing, even if just for an instant, Jupiter in his happiness. It was Jupiter who, in giving up his love for Thetis, allowed Peleus to fulfill his desire. This is the ideal, just as the opening lines of *70* and *72* express in personal terms what Catullus' view of perfect love was. Momentarily he is greater than Jupiter because Lesbia loves him, just as Peleus, in the bliss of his marriage with Thetis, seems almost equal to the chief of the gods.[51] The second halves of both *70* and *72* take up the real, what actually comes of the dreams (on Catullus' part) and expression (on Lesbia's) of perfection, dreams which are shattered by the reality of her vulgarity. The reference to Jupiter, as an aspect of the perfect marriage defined by the short poems, offers a further hint that the contrasting section of *64*, devoted to Ariadne, is indeed the reenactment of the second halves of both *70* and *72*, the truth of reality after the fleeting hope of gaining the ideal goal. This hope finds a strikingly vivid, truthful, and Roman portrayal in *61*. The episode of Peleus and Thetis is its epic counterpart.

The poet is so taken with the picture he has drawn that he bursts in with an aside of his own (lines 22–23):

> o nimis optato saeclorum tempore nati
> heroes, salvete, deum genus!

When Catullus does this in epic statement, as at the end of *63*, it means much as a disclosure of his personal involvement. Here once more the thought reflects that of the closing lines of the poem. This was the great age of mankind, this the *optatum saeclorum tempus* in which men married happily and the gods blessed the union. Peleus will be happy (lines 25–26):

> teque adeo eximie taedis felicibus aucte,
> Thessaliae columen, Peleu, . . .

In much the same words the Fates begin their song to Peleus.[52] It would seem that Catullus can, like the Parcae, detach himself and admire the beauty and happiness of Peleus' love. The question with which he concludes the opening section (lines 28–30) almost implies amazement at the good fortune of the lovers. Could such a thing really happen to a mortal? the poet asks, repeating the *te* of direct address in lines 25, 28, and 29. He can separate himself from this love and admire. He can only partake in Ariadne's sadness.

The scene changes in line 31, and the generalized statement of line 22 becomes the particular. The poet's universal feelings about the age become centered on the special event about to take place. The six lines which follow (lines 32–37) paint a portrait which could without exaggeration be called Catullus' ideal setting, uniting the beauty of home with the pleasure of arrival, which in this case is doubly gratifying because of the future wedding. All Thessaly crowds the house (lines 32–34):

> advenere, domum conventu tota frequentat
> Thessalia, oppletur laetanti regia coetu:
> dona ferunt prae se, declarant gaudia vultu.

Much of the imagery recurs shortly. It was even of his *ianuae frequentes* that Attis thought, as symbolizing his lost home. The throngs of people mean as much to the poet as the joy which they display.

Catullus places the reader as an onlooker upon the threshold who is to behold the palace receding (line 43) in its brightness.[53] It gleams with gold and silver. The ivory glistens, the goblets flash. Indeed (line 46),

> tota domus gaudet regali splendida gaza.

The house has become for the moment a person, capable of displaying the same emotion as the guests. Exactly such an emotion Catullus imputes to a personified and rejoicing Sirmio at the end of *31*. Nor are the events dissimilar, for he is also arriving home, back to his beloved peninsula. He has left the fields of Bithynia to return, and his home displays obvious pleasure at the advent of its master, just as the house of Peleus glories in the arrival of the wedding visitors.[54]

So begins the poem. From the top of Pelion to the meeting of the lovers to the bright colors on the wedding couch, all the scenes are delightful. The poet conveys thus his own happiness, and makes the outer situation mirror the ideal beauty of such a perfect union among lovers. When the poet returns to this picture, after the digression on Ariadne, the mortal guests are departing and the gods beginning to arrive. The poet is true to his initial statement that the event shows the unity of gods and men. After a beautiful simile comparing the departing mortals to the sea at dawn ruffled by the rising winds which, in turn, make the waves glimmer as they recede into the distance (sight and sound could scarcely be unified imaginatively to greater effect), the poet turns to the gods. Chiron is the first to arrive (like the Argo, *e vertice Pelei*) bringing *silvestria dona* (lines 280–83). The imagery lends much to the atmosphere already established, but also adds a new note of youth and bloom, preparing the reader for the wedded joys to be described in the song of the Fates. Once again it is upon the house that Catullus, resorting to words of sound to convey the excitement of a lovely odor, centers his feelings (line 284):

> ... permulsa domus iucundo risit odore.

Catullus maintains this mood up to line 302, as the home of Peleus gradually grows green with the gifts of nature brought by the divine guests.

Even here, however, the bliss of the wedding does not remain unbroken, for the appearance of Prometheus, which has never been adequately explained, somehow breaks the enchanting spell, as the description of Achilles does again later. Critics seize rather lamely upon two minor versions of the Peleus and Thetis myth which make Prometheus the person who warns Jupiter that whoever marries Thetis will beget a son stronger than himself. The lines devoted to him run as follows (294–97):

> post hunc consequitur sollerti corde Prometheus,
> extenuata gerens veteris vestigia poenae,
> quam quondam *silici* restrictus *membra* catena
> persolvit pendens e verticibus praeruptis.

The description seems needlessly verbose unless one compares the lines where Catullus describes Attis' act of emasculation (63.5–6):

> devolsit ili acuto sibi pondera *silice*,
> itaque ut relicta sensit sibi *membra* sine viro, . . .

Not only are the italicized words repeated, but there are parallels between *persolvit* and *devolsit*, *restrictus* and *relicta*, *pendens* and *pondera*. It is as if the poet himself wanted to appear at the wedding, a bit of the present in the happiness of the past, to show just what the evil power of woman is.[55]

Thus far it is basically atmosphere and mood which the poet has sought to convey. He has been building up a setting for the song of the Fates, who make their appearance in line 303.

V. The Song of the Fates

The song of the Fates is of course the wedding hymn itself, and should be designed to elaborate the future happiness of Peleus and Thetis and magnify their glories. Yet, at the same time, it takes one of their proudest boasts, their future son Achilles, and identifies him (despite the heroic attributes attached to him) with the bloody brutality of war. Moreover, the song stands apart from the symmetry of the whole.

The song itself, however, is finely symmetrical, and close analysis shows that it is constructed in the characteristic form of a digression. It starts off in lines 328–37 with a further allusion to the ideal love. The personal frame of reference gives way to abstract statement in lines 334–37, where the *domus* is said to roof over the two lovers and yet is conjoined symbolically with *amor* of the next line — the house symbolizes the structure of love. Just as the house *contexit*, the love *coniunxit*.[56] The result is a compact noteworthy for its concord.[57] These same thoughts are resumed at the end of the song (lines 372–81). The lovers are urged: *optatos . . . coniungite amores* in a *felici foedere*. There is no worry that Thetis will be *discors* (line 379).

Just as the Peleus-Thetis episode surrounds the Ariadne digression, a happy event framing a sad, so these groups of ten lines each, which begin and end the song, form a distinct contrast with the intervening section. This deals with Achilles, the tragic offspring of the happy pair. The reader at first wonders why Catullus adds this episode. (He warns of its violently contrasting nature by the mere outward technique of the digression, which resumes the feelings of joy at the end without allowing any excessively bitter taste to remain.)

However, there is no doubt that the poet is carried away by the picture he is creating. Our sympathy never lies with the hero Achilles. He is fearless, brave, and fleet of foot (how finely the poet gives metaphorical expression to the Homeric epithet in lines 340–41!).[58] No hero can compare with him, when the Phrygian fields are steeped with gore.[59] The poet seems almost sarcastic in the next stanza (lines 348–51) when he says that the mothers recognized his *virtutes* as they beat their breasts during their sons' funerals. The situation reminds us of Aegeus in line 224. Just as the reader's mind is scarcely centred on the *fervida virtus* of Theseus there, so also our sympathy rests with the aged women in their grief, and not with the ruthless hero.

Catullus gives symbolic form to this characteristic in the effective simile which follows (lines 353–55):

> namque velut densas praecerpens messor aristas
> sole sub ardenti flaventia demetit arva,
> Troiugenum infesto prosternet corpora ferro.

Similar imagery was used in 48.5 to depict an overwhelming number. The *aristae* are the bodies of the Trojans whom Achilles mows down indiscriminately.[60] The hot sun places the warriors in the prime of life, while the violence of the scene is enhanced by the verb *prosternet*.[61]

The imagery in the next stanza changes from land to water, but the same ironic tone still remains. It is now the wave of the Scamander which bears witness to his *magnis virtutibus* (line 357). The river bears the bodies. But the poet does not allow us to forget the reaping imagery of the previous stanza, because the carnage is pictured as rife with *caesis* . . . *corporum acervis* — slaughtered piles of bodies which, like heaps of grain, block the passage of the river and warm it with gore.

And the final witness to Achilles' prowess, the one particularly gruesome achievement singled out from the nameless heap, is the death of Polyxena, a murder especially "heroic," the poet ironically implies, because accomplished after the hero's death (lines 362–64):

> denique testis erit morti quoque reddita praeda,
> cum teres excelso coacervatum aggere bustum
> excipiet niveos perculsae virginis artus.

The tomb is as lofty as the river is deep,[62] and the previous imagistic strand is again carried on as the *acervi* of the slaughtered foemen become the tomb *coacervatum*. The image is so skillfully wrought by the poet that the reader's eye climbs the tomb — which instead of being polished or round becomes a heap of blood-red carnage — only to find the white-limbed virgin on the top, sacrificed to the ideal of heroism which lives in spirit though dead in the flesh. The poet elaborates further on the picture (lines 368–70):

> alta Polyxenia madefient caede sepulcra
> quae, velut ancipiti succumbens victima ferro,
> proiciet truncum summisso poplite corpus.

The lofty tomb is soaked in her blood. She is both an offering sacrificed on an altar and a victim of war. The word *ferro* recalls the *infestum ferrum* which Achilles himself had used (line 355), and the fact that it is *anceps* but adds to the ambiguity, for the war ax of the Romans was also usually double-bladed. She is just one more body among the other dead, only more pathetic than the rest. So ends the Achilles digression, and with it we return to the happy bridal couple.

One can only guess why the Achilles passage was written at all. The triumph of brutality over gentleness is another way of expressing the contrast between vulgarity and chastity which is nothing new to Catullus. The purity of the virgin is only further emphasized when put in contrast with the overwhelming masculine rage of Achilles. The plough always defeats the flower. Perhaps there is another reason. Troy means one event of special importance to Catullus — the death of his brother. When he thinks of the Trojan war in *68* the result is a repetition of the lines earlier in the poem on the sad loss of the brother. The atmosphere is much the same in each case. The men are summoned away from home to battle around the walls. The Parcae knew of the results beforehand (68.85) as they sing of them in *64*. And in the end only *sepulcra* remain. Out of all the virtues (*omnium virtutum*: 68.90) the only thing left is *acerba cinis*, and the bitterest is that of Catullus' brother. This is what Troy and the Trojan war meant to him. *64* touches upon the prowess of Achilles in epic terms, but the personal events of his own life may well be at the root of Catullus' elaboration.

At any rate, the song of the Fates is bitter and sorrowful. It is a lament for the loss of purity and the former contact men had with the gods.

Though Achilles is associated with the glorious marriage of Peleus and Thetis, nevertheless the brutality of his actions somehow helps bridge the gap between the ideal/past section of the poem and the real/present. He is part of the heroic age, yet the brilliance of his deeds is tainted by a certain unheroic quality. Unnecessary blood was shed in his honor. Though by no means specifically referring to civil war, the poet seems almost to create the same aura in picturing the murderous deeds of Achilles as he does through the description of the shedding of fraternal blood in the poem's conclusion. Certainly Polyxena becomes an almost symbolic Ariadne, sacrificed to the brutality of the heroic/masculine soul. And in this respect she is a figure of Catullus himself, the feminine flower of *11* sheared by the violence of the plough which, caring nothing for its beauty, cuts it heedlessly down.

Whatever the connection, Achilles' delight in the shedding of blood and the horrors of war leads directly into the lines which commence the description of the present in the poem's epilogue (lines 397–99):

> sed postquam tellus scelere est imbuta nefando
> iustitiamque omnes cupida de mente fugarunt,
> perfudere manus fraterno sanguine fratres, . . .

The word *imbuta* implies the drinking up of gore, a fact the poet specifies a few lines later with the phrase *sanguine fratrum* (and *perfudere* has an ironic connection with *perfundat* in line 330). Hence the sadness which the reader feels in the song of the Fates is deliberately made explicit, for it also, like the lament of Ariadne, is a commentary on the evils of the times.

VI. Epilogue and Conclusion

The two sections into which the epilogue divides, lines 382–96, detailing the attendance of the gods in the ceremonies of mankind during the heroic age, and lines 397–408, picturing the present ways of the world, which through evil have driven the gods far hence, seem strangely un-Catullan in theme at first and much more akin to certain passages in the *Georgics* where Virgil inveighs against the civil wars. But so strong and clear is the stamp of Catullus upon these verses that we cannot help finding therein an epic statement of his own thoughts. The heroic age contrasts with the present decay, and it is in terms of sexual purity or foulness that the poet interprets the division. The gods were accustomed to visit the houses of men when they were *castae*, and to show themselves willingly before *pietas* was spurned. Nemesis and Minerva, Mars and

7*

Bacchus, all joined in religious worship and daily life. Afterwards the earth was imbued with *scelus*, and *iustitia* was put to flight. This seems to be the only deliberate reference to civil war.[63] The lines which follow detail in abundance the manifold sexual aberrations in which Catullus found the key to the degradation of the times. A father desires the death of his son in order to marry the son's bride. A mother loves her son, to the defilement of the household gods. *Pietas* has become *impietas* (lines 403–4), *fanda* are confused with *nefanda*, justice is no longer at hand (line 406).

The relationships are all perverse, all involving parents and their children, as if to Catullus this were the worst type of offense against moral purity. When the intense spiritual affection between parents and children is violated for mere sensual ends, the worst of evils has occurred.[64] The mother bears the burden of a double impiety — she is first called *impia* (line 403) because of her relations with her son and then (line 404) because she had no hesitation to *divos scelerare parentes*. The total picture has much in common with the father's accomplishments in 67.23–24:

> sed pater illius gnati violasse cubile
> dicitur et miseram conscelerasse domum.

Again it is noteworthy that the *domus* possesses a twofold nature: it is the *cubile* of 67.23, a symbol of sensual pleasure, yet it also stands for the *divos parentes* of 64.404. This spiritual quality of reverence and awe is also concentrated on the *penates* of 9.3 and *lar* of 31.9. The father hence performs a double breach of piety by his unnatural act in 67, for he is said not only to *violasse cubile* of his son but also to *conscelerasse domum*, to have violated the symbol of true relations between parents and children. To make the idea even clearer, Catullus calls the house *miseram*, as if it were a person in actual pain at the act of force. He adds that it was only an *impia mens* (line 25) which could have perpetrated such a deed, and cries later in sarcasm (line 29):

> egregium narras mira pietate parentem.

The *mira pietas* of the father could not be better scorned than by the explicit description of his crime that follows.

And all this, though lacking deliberate application, suggests Theseus' treatment of Ariadne, not in regard to the seduction (hardly a crime in the Roman calendar), but to his subsequent lack of *pietas* and *iustitia*. The ideal past can in no way be found in the all-too-real present. Like the bronze age, as delineated in Hesiod's pessimistic progress, the gods no longer deign nor desire to partake in the ways of men (lines 407–8, reflecting 384–85). When *pietas* is spurned, the result is not limited to a new lack of worship for the gods. Piety no longer exists on the human level, because men fail to be chaste in their dealings with each other.

The body of the poem, leading up to the lines of the epilogue, reveals exactly the same distinction that divides the final verses, and only when the analogy is pressed does the poem fall into a unified whole. The steadfast happiness of Peleus and Thetis, which contrasts with the infidelity of Theseus, is the product of that ideal age pictured in the first part of the epilogue. In the story of Ariadne we find the poet describing himself, but in so doing he becomes an example of the spirit of his own times. The very point which Ariadne makes in lines 143–48, with specific reference to Theseus, is here generalized into the lack of justice which pervades the modern world.

Indeed, Catullus found himself constantly surrounded by, and fighting against, that degeneracy of which the vulgarity of Lesbia was but a small part. Perhaps a brief word of further explanation is in order for such a claim. There is no denying that Catullus was very much a part of the press of life which swirled around him, but this in no way categorizes him as a cleverly gifted *debauché*. That he enjoyed life and described some of its more sordid aspects does not necessarily mean that he ordered his own existence in the manner he imputes to others. Indeed he protests against this very accusation when he says, in his oft imitated statement,

> nam castum esse decet pium poetam
> ipsum, versiculos nihil necesse est.

He also gives abundant evidence that his age was marked, amid its countless expressions of individuality, by the longing and search for some *modus vivendi* which transcended day-to-day life. The ideal, which was ever before his eyes but only briefly seemed attainable, takes its shape in this poem in the relationship between Peleus and Thetis.

The final lines are thus another unifying factor for the whole poem. They are of a rare sort for Catullus. To moralize was not his usual bent, even though here was one of the few occasions in his poetry where he could suitably do so. We have seen Catullus' deep involvement in the characters of Ariadne and Aegeus and traced his violent reaction to the figures of Theseus and Achilles. The organic links between the various episodes of the digression are found in the experience of the poet. Yet it is the final lines which make clear the design of the poem as a whole, and show exactly what goal the poet had in mind by the abrupt juxtaposition of two such seemingly diverse stories. The moralizing is for a purpose and is in order. The particular structure of *64* almost demands it for completion.

The fact that the Theseus-Ariadne episode adorns the marriage couch is scarcely an argument against the time differentiation which we have proposed. It is not the actual chronological sequence of events which is important, for this is gradually lost sight of in the vivid contrast which arises between the two episodes. The mere fact that the poet breaks into the happy story of Peleus and Thetis with a tale of profound sadness is proof enough that his thoughts were centred not on external temporal regularity, but rather upon the internal emotional effect which the juxtaposition caused. It is only by visualizing the resulting contrast as the tension between ideal and real that the full effect of the poem's balance is achieved.

Moreover, it is just because Catullus never states his direct involvement that he can write the final lines at all. If he were telling the tale of his own woes without the facade of epic to hide the personal intensity, he could never sit back and moralize. Yet unless we realize Catullus' own participation in the character of Ariadne and grasp the fact that it is indeed his own present story he is unfolding, the ending makes sense only as a prosaic moralistic appendage. As it is, this is the only place in the whole of Catullus where he could point a moral of such a sort, and its appropriateness is not only undoubted but demanded, because it unifies the poem and makes clear the design of the whole.

The ending is like a coda which draws together the many themes of a gigantic musical exposition. Catullus may seem here to sacrifice some of his usual Mozartian combination of tenderness, delicacy, and innate passion (the veil of suffering is hard to penetrate) for a Wagner-like quality of movement which depends not on lyric themes, but rather on the effect of a large and sweeping design. Since time is of little import, this poem seems mere rhetoric to those bent on interpreting it as part of a past tradition. E. A. Poe, in words limited because their direction was toward his own age, found the long poem an impossibility and documented his argument by casting a somewhat prejudiced eye on the *Iliad*, a poem which seemed to him only a series of lyrical efforts loosely joined together. Yet the admitted goal of many among the greatest of the Romantic poets (and Catullus is a "romantic," both through his own personality and through the temper of his age) was to write a long poem. The composition of short poems, beautiful in their fleeting selves, was often considered only an apprenticeship for things more grand in conception and outlook. *64* is, in a certain sense, to Catullus what *Hyperion* and *Prometheus Unbound* are to Keats and Shelley. It contains within it somewhere reflections of almost every major subject which interested him. Yet, great as are the long poems of the Romantics, Catullus here surpasses them with a sustained level of achievement which they did not maintain outside their lyric efforts.

The restless spirit of Catullus is revealed here as nowhere in his shorter poems, a spirit always yearning for a perfection which could never be achieved and at the same time partaking to a heightened degree in human emotions. Catullus could only rarely accept things as he found them, but rather propelled himself into an unceasing inquiry for what was better. In the manner of Baudelaire, he was a poet very much involved in both the sapphires and the mire of life, who yet demanded exterior exactness in everything from personal charm to the appearance of a manuscript, as a token of inner beauty. These are the two sides of the coin for Catullus. Such dichotomies also exist for Lucretius, whose self-imposed pattern ever fell victim to his personality and creative powers. In a very different and much more worldly manner, Cicero's idealism was likewise constantly shattered by the buffets of reality. *64* is the final expression of this tension in Catullus. In fact nothing less than the complete scope of the poet's own imagination is the central unifying core for the poem. To read it thus is to treat the work not as an obscure byproduct but as the copestone of Catullus' genius.

Nor are we justified in assuming that the epyllion could never be a vehicle for personal statement (an argument which seems to imply that Catullus could only be himself when writing in shorter verse forms).[65] Indeed, the trend of recent scholarship seems to suggest that the epyllion was not a stereotyped genre, incapable of flexibility to suit circumstances, if indeed it was a fixed genre at all. Yet, assuming that it was, it is often taken for granted that the epyllion, being perhaps a Hellenistic form, could never be used, however subtly, to express personal feelings, and that a poem such as *64* must be the result only of Alexandrian trends in a poet.

We have attempted to prove the opposite. This is not to say that there are no Alexandrian elements in *64*. Catullus could not and surely did not want to ignore tradition blindly. Nor, however, was he a poet to be bound by it when its appeal to him was not of a personal nature. Even those who seek to find the influence of Alexandria upon *64* are forced to admit how uncharacteristic the poem most often is. It is neither excessively learned nor obscure. It does not tell a story for the sake of knowledge displayed, but, on the contrary, turns two mythological tales into moving personal documents where personal intensity triumphs over any inherited stylistic devices inimical to the creation of fine poetry. If with *64* Catullus is making further acknowledgement of his debt to Alexandria, it is a very strange manner of expression indeed. Far from choosing the epic genre because it offered opportunity for mere literary exercise, he found that only here could he state his own situation as he now lived it, and as he hoped he might have but did not, in terms first veiled and then painfully clear.

This raises another point: if the poem is such a personal document, why did not the poet write in autobiographical fashion and tell his own tale in the first person? It would be easy to answer this by saying that Catullus was carried away by the situation of Ariadne and, merging his own feelings with hers, used her as a mask for himself. But I think that another issue could also be raised in response, the origin of the subjective love-elegy.

If the genres of Latin literature are viewed in terms of what we still possess, it is only by means of the love-elegy that Catullus in his own person could have given a lengthy description of exactly what his situation was toward Lesbia. But this genre was probably not yet developed. Catullus himself may have been in the process of evolving it.[66] We find the germs of the subjectivism in all his epigrammatical poems, and it reaches a new peak of development in *76*. The union of autobiography with myth, one of the trademarks of Propertius, appears in *68*. But much of the interest of the myth in *68*, as opposed to the subjective description, is that it tells the truth about the poet's present situation whereas the surrounding frame of reference is happy and past, false in relation to the present. He was not ready to, or perhaps could not, reinterpret the present by myth as Propertius does.

The only way Catullus could describe his situation in detail, and not in the bitter brevity of epigram, was through the long epic tale. Such a recourse as *64* would have been needless to the Augustan poets. To Catullus it was absolutely necessary, because it was only by the disguise of symbols that he could be autobiographical at such length. Epic statement remained the only means open to him, as he was still in the process of pioneering the genre which later Latin authors would find ideal as a mode in which to express personal feelings.

NOTES

1. The most recent work of any length on *64* is F. Klingner, "Catulls Peleus-Epos," *SBAW* 1956, No. 6, 1–92. Klingner's basic theme, to defend the long poems of Catullus, is akin to that presented here, but his argument looks pri-

marily to the changes Catullus has rung on traditional themes, not to the *ingenium* of the poet himself.

For a survey of other recent treatments see J. P. Boucher, "A propos du Carmen 64 de Catulle," *RevEtLat* 34 (1956) 190–202, to which add C. Murley, "The Structure and Proportion of Catullus LXIV," *TAPA* 68 (1937) 305–17. Murley quotes (p. 305) the criticism of Kroll on the Hellenistic appearance of the poem as based on four factors: the use of inserts, emphasis on the emotions of the characters, pedanticism, and metrical tendencies such as the frequent use of spondaic lines. That the poem is a translation of a Hellenistic original is an opinion proposed as early as 1866 by A. Riese, "Catulls 64 Gedicht aus Kallimachos übersetz," *RhM* 21 (1866) 498–509.

On William Blake see Northrop Frye, *Fearful Symmetry: A Study of William Blake* (Princeton 1947).

2. Its supposed lack of unity is perhaps the main stumbling block to an appreciation of the poem. See A. L. Wheeler, *Catullus and the Traditions of Ancient Poetry* (Berkeley 1934) who, p. 132, abandons "the effort to find some internal connection between the tales." Also cf. Wilamowitz, *Hellenistische Dichtung* (Berlin 1924) 2.301; E. A. Havelock, *The Lyric Genius of Catullus* (Oxford 1939) 77–78 and 187 n.32.

3. For a penetrating study of the unified artistic presence behind the short poems see J. P. Elder, "Notes on some Conscious and Subconscious Elements in Catullus' Poetry," *HSCP* 60 (1951) 101–36. A treatment which concentrates particularly on unity of style is H. Bardon, *L'Art de la Composition chez Catulle* (Paris 1943).

4. See O. Friess, *Beobachtungen über die Darstellungskunst Catulls* (Diss. Würzburg 1929) 12–13.

5. Poem *8* is the clearest example.

6. D. L. Slater, in his lecture on *The Poetry of Catullus* (Manchester 1912) makes the equation between Lesbia and Theseus, and the idea was elaborated in parts of the dissertation of L. L. Sell (*De Catulli carmine LXIV quaestiones*: New York 1918). Though Sell's initial idea is in the spirit of this exposition, the cargo of dubious additions it carries with it obscures its basic worth (see the review by B. L. Ullman in *CP* 16 (1921) 404-6, and Wheeler (above, n. 2) 267 n.28).

7. A history of various treatments of this marriage is given by R. Reitzenstein, "Die Hochzeit des Peleus und der Thetis," *Hermes* 35 (1900) 73–105. John Finley in *Pindar and Aeschylus* (Cambridge, Mass. 1955) reveals the essence of Pindar's treatment of the myth (see esp. p. 48), which seems to offer much common ground with that of Catullus.

8. Her feelings are *indomitos*, the very word Catullus uses to describe himself in relation to Calvus in 50.11.

9. Cf. 65.17–18. On Theseus' meaningless *dicta*, cf. 76.7–8 and 70.4, where once again the metaphor of winds is utilized.

10. *Immemor*: 30.1 and 64.58; *prodere*: 30.3 and 64.190. The theme of perfidy goes through both poems: 30.3, 6, 11; 64.132–133, 182, 191, etc. *Fallax* and *fallere* appear in 30.3–4, 64.56, 151; *iubebas*, 30.7 and 64.140; *obliviscor*, 30.11 and *64 passim* (e.g., 208). For the figure of the winds, see, along with the note immediately preceding, 30.10, and for the *facta* of Theseus and Alfenus cf. 30.6, 9 with 64.192, 203.

11. The word *fugit*, for example, appears in 8.10 and 37.11.

12. Cf. 61.11–12 (where Hymen almost symbolizes the bride) with 64.56–57.

13. E.g., *liquerit*, l. 123 (and cf. ll. 59 and 133).

14. With which cf. 76.22.

15. And cf. ll. 94 and 245.

16. The lines are not without their own beauties of craftsmanship. Consider, for example, the sounds of lines 59–60. The *pro* of *promissa* links with the opening syllable of *procellae*. The promises are equivalent to the breezes. But the breezes, like the wave imagery, are real as well as metaphorical. The *procul* of line 60, repeating the sound of *procellae*, tells the reader that the breezes of Theseus' fraudulent promises are indeed those which are wafting him far from her sight. And, as if to complete the circle, the final syllables of *procellae* are repeated in *ocellis* which ends the next line. The result of Theseus' perfidy is now literally apparent to her.

17. With the imagery cf. ll. 320–21.

18. The one adjective applied twice to Theseus, *ferox* (lines 73 and 247) is scarcely more than an epic epithet.

19. Cf. 61.32 and, by transference, 61.54. With the imagery of 64.86–90, cf. especially 61.58 and 62.21–22.

20. He may, of course, be reading it into a passage such as 2.7.

21. There are clear references to lines 121–23 in 133–35, e.g., the word *litus* occurs in 121 and 133; *liquerit* (line 123) becomes *liquisti* (line 133), *immemori* (line 123) *immemor* (line 135), and *discedens* appears in 123 and 134.

22. With which cf. *extremo tempore* (l. 169).

23. Cf. l. 174. For Theseus' perjury see also ll. 143, 146, and 148.

24. In her anger Ariadne surely means the word *avectam* (line 132) to have the connotations of forceful abduction, even though the previous description said nothing to that effect.

25. The same time scheme is used in poem *8*, among others. Though *quondam* warns the reader that Ariadne is looking at a happiness which is past, the theme of hope goes through the whole passage (e.g., ll. 144, 177, 180, 186, etc.).

26. One might compare, for its similarity of context, the imagery used by Dido in *Aeneid* 4. 366–67. This is picked up again and reversed in *Aeneid* 6.471, where it is she who is now like a *Marpesia cautes* toward Aeneas.

27. For similar uses of the verb *eripio* see 64.219, 65.8, etc. A comparison with the opening verses of *68* sheds further light on these lines from *64*. In line 149 Ariadne used the familiar water imagery to describe the trials of Theseus, caught in the very whirlpool of death. In such a way the poet describes Manlius' sea of troubles in 68.3–4. We would seek no further for comparisons — the image is indeed a common one — did not the phrase *spumantibus undis* of 68.3 appear also in 64.155 (and the lines show more resemblances than this). Though in *68* the poet is describing a survivor cast up on the shore while the comparison in *64* refers to a man sinking, nevertheless the metaphorical trials of the sea, in which Theseus earlier found himself, have now become Ariadne's.

28. This change from masculine to feminine, which I hope to examine more fully in a separate study, is most apparent in the long poems but occurs, under various guises, also in the shorter works (e.g., *11*).

29. In line 170, combining the breezes once more with her sense of hearing, she cries that fortune grudges ears to her wails: "fors etiam nostris invidit questibus auris." Words entrusted to the winds are useless (the similarity of sound between *aurae* and *aures* abets the ironic contrast between ll. 164 and 170).

30. Virgil offers a close commentary on these lines in the passage where

Anchises first greets Aeneas upon their meeting in the Underworld (*Aeneid* 6.687–94). Aside from many minor repetitions, l. 689 is repeated almost word for word from 64.166, with the appropriate change from *missas* to *notas*. Lines 692–93 also contain Catullan reminiscences, this time reflecting the opening line of *101*. Just as Aeneas comes to Anchises, so Catullus arrives to offer the last *munus* of love (and death) to his brother.

31. Without going into a detailed analysis here, we may observe that it is a comparison with Ariadne's situation and curse which demonstrates the unity behind the lyric *schema* of *50*. Cf. 64.54 with 50.11 ; 64.57 and 50.9, and especially 64.190–97 with 50.18–21.

32. The similarities between this passage in *68* and the opening lines of the speech of Aegeus are manifold. *Iucundior vita* parallels *vita dulcius*, *casus* is repeated in 64.216 and 68.105, and the verb *eripio* appears in 64.219 and 68.106.

33. It is noteworthy that the only appearances of the word *nuper* in Catullus are here (64.217) and 65.5, where Catullus is thinking on his brother recently dead.

34. Cf. 68.1, 13.

35. For the sensual connotations attached to *languidus*, see its use in 25.3 and 67.21 and the appearance of *languor* in 58b.9. For *saturasset*, cf. 68.83.

36. Both these images had been used previously to describe Ariadne's love. Line 71 tells that she suffered from *assiduis luctibus* when Theseus arrived in Crete, and line 97 shows her *incensam mente*.

37. The poet makes the connection explicit by using images of burial for each — the one literal, the other metaphorical (cf. 68.22, 94, 97, 99).

38. There is a similar use of *dulcis* in 64.210.

39. E. T. Merrill, *Catullus* (Cambridge, Mass. 1951) *ad loc.* claims for the word *aetas* only the meaning *tempus*.

40. The "journey" poems of Catullus show how frequently these words are associated with the joy of return, e.g., *laetus* (9.11, 31.4, 46.8, etc.) and *gaudeo* (31.12–13, etc.).

41. The phrase *laeta gaudia mente* is also employed of similar circumstances shortly after in line 236.

42. Lines 238–45 also offer an interesting example of the poet's mind at work. As Aegeus looks out from the citadel, the poet tells how he was (line 242): "anxia in *assiduos* absumens *lumina fletus*, . . ." In much the same words he portrays his own love-sick state in 68.55–56: "maesta neque *assiduo* tabescere *lumina fletu* / cessarent . . ." The lines which follow in *68* are a simile which has the twofold effect of describing both the poet's tears and the assuaging help which Manlius gave him. Yet the words of the opening lines of the simile are not unlike those which describe Aegeus' suicide (*praeceps* appears in 64.244 and 68.59; *vertice* in 64.244 and 68.57; *iecit* is parallel to *prosilit* in 64.244 and 68.58, and *scopulorum* to *lapide* in the same lines). What makes a subconscious (or even conscious) connection between these two sets of lines more plausible is the simile which preceded this description in *64* by a few lines, where the commands of Aegeus, at first remembered faithfully by Theseus, are said to leave him in the end (ll. 239–40): ". . . ceu pulsae ventorum flamine nubes / *aereum* nivei *montis* liquere cacumen." This is an elaboration of one of Catullus' favorite comparisons dealing with the lack of constancy in love. Yet in line 240 we have two crucial words repeated from 68.57: "qualis in *aerii* perlucens vertice *montis* . . ." The close juxtaposition in the repetitions in actual description and in simile must surely be

more than fortuitous. The feelings of love experienced by Catullus and Aegeus are once more described in terms of the same imagery, and here we have a chance to show the poet's mind at work upon the same imagistic pattern in two quite different poems.

43. The connection is most explicit in line 127, where Catullus tells how Ariadne climbed the sheer mountains "unde aciem (in) pelagi vastos protenderet aestus, . . ." So also Attis, while standing on the edge of the sea, begs in pitiful prayer to be told whither he should direct his eyes to find his fatherland (63.55–56).

44. *Anxius*, ll. 203, 242; *luctus*, ll. 71, 226; *assiduus*, ll. 71, 242. The word *anxius* appears often elsewhere in descriptions of love, e.g. 68.8.

45. And we recall that the same images of fleeting feeling and forgetfulness, which she uses in ll. 142–43, recur when applied to Theseus' obedience to the commands of Aegeus.

46. See F. O. Copley, "Emotional Conflict and its Significance in the Lesbia-Poems of Catullus," *AJP* 70 (1949) 22–40.

47. Poem *61* comes close to picturing in fact what must have been to Catullus the perfect marriage. But even throughout it are scattered occasional remonstrances to the happy couple concerning the preservation of marital bliss, as if the poet knew the pitfalls and was worried that the picture he was sketching could scarcely endure.

48. The same image suggested by *incanuit* is continued in *candenti e gurgite* (l. 14) and *e gurgite cano* (l. 18).

49. For other examples of imagery of whiteness in a happy setting cf. 68.148, 107.6.

50. In both 72.2 and 64.28 the verb *teneo* is used with the same sexual ambiguity.

51. A similar profession, this time made by the poet himself, is found in the opening lines of *51*.

52. Cf. ll. 25–26 with 323–24.

53. A very similar effect is achieved again in l. 273.

54. This event is similar to that Catullus expects when, in 35.3–4, he summons Caecilius to leave Novum Comum and come to Verona (cf. the sound of 35.4: "Comi *moenia Lari*umque litus" with that of 64.36: "Crannonisque domos ac *moenia Lari*ssaea").

55. One might compare with this the appearance of Shelley in stanzas 31ff. of *Adonais*.

56. Cf. also ll. 329, 331, 372–73.

57. Line 335 (and cf. 76.3 and 87.3–4).

58. Ellis (on l. 341, p. 335) quite rightly compares also Pindar *Nem.* 3.51.

59. *Campi*, a reading suggested by Statius to fill the gap in line 344, is especially apt in the light of 46.4.

60. For further instances of *carpo* see 62.36, 37, 43.

61. And we also recall the use of *substernens* in ll. 332 and 403.

62. With *alta madefient* of l. 368 cf. *alta tepefaciet* of l. 360.

63. L. Herrmann, "Le poème 64 de Catulle et Virgile," *RevEtLat* 8 (1930) 211–21, maintains that the last lines of *64* do indeed refer to contemporary events, a valuable corrective to former opinion.

64. Catullus emphasizes his point by repeating line endings such as *parentes* (ll. 400, 404), *nati* or *nato* (ll. 401, 403).

65. As does, e.g., C. J. Fordyce in a review of E. V. Marmorale, *L'Ultimo Catullo*, in *Class. Rev.* N.S. 4 (1954) 132.

On the epyllion see Walter Allen, Jr., "The Epyllion," *TAPA* 71 (1940) 1–26, and the salutary criticism of it by C. W. Mendell, "Epyllion and *Aeneid*," *Yale Cl. St.* 12 (1951) 205–26. For a more detailed history of the whole problem see L. Richardson, Jr., *Poetical Theory in Republican Rome* (New Haven 1944), and J. F. Reilly, "Origins of the Word 'Epyllion'," *CJ* 49 (1953) 111–14, with full bibliography.

66. On this much-debated problem, see A. A. Day, *The Origins of Latin Love-Elegy* (Oxford 1938), esp. 107–11, and E. Paludan, "The Development of Latin Elegy," *Classica et Mediaevalia* 4 (1941) 204–29, who agrees with those who find the origin in Catullus. One should, however, approach this judgment with caution, as G. Luck, *The Latin Love Elegy* (London 1959) 58 warns. Wheeler (above, n. 2) ch. 6, argues, quite rightly, that if Catullus had had the developed genre before him he would have made use of it.

CATULLUS 66. 75–88

MICHAEL C. J. PUTNAM

Lines 79–88 break into Catullus 66 in a form which seems clearly a digression. In the preceding distichs, Catullus and his model Callimachus describe the attachment of the lock for her mistress. In Callimachus, the personified lock, though missing the oils she had previously possessed, complains that she never had the chance to partake in the richer γυναικείων μύρων (l. 78). Therefore, what the reader expects to follow immediately (and does find in ll. 89ff. of both poems) is a request by the lock to receive, in the form of libations to a deity, the unguents which she lacked when a tress on the head of the unmarried Berenice. These thoughts are connected by a mere *vero* (l. 89). The intervening episode has, superficially, little to do with the story which surrounds it. Of a sudden, the lock breaks off talking of her mistress and addresses lines to all newly married couples, urging them to offer her libations and remain chaste in fidelity toward each other.

The evidence of the papyrus is strongly in favor of a digression. As Pfeiffer says, "Catulli vv. 79–88... nihil deest inter finem fr. 1ᵛ et primum versum fr. 2ᵛ, si L. [= Lobel] fragmenta huius folii recte coniunxit."[1] The sense of the original was undoubtedly unbroken between lines 78 and 89. Indeed, as we

said above, lines 77–78 of Callimachus and 89–90 of Catullus (we have only the opening letters of Callimachus ll. 89–90) form a perfect unity.

The problem of interpretation posed by lines 79–88 remains, then, threefold: Are the lines a later addition of Callimachus, translated by Catullus as part of a whole manuscript he had before him?[2] Or are they, though likewise a translation, an addition by Catullus of verses he found elsewhere in Callimachus and, noting their appropriateness, inserted here?[3] Or, finally, are they the original work of the Latin poet himself? We shall here consider the last question[4] and shall demonstrate the very Catullan qualities of these lines, qualities which are apparent in content, style, and that subtle imagery which can only result from the imaginative processes of one particular poet.

That the lines break in as a digression is typical of Catullus, who is often led by pressing feelings of the moment to add lines which could scarcely have been part of his original plan. There is evidence of such a technique in short poems (e. g., 101) as well as long. The most striking example is the reappearance of the lines on the dead brother in 68*b*. We can trace clearly therein the poet's mind at work and show how his intense personal feelings gradually led him away from his originally happy opening of 68*b* toward an expression of something highly meaningful to him, but outside his set scheme. The thought of Troy reminds him of his dead brother, and this, in turn, drives him to reiterate the sorrowful lines which made their first appearance in 68*a*. The result is a repetition which at first seems out of place but remains the only thing that the reader would expect of Catullus.[5]

With the exception of the Theseus–Ariadne episode in 64, this is the longest digression in Catullus. Lines 79–88 of 66 are a similar instance, if on a smaller scale. To show why the poet added these ten lines, we must first turn to the four preceding lines and follow the thought processes of the poet as he works with the words before him. I quote first the lines of Catullus (in the text of Ellis, which comes closest to the received tradition of the manuscripts):

non his tam laetor rebus, quam me afore semper,
afore me a dominae vertice discrucior,
quicum ego, dum virgo quondam fuit, omnibus expers
unguentis, una milia multa bibi [66. 75–78].

These lines are a translation of the following from the *Aitia* of Callimachus (ed. Pfeiffer):

οὐ τάδε μοι τοσσήνδε φέρει χάριν ὅσσον ἐκείνης
ἀσχάλλω κορυφῆς οὐκέτι θιξόμενος,
ἧς ἄπο, παρθενίη μὲν ὅτ' ἦν ἔτι, πολλὰ πέπωκα
λιτά, γυναικείων δ' οὐκ ἀπέλαυσα μύρων.

A detailed examination of the many differences between the two poets will lead us to more general conclusions on what changes Catullus has wrought and on his reasons for doing so.[6] In this we shall find at least one motive for the digression which follows.

The first divergence is that between φέρει χάριν and *laetor*, the difference between the idiomatic "bring pleasure" and the more decisive "I rejoice." The Greek equivalent of *laetor* is, as Barber's

magnificent attempt shows, ἀγάλλομαι.[7] What Catullus adds is an intensity built up, above all, from personal feeling.[8] For this very reason, the verb contrasts vividly with *discrucior* in the next line, providing a balance which Callimachus lacks. It thus serves to emphasize the suffering of the lock, which is now discovered to exceed even her new-found joy and honor.

In spite of Barber, ἀσχάλλω is hardly replaced by *discrucior*. The one is a verb more associated with annoyance than tribulation, while *discrucior* registers the almost physical pain the lock undergoes at being separated from her mistress. This is a motif entirely of Catullus' creation, and appears obviously or inherently in most of the changes he makes from his original in the last two of these four lines. None is more important than the way he elaborates θιξόμενος into the powerfully repeated "me afore semper/afore me."

Callimachus is describing the lock's annoyance that she cannot ever partake in the oils of married life.[9] She drank many λιτά when her mistress was a virgin. This was bad enough, it is suggested, but now to be deprived of the unguents of married life is much more vexing. Catullus alters the emotion entirely and centers it, not on any selfish desire the lock might harbor on her own behalf, but upon her love for her mistress, which has become all the more alive since their separation began. Here, as in every poem Catullus wrote bearing even remotely on the subject, absence heightens the emotions of love and desire. Separation is a theme which haunted him, appearing in humorous guise in the sparrow lyrics and with the most serious intent throughout the poems devoted to his loss of Lesbia (caused by infidelity) and of his brother (the result of death).[10]

Two details serve to enhance this disparity. Catullus translates the demonstrative pronoun ἐκείνης of the Alexandrian poet with the much more specific *dominae*. This establishes that the relationship is between servant and mistress, in this case her queen; but the effect is again to personalize and show the devotion the lock bore Berenice, rather than let the reference pass with a mere "her." Furthermore, the poet adds the word *semper*, which is not paralleled in the Greek text. The separation is irrevocable and will last forever.[11]

The next two lines, 77–78, continue in the spirit of the previous distich, for they offer further explanation of why the lock yearns for her mistress. Catullus begins line 77 with *quicum* rather than ἧς ἄπο, a subtle distinction, but one which bears notice. To Catullus, the actions and feelings of the tress depend not so much on getting something from somebody as on participating in an action and deriving companionship therefrom. It is the same difference as between ἀσχάλλω and *discrucior*: the emotion of love triumphs over that of pleasure or (one might even say) selfishness, that of deep-felt sorrow over annoyance.

The word *una* (which is also a special addition by Catullus) of line 78 should be taken in close conjunction with *quicum*, thus clearing away any doubt as to its authenticity. The construction is not without parallel in Catullus, for the phrase *tecum una* appears no less than four times in 68 (ll. 22, 23, 94 and 95). The emotions described there, caused by the brother's death, are not dissimilar (though, of course, on a much grander scale) to those which the lock experiences upon separation from her beloved mistress. The phrase *quicum una* consequently adds further to the

effect of personalization which we have traced.

This is displayed once more in the phraseology of line 77. παρθενίη μὲν ὅτ' ἦν ἔτι becomes "dum virgo quondam fuit." The abstraction is humanized, so to speak, by the Latin poet, who centers the lock's emotions not on any impersonal status of her mistress (through which she gains or does not gain her coveted unguents) but on the mistress herself, thus enhancing the idea of the affection the lock bears her.

The received text of Catullus ends line 78 with the words *milia multa bibi*, the first word of which Lobel would like to see changed to *vilia* as closer to the λιτά of the original. Yet surely we have found enough alterations by Catullus to justify assuming another, especially one which fits so well into the pattern we have indicated. The phrase *milia multa* recurs constantly to Catullus' mind in contexts where exaggeration is used as a proof of affection.[12] Yet even this is not as important as the fact that Catullus is emphasizing the lock's joy in her past life, affection for her mistress and hence sadness in the present. Though she drank no unguents, still she enjoyed *milia multa* of oils from Berenice. It really made no difference, so long as she enjoyed Berenice's company. Such were the *omnia gaudia* in which the poet delighted during his brother's lifetime (68. 23). Thus *milia multa* fits the mood of affectionate attachment much better than the more literal, though far less Catullan, *vilia multa* does.[13]

To summarize Catullus' departures from the text of Callimachus, the Roman poet makes a distinct effort to personalize the story and heighten the emotion. The lock stands as a true individual whose love for Berenice becomes the more poignant through the poet's added emphasis on their joy when together and sadness when separated. Indeed, it can only be the poet's deep involvement in the theme of separation which impelled him to write the lines which follow. To these we now turn.

From the very opening words, the reader is constantly reminded of similar thoughts and imagery occurring elsewhere in Catullus' poetry. The *optato lumine* recalls the happy marriage of Peleus and Thetis, as does the mention of the *taeda*.[14] The situation of lines 80–81 echoes the verses of 64 where the poet says:

illa, atque haud alia, viderunt luce marinas
mortales oculis nudato corpore Nymphas
nutricum tenus exstantes e gurgite cano [64.
    16–18].

The subject is love which leads to marriage (the word *luce* similarly prepares the way for *taeda* in l. 25) and the wedding ceremony itself, which is the start of the ideal marriage.[15] And apropos of line 81, 61. 101 must be mentioned. The entire stanza of 61 in fact deserves quotation:

> non tuus levis in mala
> deditus vir adultera,
> probra turpia persequens,
> a tuis teneris volet
>   secubare papillis, ...

Here, too are pictured the actual physical attractions of sex, the poet's desire for fidelity in love, and his abhorrence of adultery (note the parallels between *deditus* and *dedit*, and between *adultera* and *adulterio*). The real point of the ten lines in 66 is not so much the description of an *aition* as an exhortation to fidelity (of which the *aition*, if it is one, is only a minor part). The *raison d'être* of the passage comes at its center (as it does on a grander scale in 68) in the contrast between *casto cubili* and *impuro adulterio*. This forms the major basis for the Song of the Fates and the epilogue

of 64.[16] Likewise, the imagery of line 85, descriptive of the actual fact of adultery (symbolized in the earth's failure to receive the offerings of an unfaithful wife), is used metaphorically several times, in varying ways, by the poet to denote infidelity.[17] The vanity of the lover's wishes is equivalent to the lightness of the earth and the fleetness of the winds.

The sentiments of lines 87–88 return us once again to 64. 334–36:

nulla domus tales umquam contexit amores,
nullus amor tali coniunxit foedere amantes,
qualis adest Thetidi, qualis concordia Peleo.

There is no fear that Thetis will be *discors* (l. 379); rather, love and harmony will typify her union. The same sentiment permeates the lines from poem 66. The maidens are joined together to husbands who are *unanimi*.[18] It is a *concordia* which will last forever.[19]

It is in this crucial respect that the lines are not only distinguished from those which introduce them but also are intimately connected with them. In lines 75–78, Callimachus concentrated on the lock's annoyance at being deprived of unguents, whereas Catullus stressed the torture absence from Berenice caused. The lovers will always be united, whereas the lock's parting is eternal (the occurrence of *semper* in l. 75 and then twice in 87–88 adds to the effect).[20] In this contrast between eternal separation and perpetual concord lies the origin of the Catullan digression.

The theme of separation had played an important role earlier in the poem. The departure of Ptolemy from Berenice is a situation which almost exactly parallels the departure of Protesilaus from Laudamia in 68 (and many imaginative links between the two poems can be adduced). Thoughts doubtless suggested by the situation itself here come into the poet's mind and lead him into ten lines of reminiscent moralizing on the necessity of fidelity for concord in love. Ptolemy returned to Berenice; Protesilaus died at Troy, just as did the brother (a figure who, in the simile of 68, merges with that of Protesilaus so that he becomes at once both brother and beloved). The brother's death was a kind of infidelity, as were the departures of both Ptolemy and Protesilaus. The same characteristics are compounded in the person of Theseus in 64, who deserts Ariadne and, also, by another kind of "desertion" (forgetfulness) brings about the death of his father.

The parallel with Protesilaus is even closer. We may compare, out of several examples, 66. 11–12 with 68. 79 ff. The setting is a leave-taking for war. The emotional effect is yearning for a departed beloved. The love of each for the other was as lasting as it was new.[21] Yet, at the same time, the poet pictures the event as a kind of desertion.[22] Just as Catullus is distressed in 68 by a twofold desertion of his brother and Lesbia, so in 66 the poet represents Berenice as mourning especially for the absent Ptolemy, since he is both brother and husband.[23] The love vocabulary which follows in lines 23–25 is thoroughly and typically Catullan; here, unfortunately, we lack the lines of Callimachus for comparison.

Catullus had had ample opportunity in the story which opened the poem to ponder the fact of desertion and its opposite. Much the same emotional pattern appears once more in the relationship between the lock and Berenice. Consequently, even though they are specifically applied to newly-married brides, lines 79–88 provide a commentary on both episodes, centering as they do upon love and desertion. Surely Catullus was not idly passing the time of day in translating any piece of Callimachus which lay before him, to fulfill the request of Ortalus. Rather, he was moved, consciously or not, by the various relationships between Ptolemy, Berenice, and the lock, just as he had become personally involved in a similar event in the lives of Protesilaus and Laudamia because it reminded him of Lesbia and of his brother. Berenice's bliss returned. Laudamia's love and his own twofold happiness were lost. But just as the Roman poet takes the occasion offered by the marriage of Manlius and Vinia in 61 to offer advice to the happy couple and warn them that the felicity of their present state can be maintained only if they preserve their purity and fidelity toward each other, so here, as a kind of moralizing appendage, by the device of the lock he warns Berenice and all happy lovers to preserve their *castitas* and *puritas*. For only thus will they remain united, preserving that *concordia* which, to Catullus, was the basis of all love.

NOTES

1. R. Pfeiffer, *Callimachus*, I (Oxford, 1949), 120. Lobel has since published the new fragments himself in *The Oxyrhynchus Papyri*, XX (London, 1952). On p. 92 he details the reasons why he believes there was no break in the papyrus between ll. 78 and 89. His judgment of the aesthetic merits (or, rather, demerits) of the Catullan insertion may be found on p. 98 ("If 10 vv. which are in the Latin were not in the Greek, 79–88 are easily separable and to my taste their equivalent is gladly to be dispensed with").

2. So Pfeiffer (*op. cit.*, I, 121): "hunc 'ritum nuptialem', cuius αἴτιον in disticho praecedente indicatur, Catullum de suo addidisse veridissimillimum est; nisi per errorem decem vv. in p omissi sunt, Callimachum eos addidisse suspicor, cum 'Comam' Aetiorum l. iv insereret ..., et omisisse 'epilogum' 94a, b." Yet, as we show above, Catullus changes

the text of Callimachus to the point where Pfeiffer's first statement seems unlikely. Even then, is the oil poured on the ground as a libation by newly married girls at all similar to the unguents with which Berenice might have enriched the lock, had it remained after her marriage? Though the *aition* is completely different, the emotional reasons whereby the poet was impelled to write ll. 79–88 are inherent in 75–78.

3. This is the approach taken by H. J. Mette in the most recent treatment of the subject: "Zu Catull 66," *Hermes*, LXXXIII (1955), 500–502. Mette finds in Pfeiffer's F 387 the source of the Catullan insertion. Though Mette's argument runs counter to a judgment elsewhere expressed by Pfeiffer (see P.'s comments on F 387, *op. cit.*, I, 320), the main arguments against his view may be found in F. Della Corte's *Due Studi Catulliani* (Genoa, 1951), p. 33 (the fragment "deve tuttavia appartenere a un carme posteriore alla 'Chioma,' perchè dell' astro parla come di cosa nota e da un tempo già conosciuto").Mette's paraphrases are, it should be noted, based on the text of Callimachus, not on that of Catullus.

4. Della Corte (*op. cit.*, p. 33) suggests that the nuptial-rite verses are Catullan "a meno che il Papiro callimacheo abbia omesso proprio questa parte, e cioè una decina di versi." See also his remarks in *Riv. fil.*, XXIX (1951), 274 (in a review of D. Braga, *Catullo e i poeti greci*).

5. Cf., however, F. O. Copley ("The Unity of Catullus 68: A Further View," *CP*, LII [1957], 29–32), whose stimulating views I cannot accept. In my view the slight impairment of *formal* unity occasioned by the repetition of this theme is simply evidence of the depth of the poet's grief over the loss of his brother. See H. W. Prescott "The Unity of Catullus LXVIII," *TAPA*, LXXI (1940), 475, n. 4.

6. The lack of attention which the original qualities of 66 have received is regrettable especially in view of the abundance of literature devoted to Catullus' only other known translation, 51. In each poem Catullus adds and subtracts words, changing imagery and thought to suit his own devices. 51 thus becomes much more the product of the Catullan imagination than a mirror of the lyric of Sappho. The case of the translation of the *Coma* is no different. On 51, see the sensitive and judicious treatment by E. A. Havelock in *The Lyric Genius of Catullus* (Oxford, 1939), pp. 145–49 (with which compare the same author's remarks on 66 on pp. 77 and 185).

7. E. A. Barber "The Lock of Berenice: Callimachus and Catullus," in *Greek Poetry and Life* (Oxford, 1936), pp. 343–63.

8. Cf. the powerful emotions which swarm around Catullus' use of the word *laetus*, e.g., in 9. 11, 31. 4 or 46. 8.

9. Cf. ἀπέλαυσα, l. 78.

10. The same device is used in 63. 59–60 with a repetition of the same verb, *absum*, again in the future (the one indicative, the other infinitive). Moreover, the emotions involved in each case are nearly equivalent, for in 63 Attis

is giving vent to his distress at being torn from his home and family (which parallels the lock's dismay at being torn from her mistress).

11. Cf. *semper* in 63. 90. Attis will now always be separated from his home or, worse still, will be for his whole life the slave of Cybele.

12. Cf. 5. 10 and 61. 203.

13. For bibliography on the textual difficulties of these lines, see L. Ferrero, *Interpretazione di Catullo* (Turin, 1955), pp. 451–52. A brief discussion of l. 78 is given by D.N. Levin, "Ambiguities of Expression in Catullus 66 and 67," *CP*, LIV (1959), 109. A. L. Wheeler deals with the erotic content of these lines and of the poem as a whole in "Catullus as an Elegist," *AJP*, XXXVI (1915), 155–84, esp. 171–73 (with which compare the same author's *Catullus and the Traditions of Ancient Poetry* [Berkeley, 1934], pp. 174–78). Yet his treatment of the poem in both works (see *Catullus and the Traditions*, pp. 113–14, 264, n. 61) as the closest of translations precludes any analysis of the Catullan temper at work.

14. Cf. 64. 22 (*optato tempore*) and 31 (*optatae luces*) as well as 64. 141 (*optatos hymenaeos*) and 64. 372 (*optatos amores*). The use of *optata* in 64. 328 also should be noted (and, through Hesperus, its connection with 62. 30). *Lumine* here seems to have the connotations both of time for the wedding and time of day, as well as reflecting the glimmer of the marriage torch itself. Since *taeda* occurs in 64. 25, the whole atmosphere of 66. 79 seems to reflect that with which 64 opens.

15. 64. 16–18. Ariadne is in the same dishevelled state in ll. 64–66 when Bacchus sees her and falls in love. There is a difference in mood, but the setting and result are similar.

16. E.g., l. 384, *domos castas* (with which cf. the sentiments of 67. 23–25). With *iura* of l. 83 cf. 64. 143 and 146 (and, secondarily, 135 and 148). This is the lack of justice which follows close after unchastity.

17. Cf. 64. 59 and 142, and 30. 10. It is interesting that the words *levis* and *mala*, which appear in 66. 85, both return in the stanza from 61 quoted above. The light dust is somehow akin to the flighty changeable temper of the adulterous man in 61, and it will not receive the gifts of the treacherous wife in 66. For a further parallel use of *levis*, see 72. 6.

18. For the importance of this word to Catullus, cf. the contexts of 9. 4 and 30. 1.

19. With this use of *assiduus*, cf. 61. 227.

20. Cf. the obvious verbal contrasts between the two sections, such as that between *afore* and *iunxit*.

21. Cf. 66. 11, 15 and 20 with 68. 81.

22. Cf. 66. 21, *orbum ... deserta cubile*, with 68. 29, *deserto cubili*.

23. Cf. 66. 19–22. Cf. the amalgamation of both the brother and Lesbia into the figure of Protesilaus. There may be overtones of infidelity in the word *discidium* of l. 22 (cf. 64. 123 and 134).

Horace

HORACE *CARM*. 1. 5: LOVE AND DEATH

No poem of Horace will continue to attract the attention of critics more magnetically than his ode to Pyrrha. In hazarding a brief supplement to a series of fine, recent appreciations, I offer proof only of the critic's never-ending task.[1] Horace's boundless imagination, while ever attracting the reader, provides sufficient reason to despair of completeness.

A slender youth is making love to Pyrrha in a delightful grotto. In his ignorance of love's fickleness he expects her to be his forever. He has sympathy from the speaker (presumably Horace), wiser in Cupid's ways. The poet himself has just hung up a tablet to Neptune for safe escape from shipwreck. There is a pointed irony in the final stanza.

1. Three new readings are of special interest: K. Quinn, "Horace as a Love Poet: A Reading of *Odes* 1. 5," *Arion*, II (1963), 59–77; V. Pöschl, "Die Pyrrhaode des Horaz," *Coll. Latomus*, LXXX (1964), 579–86; and E. Fredricksmeyer, "Horace's Ode to Pyrrha (*Carm*. 1. 5)," *CP*, LX (1965), 180–85. I am grateful to Professor Fredricksmeyer for his criticism of this Note.

Though Horace is now knowledgeable in amatory matters, he paid the price by a narrow escape from death. He was in such difficulties that he had to offer a vow to save his life. His waterlogged garments prove how much he was at the mercy of the sea and its powerful god. His adventures on these particular waters are over, but he still must be listed among the *miseri* who have experienced unsuspected misfortunes from Pyrrha's wiles. What of the *gracilis puer* who seems in a position of such bliss?

"Miseri, quibus intemptata nites" is a focal phrase. They deserve pity who are lured in ignorance by her gleam. Those who put Pyrrha to the test learn love's wantonness from her perverse ways and suffer for it. We have the final example of Horace himself. What will become of a slender boy faced with such wiles?

The verb *nites* suggests an answer. Its cognates are used often by Horace of seductive beauty. The *nitor* of Glycera burns Horace (1. 19. 5) and that of Liparean Hebrus has the same effect on Neobule in another poem (3. 12. 6). Horace can speak of *nitido . . . adultero* (3. 24. 20) and commiserate with Albius (Tibullus?) that in Glycera's eyes someone younger has outshone him (*praeniteat*: 1. 33. 4). In these examples human charm finds metaphorical parallels in dazzling light. This quality can also be found in landscape. Horace prays to his ship (1. 14. 19–20): "interfusa nitentes / vites aequora Cycladas." He can later include *fulgentes Cycladas* among precincts specially dear to Venus (3. 28. 14).

The idea of bright beauty in person and landscape can on occasion be unified into a single metaphorical pattern. It forms a theme in 2. 8. The treacherous Barine gleams charmingly (*enitescis*, line 6), now committed to faithless vows. She strikes terror into those who could be victimized by her charms (21–24): "te suis matres metuunt iuvencis, / te senes parci, miseraeque nuper / virgines nuptae tua ne retardet / aura maritos." Not only does she gleam enchantingly, she sends out a "breeze" that could slow a ship from its ordinarily true course.[2] But *aura* can also

mean "gleam." We need think only of the glitter emanating from Virgil's golden bough, *discolor . . . auri . . . aura* (*Aen.* 6. 204), a phrase Servius glosses as *splendor auri.*

The same metaphorical patterns run through the Pyrrha ode. They have often been traced but rarely concentrated. As her fiery name implies, she flashes, with blonde hair and a "golden" character (*aurea*, 9) which entices the unwitting. But she is like a Siren on a Siren's rock, drawing human ships to their undoing. Like the living-dead golden bough, her breeze is fickle, her glint deceptive. She rouses love but causes death. She is akin to the *nitentes Cycladas*, islands which attract and then destroy.

Here the sea is not so much a symbol for love itself as it is specifically for the dangerous journey into Pyrrha's affections. From the first stanza we can assume that sometimes the journey can be accomplished with apparent safety. The boy does enjoy her now, we learn from line 9. But after describing the initial, happy scene Horace's first word is *heu*. Weeping will soon come, first for lost *fides*, the faith she had offered him or that he had taken for granted in her or in the gods. They too change for they promise now a safe, calm trip yet suddenly send dark winds over roughened seas. The lover-sailor would have recourse at such moments to Neptune, not sea-born Venus. Landing is better than shipwreck, but under such circumstances the voyager should be thankful for any escape from death.

A slim youth now enjoys Pyrrha and hopes for ever-enduring love. If her breeze were to change he might be shipwrecked, like the poet. But even for him the gleam is false. Those for whom she is untried are worthy of pity. And the opening stanza has a secondary undercurrent of meaning which suggests that the present happy condition of the boy could serve as preparation for (or symbolic precursor of) an event of greater durability but less happiness, death.

Love scene it certainly is. We can compare the situation of Horace and his friend Quinctius Hirpinus in 2. 11. 14–17, "rosa / canos odorati capillos / . . . Assyriaque nardo / . . .

2. As Fredricksmeyer, *op. cit.*, p. 185, n. 8.

uncti." They call for wine and the presence of Lyde, *devium scortum* (22–24): ". . . eburna, dic age, cum lyra / maturet, in comptum Lacaenae / more comas religata nodum." *Carm.* 3. 14, in honor of Augustus' return, shows a servant ordered to fetch perfume, garlands, wine—and Neaera (21–22): "dic et argutae properet Neaerae / murreum nodo cohibere crinem . . ." In a later ode Horace can offer ivy to Phyllis "qua crines religata fulges" (4. 11. 5).

But elements of careful exaggeration make the reader suspect that more is involved than merely love-making. *Urgeo* is rarely used in such an amatory sense and in Horace regularly appears in very different contexts.[3] Moreover Horace stresses the quantity of roses present (in the form of garlands more likely than bushes or some even more romantic bed of roses) by the addition of *multa*.[4] And perfumes on the locks of the young lover are insufficient. He is *perfusus*, "drenched all over."

Any suspicions of overstatement vanish if we consider the scene as anticipation of the burning of a corpse on a funeral pyre. At any such event flowers and perfumes would be much in evidence. Moreover we would expect the body ready for the flames to be *perfusus*, "poured over with perfumes."

The most important parallel for roses as part of a cremation ceremony comes from a passage in Propertius that has puzzled commentators. Had he died at home, the poet cries, Cynthia would have performed the funeral rites (1. 17. 21–24): "illa meo caros donasset funere crines / molliter et tenera poneret ossa rosa; / illa meum extremo clamasset pulvere nomen, / ut mihi non ullo

pondere terra foret." This cannot refer to placing bones in an urn but must look to the actual moment of burning, before the bones have become *pulvis*.[5] Statius (*Sil.* 2. 1. 159) calls the *agger* of Glaucias' pyre *purpureo* (and then lists the scents and *liquores* that "washed his burning hair"). Vollmer sees the pyre covered with red tapestries (at *Aen.* 6. 221 Misenus' corpse is placed *purpureas . . . super vestis*). But flowers could equally well be involved as they may also be at *Aen.* 6. 884, where Anchises prays that purple flowers be strewn at the death of Marcellus.[6] Out of many instances of roses on a tomb we may note Ausonius *Epitaph.* 31. 1–4: "sparge mero cineres bene olentis et unguine nardi / hospes, et adde rosis balsama puniceis. / perpetuum mihi ver agit inlacrimabilis urna / et commutavi saecula, non obii."[7]

The anointing of a corpse and the pouring of unguents are thoroughly exampled. The latter took place before as well as during and after cremation (and of course later still on the tomb itself). Propertius is assured that at his death Cynthia will beat her breast and call on him by name (2. 13. 29–32): "osculaque in gelidis pones suprema labellis, / cum dabitur Syrio munere plenus onyx. / deinde, ubi suppositus cinerem me fecerit ardor, / accipiat Manes parvula testa meos . . ."[8]

Hence Pyrrha, blonde seductress, becomes a beacon fire that lures ignorant seafarers to their destruction and the pyre on which they suffer the *ardor* not of love but of death. The *gracilis puer* is no innocent sailor, no Archytas washed ashore and awaiting a handful of dust. He is the prey and then the victim of Pyrrha, not left to rot but laid out for burial by his

3. Cf., e.g., *Carm.* 1. 15. 23; 1. 24. 6; 2. 9. 9; 4. 9. 27. For *urgeo* in contexts directly associated with death, see L. C. Curran "Propertius 4. 11: Greek Heroines and Death," *CP*, LXIII (1968), 137, n. 16. It is possible that the phrase *herbosos rogos* at Prop. 4. 11. 8 may offer a further connection between flowers and the funeral pyre (see below on Prop. 1. 17. 21–24).

4. Cicero twice uses the phrase *in rosa* apparently of garlands at a banquet (*Fin.* 2. 65 and *Tusc.* 5. 73). For Horace also roses were common in such circumstances (e.g., *Carm.* 2. 3. 14). We are dealing neither with Marlowe's beds of roses nor with Shakespeare's souls couching on love.

On the Roman fondness for roses, see M. P. Nilsson *RE*, Zw. R. I a 1 (1914), 1111–15 (*s.v. Rosalia*).

5. The first is the contention of Enk, *ad loc.* (*in urna rosis plena*). Camps calls it a "practice otherwise unknown."

6. At *Aen.* 5. 79 the same phrase, *purpureos flores*, is definitely associated with a tomb (see Williams, *ad loc.*). Whether tomb or pyre at 6. 884 is an open question (though Norden opts for "Grabesspende," "Grabschmuck.")

7. Ausonius may well have in mind a prayer of Juvenal at *Sat.* 7. 207–8: "di, maiorum umbris tenuem et sine pondere terram / spirantisque crocos et in urna perpetuum ver." The comments of Mayor, *ad loc.* (I, 322, and esp. 459), are most helpful.

8. See Enk *ad loc.*, Smith on Tib. 1. 3. 7 and 2. 4. 44, Mayor on Juv. 4. 109 (I, 234 and 410), and Daremberg-Saglio, 1394–95 (and n. 15), *s.v. funus* for further references. We may note esp. Prop. 3. 16. 23 (where *huc* refers to the pyre itself), and Pers. 3. 104.

destroyer. He is already an example of her awesome power.

Stanzas one and four do not merely offer antithetical pictures of a boy making love in a cave and a sailor-poet dedicating garments in a temple. The poet has escaped alive (and offers homage to Neptune, not Venus), but this fact suggests that we might see the opposite, not so happy, fate in store for the youth. The opening stanza may not be as light —even ironically light—as it first seems.[9]

MICHAEL C. J. PUTNAM

BROWN UNIVERSITY

9. The love scene takes place *grato sub antro*, in a purportedly pleasant grot. But, at least by the time of Lucan, *antrum* means sepulcher or tomb as well. It is possible that this sense was in the back of Horace's mind as he composed. The new *OLD* gives three examples of this use of *antrum*: Luc. *Phar*. 8. 694 and 10. 19; and *CIL* VI, 28239. *TLL* adds *Vulg. Gen*. 23. 30; *Ier. Ep*. 108. 33; and *carm. epig*. 1362. 4.

MERCURI, FACUNDE NEPOS ATLANTIS

Horace's first Ode to Mercury (1. 10) is, in Porphyrion's terse opinion, *ab Alcaeo lyrico poeta*. Critics have long speculated on the extent of the Roman poet's indebtedness, the general sentiment usually favoring his originality.[1] Conjecture is replaced by fact, however, in the case of the first stanza. Hephaestion preserves for us the opening lines of a hymn by Alcaeus, apparently the poem Horace "imitated" (308b L.-P.):

> χαῖρε, Κυλλάνας ὁ μέδεις, σὲ γάρ μοι
> θῦμος ὕμνην, τὸν κορύφαισιν †αὐγαῖς†
> Μαῖα γέννατο Κρονίδᾳ μίγεισα
> παμβασίληï.

Comparison with Horace's opening lines points up some notable differences:

> Mercuri, facunde nepos Atlantis,
> qui feros cultus hominum recentum
> voce formasti catus et decorae
>   more palaestrae,
>
> te canam, . . .

Whether or not Alcaeus went on to treat the god's affectionate involvement with mankind's cultural development we may never know. But we can observe two changes of emphasis concerning nomenclature and genealogy. In Alcaeus' initial stanza, though the god is greeted and his immediate parentage explained, he himself is never named. Horace, by contrast, apostrophizes Mercury in his poem's first word. This might well have forewarned a Roman reader that the poem, whatever its

Greek elements and even specific borrowings from Alcaeus, was directly concerned with Mercury as god of barter and exchange—the implications of his name. This the poem proceeds to show, on levels ranging from humorous to deeply serious.

The second alteration is of equal importance. Instead of Alcaeus' more expansive look at Zeus's encounter with Maia on Mt. Cyllene, Horace briskly alludes only to the god's maternal grandfather, Atlas. Though commentators offer no reason for Horace's choice beyond the honorific genealogy proper to a hymn, a clue is furnished by Servius Auctus annotating *Aeneid* 1. 741. Virgil has introduced at Dido's banquet the singer Iopas *docuit quem maximus Atlas*. After telling us that Atlas was the son of Iapetus, Servius adds: "hic quod annum in tempora diviserit et primus stellarum cursus vel circulorum vel siderum transitus naturasque descripserit, caelum dictus est sustinere. qui nepotem suum Mercurium et Herculem docuisse dicitur." That Atlas "taught" his grandson is not attested elsewhere. His instruction of Hercules—an easy rationalization for "sharing the burden" of the heavens—is mentioned as early as Herodorus.[2] In literature previous to or contemporary with Horace we can call as further witnesses to the more general allegory of Atlas as astronomer-philosopher Xenagoras,[3] Cicero, Diodorus Siculus,[4] and Vitruvius. Cicero, linking Atlas and his brother, details the tradition which by his time would also have had Stoic and Euhemeristic overtones (*Tusc.*

---

1. As Wilamowitz, *Sappho und Simonides* (Berlin, 1913), p. 312; E. Fraenkel, *Horace* (Oxford, 1957), p. 162; G. Williams, *Tradition and Originality in Roman Poetry* (Oxford, 1968), pp. 146 f.; R. Nisbet and M. Hubbard, *A Commentary on Horace: Odes, Book I* (Oxford, 1970), p. 126.

2. F. Jacoby, *FGrH* 31 F 13 (pp. 218, 504, and supp. pp. 549-50).

3. *FGrH* 240 F 32 (pp. 703, 1010).

4. 3. 60 (cf. 4. 27 for Atlas as teacher of Hercules).

5. 3. 8): [5] "nec vero Atlas sustinere caelum nec Prometheus adfixus Caucaso nec stellatus Cepheus cum uxore, genero, filia traderetur, nisi caelestium divina cognitio nomen eorum ad errorem fabulae traduxisset." Vitruvius likewise points to a "history" behind the myth of heaven sustained (*De arch.* 6. 7. 6): "Atlas enim formatur historia sustinens mundum, ideo quod is primum cursum solis et lunae siderumque omnium versationum rationes vigore animi sollertiaque curavit hominibus tradenda . . ."

Of the post-Horatian authors who allegorize the tale of Atlas, Pausanias is of particular pertinence for returning us to the source of both myth and allegory.[6] The periegete tells us (9. 20. 3) of a place called Polus (itself a rationalization?[7]) near Tanagra, where they say Atlas sat and pondered τά τε ὑπὸ γῆς . . . καὶ τὰ οὐράνια. He goes on to quote Homer (*Od.* 1. 52–54) as if he felt the context lent unquestionable authority to notions of allegory. Homer is speaking of Calypso,

> Ἄτλαντος θυγάτηρ ὀλοόφρονος, ὅς τε θαλάσσης
> πάσης βένθεα οἶδεν, ἔχει δέ τε κίονας αὐτὸς
> μακράς, αἲ γαῖάν τε καὶ οὐρανὸν ἀμφὶς ἔχουσι.

Homer is the initial source for the interpretation of Atlas as prototype of the natural scientist.[8] But a word is in order about the epithet ὀλοόφρων. It is usually translated "of wicked mind," reading into Homer (and back into the figure of Atlas) the Hesiodic portrait of the Titan who opposes the Olympian regime. Yet, though the adjective is used in the *Iliad* only of wild beasts, in the *Odyssey* it is applied to men, specifically Aietes (10. 137) and Minos (11. 322). For the latter, model of lawgivers, the attribute can only mean something like "sagacious."[9] Aietes, king of Colchis, has impressive family credentials as a sage—grandson of Oceanos, son of Helios, brother of Circe, father of Medea ("the contriver," "inventor") by Eidyia ("the knowing one").[10] It would seem inconsistent of Homer in a single work to vary the meaning of a rare adjective applied only to three people in such a way as to ascribe craft negatively to one, yet wisdom positively to the other two.

Hesiod's vignette (*Theog.* 517 ff., 746 ff.) is of course that of the Titan overthrown. Atlas comes between Menoitios and Prometheus when their punishments are described, but his torture is noticeably different. Menoitios was sent to Erebus, transfixed by a thunderbolt; Prometheus was bound, pierced by a shaft, his liver continuously devoured by a bird. One could easily postulate another tradition operating for their fellow Titan who by contrast now upholds the wide heavens for his crime.[11] Hesiod calls Atlas κρατερόφρων (509), an adjective which may punningly allude to his physical posture but which Homer applies to Hercules (*Il.* 14. 324) and Castor and Pollux (*Od.* 11. 299), heroes who later enter the lists of traditional benefactors of mankind.[12]

Horace's treatment of Atlas' brother Prometheus shows the same double tradition operating. He is both the punished opposer of the Olympian order, and, at the same time, the culture hero and "molder" of early man. He is tortured by Jupiter's eagle (*Ep.* 17. 67) and placed in the underworld (*Odes* 2. 13. 37), whence in his cleverness he once tries to escape (*Odes* 2. 18. 35, an event in the legend not attested outside of Horace). Yet at the same time he is noted as the giver of fire to humans (*Odes* 1. 3. 27) whose characteristics he is said to have formed from primal clay (*Odes* 1. 16. 13 ff.).[13]

Atlas' intellectual pedigree also presents

---

5. Virtually the same point is made by August. *Cir. Dei* 18. 8 (cf. 18. 39 for the relationship of Atlas to Hermes and Hermes Trismegistus).

6. For additional post-Horatian allusions to Atlas as scientist, K. Wernicke, *s.v.* "Atlas," *RE*, II.2 (1896), 2124.

7. See Frazer *ad loc.*

8. The column which holds up the heavens is a universal symbol for that which links man with the transcendent, saving him from chaos. Cf. M. Eliade, *The Sacred and the Profane* (New York, 1959), pp. 34 ff.

9. Cf. Liddell and Scott, *s.v.*; Stanford *ad Od.* 1. 52. For

Homer's opinion of Minos: *Od.* 11. 568 ff. For the later ancient etymologies (from ὅλος instead of ὀλοός), see H. Ebeling, *Lexicon Homericum* (Leipzig, 1880), *s.v.*

10. For further details, see Pease *ad* Cic. *Nat. D.* 3. 48.

11. See West *ad Theog.* 509, 516.

12. As, e.g., Hor. *Odes* 3. 3. 9; 4. 8. 30 f.

13. For further examples of Prometheus as culture hero see Nisbet–Hubbard *ad loc.*; West *ad Theog.* 507–616 (p. 306); and the bibliography in Eliade, *The Forge and the Crucible* (New York, 1971), pp. 204–205.

this double inheritance.[14] Virgil sees him not only as the bearer of the heavens (*Aen.* 4. 247 ff., 481 f.; 6. 796 f.; 8. 135 f., 140 f.), but as teacher of Iopas who sings *de rerum natura.*[15] Mercury may have absorbed some of his traditional cunning from his grand-uncle Prometheus. The presence of his grandfather Atlas in the opening apostrophe of Horace's Ode points more specifically to Mercury's role as educator of mankind's mind and body through words, music, and athletics. It is to such an accomplishment that Horace directly turns, having made one brief but important allusion to another "teacher" in the god's past.[16]

Michael C. J. Putnam

Brown University

14. The first mention of Atlas in Latin is Liv. And. *Od.* Frag. 29 Mariotti: "apud nympham Atlantis filiam Calypsonem . . ." Mariotti refers to *Od.* 4. 557 (= 5. 14; 17. 143): νύμφης ἐν μεγάροισι Καλυψοῦς, ἥ μιν ἀνάγκῃ . . . We might with equal plausibility expect the phrase *Atlantis filiam* to define Calypso near her first appearance, i.e., *Od.* 1. 52: Ἀτλαντος θυγάτηρ. See S. Mariotti, *Livio Andronico* (Milan, 1952), p. 47, n. 1, for the possibility of "contamination."

15. For a detailed discussion of its contents, see C. Segal, "The Song of Iopas in the Aeneid," *Hermes*, XCIX (1971), 336–49.

16. See also *Odes* 3. 11. 1 ff. for another example of Mercury's power as teacher.

HORACE *c.* 1.20

Horace invites his patron Maecenas to drink his Sabine wine. The wine is special, put up by himself on a date Maecenas will remember. His return to health after a difficult illness found him greeted by the applause of those attending the theatre. Maecenas will drink wines such as Caecuban or Calenian, Falernian or Formian. The latter do not temper Horace's goblets.

Fraenkel, in his comments on the poem, quotes with approval Dacier's remarks that the goal of the poem is to help Maecenas remember the shouts of approval which communicated the urban mob's esteem. "Primarily Horace wanted to cheer his friend by reminding him of the scene in the theatre, but in doing so he produced a lasting picture of his own affectionate care."[1] Commager, rightly I think, sees a more symbolic intent in the poem: "Roman content, Greek container, modest cups, the emphatic *ego ipse*—the phrasing suggests that Horace's real gift to his patron is not so much the promised wine as the poem itself."[2]

If not the poem itself, at least the wine that Maecenas will drink when he visits Horace bears the tokens of poetry.[3] Both the situation and the vocabulary suggest this. Horace, the Sabine craftsman, himself puts his humble thoughts in Greek metrical guise and utters them in understatement, fit emblem of the way he lived. There is a further sense to both *conditum* and *levi* which encourages the *double-entendre*. *Condo*, on the surface, means to put wine in a jar and preserve it for future use. It also means to compose poetry to be "broached" at the proper moment. The most obvious metaphorical link between storing wine and crafting verse in Horace occurs at the opening of his first *epistle* where he says of his own present career: *condo et compono quae mox depromere possim* (*e.* 1.1.12). But elsewhere he speaks of someone who *mala condiderit in quem . . . carmina* (*s.* 2.1.82); to Julius Florus; *condis amabile carmen* (*e.* 1.3.24); to one of the Pisones: *carmina condes* (*A.p.* 436).[4]

Lino carries the same ambiguity. The wine maker seals his jars with pitch. The poet, if he is good, literally (and then symbolically) writes *carmina* which *posse linenda cedro et levi servanda cupresso* (*A.p.* 332). If he is a poetaster, he can "smear" (and hence "ruin") outstanding content by bad craftsmanship and expression (*e.* 2.1. 235–37):[5]

[1] E. Fraenkel, *Horace*, 214 f. R. Reitzenstein ("Horaz und die hellenistische Lyrik," *Neue Jahr.* 21 [1908] 96–7) draws a parallel between *c.* 1.20 and *A.p.* 11.44 (see also G. Pasquali, *Orazio lirico*, 325–29).

[2] S. Commager, *The odes of Horace*, p. 326.

[3] On the symbolism of wine in Horace's poetry see Commager, *op. cit.*, pp. 264 and 337, and "The function of wine in Horace's odes," *TAPhA* 88 (1957) 68–80.

[4] Cf. also Lucr. 5.2; Cic. *Rep.* 4.12; Vir. *ecl.* 10. 50 (on which see Quint. 10.1.56 and 95). The metaphor is particularly common with *recondo*, as Cal. Sic. *ecl.* 1.16.

[5] Cf. also Horace's uses of *allino* (*A.p.* 446); *illino* (*s.* 1.4.36); and *oblino* (*e.* 1.19.30).

sed veluti tractata notam labemque remittunt
atramenta, fere scriptores carmine foedo
splendida facta linunt.

Conditum serves a careful structural purpose as well. Its link with the subsequent *datus . . . cum*, which both chiasmus and etymology emphasize, connects the first two stanzas. The juxtaposition announces one of the poem's chief points. While Horace was putting up his wine, Maecenas was being applauded in the theatre. The initial correspondence is between Roman theatre and Greek jug, between urban applause and rustic Sabine wine. But the metaphorical power of *conditum levi* thrusts over to the subsequent words. The humility of Horace's "poor" accomplishment, refined and restrained, is scarcely compatible with the outburst of public approval which Maecenas receives from the city's populace.

The same metaphorical coloring of literal with figurative, seen with respect to the constructs of poetry, recurs here also. *Redderet laudes* refers initially to the reechoed shouts which return from the *mons Vaticanus* to Maecenas' ears. Yet on another occasion Horace gives the phrase *reddidi carmen* to a *nupta* trained to commemorate Phoebus, after the poet's fashion (*c*. 4.6. 43). And *laudes* for Virgil (*ecl.* 4.26; 6.6) as for Horace (*c*. 4.8.20, 28) often imply the recounting of heroic achievement in prose or poetry. As most commentators note, the phrase *iocosa imago* is also used at *c*. 1.12.3–4—*cuius recinet iocosa/nomen imago*—while the poet thinks of what man, hero or god he will glorify. It is the praises of Augustus with which that poem is chiefly concerned. Such, too, is the epic grandeur of Maecenas' prestige as expressed by the people of Rome.

The attributes of Maecenas are chosen for special purpose. Maecenas is an *eques*. The Tiber, whose banks help resound his praises, can be called his ancestral stream (*paterni fluminis*). These are the superficial attributes of his status, which Horace speaks of in poem after poem—*Maecenas atavis edite regibus* (*c*. 1.1.1); *equitum*

decus (*c*. 3.16.20); *Tyrrhena regum progenies* (*c*. 3.29.1); cf. Propertius 3.9.1: *Maecenas, eques Etrusco de sanguine regum*. The opening of *s*. 1.6 is a good summary of Horace's feelings on the subject:[6]

non quia, Maecenas, Lydorum quidquid
  Etruscos
incoluit finis, nemo generosior est te,
nec quod avus tibi maternus fuit atque
  paternus
olim qui magnis legionibus imperitarent,
ut plerique solent, naso suspendis adunco
ignotos, ut me libertino patre natum.

The actual situation of the *eques* Maecenas in the theatre is one of the many examples of Horace's making theatrical stance the measure of social or economic importance. He was preoccupied with the Roscian law.[7] We have, for instance, the upstart in *e*. 4, of whom he says (15–16): *sedilibusque magnus in primis eques/Othone contempto sedet*. The very event touched on in *c*. 1.20 is alluded to in *c*. 2.17, a poem also addressed to Maecenas, *mearum grande decus columenque rerum* (3–4). Poet and patron have been saved from death, *cum populus frequens/laetum theatris ter crepuit sonum* (25–26). The reason is never given, only the reaction to his recovery. Horace escaped being injured by a falling tree. The poet marvels on the fact that *utrumque nostrum incredibili modo/consentit astrum*. Yet there are more differences than similarities. Jupiter protects Maecenas, the mob responds to him, he should remember to offer victims and build a votive shrine. Horace, saved by his rustic Faunus, will sacrifice a humble lamb. The wit and irony

---

[6] For a full and careful treatment of their relationship see K. Reckford, "Horace and Maecenas," *TAPhA* 90 (1959) 195–208.

[7] In one poem dedicated to Maecenas, which he concludes by chiding his patron for over-dependence upon mere appearances, Horace asks (*e*. 1.1. 62–3):

Roscia, dic sodes, melior lex an puerorum est
nenia, quae regnum recte facientibus offert. . . ?

See also *s*. 1.6.40 f.; 1.10.76 f.; *e*. 2.1.185; *A.p.* 113. There is a further allusion to Horace's feelings on the superficiality of applause at *s*. 2.3.185 f.

of the poem lie in the challenge, not in the agreement, between Horace and his patron, and in the challenges between poverty and wealth, humility and power, and poetry and shallow achievement.

Similar themes are raised in *c.* 3.8 and *c.* 3.29, both dedicated to Maecenas. *C.* 3.8 announces a celebration on the Kalends of March to which Maecenas is invited; once more Horace opposes his world to Maecenas' hectic life; instead of worrying, he should be *neglegens ne qua populus laboret* (25). What is expressed here as a hope becomes virtually an accusation in *c.* 3.29. 25–26: *tu civitatem quis deceat status/ curas et urbi sollicitus times.* The reaction of the *frequens populus* in *c.* 2.17, the *plausus* of the masses in *c.* 1.20, is a specific instance of mob response apparently reflecting the trite attainments of the politically ambitious. In our search for governing power, how much attention are we to pay to the *mobilium turba Quiritium* (*c.* 1.1. 7), to the *malignum* (*c.* 2.16, 39–40) or *profanum vulgus* (*c.* 3.1.1)? In his strongest exhortation toward a philosophic *nil admirari* Horace directs his reader to ask (*e.* 1.6.7–8):

> ludicra quid, plausus et amici dona Quiritis
> quo spectanda modo, quo sensu credis et ore?

The reader of *c.* 1.20 notes with interest the connection between *ludicra* and *plausus*.

Maecenas is called glory of the equestrian rank at *c.* 3.16.20. The context is instructive:

> crescentem sequitur cura pecuniam
> maiorumque fames: iure perhorrui
> late conspicuum tollere verticem,
> Maecenas, equitum decus.

Horace reads the lesson to himself, apparently (*perhorrui*). It is oriented more obviously at the knight. The words would have a resonance from an earlier poem, also directed to him, as we have seen (*s.* 1.6.23–24): *sed fulgente trahit constrictos Gloria curru/non minus ignotos generosis.*

There is a further turn on the same theme in *c.* 2.12, likewise a homily to Mae-

cenas: one should not write of Hannibal's deeds in the soft measures of lyric; let Maecenas detail Caesar's wars in prose; Horace will sing of Licymnia's charms. Would you exchange, Horace asks Maecenas in conclusion, one lock of her hair for the wealth of Phrygia or Persia? What is wealth (and, by symbolic extension, the exploits of warriors and statesmen) in comparison to love and beauty, the inspirations of a lyric Muse?

Another variation occurs in the final ode of book 2. The *vates* Horace, already assured of immortality, is about to become a swan and soar above the concerns of men (5–7):

> . . . non ego pauperum
> sanguis parentum, non ego, quem vocas,
> dilecte Maecenas, obibo.

Horace, of poor familial stock, is Maecenas' protégé nonetheless. Maecenas is beloved by him and returns the sentiment. Lack of external wealth is of no importance in determining personal worth and final accomplishment. This is the only warning to *dilecte Maecenas* here.

The ambiguities of *care eques Maecenas* at 1.20.5 are more potent.[8] *Care* has its similarity to *dilecte.* Maecenas is held in affectionate esteem by Horace. He is also *carus* in another sense. He holds the title of *eques*, a man to be valued for his property and rank. He is "dear" to the mob, of noble ancestry, for whom the Tiber can be called *paternus* because of its origin near Arretium, home of the Cilnian *gens.*

But the special purpose of *care* in the poem is illuminated by its placement. Not only does it receive stress as the first word in the stanza; it is a carefully chosen anto-

---

[8] At line 5 *clare*, a correction proposed by Bentley, has been accepted by Klingner (in the Teubner text) and defended by Fraenkel (*op. cit.*, n. 1, p. 215 n. 4). However plausible such a reading might be, the virtually universal manuscript tradition need not be altered. Nor need any changes be made at the opening of line 10. Pasquali (*op. cit. supra.* n. 1), 327, is unduly restrictive when he states "*care* mostra che Orazio, pure suo cliente, non si considera qui inferiore ma amico."

nym for *vile* which holds the same position in the preceding, initial stanza of the poem. The contrast clarifies what seems to be the essence of their theme. Maecenas, *carus*, receives Horace's affection and absorbs, as well, the homage of Rome's citizens, as knight and confidant and advisor to its prince. The mob shouts its approval, which reverberates through the landscape. Horace's wine is common and poor (*vile*). It is a combination of Sabine and Greek elements—"rustic" thoughts confined within an "imported" container, quite different from the expansive reaction of Rome's theater. His lyric vintage is the opposite of the city's epic praise. It is cheap instead of dear; modest instead of overwrought; underplayed, not broadcast.

Yet, though he does so elsewhere, Horace does not here content himself with a challenge between the modest means whereby he expresses his "meager" affection and the mob's effusive response. This could scarcely be expected of the Horace who once styled himself *a vulgo longe longeque remotos* (*s.* 1.6.18). The unannounced question, posed before the third stanza, concerns the importance of the *imago*. Is it a reflection of truth, an acknowledgement of love and understanding in depth or is it a wraith, a false and fickle echo, loud and valueless?[9]

We have yet to ponder the sentiment of *e.* 1.1.52—*vilius argentum est auro, virtutibus aurum.*—or what Ulysses outlines to Tiresias (*s.* 2.5.7–8): *atqui/et genus et virtus, nisi cum re, vilior alga est.* What should be honest *res* to Maecenas? Should he batten on external applause or listen to Horace's more subtle music?

The last lines seem to support the poet's expressed thesis. Maecenas will drink choice Caecuban and Calenian. No vintage from the *ager Falernus* or the hills of Formiae tempers Horace's goblets. We appear to rehearse a variation on two themes already stated. The good wine that Maecenas will drink is at first equated by the reader, at least externally, with the theatre's applause. Nothing distinguished lends grandeur to the goblets Horace is to offer his friend. Once more Horace seems to downgrade his own achievement while lavishing praise on the mob's shouts—as if they should and did seem equivalent in Maecenas' thoughts to a fine vintage.[10]

The metaphors, I venture, tell one part of another story. We may begin with *temperant*. In connection with wine it signifies two things, both of which are operative here. It means (as we would initially expect here) to temper the tartness or bitterness of a bad wine with one of greater sweetness and quality. Yet it also connotes the mollification of a wine's strength by the addition of water or a vintage of

---

[9] The name *mons Vaticanus* comes into question here. Commager, *loc. cit.* n. 2, speaks of "a punning reference to *vaticinor*, and the 'Mount Vatican' that returns the praise of Maecenas may have some suggestions of the poet's sacred mountain." Certainly the ancient etymology connected the word with *vates* (Paul. Fest. 519.24) and *vaticinium* (Gell. 16.17.1–2). But *vaticinor* means "to rave" as well as "to celebrate in song" (Cicero, *Sest.* 10.23, conjoins it with *insanire*). If appeal is to be made to etymology, this ambiguity, of some value in an interpretation of the poem, should be operative.

Two further points. First, antiquity was unsure of the specific rise in the Janiculum massif to which the name *mons Vaticanus* should be given (see A. Elter, "Vaticanum," *RM* 46 [1891] 112–38, whose conclusion is corroborated by G. Radke, *P-W* 2.15, *c.* 490–91, quoting Ps.-Acro and Porphyrio *ad loc.*). Secondly, at least by Martial's

time the wine from the Vatican hills was notoriously bad (1.18.2; 6.92.3; 10.45.5; 12.48.14). If there is a reference ahead to the *Formiani colles* (and the quality of their wine) or back from them to the *mons Vaticanus*, it can only strengthen the ambiguous irony of any connection between *Vaticanus* and *vaticinor*. The shouts of the people could be heard by some as ravings of indifferent merit.

[10] Both Caecuban and Calenian are, to Horace, choice wines, to be reserved for special occasions (see, e.g., *e.* 9.1.36; *c.* 1.31.9; 1.37.5). A. W. Verrall (*Studies in Horace*, pp. 143–45) offers special reasons for a reference to Formiae here and shows its bearing (and that of *s.* 1.5.38 and *c.* 3.16.17–20, 33 f.) on *c.* 3.17. His reading *invides* at *c.* 1.20.10, defended on pages 146–49, is unconvincing.

less potency.[11] His wine, Horace is also saying to Maecenas, is of such nobility that Falernian, or any supposedly extraordinary wine, would only dilute its true power.

When *temperant* is taken in this sense, it follows more naturally upon *prelo domitam*. The choice draughts of Caecuban and Calenian, drunk by Maecenas, and elsewhere in Horace synonymous with good fortune and rejoicing, are actually "tamed" (domitam) and "suppressed" (*prelo*, root *prem-*) when compared to Horace's "cheap" Sabine. We need not search far to find allied words in combination. For example, looking at the first book of the *Aeneid* alone, we learn in line 54 how Aeolus suppresses the winds by his rule (imperio premit) and in line 57 how he tempers their wrath (temperat iras). Soon thereafter Jupiter tells Venus that the time will come (284–5)

> cum domus Assaraci Phthiam clarasque
> Mycenas
> servitio premet ac victis dominabitur Argis.

The last lines, therefore, bring the poem full circle and expose a deeper importance to the first two stanzas.[12] Horace's wine,

instead of being "buried," to be received diffidently and in retirement, is really of supreme quality, more tasteful and exuberant than any other. Maecenas thinks he imbibes the best. He puts faith in the plaudits of the people. But what may seem externally noteworthy—the mob's shouts and the richest vintages—are in actuality hemmed in, suppressed, and in the end valueless. Horace's own wine, the quality of himself and his poetry, could at first be characterized as cheap, rustic, put away by the poet (ordinarily a slave's task) and served *modicis cantharis*, in goblets which, because they are small, reflect a temperate nature. The unstinted force of its true worth, unsurpassed in importance and strength, is revealed only in the irony of the last stanza.[13] The poet compliments himself, to be sure. Maecenas, connoisseur of people and ideas, could perhaps draw deeper insights on the inner nature of man.

MICHAEL C. J. PUTNAM
Brown University

---

[11] As, e.g., Mart. 9.11.7.

[12] Stanzas 1 and 3 are deliberately connected by the echo of *potabis* in *bibes*. Of the many interconnections between stanzas 2 and 3, sonantal echoes and word placement stress the relationship of *laudes* (7) to *vites* (11) and of *Vaticani montis* (7–8) and *Formiani colles* (11–12). *Falerniae vites*, the producers of the finest vintages, seem to be the symbolic equivalent of the resounding *laudes*, the height of public acclaim, while Formian hills supply a metaphorical substitute for that which rebounds off the Vatican mount. In the matter of popular judgment, each appears to equal the other in value and be of the highest worth.

For further comments on word placement and construction see W. Wili, *Horaz*, p. 163.

[13] In *c.* 1.15 Horace pokes fun at himself by undercutting his own devotion to the theme of *c.* 1.20. In lines 17–18 his analogue is wine:

> rure meo possum quidvis perferre patique;
> ad mare cum veni, generosum et lene requiro.

Sabine wine will do when in the Sabine country. When Horace mingles with the well-to-do at the seaside (which he claims to prefer whenever the chance comes along), then he craves a wine to go with his situation, *generosum*, of good-breeding and ancestry (like Maecenas at *s.* 1.6.2 and, by implication, 24). A truer Horace, speaking at the end of *c.* 3.1, would not exchange his *valle Sabina* for *divitias operosiores* (among them *Falerna vitis*, 43).

HORACE ODES 3.9: THE DIALECTICS OF DESIRE

Michael C. J. Putnam

Donec gratus eram tibi
   nec quisquam potior bracchia candidae
cervici iuvenis dabat,
    Persarum vigui rege beatior.

donec non alia magis
   arsisti neque erat Lydia post Chloen,
multi Lydia nominis
    Romana vigui clarior Ilia.

me nunc Thressa Chloe regit,
   dulcis docta modos et citharae sciens,
pro qua non metuam mori,
    si parcent animae fata superstiti.

me torret face mutua
   Thurini Calais filius Ornyti,
pro quo bis patiar mori,
    si parcent puero fata superstiti.

quid si prisca redit Venus
   diductosque iugo cogit aeneo,
si flava excutitur Chloe
    reiectaeque patet ianua Lydiae?

quamquam sidere pulcrior
   ille est, tu levior cortice et inprobo
iracundior Hadria,
    tecum vivere amem, tecum obeam lubens.

While I was pleasing to you nor did any youth, more preferred, put his arms around your white neck, I flourished more
blissful than the king of the Persians.

While you did not burn more for another nor was Lydia second to Chloe, I, Lydia of great repute, flourished more famous than Roman Ilia.

Now Thracian Chloe, learned in sweet songs and skilled on the lyre, rules me, for whom I will not fear to die, if the fates spare her, my soul, surviving.

Calais, son of Ornytus of Thurium, burns me with a flame he shares, for whom I will twice suffer death, if the fates spare my boy surviving.

What if our old love returns, and compels us, driven apart, under a brazen yoke, if blonde Chloe is expelled and the door is opened for rejected Lydia?

Although he is more beautiful than a star, you more fickle than cork and more temperamental than the unruly Adriatic, with you I would love to live, with you I would gladly die.

Though its antiphonal form is unique in the remains of ancient literature for such a lyric theme, Horace's delightful dialogue between two lovers has aroused little critical comment.[1]

[1] The most sensitive, percipient discussions of *Odes* 3.9 are by S. Commager, *The Odes of Horace* (New Haven 1962) 57ff., and M. Owen Lee, *Word, Sound and Image in the Odes of Horace* (Ann Arbor 1969) 103ff. My debt to each will be patent. The novelty of the dialogue form in *Odes* 3.9 and Catullus 62 is considered by G. Williams, *Tradition and Originality in Roman Poetry* (Oxford 1968) 210f., who also summarizes the poem in *The Third Book of Horace's Odes* (Oxford 1969) 75-6. N. E. Collinge (*The Structure of Horace's Odes* [London 1961] 58ff.) analyzes the highly patterned (for Horace) strophic arrangement in an ode to whose thought processes he allots the term "progressive."

The notion of the poem as dance is developed by W. Wili, *Horaz* (Basel 1948) 184, who feels that Horace couches his poem "in einem . . . volksliedartigen Ton." This idea was hinted at in their commentary by A. Kiessling and R. Heinze (*Q. Horatius Flaccus, Oden und Epoden* [Berlin 1958] 301) who speak of "Die Form des volkstümlichen Streit- und Neckgesprächs . . ." and has been elaborated by H.-P. Syndikus *Die Lyrik des Horaz II* (=*Impulse der Forschung* VII) (Darmstadt 1973) 112f.

I am particularly happy to offer this small token of appreciation to the honorand of the present volume who has been an unfailing source of encouragement for many years. I also owe thanks, once again, to Professors K. Geffcken and K. Reckford for their gentle tutelage.

One reason is not far to seek. A simple directness of structure, nearly anomalous in a collection of otherwise complex poetic statements, fosters in the reader an equally easy reaction. Content and style are at one. In the course of six exactingly balanced strophes we learn that boy and girl once loved each other. There was a falling out as new arrangements with new partners were adopted. Yet what if former Venus returns? he asks. Though my new lover is an attractive sort, she responds, and you addicted to fickleness and cursed with a hot temper, I would still like to be yours—and forever. Happy, straightforward stuff, turned out with suitably engaging facility, the relieved critic concludes. But such a plot summary remains puzzlingly insufficient. Though the lovers seem bent on returning to each other, the poem is based as much on change and experimentation as on continuity. And though the way she caps his words is a regular feature of any amoeboean interchange, and betokens allegiance as much as idiosyncratic challenge, there are subtle tonal and psychological distinctions between the two protagonists that argue for their autonomy as well as their unity. To analyze this verbal play is my present purpose.

Seen as a cycle, the lyric stretches from past to future, from unity then, to other dalliances for each in the poem's present, to potential renewal of old love in the hereafter. It is also a debate, a mimesis of lovers' verbal play, an intellectual game leading in a brilliantly modulated crescendo to her final affirmation of a shared desire his opening words already betray. Yet in the course of this little interplay, as argument vies with agreement, evolution challenges stability, and individuality is at odds with imitation, there never occurs the possibility of total collusion between rhetoric and emotion. The antiphony serves as much to differentiate as to equate the protagonists while the poet's sharp structuring of this give and take offers reason enough to approve the presence of a brazen yoke, however lightly worn, to hold them together. Three works against two, odd against even, to keep on edge the reader's expectations of a balanced amatory order reached through spoken word. The meter, with its alternating short and long lines, seems at first to favor unity. It repeats in miniature the patterned interchange of male and female in six stanzas, he beginning and leading, she following and concluding. Yet its lines suggest inequality as much as balance, while the uneven triadic grouping around three time periods arouses suspicion that disenchantment might well set in again, as it had before, in the lives of this strangely matched pair.[2]

Though he initiates the colloquy, the male protagonist forthwith announces his dependence on her and sees their former relationship in terms of the *gratia* in which she held him.[3] The reader assumes from *tibi* what might be a plausible outcome of the poem, one which the speaker may even be anticipating. Whatever the case, his reaction to her former devotion is also seen in subjective terms—a Persian king's wealth metaphorized into a state of *beatitas*. Analogy to regal stance also proves that power, whether active or passive, is much in his thoughts. Aesthetic considerations combine with notions of physical potency in his extraordinary sketch of her putative young lover. He savors the exquisite beauty of her neck, yet *candidae* is the central feature of a chiastic deployment of words which catches this whiteness between *bracchia* and *cervici, potior* and *iuvenis,* even *quisquam* and *dabat.* His language displays the erotic force he holds in value.[4]

She by contrast lives more for surfaces. In exchanging his *beatior* for *clarior,* she chooses bright fame and public acknowledgement over inner riches and personal strength. She finds a likeness for herself not in some anonymous exotic king, devoted no doubt to a life of delicate abundance. Instead she opts for a more immediate Roman Ilia whom all would know. Titles fascinate her. Where we never learn his name, she narcissistically thrusts hers upon us twice, and in the very act calls attention to the *nomen* that results from her

[2] We can, of course, think in terms of twos or threes when dealing with the initial pair of lovers and their later liaisons. We can also view the triadic structure in terms of amatory thesis, antithesis and synthesis which presses for unity.

[3] Many commentators assume the male voice to be that of Horace himself. The present authoritative text (ed. F. Klingner [Leipzig 1959]) even sets off stanzas 2, 4 and 6 in quotation marks, implying that her words are quotations and not his. Kiessling-Heinze (above, note 1), *ad loc.,* reason as follows: ". . . denn er will sich selbst unter dem Sprechenden verstanden wissen, der darum von den vier beteiligten Personen allein namenlos bleibt. . . ." The reasons usually given for such an equation are Horace's own revelation of his inclination toward the very faults Lydia observes in her lover, fickleness and a quick temper (cf. *Sat.* 2. 3. 323 and *Epis.* 1. 20. 25).

[4] The phrase *bracchia dabat* is ambiguous. One gives one's arms as a gesture of embrace (and hence physical control) or surrender. For the former re. Vir. *Aen.* 2. 792 (= 6. 700); for the latter Prop. 4. 3. 12.

110

repute.[5] The very sounds which run from *alia* to *Lydia, Lydia,* and *Ilia* feed on each other.[6] Naturally she thinks first of her rival and sees their interconnection as one of rank in the eyes of their common lover. Naturally, too, she exploits *arsisti,* an image of glittering presence as well as sensuality to describe his emotion.

In his reply, which initiates their differing views of the present, he seems not to have heard her. He announces, what we already knew, that Chloe is his new love. True to his fashion he chooses someone of non-Roman extraction, and sees their relationship in terms of power. She now rules him whereas in the earlier liaison there existed mutual interdependence: he was *gratus* to her and *rex* as well in his own thinking. More pointedly than before he prizes the life of the mind. Chloe's learning (twice noted) and the artistic form it takes appeal to him.[7] His proclamation of a *liebestod* is couched in terms of not fearing—an internal reaction—and, aptly enough, it is her *anima* his death would save. He values Chloe for her spiritual side, of itself but surely also for the inspiriting effect it exerts on his own mental impulses.[8]

Lydia's riposte holds true to form. She is direct where he was oblique. We learn not only her new lover's name but his father's and that of his natal town. Since Calais, apparently, means

---

[5] The unexpected use of *multi* for *magni* with *nominis* may arise from the nearness of *magis*. It may, however, also be another means for Horace to insist on her propensity for quantifying and qualifying.

[6] There is a certain deliberate shock value in someone named (and from?) Lydia drawing to herself not an eastern but a Roman Ilia. With what gesture could she grow more clearly in the public eye (or climb higher on the social ladder) than by proclaiming herself consort of Mars and mother of Rome's founding twins? He ventures east in search of an abstraction. She fixes on Rome and reality.

[7] *Modos* is, of course, ambiguous and could be seen referring as much to sexual as to musical forms of activity. In the sense of "postures'. Pichon (*Index verborum amatoriorum* [repr. Hildesheim 1966]) lists Tib. 2. 6. 52; Ovid *Am.* 3. 7. 64, 2. 14. 24; *A.A.* 2. 680, 3. 771, 787. Horace nears the meaning "wiles" at *Odes* 3. 7. 12 but the large majority of his uses, some fifteen instances, concern the measuring rhythm and sound, "sweet" though this be and doubtless alluring.

The combination of *Thressa* and *cithara,* of Thrace and lute, recalls Orpheus to our attention, surely the highest compliment our male protagonist could pay to Chloe (cf., e.g., Vir. *Aen.* 6. 119-20).

[8] For the interconnection between the *gratia* that he prizes and song, re. *Odes* 1. 15. 14-15, 3. 4. 23-24, 4. 13. 21-22. In the end, of course, he veers toward Lydia's physicality.

turquoise, the dazzling object again lures her eye.[9] We are also ready for the double metaphor of burning and the protests of mutuality (no gradations here) with which she introduces her new amour.[10] In capping *non metuam* with *bis patiar* she hyperbolically rejects fear imagined in favor of torture felt. And in replacing *animae* with *puero* she yet again chooses the physical over the metaphysical, immediate literal sexuality instead of some deeper more intellectual design.

If his previous lines had betokened a certain inner-directedness by not addressing her face to face, he now withdraws still more completely into analysis of his own intellectual processes by presenting two neatly balanced hypotheses. Alternatives are his to manufacture out of life's possibilities. His language is riddled with conceits. *Venus* is a metonymy, *ianua* a synecdoche. *Iugo, diductos* and *excutitur* are richly metaphoric. Chloe is "shaken off" or "out" like a disease or a mental attitude. Lydia's reacceptance is the opening of a door.[11] This energetic world of going and coming, expelling and receiving, rejecting and accepting, separation and compulsion, is reflected in the careful, calculated pattern his thoughts receive. He still deals in positions of strength and, as in previous stanzas, wavers between active and passive. We have both a Venus who commands and a lover who opens the door. He is the controller and the controlled, the verbal leader who at times is also the emotional follower.[12] It is appropriate that the first person to hint at the restoration of prior affections should draw on symbols

[9] For *cal(l)ais* meaning "turquoise" or "topaz" see Pliny *H.N.* 37. 151: "Callais sappirum imitatur candidior et litoroso mari similis." (The only other use of the word in classical Latin is in the catalogue of the same book, 1. 37. 56.) The Greek spelling varies between κάλαις and κάλλαις, though Liddell and Scott put the former first. A listing of its usage as a slave's name, particularly at Rome, is given in *TLL* onomasticos *s.v.*

For further possible plays on the names in his pedigree see I. Düring, "Thurini Calais filius Ornyti: A Note on Horace, *Carm.* III, 9," *Eranos* 50 (1952) 91-97.

[10] The slight alliteration in *me torret face mutua* may itself betoken mutuality.

[11] His control of the housedoor is noteworthy. Door and house are common enough symbols of the female, and his authority over them implies a reversal of the regular Roman amatory posture of the *exclusus amator* and the *domina* who exerts power over the door, its keeper and the lover beyond. The implications, literal and generic, are that the man has taken over for a moment even the woman's position of authority.

[12] Yet there are anomalies in his presentation. He uses the present tense instead of an expected future (she at least makes a gesture in that direction with the concluding subjunctives). It is as if generalization, not assurance, were his policy. And in his reliance on passives he seems as well to shirk the responsibility of direct action.

of stability and force centralized, as well as of sexuality, such as the yoke and the door.[13] The very posture he had imagined and dismissed for her new lover in the opening lines is in fact a yoking. It is likewise appropriate that such strength of purpose be displayed in the steady ordering of the conditions on which he meditates, apparently to himself in spite of her assumed presence.

If he lays down conditions, she makes concessions, and by the act of answering his question suggests through grammatical enjambement that reestablishment of intimacy he adumbrates. But even in this dialectic of proposal and disposal, suggestion and submission, she remains herself, direct where he is oblique, passionate where he is contemplative. Her analogies are brisk and revelatory. She sees her present suitor as *sidere pulchrior,* a stable object of attention, physically attractive, tailored to her interests. For her former lover and present interlocutor, she finds two similes, dedicated appropriately to psychic, not physical characteristics: his fickleness (at least in her view) and his changeable temper. The final comparison—*improbo iracundior Hadria*—gains special prominence. By breaking the chiastic balance she had created between *ille* and *tu,* it offers animated proof of the infidelity we assume she now forgives, as well as further contrast to the stately rigor of his preceding sentiments.

Yet her last line with its intense intertwinings is a bow to his propensity for order—ABC, ABC in terms of idea; nearly ABC, ACB in terms of grammar.[14] His final lines, it would appear, aim for unity of the whole by taking to themselves the structuring echoes and reechoes of the previous four stanzas. But her replies, after all, made these very resonances possible, and it is reasonable that her last lines should draw strands from both their worlds together at the end. Her three comparatives, *pulchrior, levior, iracundior,* renew in the reader's attention the related juxtapositions of the opening lines (*potior, beatior, clarior*). Likewise her

[13]The ancient commentators concluded that Horace chose brass for his yoke because something literally metallic would be of long duration: "ad perpetuitatem revertentis gratiae iugum aeneum posuit; aes enim non sicut ferrum robigine consumitur" (Pseudo-Acron *ad loc.*); "Si rursus, inquit, nos Venus iungit ac firmat perpetua coniunctione. Hoc enim per iugum aeneum dicit. Aeris namque materia non sicut ferrum robigine consumitur" (Porphyrion *ad loc.*). Endurance under particular emotional stress was not in their mind.

[14]Nearly but not totally, because *vivere* and *libens* are not parallel. On this curious and important line see further Lee (above, note 1) 105.

concluding wish to live or die with her old amour corresponds to their earlier individual protestations of altruistic suicide in the middle segments of the poem. All of which would lead the reader to believe that she sees the poem as a cycle of reunification from *tibi gratus* to *tecum lubens,* and the dialogue that is its form, as a means of working out (and into) a relationship toward a final rapprochement.

But her terminal play on *amem*—"like" instead of "love," desire in the place of fruition—proves the dialectic still inconclusive.[15] Instead of tragic collapse or comic fruition the poem concludes only with a redoubled affirmation of her yearning. At the same time her words provoke the theory that any rhetorical exchange among personages so disparate is Venus' way of utilizing language itself as a brazen yoke to govern competitive energies. The only other lyric where Horace uses the image of the *iugum aeneum, Odes* 1. 33, is equally concerned with the all-too-regular mating of opposites. There the poet as abstracted commentator on the human scene to the constantly committed, constantly hurt elegist Tibullus, uses oxymoron, aptly enough, to figure his insight: "sweet" Glycera is harsh to him, the freedwoman Myrtale holds him in thrall—all part of Venus' "harsh joke." A "better Venus" is regularly displaced by someone less apt. In *Odes* 3. 9 words alone are sufficient indication of dissimilarity. Horace's humorous self-distance grants that for each individual, including himself, there is always a *melior Venus,* a more appropriate, kindred attachment, which could replace one's present antonymy, but such perfection one is rarely allowed to choose, not to say maintain.

Odes 3. 9 presents an evolving documentation both of the "better Venuses" each lover at present possesses and of the once and future mate with whom each now converses. We have seen something of the disparity of the one set and the natural attraction of the other. The male protagonist, with his feeling for love as power and penchant for the aesthetics of grace and happiness,

---

[15] The play on *amem,* extended by *libens* as well, is clarified by comparison with Catullus' *vivamus, mea Lesbia, atque amemus* (5. 1), where the verbs are equal and coordinate. The verb *obeam* is an important replacement for *mori* here. It is possible that the fourth line of Catullus 5 influenced Horace's word choice: *soles occidere et redire possunt.* Since *obire* is used for the setting of celestial bodies as well as for the death of humans, Horace and Lydia may be telling the male protagonist that he has a certain kinship with a *sidus* after all.

would naturally enough be magnetized by the spiritual rule of musical Chloe. Physical Lydia, attracted by externals and a name, should no doubt find fulfillment in shining Calais, more alluring than a star, who is equally enthralled by her. Instead, Horace, not unexpectedly, binds his speakers together with a verbal chain that would have to be firm indeed.[16]

Their personality differences have been easy enough to trace. It could be said that each uses language apposite enough to individual characteristics. His language is obsessional, as befits the subjective, solipsistic contemplative, hers compulsively directed to externals, reacting, not proposing.[17] Over and above these differentials the poet establishes his own principle of orderly disorder as comment on their union. I refer to the striking manner in which she chooses to parallel or fails to mimic his utterances.

The first two stanzas, with the repetition of *donec* and *vigui*, the reverberation of *eram* in *erat* and the corresponding comparatives, betrays a certain linguistic conformity, and hence erotic intimacy, which the two parties have disturbed but have not replaced. The third and fourth stanzas, however, are paradoxical. Close reiteration advises that his manner of expression is hers, that an expanding mode of familiarity has been achieved in a fabric of words that still conveys appropriate personality differentiations. To reproduce as closely as she does the architectonics of his stanzaic construction postulates a certain kindred imaginative ordering and spiritual interdependence. Her selfhood is defined most clearly as an expansion of his proclivities. Her attempt at greatest freedom is framed in terms that refer as much to him as to herself.

[16]For further discussion of the differentiation between the two characters see Lee (above, note 1) *loc. cit.* and H.-P. Syndikus (above, note 1) 115, and, as part of a larger panorama, R. W. Minadeo, "Sexual Symbolism in Horace's Love Odes," *Latomus* 34 (1975) 411ff.

[17]Linguistic differentiation between obsessional and hysterical speech is made in an interesting article by L. Irigarey, "Approche d'une grammaire d'énonciation de l'hysterique et de l'obsessionnel," *Languages* 5 (1967) 99-109, a reference I owe to Professor Eugene Vance. I am not concerned here with any putative difference in the use of language between male and female as such, a subject of growing interest among scholars. See, e.g., M. R. Key, *Male/Female Language* (Methuchen 1975), esp. ch. 8 ("Subjects, not objects: Linguistic structures"), and *ibid.* "Linguistic Behavior of Male and Female," *Linguistics* 88 (1972) 15-31.

Yet the message of the words themselves speaks of an emotional break, of committed affections elsewhere. At the same time, ironically but suitably, the iterated appeal to suicide, though the height of devotion, is likewise the height of the non-erotic. It presupposes the death of one's closest partner—an intellectual, fabricated posture, a quasi-romantic pose that exchanges masochism for reciprocity. One need scarcely add that the humor Horace elicits from such overstated seriousness does much to undercut the very protestations themselves.

The interrelationship between the last stanzas is even more problematical. The linguistic enjambement provided the answered question would seem to recreate amatory harmony, but its total restoration is cast in doubt by her hesitant use of "like" for "love," as if her willingness did not quite match his stipulations. If syntax offers reason for dialectical unity, extreme verbal disjunction intimates a contrary course. In the development of the most rational, calculated stanza in the poem he relinquishes his former preference for artistic Chloe and opts for passionate, self-projecting Lydia. Reason and sexuality are at odds. And her response, which releases her from his framings, with equal irony presents the greatest distinction of verbal play, the strongest divagation from previous structures, and hence the most patent self-assertion in the poem. These final lines, for example, contain the greatest number of liquids of any stanza in the poem (twenty-five in contrast to eight in his preceding verses). She voices the only two and seven word lines in the poem—its extremes of brevity and length—and *iracundior* is its longest word. His last stanza was noteworthy for its regularity. Each line is self-contained. Nowhere else in the poem are balanced meter and balanced sense so tightly merged. She, on the contrary, in the course of indulging in broken chiasmus, strange emphases, patterns worked and unworked at the end, presents one of the two stanzas in the poem with three lines that cannot stand alone (her way, perhaps, of pointing up *pulchrior* and *iracundior,* the distinction between her two lovers, as well as of proving her excitability).

Verbally, then, she manifests aspects of disorder that she finds patent in his character. Yet there is also a reductive humor to this realistic appraisal of her turned-about lover. His character is partitioned between the cork, that trivializes, and the Adriatic, which presses toward hyperbole. Such earthy analogies, distinguished from his careful calculations, assess facts. No theories here, merely the straight truth, dispelling any illusions, yet not, however, without an element of surprise, since the reader waits in suspense for the main clause until the last line and within that clause every word is given due weight.

Briefly, in the finale, as old love is almost renewed, his controlled pondering of alternatives, his balanced weighing of possibilities is directly challenged by her sharp excitement and intricate likenings. Where we most expect congruence in language we find variance, just as in the previous pair of stanzas close imitation complements the proclamation of extreme erotic distinction.[18] There are no verbal echoes at the moment when greatest intimacy should be espoused. There is most individuality at the instant where reinforced allegiance would be in order. Which is to say that in the complex amalgam of unity and differentiation by which he defines amatory coupling, Horace sees patterns of sexuality constantly challenged by patterns of language. The poem's dialectic is the actual working out of an oxymoron, proving how opposites attract—a favorite Horatian principle. But Horace is wiser than to end even here. In their highly idiosyncratic ways, as we have seen, both protagonists complete the poem as a cycle of their own return to each other. At the same time they intimate through structure as well as content that the dissolution of such a verbal bond is equally plausible. In the case of Lydia and her lover the pattern may be a frictional alternation of fidelity and faithlessness. One suspects, however, that Horace, learned in the nature of human foibles, would have put little trust in the permanence of such a tenuous bond, and that the very conflicts between erotic unity and verbal discord are his sympathetic way of telling us so.

Here, as often, Horace exploited Catullus as inspiration and measure of originality:

[18]Yet the compliment she pays him of close imitation and exaggerated capping may indicate an allegiance of sorts to his mental processes which could lead as well into a restoration of their previous relationship. The very parallelism of language may prefigure renewed interest in spite of the diversity of the actual statements. Language may anticipate felt, not to say expressed, desire. And one of the results of this language, of course, is that they kill each other off and in the killing end any other inchoate relationships!

Acmen Septimius suos amores
tenens in gremio 'mea' inquit 'Acme,
ni te perdite amo atque amare porro
omnes sum assidue paratus annos,
quantum qui pote plurimum perire,
solus in Libya Indiaque tosta
caesio ueniam obuius leoni.'
hoc ut dixit, Amor sinistra ut ante
dextra sternuit approbationem.

   at Acme leuiter caput reflectens
et dulcis pueri ebrios ocellos
illo purpureo ore suauiata,
'sic,' inquit 'mea uita Septimille,
huic uni domino usque seruiamus,
ut multo mihi maior acriorque
ignis mollibus ardet in medullis.'
hoc ut dixit, Amor sinistra ut ante
dextra sternuit approbationem.

   nunc ab auspicio bono profecti
mutuis animis amant amantur.
unam Septimius misellus Acmen
mauult quam Syrias Britanniasque:
uno in Septimio fidelis Acme
facit delicias libidinesque.
quis ullos homines beatiores
uidit, quis Venerem auspicatiorem?

Septimius, holding his love Acme in his lap, says "My Acme, unless I love you overwhelmingly and am further prepared to love you unceasingly for all time, as madly as any man can be in love, may I meet face to face a green-eyed lion, alone in Lybia or sunburnt India." When he said this, Love, although before on the left, sneezed approval on the right.

But Acme, lightly bending her head and kissing with her purple lips the drunken eyes of the sweet boy, says "So let us serve this one master, my little Septimius, my life, as a much greater and sharper fire burns within my soft marrow." When she said this, Love, although before on the left, sneezed approval on the right.

Now, having set out from a good auspice, they love and are loved with mutual response. Love-sick Septimius prefers Acme alone to Syrias and Britains, in Septimius alone faithful Acme takes her pleasure and delight. Who has seen any happier creatures, who has seen a more auspicious love?

The Acme and Septimius of Catullus' forty-fifth poem may also have had a period of separation and the poet joins them together again, quoting their protestations of utter devotion and giving his own carefully arranged seal of approval at the end. There are essential formulations in the discrimination between the two characters that must have caught Horace's ear. To support his claims of total allegiance in the future Septimius prays (6-7):

> solus in Libya Indiaque tosta
> caesio veniam obvius leoni.

Catullus bolsters the impression of someone attracted by the distant and exotic, as public servant, perhaps, or traveler, in his final summary of the youth's behavior (21-22):

> unam Septimius misellus Acmen
> mauult quam Syrias Britanniasque; . . .

Unique exposure to green-eyed lions (in Septimius' quoted words) and many looks at a variety of Syrias and Britains (in the poet's configuration) form a unified portrait.

While Septimius holds her, Acme bends her head and kisses his drunken eyes. If his interests in the faraway betray a bravado of sorts, hers are unabashedly sexual.[19] In her own voice she urges them both to serve love the master (15-16):

> ut multo mihi maior acriorque
> ignis mollibus ardet in medullis.

---

[19] Even her protestation of constant fidelity must be placed in an erotic context.

Catullus again confirms the picture in his authorial summary (23-24):

> uno in Septimio fidelis Acme
> facit delicias libidinesque . . .

Horace fancied this creature addicted to love's fires and pleasures as literary ancestress for his Lydia. He also clearly draws on the interaction of infidelity and faithfulness seen against a backdrop of time passing. One clear way to explain the overwrought hyperbole in each statement of future constancy is to accept it as token of a once opposite frame of mind—in Septimius' case revealed by an inclination for foreign wanderings (whether literal or figurative), in Acme's by a series of lustings elsewhere. This is born out by the implication of the refrain subsequent to each speech: if love now sneezes endorsement on the right he had previously demonstrated disapproval on the left. Catullus twice confirms as much in his envoi to the two suitors.[20] He begins (19-20):

> nunc ab auspicio bono profecti,
> mutuis animis amant amantur.—

as if to suggest that this dedicated mutuality (which the asyndeton enhances) had not always been the case, that in fact once in the past they had set out with an inauspicious omen.[21] Such a context forces the reader to take the full measure of the final questions (25-26):

> quis ullos homines beatiores
> vidit, quis venerem auspicatiorem?

Is this love only more auspicious by comparison to former times? To be more cynical, what if in reality we have seen lovers setting out more happily matched?

But the differences between the two poems are more telling than their similarities. Catullus, as we have seen, devotes himself to

---

[20]The military and political overtones of Catullus' language here are discussed by H. Dietz, "Zu Catulls Gedicht von Acme und Septimius," *SO* 44 (1969) 42-47.

[21]This is in my view still the most plausible way to explain *sinistra ut ante* in the refrain. Love had once sneezed inauspiciously on the left.

an intense "now," a crucial moment in the romance of his protagonists with only hints that there was a former history potentially ready to repeat itself. Horace devotes equal time to past,
present and future, with no illusions about love's permanence. He
allows his *dramatis personae* total freedom in the verbal evolution of their emotions. Catullus by contrast quotes directly for
only ten lines out of twenty-six.[22] The burden of the poem
is the working out of setting—the posture of the two lovers,
the refrain exactly repeated, the final pronouncement of a bright
departure into love. Their individual outbursts are embedded in a
poetic framing that is both descriptive and incantatory. Catullus
positions his characters, offers a ritual chant of love's enticing
approval and concludes with eight lines where exacting verbal
arrangements are worked out in a trio of pairings *(amant, amantur;
unam, uno; beatiores, auspicatiorem)* extending over four sets of
lines. The magical repetition of the refrain is elaborated in the
iterative techniques used to describe the final leave-taking.

In sum, Horace allows his characters to speak for themselves,
as they unfold their own peculiar parallelisms in a verbal dance of
love-making. Their inner life seems ours to behold; their ironies

---

[22] Another important difference is that in Catullus' meter, hendecasyllabic, all
lines are the same whereas in Horace's fourth Asclepiadean long lines *(versus Asclepiadeus)*
follow alternately upon short *(Glyconeus)*. Rigidity therefore contrasts with limited
variability.

It has been trying for critics of both poems to remain non-partisan in their judg-
ments. In treating their interconnection J. Ferguson ("Catullus and Horace," *AJP* 77
[1956] 12f.) finds Catullus' the more sympathetic effort (p. 13: "Horace produces the
tidier poem, Catullus is more deeply affecting. Horace moves the mind, Catullus the
heart. Horace's verses are the product of wit, Catullus' of the romantic imagination.")
Many would agree. To offer one general example, the gist of Ezra Pound's famous essay
is to dispraise Horace ("less poetic than any other great master of literature") by comparison with Catullus and Ovid (*The Criterion* 9 [1930] 217-27). For further comparisons see Commager (above, note 1) 141, and G. Williams, *Tradition and Originality* 210,
524 (". . . the excellence of poem 45 lies in the formality and precision of the description, the unemotional realization of emotion."

Sunt qui Horatium malint, among them L. P. Wilkinson, *Horace and His Lyric
Poetry* (Cambridge 1945) 49 and, more pointedly, Lucian Mueller (*Q. Horatius Flaccus,
Oden und Epoden* [Leipzig 1900] 231): "Schmeichler des Catull haben sein 45.
Gedicht mit unserer Ode verglichen. Was ich darüber denke, brauche ich wohl nicht
zu sagen."

Critics who still see Horace throwing down some intellectual gauntlet to the shade
of Catullus should review E. K. Rand, "Catullus and the Augustans," *HSCP* 17 (1906)
15-30.

self-made. Catullus, on the contrary, feels the need for a narrative of framings. He is a *coniugator amoris*, the third-party observer who as poet designs a controlling pattern for their outbursts of affection.

Perfect as this all may appear, there is nevertheless something disquieting in the tension between a poet's orderings and his creations' passionate hyperboles. The finale is a bit too neat, too obtrusively made, as if Catullus had deliberately adopted a clinical detachment or, better, as if the logic in his own arrangements was both requisite and somehow quixotic at the same time. It is requisite if we trust the poem as an idealized vision of love perfected at last. It is quixotic if we realize how fallible such a patterning is elsewhere for Catullus. Such richness of intonation allows the reader to run the emotional gamut between humor and sorrow, seeing the poet either serious or amused over his protagonists' intensities.[23] But the final reaction, surely, is one of irony toward them and toward the possibility of their, or any, happy union. We need only observe other instances of Catullus' change from past to present to realize the vulnerability of his design in poem 45. Once bright suns shone for Lesbia and himself, he intones in poem 8; now life is miserable self-torture. In poem 58 we hear that once Catullus loved Lesbia more than himself and all his own; now she satisfies the descendants of Remus in the alleys and crossroads of Rome. If we read poem 45 "straight," it offers an ideal vision of love to be preserved by all the poet's devices, or a witty parody of amatory manners. But if we ponder its inner tonal variations between quotation and setting with Catullus' own constant emotional problematics in mind, we are forced to see the poet ironizing against himself as well as his creatures.[24]

Another level of irony is raised by comparison with the Horatian ode. We find the ordinarily direct, impassioned Catullus imagining other lovers' avowals of fidelity and capsulating them as

---

[23] For appraisals of the ironic aspects of Catullus 45 see S. Baker, "The Irony of Catullus' 'Septimius and Acme,' " *CP* 53 (1958) 110-12; D. O. Ross, Jr., "Style and Content in Catullus 45," *CP* 60 (1965) 256-59; H. Akbar Khan, "Catullus 45: What Sort of Irony," *Latomus* 27 (1968) 3-12.

[24] Catullus, in a manner different from Horace, also raises many questions he fails to answer. When we have finished reading the poem the distinction between the lovers, which their hyperbolic, mock-political language only vivifies, remains as clear as their fusion. And how is the final question to be answered?

if only thus could a uniquely ideal situation be preserved. Antithetically Horace, by nature more aloof and contemplative, more concerned than Catullus with grander problems of man and his destiny, gives his duo free rein to work out their situation. Each poet, however, is actually very much himself. Horace, by allowing Lydia and friend apparent independence from a shaping voice, reveals more bluntly the cyclic vagaries of emotion between two people in the counterpointing rhetoric they use. Catullus, tracing the ardent outbursts of his lovers and touching gently on their past, takes refuge in the role of authorial match-maker but in so doing betrays as well his own deep involvement by imposing a pattern of disciplined enclosure not of their manufacture. Perhaps only a poet's artifice can capture and preserve such attitudes as Septimius and Acme proclaim. Left to themselves, as Catullus well knew, they become easy prey to wind and water.

Immediate Catullus, so fond of determined self-questioning, seems here the contriver of an ideal; more distant Horace appears the realist. Catullus, *auspex* of happy departure, attempts to abort change by freezing the status quo and to maintain its earnest immediacy. Horace urges that process in human relationships is both reasonable and predictable. Catullus, playing the third party external to their situation, yokes Acme and Septimius by his own ceremony of words.[25] As excited raconteur he intones the echoes and balances that conjoin. Horace, the more remote craftsman and tolerant as always of man's caprices, allows his disparate subjects, with Venus' help, to enmesh themselves in their own verbal toils. They create and dissolve linguistic unities of their own making, markedly in the last two stanzas where the male takes Catullus' artful correlations to himself and the female exerts her words both for and against them.

Catullus is extreme, either in the attempt to capture the ideal present or in the bitter cynicism that must lie behind knowledge of an inevitable failure. At the end of his poem we question his tone, as if it bordered on self-parody, and worry through his inner response toward such a topic. With Horace, more relaxed, more cosmopolitan, less personally tortured, aware that a poet's power need not always be direct, the human condition develops easily of itself with kindly irony from within the dialogue, avoiding any need for the author's further probing presence.

Finally, we may glance at Propertius' treatment of a similar theme. Separation and the emotions it provokes are a constant topic in the *Monobiblos,* and in its twelfth poem the elegist ruefully counterpoises his eternal constancy to Cynthia's changeableness. After commenting on the literal and spiritual distances between them, he looks at time past (1. 12. 7-8):

> olim gratus eram; non illo tempore cuiquam
> contigit ut simili posset amare fide.

> Once I was pleasing to her: at that time it happened to no one that he was able to love with equal fidelity.

We are not so far verbally from *donec gratus eram tibi / nec quisquam . . . ,* but philosophic difference is firm in the distinction between *olim* and *donec.* Each poet is observing time past but through diverse lenses. For the elegist the past was rewarding, the present desolate. For Horace's protagonist alteration is already implicit even in the heretofore. To the lyric poet *fides* is a virtue more mobile than enduring in any relationship. Propertius' last lines, however, prove that firmness and stability are as essential for the poet as they are needless or impossible for his mistress (1. 12. 19-20):

> mi neque amare aliam neque ab hac desistere fas est:
> Cynthia prima fuit, Cynthia finis erit.

> It is right for me neither to love another nor to cease loving her: Cynthia was the first, Cynthia will be the end.

Cynthia, though caught between the extremes of "was" and "will be," beginning and end, remains doubly invariable to her lover.

We may compare these doublets with the pairings in Horace's final line:

> tecum vivere amem, tecum obeam lubens.

Lydia equates love with existence (Catullus' *vivamus . . . atque amemus*), with living and dying together. Propertius equates Cynthia with love's extent, a process in the abstract defined by a name and lived out in hopeless yearning. For Horace's Lydia living, dying and loving are bundled into a concrete, sensory, emotional plea for unity. Propertius' stance teeters indulgently on the edge of self-pity, conserving with true elegiac fixity an ill-matedness he cannot or is unwilling to cure.

Wise Horace proves acutely aware of the futility of such steadfastness in his poem to Tibullus who espouses the same backward glance as his elegiac colleague—*Albi, ne doleas plus nimio. . . .* Better a brazen yoke for the unmatched, Horace appears to say, than no partner at all. Better a dialogue, noteworthy for its open-endedness as much as for its closure, than a soliloquy turning it on itself. Better, finally, a sense of humor instead of either Propertian elegiac despair or Catullan ironic idealism, in coping with the pit-falls Venus and Amor proffer to their hapless prey.

HORACE *ODES* 3. 15: THE DESIGN OF *DECUS*

MICHAEL C. J. PUTNAM

Uxor pauperis Ibyci,
    tandem nequitiae fige modum tuae
famosisque laboribus;
    maturo propior desine funeri

inter ludere virgines   5
    et stellis nebulam spargere candidis.
non, siquid Pholoen satis,
    et te, Chlori, decet: filia rectius

expugnat iuvenum domos,
    pulso Thyias uti concita tympano.   10
illam cogit amor Nothi
    lascivae similem ludere capreae:

te lanae prope nobilem
    tonsae Luceriam, non citharae decent
nec flos purpureus rosae   15
    nec poti vetulam faece tenus cadi.

HORACE, concerned as so often with patterns of order and disorder in human behavior, here limits his attention to figurations of grace and, more pertinent, gracelessness, in sexual mores. His protagonist is a mother who would emulate her daughter, a wife playing among unmarried girls, the aging beldame craving to be young.[1]

At first only her husband is named—Horace's crisp way of noting her duty.[2] After observing that she is married and that Ibycus is poor, the poet proceeds to watch her heightening spurts of emotion and each time to exhort against them. Her indulgences range from abstract (*nequitiae tuae*) to something nearer concrete (*famosis laboribus*).[3] Impropriety is glossed through those "efforts" known to all. Presumably such *labores*, because they

---

1. The best discussion of aspects of *Odes* 3. 15 is by S. Commager, *The Odes of Horace* (New Haven, 1962), pp. 249 f., 255 f., 292, though he offers no general interpretation of the poem as a whole. His comparisons with *Odes* 1. 23 are especially helpful for elucidating Horace's view of time. The poem is not treated in other important recent work by Fraenkel, Lee, Pöschl, Reckford, or West, though G. Williams gives a summary overview in *The Third Book of Horace's "Odes"* (Oxford, 1969), pp. 96–97. There and in *Tradition and Originality in Roman Poetry* (Oxford, 1968), p. 296, Williams sees the poem as an illustration of Horace's poetic commingling of Greek and Roman elements.

2. If there is anything in Horace's choice of the name Ibycus, it might lie in ironic contrast between our *pauper* and the sixth-century lyric poet of Rhegium whose eroticism was notorious. Cf. Cic. *Tusc.* 4. 71 ("maxime vero omnium flagrasse amore Reginum Ibycum apparet ex scriptis...") and the *Suda*, s.v. Ἴβυκος ("γέγονε δὲ ἐρωτομανέστατος περὶ μειράκια . . .").

3. In the elegies of Propertius and Tibullus *nequitia* can apply equally well to wantonness in male or female. *Labor*, however, in an erotic context, usually defines purely masculine enterprise (Prop. 1. 1. 9, 1. 6. 23, 2. 24. 29; Tib. 1. 2. 33, 1. 4. 47). As in the case of her daughter, Chloris also takes on a sexually incongruous *persona*.

126

are public rather than private, do not befit a wife concerned with her husband's poverty.[4] Horace urges an end to be fixed, not merely placed, to this conduct which has gone on for some length.[5] The imperative mood attacks Chloris directly and is the poet's persistent, commanding attempt at rhetorical control.

At the next moment he lures us more excitedly into both her action and his counter-remedy. We learn that her desire is to play among young girls (*inter ludere virgines*), which, to the poet, is like scattering a cloud over bright stars (*stellis nebulam spargere candidis*). These details expand upon the still vague *nequitia* and *labores* of lines 2 and 3 with verbs now added to nouns. Abstract and generalized concrete notions are elaborated first by specific, literal fact, then by analogy, with the final imaginative touch left to metaphor. A parallel heightening qualifies the poet's own exhortations. *Tandem fige modum* is drawn out into *maturo propior desine funeri*. Death is the ultimate *modus*, the finale of life itself and an especially importunate presence, we assume, for one whose iniquity is accompanied by an attempt to reverse time's progress.

This heightening from *nequitia* to *nebula*, from abstraction to metaphor, literal to figurative, makes us see the wife's idea of "playing" in terms of the poet's "scattering clouds." Her gamboling is a form of immoral exertion, the part taken by the Lucilian *nebulo*, the shady scoundrel of earlier Roman satire.[6] Horace plays dexterously on the tension between *maturo* and her name, Chloris, when it finally comes. Instead of being "green," "unripe," "immature," she is in fact an elderly wife unwilling to mature elegantly toward time's finish. For one who is forgetful that she is long past the stage of courting and can make little pretension to being a *virgo*, for one whose play is effort (especially if harlotry is involved), it is fitting that what is most ripe in her life is death. The cloud in motion against the stable background of gleaming stars denotes a time fulfilling itself toward ultimate oblivion, not only the momentary eclipse that age and ugliness and moral disrepute project on the bright and colorful territory of the young.

The association of *labores* and *ludere* helps expand our thinking into other Horatian contexts which further prove the paradoxical folly of Chloris' ways. Horace is wont to urge a limitation to *labores*. He so advises Maecenas (*Sat.* 1. 1. 92–94):

> denique sit finis quaerendi, cumque habeas plus,
> pauperiem metuas minus et finire laborem
> incipias, parto quod avebas . . .

4. Sexual prodigality is thus pitted against economic poverty in a very Roman distinction. The two should be mutually exclusive because impecuniousness, we are often told, fosters lack of indulgence. Plautus, for instance, sees *nequam* in opposition to *frugi bonae* (*Pseud.* 468; cf. 337 ff.). See also Cic. *De or.* 2. 248, *Font.* 39; and, for fuller detail, W. Ramsay (ed.), *The "Mostellaria" of Plautus* (London, 1869), pp. 229–30.

5. There is verbal heightening even here. What is initially hers (*tuae*) is soon qualified as of more universal ownership (*famosis*).

6. Lucilius frags. 468, 577 Marx. Cf. Hor. *Sat.* 1. 1. 104 (with Heinze's comments on Cicero's connection of *nebulo* and *homo nequam*), 1. 2. 12; *Epist.* 1. 2. 28.

Plancus, too, should put bounds to *labor* (*Odes* 1. 7. 17–19):

> . . . tu sapiens finire memento
> tristitiam, vitaeque labores
> molli, Plance, mero . . .

It is ironic that, in extending this wisdom to Chloris, it is for reasons of *decus* presently lost, not of past pleasure adequately enjoyed, that Horace enjoins restraint in erotic matters. What is natural play for her daughter is now effort for Chloris. Age interrupts the sexual game, and any strenuous attempt to circumvent nature becomes a matter of public concern over a blatant insult to decorum. These notions are combined again, with a bow to Lucretius, at the end of *Epistles* 2. 2 (213–16):

> vivere si recte nescis, decede peritis.
> lusisti satis, edisti satis atque bibisti:
> tempus abire tibi est, ne potum largius aequo
> rideat et pulset lasciva decentius aetas.

It is no accident that Chloris' name is revealed only in line 8, away from her husband and near her daughter, since these lines are devoted to their strange intermingling. Though grammar and thought conjoin the two opening stanzas, the second stanza has a formal unity of its own, caused partly by the anaphora of *et* and by pronounced sigmatism seen prominently at each line ending. The vague *virgines* is specified in Pholoe, daughter of the household, whose company her mother would keep. The latter, an *uxor* whose manner is in several senses cloudy, is finally and appropriately mentioned in a line contiguous to her offspring.

Horace's moralism is offered softly. Matters are open to discussion and comparison, and gentle disparagement is meted out to both, not to Chloris alone. Chloris' performance is not totally indecorous. It is only that her ways are not sufficiently seemly. Just as she is nearer death than youth, so her daughter's cavorting is only more, not unreservedly, right, and only more by juxtaposition to Chloris' actions.[7] Pholoe is no normal *virgo* by other standards, as the third stanza, which is hers alone, unmistakenly proves. We do not, for instance, find ourselves observing a fit subject for elegy, a lady demurely closeted from the onslaught of gallants by house door, parent, or nurse. Instead, adopting more a masculine than a feminine role, she acts the bellicose lover, taking by storm the houses of youths, house after house, youth after youth.[8] She is orgiastic as well as martial, behaving like an ecstatic devotee of Bacchus (as often as not an analogy for the insatiate ravings of a middle-aged lovesick matron).[9] Finally her energies are comparable to those of a licentious goat, unrestrainedly physical and animalistic.[10] To all this extremity of vigorous stimulation she is a

---

7. Perhaps, too, Horace uses *modum* instead of a more unequivocal synonym for *finis* to allow some leeway in conduct even for Chloris.

8. On the name Pholoe, a mountain in Arcadia favored by centaurs, see M. C. J. Putnam, "Horace and Tibullus," *CP* 67 (1972): 82.

9. For more detail on the meaning of Thyias see A. S. Pease on Vir. *Aen*. 4. 302; C. J. Fordyce on Cat. 64. 390–91; J. G. Frazer on Pausanias 10. 4. 3, 6. 4, 32. 7.

10. The posture is natural enough in life's spring (cf. Lucr. 1. 260–61; Vir. *Ecl*. 2. 64).

passive prey (*pulso, concita*), compelled by love to succumb to emotions beyond her wish or capacity to harness.[11]

As contrast with this excitable world of Pholoe, Horace turns to what in fact should enhance Chloris' existence: "te lanae prope nobilem / tonsae Luceriam . . . decent. . . ." *Lanae* ought to signify her life. No newfangled role-reversals or unbridled lusts for her, says the poet, merely the traditional posture of *lanifica*, the Roman *matrona* working her wool. This means, by implication here, not only keeping her house chaste and remaining faithful to her husband, but also perhaps helping the domestic economic situation by praiseworthy *labores* to replace the public and unfortunate bursts of emotion in rivalry with her daughter's erotic impulses. Tightly organized verbal structure knots this portrait of the ideal Chloris controlled by words. From *lanae* to *Luceriam* nouns and adjectives are placed chiastically yet modify each other in alternating order. The pattern of alliteration in *te lanae . . . tonsae Luceriam,* by which Horace varied a possible but trite jingle *te tonsae . . .* , complicates the unity still further.[12]

Pholoe's own climactic appearance, by suggestion at a symposium, is as stimulated as ever. Now, though mother and daughter are again juxtaposed as in the second stanza, distinction rather than unity is triumphant. The climax from *citharae* to *cadi*, in three stages yet strung together by the chain of negatives from *non* to *nec . . . nec*, is one of the more impressive in Horace. This tricolon extends from one word to three to four, from a plural noun to two singular nouns to singular and plural nouns combined. In terms of sensual perception, in the progress of *citharae* to *flos* to *cadi*, we expand first from sound to sight. Here hypallage sets in relief the flower which is first qualified by a color word and then by its species, which also posits color. Then we turn to a union of touch and taste (and sight as well, if we consider the visual impact of *faex*[13]), the most intimate, tactile sensations combined.[14] Seen emotionally this parallels a development from song (that merely entertains) to rose crowns (that deck the symposiasts' heads) to the committed act of drinking. This last is done not tamely with goblets but with whole jugs, to suggest, as elsewhere in Horace, utter emotional exhaustion and resolution.[15]

We think at first that this is merely another stage in Pholoe's rakish progress, but there is a certain finality to it that complements the concluding vignette of Chloris' proposed stability. We presume that each is now inside a house—Chloris dutifully working the dull wool of sheep habitually shorn,

11. The name Nothus may be chosen deliberately to undercut Pholoe's passionate pursuit. Is she excited over someone "false," "counterfeit"? Does his putative illegitimacy run counter to the poet's demands for familial stability? Or is he merely part of an ethically different world which he shares with Pholoe, distinguishing himself thereby from Ibycus, to whom Chloris should remain loyal? Is it that Pholoe, the product of a legitimate union whose continuity is threatened by her mother's behavior, is now taking up deliberately with the offspring of an illicit liaison?

12. It is possible that not only wool but the act of shearing should be associated with Chloris, who in fact could trim her lifestyle as well as practice the virtues of spinning. She should be, but is not, subject to diurnal and seasonal time.

13. For *faex* as dye or rouge see Hor. *AP* 277; Ovid *Ars am.* 3. 211.

14. Sound, and therefore hearing, may also be operative as a unifying rhetorical feature throughout these lines. At *Odes* 3. 19. 9–11 Horace uses *ae* sounds to suggest festive shouting at a party. Here we move from *citharae* to *rosae* to *faece*, though the last word works in two ways at once.

15. Cf. *Odes* 1. 35. 26–27.

Pholoe at last with her lovers, partaking of the colorful, volatile round of immediate feelings.[16] But whatever the role Pholoe might play in such a context or however fleeting such a situation might at first seem, we must grant also that the Horatian symposium is an event for which time usually stops. In *Odes* 2. 11, for instance, though the locks of Horace and his friend Quintius Hirpinus are hoary with age, nevertheless wine and music, roses and the wench Lyde are only part of a setting that will abstract them from the existential cares of reality. Though the accoutrements of the symposium may betoken the heightened moment of sexual fulfillment, they also reiterate the symbolism of the continuously glimmering stars behind the passing clouds—Pholoe for the moment ever young. We are made to think of aspects of life beyond mere human temporality—the rose's surpassing beauty,[17] the eternity of music, and the enduring imaginative impulses forgetful wine often gave the lyricist at work or play.

The unexpected appearance of the long postponed *vetulam* in this context is both the climax and the rhetorical masterstroke of the poem. Pholoe's animalistic, orgiastic, impetuous energy has been channeled into the passionate yet delimited emotions of the symposium. The bacchante, stirred up by beaten drum, yields to the symposiast drinking copious wine to the sound of the lute. Into the midst of the final burst of excitement, when the reader had thought she was already happily settled elsewhere, Chloris is verbally thrown by the poet, far from where grammar and ethics would ordinarily place her. Age again is projected among the young, time passing into the imaginatively eternal.[18]

The seriousness of reality forces its alien presence upon the illusions of game, that is, upon one of those self-contained festive moments defined apart from the course of ordinary events.[19] Horace's satirical eye sees Chloris finally at her most graceless—degraded into ugly, undignified age, sharply incongruous with her daughter. As a result the poem too is wrenched, generically. Analogies for Chloris' conduct come more readily to hand from comedy or invective than from elsewhere in lyric. We think, for instance, of Scapha's representation of rank old women as an object lesson to Philematium (*Most.* 274–77):

> . . . istae veteres, quae se unguentis unctitant, interpoles,
> vetulae, edentulae, quae vitia corporis fuco occulunt,
> ubi sese sudor cum unguentis consociavit, ilico
> itidem olent quasi quom una multa iura confudit coquos.[20]

16. The house is a natural symbol for continuity and stability, whether for spinning or symposia. It plays a subtle but important role in evaluating ethics through the dialectic of outer and inner, motion and calm, active and passive. On the association of woolworking and fidelity, see G. Williams, *The Third Book of Horace's "Odes,"* p. 97 and p. 87, n. 1; and idem, "Some Aspects of Roman Marriage Ceremonies and Ideals," *JRS* 48 (1958): 21, n. 20.

17. The rose here symbolizes Pholoe's intense yielding to the sensual moment rather than the fragility of beauty, often recherché, always passing with time, that it occasionally bears elsewhere in Horace. For the beauty of the rose, see *Odes* 2. 3. 14 (beauty and brevity), 3. 19. 22, 4. 10. 4.

18. *Vetulus* is associated once elsewhere with the aging crone, at *Odes* 4. 13. 25 (on which see p. 95), the last of a series of poems on the same topic which smacks as much of Archilochean diatribe as of the lyric Horace (*Epodes* 8 and 12; *Odes* 1. 25).

19. On the nature of play as described here, see J. Huizinga, *Homo Ludens* (London, 1949), passim, esp. chap. 1.

20. Cf. also *Men.* 864.

This aspect of *vetulam* is reinforced by proximity to *faece*, which equally, if less immediately, qualifies her actions as ethically out of place. Though, for Pholoe, wine lees connote the culmination of spent emotion, they also reflect onto the promiscuous finality of Chloris' old age an association with the lowest refuse of society whose evil influence on the ethical standards of contemporary Rome Cicero and later authors expound.[21] She would in fact also attempt to drain life to the dregs but is herself used up. Instead of "drinking" or "revelry" as unsuitable for Chloris we have the striking passive *poti cadi*. She is neighbor to something thoroughly exhausted, one step even beyond the diminished pretensions of Lyce (*Odes* 4. 13. 2–6):

> . . . fis anus et tamen
> vis formosa videri
> ludisque et bibis impudens
>
> et cantu tremulo pota cupidinem
> lentum sollicitas . . .

For Lyce, feebly at play, love comes slowly and only when she is drunk. She is now a subject of amusement to the young, a torch turned to ashes, in her own way, too, aging inevitably toward the grave.

We have been prepared for this final interruption of Chloris, but scarcely for its poetic power. The phrase *inter ludere virgines*, with Chloris' "playing" forced between preposition and noun, structurally among the maidens (and, we soon learn, specifically with her daughter), sets the pattern which is followed immediately and more expansively by *nebulam spargere* interposed between *stellis candidis*. This cloud, the unseemly presence of a creature incapable of living out her life decorously within bounds proper for an aging mother and wife of a poor husband, is itself fragmented and scattered throughout the poem. The consonants of *nebulam* reappear in *nobilem*, the vowels in *vetulam*. The latter is the realistic, disordering detail that emotionally inflicts time on the youthful. The first draws Chloris toward noble Luceria, toward wool from a spot known for its uprightness—an abstract, ethical ordering of her life through symbol. Chloris' untimely ways and impecunious background challenge the sumptuous circles into which her daughter has maneuvered. Wool, emblem of inner nobility and external parsimony, is her fit companion, suggesting wifely duties seriously undertaken and a mature understanding of human mortality.[22]

Upon these flashes of emotion and disorder Horace imposes another verbal pattern which has a steadying influence over and above the poem's many tensions. He achieves this effect more through repetition than novelty or displacement. The possibility of order appears most prominently in the reiterated appeal to Chloris—*non . . . te . . . decet, te . . . non . . . decent*—to understand that what is more appropriate for her virginal daughter is not so suitable for her. This design for *decus*, for the fitting in life, takes further poetic shaping in the chiastic iteration of *propior* and *prope* at the end of the

21. See, e.g., Cic. *Pis.* 9; *Att.* 1. 16. 11, 2. 1. 8; *Fam.* 7. 32. 2; *QFr.* 2. 4. 5.

22. *Nobilis* is complementary to *pauper*, antonymical to *famosus*. *Paupertas* is the external sign of inner *nobilitas*, while something *famosus* remains morally suspect. True uxorial "labor" has nothing to do with notoriety.

first and the commencement of the fourth stanzas and of *ludere,* opening the second and concluding the third stanza. Chloris does play among the maidens, and should not. Pholoe behaves like a lusty she-goat—and more becomingly, too. For Chloris, however, approaching a ripe death, wool sheared near renowned Luceria is a likely companion.

Hence, seen ideologically and rhetorically in the poem's thought as outlined in its verbal structure, life's patternings are all relative, whether they compose or interrupt, complement or challenge each other. Since metaphor itself implies a way of viewing experience by verbal relativity, the whole poem is a metaphor for *decus,* generating one abstract definition of grace by relating two different but interreacting manifestations of its presence (or absence). The ordered words themselves are the final exemplar of truth and propriety.

Horace further implies that as individuals we are constantly suffering a multitude of comparisons but that at any given moment one individual *decus* is most applicable and no other, a *decus* that can be conceived, say, in terms of ethics and personal obligations, of economics, or merely of time. Chloris is placed near her daughter when she is first addressed by name and makes one final, brilliant sally into Pholoe's realm of immature life at play. Her better role, because she is in reality nearer mortality, ripe for the funeral pyre, not for adolescent sexual adventuring, is to busy herself at home. To do so would restore her to her proper sphere as submissive, senescent wife to poor Ibycus and prevent her from the perversion of her own and the obfuscation of her offspring's *decus* which the poem illustrates. The point is both natural and universal. For Chloris it means the moderate, aware acceptance of time's passage and a wise initiation into death.

In all this we find revealed one brief but glittering example of Horace's sometimes desperate need for order in himself and in existence around him. The poet who framed Chloris and Pholoe into one picture knew instinctively the necessity for those stabilizing graces in life that help each being accept fearlessly, if on occasion ironically, temporal change and physical diversity, the pressures of history and society. Perhaps more even than wrapping oneself in virtue, marrying poverty, or sailing life's stormy Aegean in a two-oared skiff, the conjunctive imagining of the writer's external and internal worlds into the precise expression of poetry is the final gesture toward creative *decus.* It is this affirming configuration of life through art which makes Horatian lyric so finely revealing of its author's conscience and of our own continuing foibles revealed and molded through his words.[23]

Brown University

23. I am grateful to Professors Katherine Geffcken and Kenneth Reckford for their careful criticism.

HORACE C. 3. 30: THE LYRICIST AS HERO

Michael C. J. Putnam

Exegi monumentum aere perennius
regalique situ pyramidum altius,
quod non imber edax, non aquilo impotens
possit diruere aut innumerabilis
annorum series et fuga temporum.   5
non omnis moriar multaque pars mei
vitabit Libitinam: usque ego postera
crescam laude recens, dum Capitolium
scandet cum tacita virgine pontifex:
dicar, qua violens obstrepit Aufidus   10
et qua pauper aquae Daunus agrestium
regnavit populorum, ex humili potens
princeps Aeolium carmen ad Italos
deduxisse modos. sume superbiam
quaesitam meritis et mihi Delphica   15
lauro cinge volens, Melpomene, comam.

(I have finished a monument more lasting than bronze
and loftier than the pyramids' royal pile, one that no
wasting rain, no furious north wind can destroy, or the
countless chain of years and the ages' flight. I shall
not altogether die, but a mighty part of me shall escape
the death-goddess. On and on shall I grow, ever fresh
with the glory of after time: so long as the pontiff
climbs the Capitol with the silent Vestal, I, risen high
from low estate, where wild Aufidus thunders and
where Daunus in a parched land once ruled o'er a
peasant folk, shall be famed for having been the first to
adapt Aeolian song to Italian verse. Accept the proud
honour won by thy merits, Melpomene, and graciously
crown my locks with Delphic bays.) (Bennett)

The extent of the 'edifice' Horace has constructed for himself as proof
of immortality is initially gauged by the meter.[1] The first Asclepiadean
is used elsewhere in the first three books of *carmina* only in the premier
ode of book one. These two poems, each using a rhythm of stately power,
frame their creator's 'monument'.[2] The introductory song examines
Horace's potential career as lyric poet by comparison with a series of

more practical and competitive lifestyles. It also acknowledges Horace's dependence on the opinion of Maecenas—powerful, charming descendant of Etruscan kings—about his rank among writers of lyric. The final ode, alluding to no patron, assumes instead a prideful stance which does not hesitate to command the muse herself with personal assurance. In between Horace has reared his fabric of words whose endurance, because it is constructed of words alone, must be calculated in terms which exceed categorization by time and space.

The architectonics which outline this spiritual design are not limited to unifying parallels between the beginning of the series and the end. The valedictory of the second book likewise stakes the claim of poetic immortality while the concluding ode of book one suggestively turns the appurtenances and setting of creativity into a critique for poetry itself, the myrtle of love and the wine of inspiration merged in an environment which seeks out simplicity over complexity, 'tightness' over elaboration.[3] There are careful links, moreover, with the initiatory ode of book 3 where Horace establishes his role as priest of the Muses, singing to virgins and unwed youths a song of kings and of Jupiter still more royal. And both these notions, the continuities of religious ceremonial action presided over by a priest and his vestal, and a sense of surpassing regality, help inform the standards through which Horace measures his own accomplished pattern in the valedictory poem.

Exegi monumentum aere perennius: the impressive measure of the rhythm complements the assured, confirmed ease of the poet's announcement—verbal action precedes noun which only then is qualified. The first word receives special weight. This is the first occasion in Latin literature where *exigo* bears the meaning 'complete' in reference to a work of literature. What has hitherto been worked within a temporal scheme is now finished, not past but eternal, out of time. Yet the verb involves as well as distances both author and reader. It does not lose its commanding ring—'I have demanded'—and this projected stance of poetic power resonates through the subsequent verses, culminating in two final imperatives extorted from the poet's source of inspiration. The first meaning, 'I have brought to conclusion', also draws associated with it a more specially literary metaphor, restricted especially to style: 'I have refined . . .' Propertius, in a contemporary elegy replete with apparent echoes of Horace, can speak of his verse polished with slender pumice stone *(exactus tenui pumice versus)*, and Horace will cause us to think again later in the poem of the 'polish' of his song.[4] Assurance of mind is an essential prerogative for fineness of song.

Another aspect of this architecture of the spirit is revealed by the initial comparison to which Horace opens his poetic memorial.[5] It is *aere perennius*, more enduring than the most (supposedly) indestructible metal, used by the Romans for statues and for the engraving of important documents such as laws or *res gestae*. This aloofness from temporality, a splendid unconcern with the horizontal line of time's passage, would, I suspect, gain particular importance to an Augustan reader, aware of his Latin poetic heritage, from the word *perennius*. In meditating on his originality, viewed within the spiritual context of his literary inheritance, Horace would have us recall both Catullus and Lucretius.

Catullus at the end of his first poem (the balancing position is again important) had, with modesty forced or true, prayed that his slim volume endure beyond one generation *(plus uno maneat perenne saeclo)*. He entreats fleeting life from a nameless muse who possesses the status of his *patrona*. The dedicatee of the poems, Cornelius Nepos, is an Italian whose Horatian daring embraces *omne aevum*, while Catullus, unlike his self-possessed follower, does not demand but merely bestows. This glance at the past, however, may be one reason (we will observe others as well) why Horace, as he reaches the crucial moment of testing his own modernity against tradition, styles himself *princeps*—salient lyricist but not in every sense first.

There is another reason, related only to tradition and not to innovation in a specific poetic genre, why the Italian Horace must of necessity remain only *princeps*, and that is the accomplishment of Ennius. It is Lucretius who speaks of (1. 117-19):

> Ennius ut noster cecinit qui primus amoeno
> detulit ex Helicone perenni fronde coronam,
> per gentis Italas hominum quae clara clueret.

> (. . . as our own Ennius sang, who first bore down from
> pleasant Helicon the wreath of deathless leaves, to win
> bright fame among the tribes of Italian peoples.) (Bailey)

Ennius—the pun is unmistakable and may well reverberate in Horace's *perennius*—was the first immortal Italian poet.[6] Even Lucretius follows in his wake. Yet the author of *de rerum natura*, to whom Epicurus was *primus* as a thinker (1. 66, 71; 3. 2), did consider himself also a poetic *heuretes*, the first Roman promulgator in verse of philosophy and of a philosophical vocabulary. He twice elaborates on this position as premier, the second occasion, centering around 5. 336-37, being of some importance to the student of Horace *c.* 3. 30:

> . . . et hanc [naturam rerum rationemque] primus
> cum primis ipse repertus
> nunc ego sum in patrias qui possim vertere voces.

(. . . and I myself was found the very first of all who could turn it [the nature and philosophy of things] into the speech of my country.) (Bailey)

Lucretius' argument is on behalf of the novelty of his task and of our world (*recens,* 330), but to prove his point he must embed his discussion in a catalogue duly observing time's devastating progress. Do you not see, asks the poet, high towers falling in ruins (*altas turris ruere,* 307), the monuments of men collapsing (*monumenta virum dilapsa,* 311), stones wrenched from high mountains tottering headlong (*ruere avulsos silices a montibus altis,* 313)? Among the casualties are the deeds of men sung by poets before the Theban and Trojan conflicts (328-29):

> quo tot facta virum totiens cecidere neque usquam
> aeternis famae monumentis insita florent?

> (Whither have so many deeds of men so often passed away? Why are they nowhere enshrined in glory in the everlasting memorials of fame?) (Bailey)

These 'memorials', like the *monumenta* mentioned at line 311, may well be tangible, but the context suggests otherwise. The human achievements to which poets give eternal fame are *insita,* grafted on to the tree of flourishing tradition, not engraved upon or moulded from more perishable materials. It is to these latter which, as Lucretius reinforces his listing of destructive elements in nature, we are subject, to ravaging heat, tremendous upheavals or gnawing rivers swollen from unceasing rains (*ex imbribus assiduis rapaces amnis,* 341-42).

Against this background and much in these terms Horace views the immortality of his poetry. The analogies he offers likewise have their forebears in poetic tradition. Reference is usually made to Pindar and Simonides, and here again it is important to stress the contexts of the allusions.[7] The Theban poet boasts that he has reared for Xenocrates of Acragas a treasure-house (*P.* 6. 10-14).

> τὸν οὔτε χειμέριος ὄμβρος ἐπακτὸς ἐλθών,
> ἐριβρόμου νεφέλας
> στρατὸς ἀμείλιχος, οὔτ' ἄνεμος ἐς μυχοὺς
> ἁλὸς ἄξοισι παμφόρῳ χεράδει
> τυπτόμενον....

> (. . . . which neither wintry rain with its invading onset, the pitiless host launched from deep-thundering

clouds, nor the storm-wind with its swirl of shingle, shall buffet and sweep away into the recesses of the sea.) (Sandys)

Pindar, in telling of a Pythian victory (the θησαυρός is Πυθιόνικος), announces his own poetic defeat of elemental wind and rain. Likewise Simonides (fr. 531P), lauding those fallen at Thermopylae, vows to create by his words an ἐντάφιον, a 'shroud' which neither decay (εὔρως) nor time (χρόνος) will lessen. Each poet treats of heroic events but Pindar's is a doubly forceful vision, proclaiming the prowess of both the subject and his eulogizer. Hence it may be that when Horace, in one of his ode's more strikingly original and influential notions, orders the muse to crown him with laurel from Delphi he is bowing specifically toward his great Greek predecessor as well as toward his Hellenic heritage or some still vaguer vatic, Apolline stance.

Yet in Horace the victor and the writer merge completely. Epinicean hero and bard are one, and eternal youth is assured the craftsman and his 'monument'. This hero's progress is in an intangible art, not tested in any literal, measured course. The ambiance of Delphi is metamorphosed into a setting for spiritual competition and reward. The curiosity is that as a result of this victory Aeolian song is led in triumph (*deducere*) to an Italian step. This in turn proposes a near paradox of symbols to be examined later: the Delphic laurel crowns an Italic victory in a rite the Hellenic muse performs in the Roman temple of Jupiter.

Horace has echoed the poetry of Pindar and Simonides in listing the instruments of destruction against which he claims permanence—wind, rain, time and rust. This last, we note, enters in the guise of an important pun. Horace's monument is more lasting than bronze and taller than the royal shape of the pyramids. Time and space, horizontal and vertical thrusts, compete and interconnect in the analogies. The word *situs* is focal for the conjunction, carrying implications of decay as well as bulk. Grand though the pyramids be in size, they are still subject to time's tooth. The analogies seem at first positioned chiastically. *Aere perennius* ('more lasting than bronze') anticipates *innumerabilis annorum series* ('the countless chain of years') in sound and sense while the pyramids reach against the wind and rain which descends upon them. But intangible can no more be measured by tangible than spiritual can appraise physical. The mind's monument endures incomparably beyond temporal, visual standards of achievement. History's progress, the interlocked dance of the years or the flight of time, has no effect, in Horace's view, on the mind's autocratic, apocalyptic creations. Even the north wind, 'uncontrolled' (*impotens*), is in this case 'powerless', no match for a personage who is truly 'master of himself', in the words of the preceding poem (*potens sui, c.* 3. 29. 41) or, in a still more grand manner, *ex humili potens.*[8]

The comparison of poetry to pyramids, regal and lofty, is in itself a provocative novelty.[9] Perhaps Horace would have sensed in their conic shape the symbolism which they probably presented to an Egyptian—a 'mountain' whereby the pharaoh climbed toward immortality, ascending step by step toward the sun's rays and eternal union with Osiris.[10] The contemporary Roman would probably have sensed a still more pertinent reason for the simile. Pyramids would mean Egypt and Egypt would serve as a reminder of queen Cleopatra, a *regina* who in Horace's words elsewhere was powerful and yet *impotens* (1. 37. 10), the plotter of mad ruin for the Capitolium (*dementis ruinas,* 1. 37. 7) finally herself ruined.[11] But it is a noble fall, one whose virtues Horace draws subtly to himself (1. 37. 30-32):

> saevis Liburnis scilicet invidens
> privata deduci superbo
> non humilis mulier triumpho.

> (plainly scorning the thought of being carried, no
> longer a queen, on hostile galleys to grace a glorious
> triumph—no humble woman she.) (Bennett)

Cleopatra's triumph is within herself, to realize the courage for an heroic suicide and avoid participation in a Roman conqueror's more immediate, literal moment of glory. Her inner lordliness (she is, after all, *non humilis*) scorns obeisance to Octavian's external triumph (*superbo triumpho*). Horace, though 'humble' once, now claims his own triumph, offering in evidence for his pride—to anticipate for a moment—the tamed parade of Greek song marched to an Italian beat. It too is an internal achievement, yet, perhaps simply because it is spread by words (*non moriar* becomes the positive *dicar*), more enduring than Cleopatra's victory of the spirit as it is immeasurably more lasting than the pyramids and independent of local, temporal prizes. And while Cleopatra in wildness planned the actual destruction of the Capitolium, Horace sees a more rational symbol for his poetry's continuity in 'action' also centred around Rome's citadel but now become the focal point for ceremonial silence and slow time, not history's passing immediacies, be they destructive or momentarily honorific.

There is one further aspect of Horace's pride, linking poetic monument with its setting for immortality. Not only will a large part, the immortal part, of Horace escape the goddess of funerals but 'ever will I grow fresh with the future's praise'.[12] What at first seems paradoxical

—growth retaining continued freshness, eternity imposed on futurity—only certifies the initial programme of a *monumentum* espousing stature beyond space and time. Horace does not say 'I will always remain' but 'I will ever grow, fresh. . . .' The spatial image of continuous growth is counterpoised against the miraculous spectacle of spontaneity outside the cycle of seasonal recurrence. The *laudes* Horace will receive, the praises of posterity for grand endeavour, are in fact beyond time, and the physicality which *crescam* implies is non-corporeal, incapable of restriction to the destiny of bronze or pyramid, vernal beyond life's regular springs.

Paradoxically, the analogy for immortality is put in terms of motion which implies change viewed through alteration of place and time: a priest and his vestal climb—always climb—the Capitoline, we may assume to perform rites at the temple of Jupiter Optimus Maximus. No doubt the phrase resonates with patriotic particularity. The poet's work will survive as long as the core of Rome's pretensions to empire remains intact.[13] But there are other aspects of this setting which transform Roman specifics into a more universal spectacle. A walk up the Capitoline would presumably have taken priest and virgin from the Regia and the *atrium Vestae* to the temple of mighty Jove. A Roman would have known or sensed the regality of the pontifical inheritance. He might also have reasoned that such an aspiration as Horace makes, the ascent toward acclaimed perfection, combines Vesta and Jupiter, earth and sky, female and male, and intimates, in the journey from one to the other, the poet's hopes for an immortality outside any temporal accomplishments—the lyric bard, in fact, finally striking his head against the stars. It is religion that provides the closest approximation to what Horace expects of his imagination's rituals. The priest of the Muses, singing to virgins and youths, who introduced the book by adopting a stance above yet acutely perceptive of mortal doings, can at the end with justice embrace the same notion to embody symbolically the enduring results of a perspective which views the expression of poetry as a rite.

Horace, in analogizing his eternity, adds a further dimension to the previous notions of time he had raised. His poetry surmounts the disordering time of history or even the cyclic time of seasonal change and renewal wherein decay and growth counterbalance each other. His ascription to divinity, to the hyper-reality his art creates and maintains, is hypostasized in the climb of priest and virgin—a religious rite performed by male and female which, however, has no intimations of sexual union. The sexual act is a necessary part of both the linear time of individual life or history's course and the periodicity of organic time. The purposes of religion, the mystic search toward a superterrestrial, cosmic consciousness, depend on a purely spiritual 'bond' linking men and gods. The action of the imagination's priest becomes directly numinous as the poet's private ego is fused into a process of creativity beyond rational time as well as human enterprise. For Dante this third dimension of time would gain definition in the concept of transcending love; for Horace it is visualized in a ritual of words, presided over finally by the songstress muse, inspiriting, incorporeal daughter of memory.[14]

The myth of poetic immortality explained through religion's victory over time also implies that the poet has surmounted his own selfconsciousness as creative being. To demonstrate this Horace now remembers his earthbound, secular origins where the raging Aufidus resounds and arid Daunus governs rural peoples.[15] The paradox—destructive river in a waterless land—challenges the reader's attention. The attributes suggest that Horace is fully aware how changeful has been the road to Rome, the way toward eternity, from country birth to urbane perfection. The dry land of Apulia has yielded an artist ever fresh; the impetuous Aufidus' roar has become a virgin's silent climb with only the poet's words (dicar) to intervene. King Daunus has fathered a poet whose monument is loftier than any other structure of regal proportions.

But at the same time Horace would not forget the power intrinsic to this epic inheritance of rivers and kings.[16] He would combine them once again in a later analogy for conquering Tiberius' onslaught against the Vindelici (c. 4. 14. 25-30):

> sic tauriformis volvitur Aufidus
> qui regna Dauni praefluit Apuli,
>   cum saevit horrendamque cultis
>   diluviem meditatur agris,
>
> ut barbarorum Claudius agmina
> ferrata vasto diruit impetu . . .

> (So does bull-formed Aufidus roll on, flowing past the realms of Apulian Daunus, when he rages and threatens awful deluge to the well-tilled fields, even as Claudius o'erwhelmed with destructive onslaught the mail-clad hosts of savages . . .) (Bennett)

The rage of the river itself, the acer Aufidus, is noticed by Horace early in his career (s. 1. 1. 58), but in c. 3. 30 and again in c. 4. 9 it is directly linked to his birthplace and to the epic resonance of his song:

> ne forte credas interitura quae
> longe sonantem natus ad Aufidum

> non ante volgatas per artis
> verba loquor socianda chordis . . .

(Think not the words will perish which I, born near
far-sounding Aufidus, utter for linking with the lyre,
by arts not hitherto revealed . . .) (Bennett)

The poet also connects his inspiration with the landscape of his birth.
He is the grace of the Daunian muse (*Dauniae decus Camenae, c.* 4. 6.
27). His other references, however, associate Daunia with martial prowess. In the ode to Lalage Horace gives Daunia the epithet *militaris* (*c.*
1. 22. 13) and to Pollio he can single out his countrymen to exemplify
those fighters slain in recent Roman civil strife (*c.* 2. 1. 33-36):

> qui gurges aut quae flumina lugubris
> ignara belli? quod mare Dauniae
>   non decoloravere caedes?
>   quae caret ora cruore nostro?

(What pool or stream has failed to taste the dismal
war? What sea has Daunian slaughter not discoloured?
What coast knows not our blood?) (Bennett)

Horace, therefore, first tests himself against place, viewing in his
earthbound origins a force and strength which he was to tame and
channel. From his initial proclamation of an elitist spiritual authority of
universal importance he can turn back to his secular source and review
a temporal, national background, the physical starting place for a metaphysical journey. The ethereal conquest of immortality, the search for an
apocalyptic stance outside of time, still commences with a sense of
place, for a sense of self and a sense of place are indispensably interrelated.[17]

A second touchstone against which Horace appraises the uniqueness
of his personal vocation is his heritage from his intellectual forebears.
This change from physical to psychic identity—from an inheritance of
body to a relationship with literary history and the imagination's past—
is executed partially by the words *ex humili potens princeps. Humili,*
coming as it does closely after *agrestium* yet anticipating *superbiam,* by
pun lifts the poet from his mundane origin toward abstract assurance.
Potens, too, by recalling the wind and rain *impotens,* palpable forces
powerless to destroy Horace's spiritual grandeur, moves the reader away
from the poet's literal background into consciousness only of mental
power. The process culminates in the word *princeps.*

Since the reader would perhaps expect *primus*, emphasis is directed to the special overtones of *princeps*.[18] These are notably of a political nature. Three times in his lyric poems Horace styles Augustus *princeps*, a title the emperor specifically espouses in his *Res Gestae*.[19] By drawing such connotations to himself Horace makes it clear again, as he had in the opening lines, that he too possess sovereign power. But his heroic adventures, his voyages of discovery, are of the mind, his potency such as to be contrasted not equated with any visible evidence of military or civil status. Horace had carefully associated himself with Augustus earlier in the book, particularly in the fourth ode. Now he proves himself an Augustus of the spirit whose feats are parallel with, but incomparable to, those of his patron.

This spiritual power is manifested in one special way. Horace was the foremost to lead Aeolian song to Italian measures (*Aeolium carmen ad Italos/deduxisse modos*). The phrase is striking because the poet at first seems to be saying the opposite of what we expect. We anticipate a proclamation that the rhythms were Greek, the imagination Italian. Instead we are told that Greek song (and even the word *carmen* is Latin) has been led forth to an Italian 'beat', and this reversal highlights the ambiguities of *modos* and *deduxisse* which enrich the poem.[20] Horace, Orphic bard gifted with the charm to draw words on,[21] uses a term that could be applied to a procession in marriage or triumph, to troop movements or the leading forth of colonies, to drawing wool down from a spindle and crafting a fine-spun song.[22] We have already been assured of the poet's 'power' and are preparing to envision his 'triumph'. Horace's winning of Alcaeus and Sappho leads from Aeolia to Italy, the journey on which conquered song is marched. But this progress also parallels his own refining way of endeavour, from Daunia to Roman Capitolium, from birth at the core of Italy—land of headstrong streams and mythical kings—to everlasting fame at ritual's centre. And all these paths have as their ultimate goal what the poem's first word, *exegi*, suggested—not only a sense of heroic feats concluded but the polishing and crafting of the soul's memorial as well, the production, in Virgil's words, of a *carmen deductum*, a controlled song of perfect finish.

The suggestiveness of the word *modos* is also forced by its context to expand from the strictly prosodic, 'rhythms', to more general notions of 'method' and 'form'. It is Italian artistry, Italian ways of thinking and means of statement, to which Greek lyric expressiveness must now adhere. Here, too, the implication is of a challenge overcome, of dynamic motion stabilized, of stasis born out of continuity. Art now obeys new exigencies of structure and Horace reforms the designs inherited from his Hellenic past—his vocation from history—through the medium of his own intellect.[23] Horace portrays the final ritual stylization of his experience as a human, of his descent in time from Daunus to the present, in space from the Aufidus to Rome. And this journey from birth to immortality is also the journey out of the literal into the figurative, as the wild is tamed, the primitive rustic learns sophistication, a king of one sort becomes *princeps* of quite another. Who, however, we finally ask, as Horace does elsewhere, is the civilizer, who the civilized? Does violent, rustic Italy really tame Aeolian song or does the Delphic crown presuppose that in a very different way this 'wild victor' has himself learned *artes* at the feet of the 'captive' Greeks?[24] Whatever the answer, these aspects of Horace's life are the 'means' through which the poetic monument is finally ordered and, if they are 'rhythms', it is because they call the step that ceases only at the moment when a Roman is crowned by a Greek muse who usurps, now paradoxically, the place of an Italic god and does honour to a poet-hero who controls the elements, overpowers death and superannuates time.[25]

The ceremony of triumph that salutes this poetic feat expands such a double notion. This is no ordinary rite. Where a regular *triumphator* would make an offering of his (literal) wreath Horace demands that an abstraction, his pride, be accepted as gift while he receives (now as symbol) what the *triumphator* would according to custom bestow.[26] And it is no haughty, almighty Jupiter demanding prayerful supplication whom Horace confronts at the culminating moment, but a Greek muse, Melpomene, whose willingness to accept and to bind he, instead, can command.

But to offer even *superbia* implies a gesture of humility. Whose merits—his or hers—have won this pride remains appropriately ambiguous. Horace will declare his dependence on Melpomene in the third ode of his fourth book, a poem which bears a close resemblance to *c*. 1. 1 and 3. 30 in contrasting humankind's external ambitions with a poet's inner awards:

> Quem tu, Melpomene, semel
>   nascentem placido lumine videris
> illum non labor Isthmius
>   clarabit pugilem, non equos impiger
>
> curru ducet Achaico
>   victorem, neque res bellica Deliis
> ornatum foliis ducem,
>   quod regum tumidas contuderit minas,
>
> ostendet Capitolio:
>   sed quae Tibur aquae fertile praefluunt

et spissae nemorum comae
　　fingent Aeolio carmine nobilem.

> (Whom thou, Melpomene, hast once beheld with fav-
> ouring gaze at his natal hour, him no Isthmian toil shall
> make a famous boxer, no impetuous steed shall draw
> as victor in Achaean car, nor shall martial deeds show
> him to the Capitol, a captain decked with Delian bays,
> for having crushed the haughty threats of kings; but
> the waters that flow past fertile Tibur and the dense
> leafage of the groves shall make him famous for
> Aeolian song.) (Bennett)

The person upon whom Melpomene looks kindly at birth will not gain fame as a victor in games or because, as *dux*, his military skills have displayed him in glory on the Capitolium. Yet he will be *nobilis* in another sense, ranked through the prestige of Aeolian song, having at last gained a spot fertile in water and thick with shade.

The final apocalypse, then, is of a Greek muse crowning an Italic poet with Parnassian laurel, presumably in a Roman setting. The distinction presents for the last time the poet's own spiritual travels whose end result is an amalgam, merging in one universal spirit a double heritage. Delphic laurel is the unifying symbol for this achievement. Horace thought of it elsewhere—and has readied us to accept it here—as symbol of regal power (*c*. 2. 2. 22) or of a triumphant statesman (*c*. 3. 14. 2, of Augustus). [27] When he thinks of himself as an *animosus infans*, the secure bard already as a child free from nature's menace, his protection is the poet's sacred laurel (*c*. 3. 4. 18-19). Specifically we think of Apollo and of the Boeotian Pindar, lyric singer of Delphic victories, the one poet Horace singles out as gifted with Apollo's laurel (*laurea donandus Apollonari*, *c*. 4. 2. 9). [28] Apollo himself is god of quiver and lyre, martial glory and poetic song. Pindar is the most heroic of lyricists whose song is akin to the Aufidus, a mountain torrent overflowing its banks (*c*. 4. 2. 5-6). It is from him that Horace has already carefully drawn his opening analogy for the eternal endurance of his verse. Hence, as Parnassus and Capitoline, Delphi and Rome, converge to symbolize the poet's eternity, it is of Apollo and Pindar that Horace thinks at the end, embracing not only Aeolian song but Delphic inspiration as well in his multiform triumph.

Hence the modern and the traditional—the poet as potent inventor (*princeps*) cognizant of his double legacy of body and mind, Italian birthright and the Greek literary past—vie in formulating a brilliant portrait of the lyric artist as genius. Fully knowing his place from and in history, Horace is likewise aware that true genius is outside of time, beyond any cycles of recurrence, whose stability goes even beyond 'a marble or a bronze repose', whose endurance finds analogy only in an eternal continuity of ritual. This splendid monument, edifice of the mind, higher than anything tangible, loftier in style and tone than anything lyric imagined before, comes from exactly this merger of Capitolium and Parnassus, of a steady, instinctual climb toward a muse who gives recognition to the triumph of words not deeds. Horace's particular vatic stance, the poet as priest and maiden, as spokesman for mankind to and from divinity, eases away from *moriar* to *dicar*, from mortality subject to wind and rain, to an autonomy based on language alone. This transition from flesh to spirit, from man's momentary existential involvements as a creature in time to eternal converse with the gods—to immortality of imagination, in a word—is effected by that verbal ceremony we call poetry.

In conclusion we may turn back briefly to *ode* 1. 1, to look again at the two poems as complementary, the second fulfilling the promise of the first:[29]

Maecenas atavis edite regibus,
o et praesidium et dulce decus meum:
sunt quos curriculo pulverem Olympicum
collegisse iuvat metaque fervidis
evitata rotis palmaque nobilis   5
terrarum dominos evehit ad deos;
hunc, si mobilium turba Quiritium
certat tergeminis tollere honoribus;
illum, si proprio condidit horreo
quidquid de Libycis verritur areis.   10
gaudentem patrios findere sarculo
agros Attalicis condicionibus
numquam demoveas, ut trabe Cypria
Myrtoum pavidus nauta secet mare;
luctantem Icariis fluctibus Africum   15
mercator metuens otium et oppidi
laudat rura sui: mox reficit rates
quassas indocilis pauperiem pati.
est qui nec veteris pocula Massici
nec partem solido demere de die   20
spernit, nunc viridi membra sub arbuto
stratus, nunc ad aquae lene caput sacrae;
multos castra iuvant et lituo tubae
permixtus sonitus bellaque matribus

detestata; manet sub Iove frigido 25
venator tenerae coniugis immemor,
seu visa est catulis cerva fidelibus,
seu rupit teretes Marsus aper plagas.
me doctarum hederae praemia frontium
dis miscent superis, me gelidum nemus 30
Nympharumque leves cum Satyris chori
secernunt populo, si neque tibias
Euterpe cohibet nec Polyhymnia
Lesboum refugit tendere barbiton.
quodsi me lyricis vatibus inseres, 35
sublimi feriam sidera vertice.

(Maecenas, sprung from royal stock, my bulwark and my glory dearly cherished, some there are whose one delight it is to gather Olympic dust upon the racing car, and whom the turning-post cleared with glowing wheel and the glorious palm exalt as masters of the earth to the very gods. One man is glad if the mob of fickle Romans strive to raise him to triple honours; another, if he has stored away in his own granary everything swept up from Libyan threshing-floors. The peasant who loves to break the clods of his ancestral acres with the hoe, you could never induce by the terms of an Attalus to become a trembling sailor and to plough the Myrtoan Sea in Cyprian bark. The trader, fearing the southwester as it wrestles with the Icarian waves, praises the quiet of the fields about his native town, yet presently refits his shattered barks, untaught to brook privation. Many a one there is who scorns not bowls of ancient Massic nor to steal a portion of the day's busy hours, stretching his limbs now 'neath the verdant arbute-tree, now by the sacred source of some gently murmuring rill.

Many delight in the camp, in the sound of the trumpet mingled with the clarion, and in the wars that mothers hate. Out beneath the cold sky, forgetful of his tender wife, stays the hunter, whether a deer has been sighted by the trusty hounds, or a Marsian boar has broken the finely twisted nets.

Me the ivy, reward of poets' brows, links with the gods above; me the cool grove and the lightly tripping bands of the nymphs and satyrs withdraw from the

146

vulgar throng, if only Euterpe withhold not the flute,
nor Polyhymnia refuse to tune the Lesbian lyre. But if
you rank me among lyric bards, I shall touch the stars
with my exalted head.) (Bennett)

Horace's dependence on Maecenas, lofty descendant of ancient kings,
has already been noted. Maecenas is a bastion against life's real pressures and also bestower of a poet's necessary grace. His ranking, which
brings the poem full circle, bestows heaven on the lyric bard. The list
of occupations following upon the initial apostrophe begins with the
Olympic victor, also heaven-bent. Once more we think of Pindar, not
only as the author of epinicean odes honouring contestants at Olympia
but, in particular, for a fragment (221) containing kindred vignettes
and beginning similarly:

ἀελλοπόδων μέν τιν' εὐφραίνοισιν ἵππων
τιμαὶ καὶ στέφανοι,...

(One man is gladdened by honours and crowns won by
wind-swift steeds; . . .)

With Horace's help the reader also connects the winning racers — raised
to divinity by turning-point shunned and honorific palm—with the poet
himself whose symbolic ivy mingles him also with the gods.[30] But there
is nothing in the final picture of Horace that suggests the intensity of
active competition which ultimately conveys apotheosis to the victor.
Horace is already immortalized because of his 'learning'; the victor, on
the contrary, must be drawn heavenwards by his physical prowess.

And there are disturbing elements in the portrait which confirm
those critics who view much of what follows as either negative or, at
best, ironic. The collecting of dust, even Olympic dust, does not appear
the most ennobling of pursuits. Dust, to be sure, can stand as evidence
for the athlete's strain. Yet it can equally look to the futility and meaningless of human aims.[31] And a personified turning-point is a strange
creature to assure divinization. When we look to the second field of
endeavour, the flitting fickleness of the Roman mob in its struggles is
supported poetically by the word *turba* ('crowd' or merely 'uproar'?)
and the dubiety of its blessing glossed by *tollere* ('raise up' or 'destroy'?).
And the man who would sweep all Libya's grain production into his
own barn is the victim of the poet's hyperbole as well as of his own self-
aggrandizement. On the other hand Horace seems to mete out praise to
the hoer content with his fathers' land,[32] but such a figure, should en-
joyment yield to restlessness, could become a fearful sailor, 'cutting'

water instead of land. The untaught *mercator,* ignorant that endurance of one's lot, however poor, is a virtue often imposed as a necessity, is victimized, himself and his ships, by a conflict between wind and sea.

Then, at line 19, Horace breaks both the poem (at its centre) and the progression of activists with a look at one who does not hesitate to 'break up' his own full day. *Solido die,* life's continuous glare, the poem's stream of competitiveness, is severed by a man who drinks old Massic (*oblivioso Massico,* c. 2. 7. 21, the eraser of cares) and lies under a green arbute near a soft fountainhead of sacred water. This *locus amoenus* generally suits one whom a chill grove and choruses of nymphs and satyrs (and a *praesidium* of some strength) separate from the people. Attributes of shade and fountain are particularly fitting for a poet.[33]

The spell is shattered as we return to the *vita activa,* to soldier and hunter. From the fountain's softness we are plunged into a world of noise, from a sacred spot into an existence cursed by mothers. Then, the contrast continuing into the next episode, we find ourselves instead of *viridi sub arbuto* ('beneath the verdant arbute-tree') transported *sub Iove frigido* ('beneath the cold sky'). Green gives place to chill, verdant freshness with all it suggests of youth and strength yields to frigidity, to a man whose professional impulses lead him to forget his wife (our sympathy is aroused by the adjective *tenerae*). And, paradoxically, while he is neglecting his wife, his hounds are faithful to him, and while he is careless of the one to whom he is 'joined' the Marsian boar 'breaks' his nets. As in the case of the *mercator* there seems a measure of futility in each enterprise. The doe is merely sighted while the boar rips through the trap.

In the end this round of ambition ceases, as it had momentarily at the centre, this time with a direct look at the poet. Bacchus' ivy, like the victor's palm, divinizes the poet but instead of drawing him to heaven it only mixes him with the gods above, in this new golden age of the imagination.[34] The chill grove and the entourage of Bacchic creatures offer further symbolic evidence of poetic immortality. The wine, arbute and spring of lines 21-22 have suffered final transformation into Bacchus' ivy and grove, and the water's soft sound becomes the company of the muses (their names betoken both pleasure and song), the one granting the flute, the other the lyre.

Horace, then, in scrutinizing his professional ambitions, lifts us out of a world of superficial immediacies into a spiritual realm where poets consort with gods. As the final ode of the third book glances at the poet's progress from Aufidus to Parnassus, from literal birth near resounding rivers to immortality assured by Delphic laurel, so here the poet extends his approbation with growing strength to the actual farmer, who in stability tills inherited acres, to the man who escapes away from life's pressures into a quasi-symbolic setting for leisure, and finally to a purely mythic landscape with a poet reaching from earth to stars through the grandeur of his vocation. Nor do the negative overtones in Horace's description of the Olympic victor's perfervid course lessen his allegiance to Pindar. Horace's victory is poetic, not mundane, a journey to heaven that depends for confirmation not on Olympic dust or the crowd's plaudits but on the maintenance of aloofness coupled with the bestowal of charm—a combination Horace finds in Maecenas.

In fact the vatic hero's development in the initiatory ode, with its merger of Pindaric elements and a plea that Polyhymnia string the lyre of Lesbos, clearly anticipates the balancing ode's boast of crowning with Delphic laurel and leading Aeolian song in triumph. It also anticipates the same careful mixture of Greek and Roman elements—racer at Olympia and Roman mob; Massic wine and Marsian boar, yet Cyprian boat and the seas around Myrto and Icaria; above all a poet relying on Greek muses to string a Greek *barbitos* from Lesbos, but himself to be ranked among (Italic) *vates* by a descendant of (Etruscan) kings.[35]

The chief difference between these two ways toward apotheosis— the priestly climber who strikes the stars—seems to rest on the level of symbol as the ivy of Bacchus, central to the first ode, is changed in the last to Apollo's laurel. Bacchus' provocative setting, cool groves populated by dancing nymphs and satyrs—the source from which poetry emanates—becomes that measured pace which finally claims the Delphic laurel. The poet introduces himself pitting his own vocation against other motley careers and leaning on his patron's opinion. His envoi hymns a total self-assurance. Bacchic inspiration has given birth to a monument endowed with Apolline authority.[36]

Brown University

NOTES

1. For another recent critique of this poem see V. Pöschl, 'Die Horazode *Exegi Monumentum* (c. 3. 30)', *GIF* 20 (1967), 261-72 (reprinted in *Horazische Lyrik: Interpretationen* [Heidelberg, 1970], 248-62).

2. A point made by S. Commager, *The Odes of Horace* (New Haven, 1962), 313.

3. On *c.* 1. 38 see especially K. Reckford *Horace* (New York, 1969), 12ff.; M. Owen Lee, *Word, Sound, and Image in the Odes of Horace* (Ann Arbor, 1969), 90ff.

4. Prop. 3. 1. 8 *Cf.* Hor. *e.* 2. 1. 7; Ovid *M.* 15. 871. For *exigo* specifically in relation to time see *c.* 3. 22. 6 (*exactos annos*). The many parallels between *c.* 3. 30 and Prop. 3. 1 and 3. 2 have been discussed by Butler and Barber (*The Elegies of Propertius* [Oxford, 1933], xxiv) who maintain that Propertius is the imitator and

that therefore book 3 of the elegies was logically published in 22, a year after *Odes* 1-3. The relative chronology, however, must still remain in doubt.

5. On *monumentum* and the immortality of works of literature, prose as well as poetry, see W. Suerbaum, *Untersuchungen zur Selbstdarstellung älterer römischer Dichter = Spudasmata v.* 19 (Hildesheim, 1968), 327f.

6. That such a play on words was not beneath Horace may perhaps be seen at *s.* 1. 2. 36f. where the mention of a certain Cupiennius is immediately followed by a parodic reference to Ennius himself.

7. Re. Suerbaum, *op. cit.* 167; Pöschl, *op. cit.* 261f. Both add Isoc. *Antid.* 7 to the traditional citations but the orator's point is the beauty, not the endurance of bronze.

8. On the relationship of *c.* 3. 30 to its predecessor, a relationship partially defined in the change from *fugiens hora* (*c.* 3. 29. 48) to *fuga temporum*, see Commager, *op. cit.* 315.

9. Re. Suerbaum, *op. cit.* 166 and 326f. for other possible parallels.

10. For further discussion see I. E. S. Edwards, *The Pyramids of Egypt* (London, 1961), 234ff.; K. Mendelssohn 'A Scientist looks at the Pyramids', *American Scientist* 59 (1971), 210-20, esp. 218.

11. A reference to Cleopatra in *c.* 3. 30 is also suggested by I. Trencsényi-Waldapfel 'Regalique situ pyramidum altius', *Act. Ant. Hung.* 12 (1964), 149-167.

12. The topos of 'freshness' is discussed in detail by Pöschl, *op. cit.* 262-3 and n. 4.

13. The analogy of the Capitolium and immortality is used contemporaneously by Virgil (*Aen.* 9. 446-49), a point made by G. W. Williams (*Tradition and Originality in Roman Poetry* [Oxford, 1968], 152) to emphasize Horace's Romanness. See also I. Borzak, 'Exegi monumentum aere perennius', *Act. Ant. Hung.* 12 (1964) 137-47.

14. On the 'indefinitely recoverable, indefinitely repeatable' quality of sacred time, see Mircea Eliade, *The Sacred and the Profane* (New York, 1959), 68ff. For a detailed discussion of notions of eternity see H. Meyerhoff, *Time in Literature* (Berkeley, 1955), 89ff.

15. Williams, *op. cit.* 152f. and 367, evokes a lowly village where Horace was born. Re. also *ibid., The Third Book of Horace's Odes* (Oxford, 1969), 151 ('The obscure little town in which he was born') and 152 ('his humble home-town').

16. Cf. the use of *violens* of a victorious horse at *e.* 1. 10. 37.

17. Cf. G. Hartmann 'Toward Literary History', *Daedalus* 99 (1970), 355-83, esp. 369ff., reprinted in *Beyond Formalism* (New Haven, 1970), 356-86.

18. For those who see *princeps* as only *primus*, Catullus' sapphic poems are the stumbling block (see G. Williams *Horace's Odes*, 151; J. Ferguson 'Catullus and Horace', *AJP* 77 [1956], 1-18, esp. 3f.). Horace attacks the problem of his originality in *e.* 1. 19 calling himself again *princeps* (21), apparently in general, and *primus* (23), with particular reference to Archilochus and the *Epodes*. At *e.* 1. 19. 32 he singles out Alcaeus as the poet whom he especially celebrates and at *e.* 2. 2. 99 he is already known as Alcaeus. For further hints on his preferences among the Greek lyricists see *c.* 1. 32. 3ff. and 2. 13. 30.

19. See the notes of P. A. Brunt and J. M. Moore (edd. *Res Gestae Divi Augusti* [Oxford, 1967]) to 13, 30. 1, 32. 3, esp. pp. 79f. and 83f. For more general discussion see A. Gwosdz, *Der Begriff des römischer princeps* (Diss. Breslau, 1933); R. Syme, *The Roman Revolution* (Oxford, 1939), 311.

20. The reversal is treated only as an example of hypallage by M. Owen Lee in his sensitive discussions of the poem (*op. cit.* 15; *cf.* also 6, 50).

21. For *deducere* in this sense see Vir. *ecl.* 3. 46 and 6. 71 (*cantando rigidas deducere montibus ornos,* 'by singing to draw the stubborn ash-trees down from the mountains', of Hesiod's power over nature). Cf. *geo.* 3. 10-11.

22. Pöschl (*op. cit.* 268ff.) singles out the spinning metaphor. E. Maroti ('Princeps Aeolium carmen ad Italos deduxisse modos', *Act. Ant. Hung.* 13 [1965], 97-109) opts for the leading out of a colony. For *deducere* in connection with a triumph see Nisbet-Hubbard on Hor. *c.* 1. 37. 31.

23. Cf. the ambiguity of the word *modi* at *c.* 3. 3. 72 and Horace's word-play at *e.* 2. 2. 141ff.

24. The famous passage is *e.* 2. 1. 156f.

25. In all this Horace may be proposing himself as a literal *pontifex*, a spiritual 'builder of bridges' who in and through himself religiously binds together disparate worlds. The structure of lines 12-14, from *potens* to *princeps* to *deduxisse*, suggests such an enterprise.

26. For the offering of laurel by the triumphator, see *P.-W.* 7a (1939), 510. Augustus himself deposited *laurum de fascibus . . . in Capitolio* (*R. G.* 4).

27. Re. Pliny *H. N.* 15. 127 and Smith on Tib. 2. 5. 117.

28. For Horace and Pindar re. the poet's own remark at *e.* 1. 3. 10; E. L. Highbarger, 'The Pindaric Style of Horace', *TAPA* 66 (1935), 222-55; E. Harms, *Horaz in seinen Beziehungen zu Pindar* (diss. Marburg, 1936); Commager, *op. cit.* 20ff., 59ff.; Nisbet-Hubbard, *op. cit.* xiii; G. Williams, *Tradition and Originality,* 270ff.; Pöschl, *Horazische Lyrik,* 11.

29. For recent literature on *c.* 1. 1 see K. Vretska, 'Horatius, Carm. I, 1,'*Hermes* 99 (1971), 323-35 and H. James Shey, 'The Poet's Progress: Horace, Ode 1. 1'. *Arethusa* 4 (1971), 185-96.

30. This point is elaborated by D. Norberg ('L'olympionique, le poète et leur renom éternel', *Upp. Univ. Ärsskrift* 1945. 6, 3-42, esp. 24ff.) without admission of any negative elements. See, by contrast, G. Carlsson, 'L'Ode I, 1 d'Horace', *Eranos* 44 (1946), 404-20; E. Fraenkel, *Horace* (Oxford, 1957), 231, n. 3.

31. For the first association see *c.* 1. 8. 4 and *e.* 1. 1. 51; for the second, *c.* 3. 3. 21 and 4. 7. 16.

32. See also *c.* 1. 12. 43-44.

33. See H. Musurillo, 'The Poet's Apotheosis: Horace, *Odes* 1. 1', *TAPA* 93 (1962), 230-39, esp. 237.

34. Horace's references to Bacchus are analyzed by E.-R. Schwinge, 'Zur Kunsttheorie des Horaz', *Philologus* 107 (1963), 92-3, n. 4. For a detailed interpretation of the role of Bacchus in Horace's poetry see E. T. Silk, 'Bacchus and the Horatian "*Recusatio*"', *YCS* 21 (1969), 195-202.

35. This intermingling of Greek and Roman elements is noted by Nisbet- Hubbard *ad. loc.*

36. I am grateful to Professor Kenneth Reckford for his comments on this paper.

HORACE AND TIBULLUS

MICHAEL C. J. PUTNAM

Two of Horace's most incisive and witty poems, *Odes* 1. 33 and *Epist.* 1. 4, are addressed to a certain Albius. Because of correspondence especially between the latter poem and what we know of his life (from poetry and *vita*), the recipient is usually taken to be the elegist Albius Tibullus. Each poem can (and initially should) be read separately, and biographical conjectures are of little critical moment in any case. But an elegist, whose temperament battens on constant rehearsal of past suffering and aloof contemplation of unexperienced realities, seems to lurk in the background. He is likely to be Tibullus, seen through Horace's eyes. There may be something to gain from treating the poems in conjunction.

I.

Albi, ne doleas plus nimio memor
immitis Glycerae, neu miserabilis
decantes elegos, cur tibi iunior
    laesa praeniteat fide.

insignem tenui fronte Lycorida   5
Cyri torret amor, Cyrus in asperam
declinat Pholoen; sed prius Apulis
    iungentur capreae lupis,

quam turpi Pholoe peccet adultero.
sic visum Veneri, cui placet imparis   10
formas atque animos sub iuga aenea
    saevo mittere cum ioco.

ipsum me melior cum peteret Venus,
grata detinuit compede Myrtale
libertina, fretis acrior Hadriae   15
    curvantis Calabros sinus.

The Ode is a polite lecture from lyric to elegiac poet on the complexities of human relationships. Overcalculation, says Horace, is impossible. The basic rule of the game is expect the unexpected, be ready for involuntary as well as voluntary reactions away from one's ordinary procedures and affections. In the first three stanzas Horace seems to yield more and more to the commonplace (to lull us intellectually into the opposite stance he would have us ultimately believe). But in stanza four he announces, with honest humor, that he too, the apparently aloof purveyor of spiritual medication to his poet friend, is no stranger to the sexual realities which his sage analogies have hitherto sketched. The poem is a splendid example of Horatian artistry. At the risk of overintellectualizing with a heavy hand a brilliantly light poem, I should like to look at its verbal structure in some detail.

Tibullus, true to the elegist's form, sorrows unceasingly for fickle Glycera. He bases his life on memory and continued grief. Horace sees him as deliberately exaggerating his pain (*plus nimio* is nearly hyperbolic). He mourns the (implied) comparison between age (himself) and youth (the rival), between his faithfulness and Glycera's unsteadiness. He notes his rival's greater "charm" (*praeniteat* may refer to mental, physical, and moral virtues in any or all combinations). We might assume that Horace's point was "nothing *plus nimio*," μηδὲν ἄγαν, but it is the oxymoron *immitis Glycerae* which sets the tone for what follows. Glycera, untrue to her sweet name, is in reality unripe (physically) and pitilessly unkind (spiritually). She would not do for Tibullus in any case.

That he was nevertheless drawn to her, however, leads the way to the second stanza (5–7): "insignem tenui fronte Lycorida / Cyri torret amor, Cyrus in asperam / declinat Pholoen..." Lycoris loves Cyrus; Cyrus loves Pholoe. But Pholoe will sin as soon as wild goats mate with Apulian wolves (7–9): "... sed prius Apulis / iungentur capreae lupis, / quam turpi Pholoe peccet adultero." This last seems an *adunaton*, something that will never happen. Wolves are the natural enemies of goats, even wild goats, and prey destructively on them, we might first assume. But this is exactly what does occur in Venus' world (10–12): "sic visum Veneri, cui placet imparis / formas atque animos sub iuga aenea / saevo mittere cum ioco." The reverberation of *iungentur* in *iuga* is arranged with strict purpose. The mating of opposites is part of love's game. Wolves and goats get along willy-nilly when pressed into service by Venus. Her yoke must be made of bronze, not wood, however, to keep such disparate elements under strict control. Like the union of opposites that she perpetrates, this is a *saevus iocus*, a joke that is no joke at all (which, as another oxymoron, is linguistically to say the same thing).

Verbal details, in particular a series of puns on proper names, enrich the general plan. Both wolves and goats were constant

symbols in antiquity for ardent sexuality. The connotations of *lupa* in Latin need no comment. For goats we need only take note of the daughter of Chloris (perhaps another or even the same Pholoe): "illam cogit amor Nothi / lascivae similem ludere capreae" (*Odes* 3. 15. 11–12). At least on one purely physical level, the opposites are not opposites at all. In fact the first name we meet, Lycoris, "wolf-girl," is preparation enough for the appearance of *lupi* in the supposed *adunaton*. She is "outstanding" for something "thin." (This is itself a virtual oxymoron. A narrow brow was a sign of beauty in ancient Rome. Does it also follow that she was rather hirsute, as befits her nomenclature?) Cyrus does not return her love, but instead is magnetized by Pholoe who is *aspera*, "harsh." If we think back to the Cyrus who makes bold appearance in *Odes* 1. 17, we will be prepared for a certain discord between himself and his love. There Horace assures Tyndaris, "... nec metues protervum / suspecta Cyrum, ne male dispari / incontinentis iniciat manus..." (*Odes* 1. 17. 24–26). The name Cyrus may conjure up the spectacle of a barbarian potentate, but its meaning in Greek, "strength," "power," is more likely part of Horace's verbal intention. Cyrus pays no attention to Lycoris but instead veers, involuntarily or not, from the straight line (which in his case may have meant love for Lycoris and certainly implies a loss of inner firmness) toward "rough" Pholoe. And once more we have a secondary verbal play to abet the primary meaning. Pholoe was a mountain in Arcadia on the border of Elis, notorious in legend as a haunt of Centaurs. No wonder, then, that she is "rough." Apart from the erotic sense, the epithet is fully applicable to a wild piece of terrain (toward which Cyrus bends from his regular path) and especially to a mountain which harbors creatures which are a

153

combination of beast and man, half human and half animal. Such a forced conjunction of things innately antipathetic is exactly part of Venus' cruel joke.

Sooner shall female wild goats be joined with wolves than Pholoe will sin with a base adulterer ("quam turpi Pholoe peccet adultero"). Knowledge that such a yoking is in prospect makes the phrase instructive. We tend to connect the word *pecco* with some moral aberration (Cicero's definition goes: "peccare est tamquam transilire lineas"), but the literal meaning, "trip," "stumble," is also in the foreground here. Horace uses it of an old horse (*Epist.* 1. 1. 8–9): "'solve senescentem mature sanus equum, ne / peccet ad extremum ridendus et ilia ducat.'" For Pholoe to stumble, that is to be unable to continue on the road she intended, is by now nothing new in the poem. We can (and on one level we should) give a moralistic tone to *turpi* and *adultero*, appropriate companion words to *peccet.* *Turpis* could well mean "base" (looking to Cyrus' potential bad behavior) and *adulter* imply that he was leaving some more permanent liaison. But *turpis* could just as clearly refer to low birth or physical ugliness (a subject of consequence in the next and last stanza) while *peccare* and *adulter* are exampled in Horace simply as "love" and "lover." The former is the implication of the poet's words to the brother of Opuntian Megilla (*Odes* 1. 27. 16–17: "... ingenuoque semper / amore peccas"), and *adulter* has no deeper sense than *amour* at *Odes* 1. 36. 19: "... nec Damalis novo / divelletur adultero / lascivis hederis ambitiosior." Hence, looking at the phrase as a whole, if the *adunaton* does not happen, we are tempted to see everything in a moralistic way (Pholoe will never sin with a deceiving adulterer). If the *adunaton* does actually occur (as Venus' action portends), the words mean only that Pholoe is likely to "falter" with a new lover of less charm or lower social standing than herself, and this, Horace has already shown us, would be nothing out of the ordinary.

Horace himself is not immune to his own artistic reasoning (13–16):

> ipsum me melior cum peteret Venus
> grata detinuit compede Myrtale
> libertina, fretis acrior Hadriae
> curvantis Calabros sinus.

Who is this better Venus? Better than whom? The Venus who delights in uniting the unlikely? Better than Horace himself or his present love? Better in respect to attributes of mind or body or both? Better for reasons of personal congruity, or social standing, or monetary worth? This is an unusual Venus in any case because, true to a basic metaphor in the poem but strange for love, she was directing her course to him, seeking him out, acknowledging her involvement. Instead of this Venus, however, we have Myrtale, apparently a "worse" affection. But her name, because the myrtle associates her directly with the goddess of love, symbolizes a more likely Venus in terms of the poem's intent. She held him back (*detinuit*), meaning, we assume, that Horace, like Cyrus and Pholoe before him, was about to set out on his way with a love that was somehow more *à propos.* But life is not like this (at least for the poet as he writes). Horace is no different from his creations— and from his elegist friend.

He makes the point with a final series of oxymora. Myrtale, in terms of social standing, was a *libertina*, a freedwoman, once a slave. Yet, varying the metaphor of Venus, yoker of unequal beasts, she "enslaves" the poet with fetters. The bondage, however, unlike literal slavery, is *grata*, a pleasant loss of freedom, even though Myrtale herself is *acris*, sharp of character, galling like the abrasive wounds emotional fetters might cause. *Compes* is apt for another reason as well. Binding the feet will keep the poet (at least for the moment) from wandering afield to greener pastures. It puts him as a final example in the tradition of Cyrus who "veers" from one love to another, and of Pholoe who "stumbles" on her emotional way. And Horace is the most securely fastened!

The word *acrior* is itself used in an ambivalent manner. It is ordinarily applied to a lover's "grief," the bitter effects of an unhappy affair, or to the goddess who inflicts them. Like *aspera* Pholoe before her, Myrtale is becoming a type of Venus. But a sharp love is one which is in some sense unsatisfactory; we should expect someone *acris* to be brusque and uninvolved. Ironically, however, like the *melior* Venus of line 13, she too seeks out the poet. She holds and tames him. Moreover, if we may rely on the etymological connection between *fretum* and *ferveo-fervidus*, she goes about her work with "seething" passion. Bitter she may be on the one hand, but in reshaping the Horatian shore, she approaches with feeling. Hence the paradox of the word is the paradox of the person, a further, witty example of the union of oppositions within any given individual.

The final spectacle of Myrtale, the wild Adriatic *curvantis Calabros sinus*, serves as summary and confirmation. In this particular round of the eternal battle between land and water, specifically as Calabrian bays submit to Adriatic waves (and Horace to Myrtale), the latter has the upper hand. It bends what was once rigid. The metaphor is often applied to the taming of a slave. Virgil uses the adjective *curvus* to describe an elm, tamed to the shape of a plow (*Georg.* 1. 169–70): "continuo in silvis magna vi flexa domatur / in burim et curvi formam accipit ulmus aratri." Philosophically it could form part of a distinction between straight and crooked reasoning (*Epist.* 2. 2. 43–44): "adiecere bonae paulo plus artis Athenae, / scilicet ut vellem curvo dignoscere rectum . . ." In an amatory context, the verb *curvo* has the sense of "make yielding," that is, "move" in an emotional manner. All these intimations, amatory, social, philosophical (*formas atque animos* again), converge to suggest one general observation about life which Tibullus could now make, for education as well as consolation. Love joins inequities together, physical along with mental. This means that between two people, the set of oppositions could be quadripartite. Beyond this, life (and the poetry that tells us of it with honesty) is a series of unexpected tropes. In poetry the literal and figurative are in constant conjunction and competition. In life nothing, especially the singing of sad songs, mourning lost loves and time's passage, can or should be done continuously. The only paradigm for life is constant change in the emotional contours of existence. It is a principle that nothing, especially of an erotic nature, is "straight," normative, secure. The elegist who harps on sorrow in the search for time past misses the challenge of life's antinomies by not allowing himself to be "rounded," to bend with the moment's changing impetus even when this involves yielding to the sharp or turning toward the bitter, even when brighter prospects are apparently in store. The superficies of life is deceptive and things are not necessarily what they seem. External beauty may hide cruelty; ugliness may mask nobility. In the duel between appearance and reality, rarely are *forma* and *animus*, physical and spiritual, external and internal, appropriately mated in any given individual.

Elegy is by nature comparative ("now" is regularly seen in the prospect of "then") but in a melancholy tone which looks to the passage of time in contemplating the loss of youth and beauty and the crumbling of love's faith. Change is ever for the worse. Horace suggests to Tibullus something deeper and ultimately more reassuring, something closer to a lyric than an elegiac impulse (the literary pose is in part the personal stance as well). Become a lyricist, like Horace, and take love easy. Look to the future and, in the process, expect the unexpected, in the knowledge that the only true stability in love is variability. This is Horatian humor at its most humane, exemplifying the strength to see in perspective infinite variations of emotion and countless types of personality which arouse them. The final graceful touch is to avow wittily one's own participation in the same game.

II.

Albi, nostrorum sermonum candide iudex,
quid nunc te dicam facere in regione Pedana?
scribere quod Cassi Parmensis opuscula vincat
an tacitum silvas inter reptare salubris
curantem quidquid dignum sapiente bonoque   5
    est?
non tu corpus eras sine pectore: di tibi formam,
di tibi divitias dederunt artemque fruendi.
quid voveat dulci nutricula maius alumno,
qui sapere et fari possit quae sentiat et cui
gratia fama valetudo contingat abunde   10
et mundus victus non deficiente crumina?
inter spem curamque, timores inter et iras
omnem crede diem tibi diluxisse supremum:
grata superveniet, quae non sperabitur hora.
me pinguem et nitidum bene curata cute vises, 15
cum ridere voles, Epicuri de grege porcum.

Epistles 1. 4 also opens with immediate address to Tibullus. The recipient of Horace's letter is a *iudex*. In appraising his friend's *Sermones*, Tibullus displays the taste and standards necessary to judge quality. Punning lightly on his name (*nomen omen*), Horace sees him as *candidus*, clear in his thinking, forthright and honest in his opinions whether they be positive or negative. But immediately after the apos-

trophe, and with a certain irony, we begin with Horace to ponder the doings of his subject, who is himself an intellectual. He lives (at least as Horace chooses to envision him) in one of the more deserted areas of the Alban hills, amidst healthful woods. He is a theoretician and aesthetician, devoted to two endeavors, writing and thinking (each offering an aloof, abstract preoccupation). It makes little difference what the *opuscula* of Cassius of Parma were (since he was a lampooner of Octavian and the last surviving murderer of Julius Caesar, it is reasonable to see them as satiric in tone and conservative in attitude). To portray Tibullus as involved in two prime aspects of a *vita contemplativa*, removed from the bustle of Rome, is Horace's purpose.

He has received gifts in abundance (6–11). One of these gifts, the ability not only to think wisely but to express in words what he feels ("qui sapere et fari possit quae sentiat"), conspires with Tibullus' own thoughts as he paces his healthful forest, pondering what is worthy of a good and wise man (*sapiente bonoque*). The poet and his mental attitudes are at one with each other, in Horace's appreciation. We are reminded of the elder Cato's definition of an orator as *vir bonus dicendi peritus*. But Horace sees in his friend three attributes—first wisdom, then the strength to utilize it in one's moral conduct, and finally the ability to project it verbally. Horace is reminding (or enlightening) Tibullus that he is one of those rare individuals who could influence his moral stance through his intellectual virtues, who combines theory and practice, knowing and doing, in the conduct of his life. The past tenses may imply that he has lost the power so to evaluate himself in spite of such gifts. Perhaps he is in danger of losing the gifts themselves. At the very least the chronology, from the gods' gifts at birth (which are associated with the past) to a nurse's prayers for the newborn to the imminence of future death, is of some moment. But, in spite of divine benediction and nourishing affection, the recipient himself alone can have the wisdom truly to exploit his potential.

He has been showered with an amazing list of other blessings. He possesses riches in abundance which allow his manner of living to be generous. He has physical beauty (*formam*), taste (*artem fruendi*), style (*gratia*), reputation (*fama*), health (*valetudo*). Above all he combines within himself a *corpus* and *pectus* which complement rather than challenge each other. Exterior does not belie interior. Unlike the ill-mated lovers of *Odes* 1. 33—ill-mated within their individual selves as well as with each other—Tibullus has *forma* and *animus* which match, while each is also of the highest quality and the man himself is able to take advantage of a well-endowed social status.

This should mean that this cultured intellectual, a poet with the creative power to speculate and comment upon universals, should have balancing appreciative insights into human instincts and individual psychological needs, into the passions that inform any personality. Horace's next words, abruptly positive following three questions, suggest otherwise (12–14): "inter spem curamque, timores inter et iras / omnem crede diem tibi diluxisse supremum: / grata superveniet, quae non sperabitur hora." With mention of hope and sorrow, fear and anger, we enter deep into the world of the *psyche* itself. These are important polarities of human emotions, negative and positive, receptive and assertive, introvert and extrovert, which far transcend the easy distinctions between mind and body Horace has proposed earlier. Above all it is the idea of ultimate death which Horace commands his colleague to

contemplate. Horace is preaching a form of existentialism to his poet friend. The true philosopher (or poet, for that matter) is not the dedicated contemplative who watches the spectacle of life from a detached vantage. Rather he analyzes human passions in depth, recognizes the irrationality which permeates existence, and boldly faces the fact of death. Only by so doing can one live with fully heightened sensibilities, enjoying each moment for what emotional adventures, good or bad, it contains, yet always with the premonition that such moments will be cut off quickly and irrevocably. This is another paradox of the Horatian wit, that awareness of death magnifies appreciation of life's variety. And, ironically, true contemplation of the fact of mortality makes those who accept Horace's message less rather than more "serious," more capable of accepting life's foibles with benign sympathy and penetrating interest (which is one definition of a true sense of humor).

And this is to realize and accept lightly the same picture of emotional variety which *Odes* 1. 33 presents. If anything is orderly in life (besides the inevitability of death), it is a constant sense of rearrangement. Philosophers are always seeking patterns in and proposing rationales for existence (or, more negatively, wondering why they do not occur). Tibullus, according to Horace's portrait, is one such person, whether meditating in the security of Pedan woods or yielding to unceasing self-pity. In either case such metaphysical musings betray a certain lack of understanding of nature's changeability and suggest a withdrawal from life's rhythms which in a poet is not above suspicion. For Horace, the true "philosopher" espouses rather than bemoans life's variability, accepting the tension of opposites rather than imposing reasonable yet impersonal schemata on existence.

The Epistle, like the Ode, ends with Horace turning matters toward himself (15–16): "me pinguem et nitidum bene curata cute vises, / cum ridere voles, Epicuri de grege porcum." Tibullus, as we sense in both poems, needs to laugh, and Horace conjures up an appropriately humorous portrait of himself as an Epicurean pig—fat, sleek, well-manicured. Horace is no monotonous brooder on personal sufferings but a mere philosophical "animal," claiming attention only for virtues of the body, not the mind. He is someone, in other words, who, by realizing life's flexibility and deep seriousness (present emotion, ultimate death), cannot take himself too seriously at any given moment. To combine serious commitment with humorous detachment is the lesson Horace reads Tibullus in both poems.

The autobiographical equation of Horace with a pig is a purposive comic device splendidly worked out, with the dramatic power that only its position at the end can grant. For one thing it is quite unexpected. Horace lightens the melodrama of his best podium manner by turning things in on himself. Even if the pig is educated (he is an Epicurean, after all), he is still an animal, and any device that calls attention to the physical aspects of a person is comic. This is what writers on humor term "degradation" (though upgrading by comparison to objects of higher quality also has the same result): the visualizing of something in less dignified terms than it deserves. The mere shape, sounds, and propensities of a pig are diverting—the more so for having Horace, the philosopher-poet, the most exacting of craftsmen, metamorphose himself into this most indolent of animals. With engaging incongruity the deep thinker becomes a creature of the common herd, interested only in his skin and the fat it encloses. He is a superficial animal at best, but he has one fetching characteristic unknown to most pigs: he likes the way he looks, and he wants people to notice. He is, after all, *nitidus*, sleek to himself (pleasantly oily) and shiny to others, worthy of their attention as a special beast.

The metaphor turns our thoughts back for a moment into the body of the poem, to the spectacle of Tibullus "creeping silently among his healthy woods." The implicit comparison with a snake suggests someone who goes slowly along, perhaps in circles. There is one documented use of *repto* in connection with a person walking deep in contemplation, the spectacle Horace conjures up of Tibullus over in Pedum. But the implied comparison between Tibullus, the snake, and his porcine friend intimates something else. The snake is by nature a paradigm of the devious. It lurks hidden, out of sight of the world. This would mean, in a person, someone who is both unaccounting and unaccountable, even slightly sinister. When Cicero, at one of the saddest moments of his life, feels the need for complete escape from the world around him, he writes to Atticus from his property at Astura: "In hac solitudine careo omnium colloquio, cumque mane me in silvam abstrusi densam et asperam, non exeo inde ante vesperum. Secundum te nihil est mihi amicius solitudine" (*Att.* 12. 15). There is an irony, then, in Horace's application of the adjective *salubris* to Tibullus' woods. Perhaps for Tibullus they are in a certain way healthy, by offering an escape from Rome or, less productive, by fostering tendencies to evade reality already latent in the poet and visible to his acute correspondent. What Cicero finds *densam et asperam*, Tibullus finds, for different and (ironically) less healthy reasons, *salubris*.

The comic juxtaposition with the pig puts the matter lightly. In the darkness of his quiet woods, the escapist serpent Tibullus can creep along, "healthily" evading confrontation with life. The pig Horace revels in his shimmer. His shiny neatness is a joy to behold. He espouses, indeed craves, the glare of life which Tibullus shuns. The difference between the two should in itself be an object lesson to Tibullus on the multitude of diverse personal types which together form the relationships of this world. The funny vision of the philosopher-pig should bring the brooding elegist out of himself. But Horace makes a more subtle point which he hopes will not elude his friend, namely that in reality Tibullus, not Horace, is the comic character, in a double way. In the first place he is unsocial. In the second, as we learn from *Odes* 1. 33, he is rigid, unbending, unable, in Horace's view, either to look clearly at himself or examine dispassionately his relations with others. And both separatism and inelasticity rank high in Bergson's list of traits which lend themselves most easily to comic characterization. Horace's wisdom, therefore, proposes laughter as the best corrective for Tibullus' ailments in each poem. *Odes* 1. 33 takes subtle note that humor, not sadness, lies in the clash of opposites and in the idea of paradox. *Epistles* 1. 4 suggests that there is greater "health" to be found in realistic amusement at one's own foibles and acceptance of life's vividness than in escaping under some darkening shade. In both cases humor is the saving grace, one which Horace possessed in abundance.[1]

Brown University

1. I am grateful to Professors Katherine Geffcken and Kenneth Reckford for their comments.

Tibullus

Of the three surviving elegists of the Roman Augustan age, Tibullus is little read, less appreciated. Propertius fascinates by his intensity, his gnarled propulsion of idea which forces careful attention to the process as well as the wholeness of a poem. Ovid's facile warmth and smooth irony win ready admirers. With Tibullus praise was not always so faint. A younger contemporary of Virgil (he died the same year, 19 B. C.), he is mentioned twice with affectionate concern by Horace whereas Propertius receives but a passing jibe. Ovid in the *Amores* elegizes his death and on more than one subsequent occasion shows a preference for Tibullus, a judgment that Quintilian forthrightly echoes two generations later. Modern criticism, more patronizing than productive, lauds his ease and clarity of diction which serves, we are told, as suitable vehicle for a mind which delicately, if somewhat hazily, balances elegiac and pastoral subjects. But was this praiser of the past, sufferer of the moment, whose chief gods were Pax and Spes (a calm present, a stable future), as aloof from immediate concerns as he is usually envisioned? Would escape be such a necessary desire to one who had not felt, and therefore as a poet needed to expound, life's bitter side?

Though hatred of war and scorn for riches are two of his constant themes, Tibullus must have known the world well. He was a knight whose property, like that of so many others, suffered depredation during the continuous chaos of the preceding decades. He may well have taken part in the decisive battle of Actium (31 B. C.). He certainly was given military honors a few years thence, after campaigning in Aquitania with his patron Messalla Corvinus. Nevertheless, time and again his reaction as a poet, when faced with life's difficulties whether in love or war is to escape into a self-imagined and in part obviously self-deluding realm of fancy.

Yet his two books, containing a total of only sixteen elegies, were written while the *Aeneid* and Rome's most magnificent lyric poems, Horace's *Odes,* were being composed. Shy Virgil managed to recreate Rome's epic grandeur in a manner which brilliantly unifies national triumph and personal hurt, glory and horror. Horace, who sensed a sturdier past and acknowledged a corrupt present, especially in his extraordinary initial odes of Book III could reconcile political involvement and spiritual aloofness. Tibullus, who possibly saw more of activist Rome than either of his two colleagues, proposes the deepest withdrawal.

Horace echoes one aspect of Tibullus' poetic self-portrait. He represents him as a country dweller prone to quiet wanderings, a philosopher "caring for whatever is worthy of a wise and good man." (*Epis.* 1.4) Horace rightly shows him vacillating between hope and trial (*spem curamque*), fear and anger (*timores et iras*), and warns him (unnecessarily, as the elegies prove) of death. The abstracts Horace seizes upon are all grist for an elegist's mill. They may well point the way to a more sensitive reading of this equally Augustan poet. Suppressed fear of what? Discreet rage against whom?

There is also the problem of style. Conservative in thought and personality means also conservative in style, it is suggested. In both regards Tibullus is often said to follow the example of his mentor, Messalla, whom the elder Seneca called *exactissimi ingenii, Latini sermonis observator diligentissimus.* Tibullus, says Quintilian sententiously, is *tersus atque elegans,* concise in expression and careful in word choice. Herein lies another reason for Ovid's friendship. He would have sensed Tibullus, and then himself, in the mainstream of "exactness" in Latin as opposed, say, to the novelistic, emotional Propertius whose poetic predispositions (to mythology, for instance) distract and inhibit as much as they titillate and broaden. But poetry of retreat is not, at least here, poetry of unconcern, and exactness of diction in no sense betokens a simplicity, taken pejoratively, either of intellectual pursuits or their expression. "Simplicity" is as much a creative ruse as the most directly artful elaboration and ornateness.

We may draw a stylistic parallel in English letters with George Herbert. A bias toward the meditative and introspective often lays ready claim to a "plain" style. But the truly simple style, as in the case of Herbert, incorporates rather than rejects discordant elements, and wit, whatever form it takes and whatever the figures of speech toward which it most tends in any given writer, becomes an element of control instead of distraction.

Much the same may be said of the elegiac couplet, apparently straight forward, actually capable of the most intricate variations. A spreading hexameter first line (with, however, its usual, important caesural pause) leads to a more rhythmically confined pentameter. The tendency toward jingle in the latter, where an uncomplicated beat is immediately reiterated, makes it the easier to condense into the finality of epigram the hexameter's expansive idea. Yet, though initial statement is summarized and reviewed, the two lines are regularly in solution, developing and then resolving tensions through antitheses (contrasts) and balanced parallelisms. The "stiffness" (Pope's word renoted by Wimsatt) given to the English heroic couplet by rhyme is replaced in Latin by rhythm and deeper constrictions of meter. Still there is much in common, especially between the ironic Pope and the deceptively facile Tibullus. While rhythm and rhyme, by lending order and regularity, may outline and frame an abstraction, there are in each author constantly invigorating figures of speech, from the lightest pun to the darkest conceit, which enliven with alogicality.

Unlike the majority of his contemporary poets, Tibullus never talks directly about poetry, not even to establish himself in a tradition as foil for originality (on analogy with Propertius we might expect allusion to Gallus, say, or, more remotely, Callimachus). The poet's self-consciousness, assumed but unstated, manifests itself only in the power of his language. Assured awareness of the capabilities of his verse must be sought in his words themselves. Style as the method of controlling words dominates the self as well as its creations. In Tibullus' case the simple controls the complex, and the creation and utilization of such a means of communication is thus a careful moral act on the poet's part to both express and yet master a variety of tensions.

In the pages which follow I would like to illustrate this multifaceted relationship between man and style in Tibullus, first by a close examination of three couplets drawn randomly from the poems, secondly, with more general considerations on two elegies and on Tibullus' total *œuvre*. My goal is this: to offer brief illustration of how a human horizon, whose limitations are purposefully deceiving, is complemented by an intricate style with initially delusive ease — a poetics of action, in other words, under the guise of inaction. Simplicity of outlook and idea as a moral ideal may be mirrored in facility of expression. When, as here, the first is merely a veneer, the second may likewise hide subtleties of some consequence.

Let me offer as an initial example of Tibullus' splendid molding of the couplet's possibilities a moment where he is dealing with song itself (2.3.19-20):

> O quotiens ausae, caneret dum valle sub alta,
>   rumpere mugitu carmina docta boves.

> [Oh how often did the cattle dare, while he was singing within a deep vale, to shatter the learned songs with lowing.]

Tibullus is exclaiming on a sad occasion in Apollo's life when, in the forced guise of a rustic, his clever singing suffered the constant interruption of cattle lowing. The number of unfortunate occasions, the bovine daring, the location, which the hexameter outlines, are all explained in the pentameter. The challengers are cattle, their daring consists in "breaking up" wise verses with bellow. Yet the antithesis between *mugitu* and *carmina* (especially *docta*) is delineated in the structure of the couplet itself. Break in song is illustrated by break in style. The principal caesura comes after the first moment of daring, *ausae,* a word which does not receive its noun until the last word in the couplet: Apollo's song is disrupted by the pause in rhythm after *ausae,* whose sense is not completed until *boves.* There is also a necessary hesitation after *caneret,* the first mention of song itself. To turn to niceties of sound, the assonance of *valle alta,* a spot where echo would enhance music, is prefaced and broken by the monosyllables *dum* and *sub.* Their common vowel is "reechoed" in the brilliantly onomatopoetic phrase *rumpere mugitu* which begins the next line and forms, as such, the decisive moment of actual interruption.

For another example, by no means unique, of brilliant verbal usage drawn from a more amatory context we might turn to the opening of the fifth elegy of book 1. In four brisk couplets the poet first boasts of willing separation from his mistress Delia, then acknowledges lack of control, demands the torture of a slave and finally craves her mercy (1.5.7-8):

> Parce tamen, per te furtivi foedera lecti,
>> Per venerem quaeso compositumque caput.

> [Yet spare, I beg you, in the name of the stealthy agreements
> of the bed, in the name of our love and your wreathed head.]

The lofty tone (with its models in Greek epic and tragedy), the asyndeton, the displacement of *te* are all typical of an oath. This last detail is a compliment to Delia: the word *te* is not grammatically resolved until the appearance of *quaeso.* In the meantime we have had the iteration of *per* which, on its second occasion, is immediately followed by *venerem,* their love or Venus herself, appropriately ambiguous. The sequence leads from *foedera* (equally ambiguous and stressed through alliteration with *furtivi*), to bed (given the emphasis of a displaced epithet which takes us from abstract to concrete) to love to head. The latter is a common enough object in oaths and deserves its place of eminence, but it is the play on its accompanying participle, *compositum,* which most leavens legal dignity with the yeast of elegiac wit. The word means literally "ordered," "arranged" (of her hair or the position of her head near him). Yet it also connotes "agreed," "compacted," as if the *foedera* (with which *composita* would also be a commonplace) were centered specifically on her head. Finally *componere* is a technical term for the laying out of a corpse. The epithet thus anticipates the next five couplets which are devoted to a detailed exposure of various maneuvers by which Tibullus claims to have saved Delia from death during a past illness. And she is now called upon to spare him!

Tibullus can turn subtle verbal satire against those of whom he disapproves. Here is the first of three ways by which he sketches a *praedator,* a hunter after gain (and his girl) (2.3.41-42):

> Praedator cupit immensos obsidere campos,
> ut multa innumera iugera pascat ove.

> [The booty-hunter desires to possess measureless fields that he might feed numberless sheep on many an acre.]

The phraseology speaks with strength, but there are a series of acute verbal plays. *Obsidere* means "hold in one's possession," but the military technical term, "besiege," is also operative: the *praedator,* who might well acquire some of his lands by martial exploits, must still behave as if they were equivalent to a beleaguered town. The pentameter, which we would expect to say "that he might feed uncountable sheep on many an acre," — a vivid enough hyperbole — in reality conveys something more negative. The unusual transitive use of *pasco* (replacing the regular *depascere*) gives the statement a double-twist in meaning. The fields are being devastated, not nourished. Further, though the usage is common in Ovid, this is the first instance in Latin of *innumerus* with a singular noun which does not in itself denote number. But the poetic replacement of singular for plural has a particular irony in a context which characterizes other related objects as *immensos* and *multa.* How many acres, what measureless fields does a greedy owner need to foster one sheep, when even that one cannot be counted? This is witty "simplicity" at its most artful.

The imagination whose efforts such rhetorical skills enrich was possessed by one surpassing concern — the need to escape from the present, the notion that the dream of past or future is more satisfying than any other. Just as elegant simplicity in verbal choice and construction serves as superficies for considered stylistic complexity, Tibullus' search for an ordered life is illusory and self-hypnotic. It covers a basic challenge between life as it must be lived and life as a dream, between real and unreal, a challenge which is verbalized in many lesser tensions, between city and country, for example, or war and peace, turmoil and quiet, even noise and silence. This retreat from history and time passing (in spite of the enforced involvements detailed in two poems to be looked at below) takes immediate form in the stylized poses of elegy. Artistry in any case offers continuing ironic comfort to the fevered brow, spiritual regulation of psychical disorder. (And sometimes even stylistic devices, such as Tibullus' constant use of anaphora, have the quality of a mesmerizing litany.)

For Tibullus the elegist's sufferings, remote as they may seem, are relieved immediately by wine and magic, less tritely by adherence to other stabilities in the Roman world such as religious rite. Above all it was the land and its activities whose contemplation seems most to have taken Tibullus, on the one hand, out of the passing afflictions of an elegist, on the other away from the more realistic impositions of military involvements or moral decay in contemporary Roman life. For him the latter seems typified in the search, through war or otherwise, for gain and ambition's more superficial trappings. His first poem begins with the word *divitias,* riches amassed through martial exploits, which he denounces while yet hoping to retain his own still modest means. The countryside's seasonal demands, of labor and ceremony, abstract the poet from life's pressures and, especially if love smiles, absorb the urbane elegist's standard discontents into a georgic world's more fulfilling continuities.

We may illustrate in general terms the progress of typical Tibullan themes in two elegies each connected with a specific historical event — 1.7. a birthday hymn to Messalla closely connected with the celebration on September 25, 27 B. C., of his triumph over the Aquitanians, and 2.5. written for Messalla's son, Messalinus, on the occasion of his election to the *Quindecimviri sacris faciundis,* a board which presided over the reading of the Sibylline books.

First 1.7. Though his dislike of war is a sentiment which emerges frequently even in the most intimate of the elegies, Tibullus here takes a positive view of the military accomplishments of Messalla, scion of one of Rome's most prestigious families. A double element of ritual initiates the poem. Tibullus is singing of a day the fates foretold, perhaps even voicing their awesome words. He is also telling literally of a triumphal procession with the proud *triumphator* accepting the mob's devotion. It is an easy step to turn to the Gallic deeds themselves in which the poet boasts his participation. At line 13, with a vague *canam,* Tibullus orients his attention eastward without any mention of specific involvement on the part of either poet or patron. We hear of Cydnus and the source of its headwaters, Mt. Taurus which fosters Cilicia (back in space), of Astarte's Syrian doves and of Tyre, inventor of boats (back in time and still further in space). Finally we reach *fertilis Nilus,* nourishing even at the dry season, source unknown though Tibullus ponders its whereabouts. This leads to Osiris, the Egyptian equivalent of Dionysus, and to a detailed exposition of Osiris as "source" (we are dealing with time again, not place), the first to invent the plough. It is a simple step to viticulture and, still more specifically, to the making of wine and then its effects. Osiris may have invented ploughing but wine taught song and dispels care and suffering, for farmer and slave. Wine creates and wine comforts, two essentials for the elegiac poet.

The poem's supple way makes light of the artful, removing progress, spatial, temporal, intellectual, emotional, out of momentary Roman grandeur to the sources of water, wine and song. It is an easy return to the present festivities, to further praise of Messalla and his birthday spirit. One final accomplishment of Messalla is singled out at the end, his rebuilding of a stretch of the Via Latina between Rome and the Alban Hills. This is a subject of rejoicing, says Tibullus, for the man who has his ancestral Lar, his household gods, in the territory of Tusculum, or for the farmer returning home late from the city. Even here it is away from Rome, to a country home and to a farmer, whose troubles are lessened by Messalla's good works as well as by wine, that the poet's thoughts flee. From Roman triumph to public works separated by a detailed explication of the achievements of Osiris — Messalla would surely have recognized the compliment. But by stressing the farmer's trials at two crucial moments in the sweeping panorama of the actual and the timeless, Tibullus puts further emotional distance between himself and his practical Roman heritage to espouse instinctively humane poetic causes.

The amatory aspect of elegiac poetry is virtually absent from 1.7. In poem 2.5, Tibullus' longest and in some respects finest poem, it is carefully meshed with the broader sweep of the main theme which is really the foundation of Rome. Immediately at the start we are drawn out of life into the formalism of ritual. *Phoebe, fave*: the opening line (briskly dactylic) commands Apollo's favor for his new priest while attracting the reader also into his Palatine temple. Apollo is to come crowned with a victor's laurels, the same Apollo who sang Jupiter's praises at the expulsion of Saturn (i. e. the Titans). Neither Tibullus nor Horace, who makes a similar reference in the "Roman" odes, need express more explicitly the latent allusion to the battle of Actium where Octavian under the protection of Apollo (so Virgil would have it) defeated Antony and brought to an end the lengthy era of civil war.

In any case war is to give way to music and Apollo to resume a creative career as god of sound, song and prophecy (*carmina* in every sense). It is he who prompts the Sibyl (11-18) and she in turn foretells the glorious future to Aeneas at a time when the city of Rome was quite different from its present state (23-38). This last vignette is a model of intensity through limitation. Romulus "shaped" an *urbs*. In pre-Romulean days no constricting walls (*moenia*) existed to put unnatural social and military boundaries between houses, fields and people. There is a direct physical and implicit moral contrast with the present. The Palatine hill, home of Augustus and site of Apollo's glorious new temple, then offered grassy fodder for cattle. The *Iovis arx*, the later fortress of the Capitoline on which stood the temple of Iuppiter Optimus Maximus, held only humble huts.

Thoughts of the Palatine blend with references to Pales and Pan, to a shepherd's pipe offered in his honor and then to a careful description of the decreasing segments of the pipe itself. Critics grumble at the apparently unnecessary detail, but we are once again back into an ideal center in nature and of song, away from it all, intellectual concern limited to tree and pipe. To confirm the point, Tibullus concludes his picture of early Rome with a brief sketch of a country swain and his girl making love on the Velabrum, then open water but later to become the commercial center of Rome. The erotic element is rarely missing in Tibullus' idyl. In the days before civilization and history came to Rome, commerce consisted in a lover's gifts of cheese and lambs.

Suddenly (at line 39), *via* the now direct words of the Sibyl, we are back to Aeneas, brother of *Amor* (to make the transition easy) and a catalogue of his adventures culminating in the death of Turnus. This leads to the founding of Alba Longa and the liaison of Ilia and Mars, whence sprang Romulus (51-54). I see Ilia, says the Sibyl,

> Concubitusque tuos furtim vittasque iacentes
> Et cupidi ad ripas arma relicta dei.

[and your stealthy meetings and fillets left lying and the weapons of the eager god abandoned on the river bank.]

Once more the subjective element reappears as war is put aside, this time for love. The Sibyl then concludes her survey with a brief mention of Rome's sweeping future dominion. Tibullus gradually edges back toward the present through prophecy, to the prodigies which accompanied the death of Julius Caesar — comets, eclipses, speaking cattle and the like (71-78). Quickly he announces *haec fuerant olim* (79), this happened once upon a time. Here also there is no mention of Actium, crucial though the event was for resolving the tensions surrounding Caesar's murder, as if the poet found too close a look at the event abhorrent. But what follows, again with a brisk transition, is a special portrait of a countryside at peace, complete with the elegist's stock complaints of his unhappiness. We are a long way now from Apollo's Palatine. It is a country feast which is being celebrated, the Palilia on April 21, traditional foundation day of Rome. The description centers expectedly on the idea of fertility and generation. The landscape is to be renewed by ritual and ceremony.

Then back to Messalinus and a last prayer for their approval of his song to Apollo and his sister Diana, whose importance for Rome's renewal Horace would soon exploit in the *Carmen Saeculare*.

In sum, Tibullus, working from the stance of ritual and through the medium of prophecy, blends history with unreality as an idealized Roman past confronts moments of challenge which in turn form a backdrop for present festivity and the special happiness of Messalinus. The allusions to violence in Roman history — to Aeneas killing Turnus, to Romulus' need for *moenia* — find mythological analogy in Jupiter's defeat of the Titans and anticipate Octavian's defeat of Antony which Tibullus does not mention directly. But Apollo, now mild (*mitis*), again renews a career of song just as Mars must needs doff his armor for his dalliance with Ilia prior to the birth of Romulus and the initial foundation of Rome. There is no grand merger of public and private, commitment as well as retreat, such as Virgil in the *Aeneid* and Horace in his more political odes propose. No spirited announcement, such as the fourth *eclogue* trumpets, that pastoral woods and consular power will combine in a reborn golden age. Tibullus' is a quieter notion which would have been no less appealing then, I venture, than it is now. His idealistic vision is merely a moment when ritual, song, love and the rural daily round unite in an uninterrupted continuum, disdainful of history's doings. Such a dream may at first seem to have little to teach us. But the very fact that non-involvement was considered so important by one who had himself received military honors surely means that it must have tempted many at a particularly complex moment in the development of Roman civilization.

One of the striking points about Tibullus is his lack of need to demonstrate about his art. He does not feel the regular Roman poetic compulsion to worry out loud about tradition and design, to verbalize art's dialogue with itself. He is fascinated with words, not about them. A first impression of Tibullus' ease soon gives way before amazement at a verbal intricacy which in turn complements a more richly varied interior landscape than he is usually allowed. In poem 1.3, for instance, the poet makes the most of his position on Phaeacia, poised between life and death, Rome and Elysium, to treat himself as Ulysses and Delia as the faithful Penelope, with exquisite irony in each instance. Poem 1.4 is one of the most amusing parodies of didactic poetry in any language, twisting the words of such hardy and serious poets as Ennius to less elevated concerns. Poem 1.5, which beings with a simile comparing the poet to a spinning top and ends with reflections on Fortune's turning wheel and love's fickleness, is a brilliant example of poetry's control over the uncontrollable.

The refined delicacy of expression is true, the simplicity deceives. Tibullus, more understated than the Mannerist Propertius, is also a poet of the processes of emotion, and the processes are reflected in the many levels of verbal usage and the intricacies of couplet construction. External perfection masks a myriad of tensions. Tibullus' reading of human experience preaches detachment, but detachment, even when it takes its most vivid form as retreat into humility and into severe living from life's ambitious doings, has involvement as its touchstone. (Sypher speaks of the struggle in Herbert "between the poet's calm, assured piety and his agitated awareness of things in the world"). Baroque Ovid playfully decorates a stringent order. Tibullus, his Renaissance predecessor and idol, clothes inner struggles with an exquisite and exacting dress. In both cases style and content complement each other, but Tibullus may well be the more difficult poet who, by seeming on one level to retreat from reality as well as linguistic complexity, has ultimately more to tell us about a poet's commitment to confronting and expressing life's deepest necessities.

Propertius

Propertius 1. 22: A Poet's Self-Definition

by Michael C. J. Putnam

The three poems which close the first book of elegies, the *Monobiblos*, of Sextus Propertius, stand apart from their predecessors. The first of these, poem 20, appears distinct from the rest because it deals at far greater length than any before it with a seemingly impersonal, and therefore atypical, theme drawn from myth. Then the last two poems, the companion pieces 21 and 22, differ from others in the book not only because of their brevity (each is only ten lines long) but because in them Propertius puts aside amatory subjects for two sharp glances at war and its effects on people and landscape. It is to the second of these brief elegies, the poet's σφραγίς, the "seal" for his collection, that this paper is dedicated. Unlike other contemporary examples of this type of ending, Propertius' *envoi* neither contains any proud boast of his craftsmanship nor lays claim to immortality through a monument of words. His is a poem more concerned with universal mortality than with his own eternity, more about the negative price of power than a poet's upward strivings. I will first analyze this brief finale critically in detail, then relate it to the poet's literary inheritance, and in conclusion seek to place it in the context of Propertius' total *œuvre* [1].

---

[1] Poem 1. 22 has been well treated in two recent articles, my indebtedness to which will be apparent: J. T. Davis, ' Propertius 1. 21-22 ', *Class. Journ.* 66, 1971, 209-13 and W. R. Nethercut, ' The ΣΦΡΑΓΙΣ of the Monobiblos ', *Am. Journ. Philol.* 92, 1971, 464-72. Professor Davis gives a full bibliography of work on poem 1. 22 centered especially on its relationship to 1. 21, a much discussed subject which the present paper will not treat. (See n. 16 below. For a sympathetic treatment of the matter see K. Quinn ' Practical Criticism: A Reading of Propertius 1. 21 and Catullus 17 ', *Greece and Rome* n. s. 16, 1969, 19-29, esp. 22 f.). Progression of thought in 1, 22 has been briefly but acutely handled by A. K. Lake (Michels), ' A Note on Propertius 1. 22 ', *Class. Philol.* 35, 1940, 297-300.

Qualis et unde genus, qui sint mihi, Tulle, Penates,
    quaeris pro nostra semper amicitia.
si Perusina tibi patriae sunt nota sepulcra,
    Italiae duris funera temporibus,
cum Romana suos egit discordia civis,
    (sic mihi praecipue, pulvis Etrusca, dolor,
tu proiecta mei perpessa es membra propinqui,
    tu nullo miseri contegis ossa solo),
proxima supposito contingens Umbria campo
    me genuit terris fertilis uberibus.

The first word of the poem, *qualis*, suggests the richness of what is to follow by already expanding upon any literal, traditional "Who am I?"[2]. The poem is to pass beyond a mere autobiographical, egocentric precis and will deal briskly yet profoundly not so much with Propertius' past seen from the present as with his inner self pondered in relation to this inheritance. He announces native quality, viewed and clarified by experience. This distancing, in space as well as time, is already achieved and counterpoised with the here and now in the first line. The implicit "I" of the speaker, near to hand and addressing Tullus, leads to *unde*, a word capable of bridging the temporal and topographical gap between the imagined moment of composition and some different place and remoter time of birth.

As often, while Propertius establishes the setting of a poem, there is a direct confrontation between the first and second per-

---

[2] On the uniqueness of *qualis* see Nethercut, *op. cit. supra*, 465, n. 4 and *ibid.*, ' Propertius 3. 11 ', *Trans. and Proceed. Am. Phil. Assoc.* 102, 1971, 409-43, esp. 412, n. 3. We may compare Pallas' question to Aeneas, newly arrived at Pallanteum (*Aen.* 8. 114):

qui genus? unde domo? pacemne huc fertis an arma?

An answer to the last phrase would go some way toward an explanation of *qualis*.

Wilamowitz, *Sappho und Simonides*, Berlin, 1913, 296 ff., has an important discussion of the Greek inheritance behind Propertius' use of the σφραγίς and on the merger of elegy and epigram (see also notes 20 and 24 below). Cf. also the comments of A. S. F. Gow, *Theocritus*, Cambridge, 1952, II, 549-51) on [Theocritus] *epig.* 27 and of Gow and D. Page (*The Greek Anthology: Hellenistic Epigrams*, Cambridge, 1965, II, 678-9) on Meleager's "seal" poem (*A. P.* 12, 257 = Gow-Page 129).

sons, between the author and his addressee. Here the latter would have appeared especially prominent, we may hazard, to a Roman ear through the first syllable of Tullus' name. Yet the confrontation remains notable in this instance because the " I " surrounds the " you ". *Tulle* stands apart from both *mihi* and *Penates*, the poet's present and past fused around his questioner.

These two different worlds, which *unde* mediates with the help of the verb " to be " implied throughout, take us to the source of Propertius' being. Past and present are most directly juxtaposed with each other through the proper names *Tulle* and *Penates*. But the structure of the line suggests progression as well as distinction. *Qualis* (*sim*), initial and most generic, implies the linking of then and now through the character of the poet's " I " (*mihi*). *Unde genus* (*sit*) makes the continuity explicit by pointing to the origin of the poet's race. Finally *qui sint Penates*, more direct still though more remote in time, suggests an actual place as well as family and inherited traits. But here continuity and differentiation merge: the house of origin is not the present orientation of the protagonists. Though the all - embracing personality of the poet - speaker (*qualis*) links present to past, there is an equally provocative division between Propertius' present, Tullus' present (Rome?) and the poet's past, as the tripartite row *mihi, Tulle, Penates* points up. Depending on his readers to sense the power of this summary structure, Propertius will proceed further to characterize himself to Tullus through concise yet expansive notions of unity, diversity and a proximity which will regularly illuminate both.

Form counterpoints this intense, volatile fabric of words. Critics have long since proposed a parallel between the details of Tullus' interrogation and Penelope's questioning of the disguised Odysseus (*Od.* 19. 105):

> ... τίς πόθεν εἰς ἀνδρῶν; πόθι τοι πόλις ἠδὲ τοκῆες;

But any suggestion that Propertius might be casting himself in the role of an itinerant Homeric hero returned home is contradicted by the influence of another, equally pertinent poetic inheritance — the sepulchral inscription[3]. Propertius imputes to himself the

---

[3] Though Wilamowitz (*op. cit.* 296) saw the inscriptional character of the poem's

epigrammatic words on a burial monument. He becomes for a moment the stone appealing to the passer-by who is expected to pause and take quick note of death's finality in carved words. For all the verbal mobility that the pattern of the opening line suggests with its triadic and developing interplay of person, place and time, Propertius now forces his reader to reverse such stylistic impetus and see him as no epic wanderer but mortally stable with Tullus now the figurative questioner who comes and goes. This new relationship, and especially the rigorously concise poetic form it takes, will extend significantly into what follows.

Another word in the first distich, *semper*, is as striking as *qualis*, for reasons of placement as well as sense. It would at first seem logical structurally, and easeful in terms of meaning, to associate *semper* intimately with *amicitia*. Whatever possibility of tension or difference between Tullus and Propertius might have appeared implicit by the verbal arrangement of *mihi, Tulle, Penates* would now seem counteracted by the implications of *nostra amicitia*, " I " and " you " seen reconciled in " our " friendship, the unity of a personal relationship and one of some lengthy, continuous endurance [4]. But the phrase can also be considered broken

---

final distich, only recently has the influence of the sepulchral epigram on the poem as a whole been detailed. See now especially E. Schulz-Vanheyden, *Properz und das griechische Epigramm*, diss. Münster, 1969 (Münster, 1970), 30-41, a most valuable discussion of the effect of Hellenistic epigram on the form of 1. 22. On the *quaeris* formula, besides a comprehensive excursus by Schulz-Vanheyden (*op. cit.* 42-48), see O. Weinrich, *Die Distichen des Catull*, Tübingen, 1926, 99 f. (n. 14) and especially the pioneering study of W. Abel, *Die Anredeformen bei den römischen Elegikern*, diss. Berlin, 1930, Charlottenburg, 1930, 31 ff.

[4] This is the only use of *amicitia* in Propertius (he never defines *amor* through *amicitia* as, for instance, does Catullus at 109. 6). Other words in the poem also stand apart from ordinary Propertian usage. *Contego* and *uber* (as an adjective) are unique; *discordia* appears elsewhere only at 1. 2. 17; *fertilis* is used only here in the first three books.

The power of the word *semper* is drastically diminished if we seek to ally it more closely with *amicitia* than *quaeris*, as, for instance, do D. R. Shackleton Bailey, *Propertiana*, Cambridge, 1956, 60, and W. A. Camps, *Propertius: Elegies, Book 1*, Cambridge, 1961, 100. In fact its divisive value parallels the force of *Tulle* in the preceding line.

For an equally hyperbolic version of a similar sentiment cf. Hor. *epode* 14. 5 (... ' candide Maecenas, occidis saepe rogando ' ...) with commentators thereto.

by *semper* which then rivets attention for its position in the line, remote from the verb grammar makes it primarily modify and between two words whose syntactical as well as formal unity is of some importance [5]. We must therefore argue its meaning. The recurrent relationship which the *Monobiblos* seems to show between Propertius and Tullus becomes qualified by a recurrent question [6]. Why must Tullus constantly interrogate Propertius about his background before the poet can give, or his friend receive, an answer? (And in any case — to gauge only the literal intent of the words — how deep could be the bond between two people or how long a period of time could they have been associated together when one does not know even the birthplace of the other?) If the poem were meant to give information, to serve the regular autobiographical purpose of a σφραγίς, there would be no need for the rigamarole of friend and question. By their presence the poet demands of the reader that he pursue further the implications of *semper* and ask what time scheme may be implied by this " always ".

The last work in a book of poems need not be the most recently composed nor, in this case at least, is a specific date determinable by or even necessary for the critic. Nevertheless from the concluding position of 1. 22 it is reasonable to assume a late date for composition. And if for other reasons the book's publication is to be placed around the year 29, then slightly more than ten years have passed from the events which Propertius is about to describe in the " sealing " of his first book. We must also note a point to be more thoroughly investigated later, that the initial poem in the book is addressed, as are two subsequent

---

[5] For a careful, enlightening analysis of word placement in the pentameter of the elegiac couplet see J. Van Sickle, ' About Form and Feeling in Catullus 65 ', *Trans. ana Proceed. Am. Philol. Assoc.* 99, 1968, 487-508, esp. 487ff.

[6] It is no wonder that the sound of *qualis* (and *qui*) is reechoed in *quaeris*. We should also ask the meaning of *pro*, likewise a word of some importance to the sense — and sound — of the poem as it unfolds. Does it mean " because of ", looking to the past, or " on behalf of ", something preserved for the future? In this acute vignette of diverse time schemes both are implied. It is in its more tangible, local sense of " near " that the word will recur throughout the poem with growing excitement from *proiecta* to *propinqui* to *proxima* where at last spiritual (and linguistic) worlds of some consequence abut each other.

7

elegies, presumably to the same Tullus [7]. That a cycle of poems of great variety and imaginative depth intervenes between the first and last pieces adds immeasurable weight to this lapse of time, to this apparently uninterrupted interrogation of friend by friend. The reason for this lengthy pause we may only guess. Would Tullus for whatever motive fail to understand either the meaning (or effect) of his question or the potency of the answer he would receive? Was the subject one creating such bitterness and sorrow for Propertius that only time's extensive purgation would permit him to respond? The rhetoric has prepared us grandly for the climactic answer when it finally comes. In every sense this is to be a poem of finalities.

The answer comes indirectly and gains its impetus and power through this very indirection. It begins with a supposition in the form of a conditional clause which continues, expanding yet still unresolved, for six lines until it receives a main clause only in the last distich. The final two lines do in fact fulfill Tullus' request. In terms of both plot and verbal structure the first and last distichs form a unity. *Umbria me genuit* completes the cycle that had begun with *qualis et unde genus* [8]. Nothing in between literally touches on the poet's birth. Yet the intervening three couplets, the tense distance separating inquiry and answer, are the indispensable core without which the poem loses all point. From nearness we seem to move into a distance of place and time past. Yet — and here is a basic creative paradox of the poem — the distance is defined by a still more palpable nearness. It is a nearness centered not on birth but on death.

The lines begin by once more engaging Tullus with an object, or better objects, that he should have known. He cannot truly understand Propertius (*qualis*) unless he comprehends their impli-

---

[7] On the unity of the *Monobiblos* through apostrophe of Tullus see Wilamowitz, *op. cit.* 296; G. Pasquali, *Orazio lirico*, Firenze, 1920, 319; Schulz-Vanheyden, *op. cit.* 35, n. 32.

[8] Schulz-Vanheyden (*op. cit.* 36) notes the epigrammatic " framing " of the poem and the resulting contrast with the central section: " Gerade in der Spannung zwischen Inhalt und elegischen Stil des Mittelteils auf der einen und der epigrammatischen Anlage auf der anderen Seite liegt der Reiz und das Besondere dieses Gedichts ". Unfortunately he does not trace further the vital relationship between this juxtaposition of styles and the poem's content.

cations. As so often in this poem, Propertius uses sound patterns to great effect, here coaxing his reader into a belief that the transition from the opening lines was smooth and that there is unity of sense between the first two distichs. We notice, for instance, how the key word *semper* reverberates in the initial words (*si Perusina*) and, together with its preceding adjective *nostra*, suffers echoing metamorphosis into *nota sepulcra* and then *funera temporibus*. But contrary to expectation such resonances force the enormous difference between the opening couplets into the open. The change in proper names from *Tulle* to *Italiae funera* and from *Penates* to *Perusina sepulcra* (though they, too, deliberately echo each other in sound patterns) gives a further indication of this disparity. The narrow world of a poet's heritage and personal relationships is expanded to embrace a far greater dimension of existence seen through events whose meaning Tullus might only dimly measure. Such is the implication of *si*.

One person's race, household gods, friendship expand into the whole land of Italy — a fatherland for many more than two interlocutors, a spatial breadth far wider than whatever place we are for the instant to imagine the poet and his questioner (again, Rome itself?). Paradoxically, what this *patria Italia* is known for, what Tullus should know it for but apparently does not (it is, after all, a past which he could measure), is not a single poet's birth but a plurality of deaths — hard times defined by *sepulcra* and *funera*, tombs and burials. By this juxtaposition the subtler refinement of *semper* in *sepulcra* and *temporibus* becomes sharply ironic, and one's private moments of questioning are answered, through bold involution, by the public occasions, also repeated and more seriously importunate, of death. Such matters of mortality begin now to distinguish a man (*qualis* once more) who places greater stress on the universality of suffering than on an acquaintance's trite, simplistic inquiries. With *tibi* Tullus sinks beneath the surface of the poem, not even to reappear when his question is at last answered.

In this superbly paced, gradually climactic period, specificity and generality vie with each other, their parts taken by geographical nearness and a poet's personal grief on the one hand — the suffering caused by a neighbor's or relative's long past death brought piercingly present again — and the seemingly abstract, topographically more remote Roman dissension on the other. The interplay is remarkable structurally. Since the *bellum Perusinum* was only one brief moment in the civil wars, *Perusina sepulcra* is expanded both spatially and temporally first by mention of the unnamed *patria*, then through the more broadly sweeping *Italiae duris funera temporibus* [9]. Place and time are deliberately interlocked in a lasting series of disasters. Even the highly tangible *sepulcra* pass into the more ambiguous *funera* — burials, yes, but also the more general, death-dealing troubles that accompanied a whole period of civil strife.

The climax here is, of course, *Romana discordia*. *Discordia* remains more abstract than *sepulcra* and *funera*, and Rome, in one sense, still more remote and all-embracing. It is not simply another way of naming *patria* and *Italia* but incorporates both labels as a result of its paramount influence over the whole peninsula after the social wars. Yet Rome and her citizens, *Romana suos ... discordia civis* (this time abstract and concrete intertwine to categorize cause and effect with precision), are as limited and specific as they are broad and expansive. From one point of view Rome, the *communis patria* of Italy, envelopes its citizens all together: the poet's past and present, Tullus, Etruria and, soon, Umbria. From another aspect Rome is a much more confined entity, another city like Perusia, some distance further south within the Italian peninsula. This city, though it happens to be omnipotent, presents as calculated a political (and verbal) challenge to Perusia as Tullus does to the poet's " I " and as ultimately Umbria will offer to Etruria. It is this more exclusive, narrow view of *Romana discordia* which combines with the distancing inherent in *suos civis* — " her " citizens but not at the moment the contemplative poet — to make facile the transition back to *pulvis Etrusca* (of which Perusia is only a part) and to Propertius' private, personal grief (*mihi* replacing *suos*). Thus, to dilate on an earlier point, within the greater unities with which we are dealing — the poem as a whole and a central *patria* encompassing the lives and deaths of its *dramatis personae* — we must take constant

---

[9] *Patriae* is of course ambiguous: " graves of our countrymen " (Camps) or, more exact and perhaps more justly negative, " tombs of our fatherland ", the implication being that the *patria* is in some sense buried as well.

note of the welter of antagonisms forced regularly into juxta-position. In this respect too style and form will be seen to en-hance and reflect content.

The disappearance of Tullus and the rise of Rome as a prin-cipal theme of the poem brings one of these challenges imme-diately to the surface. It is not personal *amicitia* but political *discordia*, not Tullus' present friendship but Rome's past dishar-mony that is crucial to the poem as it develops [10]. After the specificity of Perusine tombs the poet's synopsis first broadens into an overview of Italy and its troubled moments, then concentrates once more, now on Rome, the apparent purveyor of tombs to the whole land as a result of its own inner fury. Again place and time are intimately, devastatingly interrelated. The deeper impli-cation of the conditional clause which opens the second distich is that, whatever Tullus' ignorance, Propertius himself has appre-hended fully and explicitly the tragedy of Perusia. From Rome, however, and the abstraction that guided her citizens the poet maintains his aloofness, as we have seen, by means of the pro-nominal adjective *suos*. If he had led us to expect protestations of patriotism at the time of writing they are now disavowed. He may thereby reveal another elusive level of intent. If Tullus is so close to Propertius and yet ignorant of the poet's birthplace, so dependent on the closeness of *amicitia* though unaware of the extensive effects of Roman *discordia*, where must we center his life? Perhaps if he pleads ignorance of the feelings which sur-round *mihi/nostra* and *tibi* he does in truth know Rome and its citizenry, vividly but myopically.

Line 6 heightens the effect of distance by forcing the reader's attention again away from the source of *discordia* and back to Etruria. Though the pentameter line, as customary, enhances the hexameter and rounds off the distich, it here has its own special intensity. The first person appears again for the first time since the opening couplet. Yet the echo of *sint mihi* in *sic mihi* marks challenge as much as complement. At the start of the second half of the poem, in a place of particular prominence where a

---

[10] Remoteness back in time is stressed by the phrase *duris temporibus*, gram-matically taken up and enhanced by a temporal clause with *cum* which need have no causal implications.

balancing echo of the initial line is not unexpected, the poet changes venue and addressee. We have seen the gradual movement from *amicitia* into *discordia* as a private relationship is glossed by public tombs. Here, with the replacement of *Tulle* by *pulvis Etrusca*, intimacy and immediacy once more gain control, and though the object of address is now impersonal, the cry of grief on the other hand springs from the most deeply personal reaction[11]. *Amicitia* is left far behind but a new, more bitter definition of proximity takes its place.

The reason for the apostrophe to *pulvis Etrusca* is not yet clear. Before reading further we might be right to think of *pulvis* as a field of battle or the " dust " that rises as the conflict at Perusia runs its course. But battling leads to death, and Propertius' grief centers on his *propinquus* who lay unburied in the aftermath of war, covered by no soil not even the traditional, symbolic handful of dust[12].

In terms of linguistic usage these three lines are closely knit together as befits their parenthetical nature. The use of labials, for instance, prominent throughout the poem, reaches a climax in lines 6 and 7 where the fivefold iteration of " p " explodes with the poet's anguish, forcing utterance outward with a violence that vocally mimes the physical event it describes. (The sounds fade away, though scarcely forgotten, into the echoes of line 9). Sibilants, too, hiss a bitterness (in anger? scorn? even sadness?) that culminates in the resonance of *perpessa es* in *miseri contegis ossa*

---

[11] It is not without point that certain sound values in the name Tullus seem to recur throughout the poem — in *sepulcra, pulvis*, the anaphora of *tu, nullo solo* (and perhaps even *fertilis*). *Tullus* and *Umbria fertilis* frame the poem and, however individually diverse, both serve to enhance the force of the central section by the contrast.

[12] For *pulvis* as the dust of war, re. Hor. *c.* 2. 1. 22; on the " ashes ", indistinct remnants of the dead, Hor. *c.* 4. 7. 16. On *pulvis* and the sepulchral epigram see the remarks of Abel, *op. cit.* 33; Schulz-Vanheyden, *op. cit.* 24.

There is a patent difference between Propertius' apostrophe and the occasional references in the Greek Anthology to the soil in which a corpse has already been buried. For examples of the latter see *A. P.* 7. 222. 7 (= Philodemus 26 in *The Greek Anthology: The Garland of Philip*, ed. A. S. F. Gow and D. Page, Cambridge, 1968), and *A. P.* 7. 315. 1 (= Zenodotus 3 in *The Greek Anthology: Hellenistic Epigrams*, ed. Gow and Page).

solo [13]. The chief unifying factor, however, is the reiteration of the apostrophic *pulvis* in *tu ... tu*, as litany appears to merge into reproach. We have come a long way from the initial address to Tullus, voiced at last and with reluctance, to this insistent cry.

It is a climax in another way as well. The preceding lines had taken note of the effects of *discordia* which might have been known to Tullus (*tibi*), namely *sepulcra* and *funera*. Again using two neuter plural nouns, *membra* and *ossa*, Propertius now takes direct personal note (*mihi*) of the special reasons for his own suffering. These sets of lines, 3-4 and 7-8, form carefully balanced pairs [14]. Yet as the generic focusses on the particular, one irony stands out. In spite of a poet's momentary personification, the dust and soil of Etruria, on which the limbs and bones lie, is inanimate and cannot respond (the way the poet can, even reluc-

---

[13] How deliberately pronounced, in fact, is the sigmatism of 1. 22 can be judged by comparison of the statistics collected by P. A. Cronin (' Sigmatism in Tibullus and Propertius ', *Class. Quart.* n. s. 20, 1970, 174-80). In the various tables which he provides, Propertius has consistently more asigmatic verses than any major Latin author. He also uses sibilants less frequently than any classical Latin poet except Lucretius and Virgil. The average number of *s*'s per one hundred lines in Propertius' first book is 268. This would mean that 1. 22, with 34 instances of *s*, contains nearly 25% above the norm. Whatever the emotional effect Propertius anticipated, it was clearly intentional.

[14] The carefully proportioned verbal and linear balances throughout the poem could be analyzed at far greater length. For example, the first and last lines stand apart from the rest (and therefore complement and lead inexorably toward each other) for their lack of any noun or adjective ending in *a*. Lines 3-4 and 7-8 have plural, neuter nouns; lines 2-5 and 6-9 are patterned around singular, feminine nouns (or in the case of line 6, an adjective). The first two of these sets, lines 3-4 and 7-8, parallel each other as paired groups. The second sets, lines 2-5 and 6-9, are objectively unified by the echo of *tibi* in the anaphora of *tu* and by the common concern with *sepulcra*. They challenge each other and propose some of the poem's ironies (friendship explained by hatred, birth by death, fertility through barrenness). We are led by chiasmus into and out of a series of paradoxes: an aspect of *discordia* is made explicit in *pulvis Etrusca* while *Umbria* helps return our thoughts to *amicitia*. The first set deals in abstractions which seem impersonal (the replacement of *amicitia* by *discordia* results in *sepulcra* and *funera*). The poetic journey from Etruscan dust to fertile Umbria is a meditation on the intimacies the poet relates (literally) by words — of place to place person to person, and (most impressive) person to place and place to person. The proximate and correlative, again paradoxically, are defined not by synonyms but by tense antonyms, basic to human life.

tantly, to Tullus). It can neither offer tangible comfort nor fulfill somehow the most minimally physical role as a symbolic agent of burial. It too purveys an abstract, *dolor*, a highly personal version of the results of *discordia* but abstract nevertheless.

Worse still it displays the evidence for what to antiquity would have been an especially barbarous act, to throw out a corpse (beyond the city walls?) and allow it to lie uninterred [15]. The results of Perusia's siege have sufficient documentation to illustrate dramatically how Italy at large was hurt by Roman strife, as Octavian ousts Lucius Antonius from the city and further avenges his adoptive father's murder [16]. The revelation is atrocious enough that no names need be mentioned to enhance the details. Even the *propinquus* (and his poet, for that matter) remains anonymous at this moment when individuality is submerged and human lives become easy victims of external forces which they are powerless to control. In this there is a purposeful break on Propertius' part from the egocentric tradition of the σφραγίς. To make this break even more forceful he puts his emphasis especially on place, not nomenclature, on the relationship of one man with another

---

[15] For documentation on the severity of such a punishment (for such it probably was), cf. R. M. Ogilvie (*A Commentary on Livy Books* 1-5, Oxford, 1965) on Livy 1, 49, 1; G. W. Mooney (ed., C. Suetoni Tranquilli *De Vita Caesarum*, London, 1930) on Suet. *Vesp.* 2. 3; E. Koestermann (ed., Cornelius Tacitus *Annalen*, Heidelberg, 1965) on Tac. *Ann.* 6. 29. 1.

On *proiecta* in relation to an unburied corpse, see commentators on Cic. *Div.* 1. 56; Lucr. 3. 882 and 6. 1155.

For a detailed discussion drawn from funeral monuments of the concern in antiquity for a final resting place and of the need for burial see R. Lattimore, *Themes in Greek and Roman Epitaphs* (*Illinois Studies in Language and Literature* 28, 1942, 1-354) esp. 199 ff., 220 ff. (on the burial of one's kindred as a matter of duty).

[16] The circumstances surrounding the siege of Perusia are detailed by R. Syme, *The Roman Revolution*, Oxford, 1939, 210 ff., and, with particular reference to Propertius 1. 22, by A. L. Frothingham, 'Propertius and the Arae Perusinae', *Class. Philol.* 4, 1909, 345-52. Syme discusses 1. 22 (*op. cit.* 466) but does not deal with the question of the unburied corpse. It is of course possible that the victim may have succumbed as a result of the infamous *Perusina fames* (Luc. *Phar.* 1. 41) which preceded Lucius Antonius' capitulation. Others see the *propinquus* as that Gallus of the preceding poem who escaped the swords of Caesar and died by unknown hands. Defenders of this interpretation must argue, somewhat implausibly, that *dispersa ossa* (1. 21. 9) must be equivalent to *proiecta membra* (1. 22. 7). The literal occasion is of only slight importance to the poet's point.

(*propinquitas*) and of both men to a certain spot. This narrowing of intent occurs not only as generalized sufferings become particularized in the poet's own hurt, when a cousin's death reveals Propertius' private grief among universal *sepulcra* and *funera* — a grief that remains still forcefully present (*contegis*). It also arises from the terrifying fact that ordinarily people who were killed in such a sad affair, or in any war not only civil, were given decent funeral rites and burial. Propertius' own personal trial, that in the wake of Roman *discordia* his relative was treated as so much carrion, would have been the more grievous.

We might envision this climactic moment as a crucial (but not, as we shall see, final) pointing of emotion through relationship. The poem began with *amicitia*, the relationship of Propertius and Tullus who asks for a poet's self-definition through ancestry and place. It expanded to treat *discordia* and the effect of place on place, of Rome on all of Italy including Etruria and particularly Perusia. Both aspects merge in the unburied figure of the *propinquus* whose very title plays on his "closeness" to Propertius' feelings. As cousin he replaces Tullus on one level, just as *pulvis Etrusca* does on another. He answers a friend's interrogation concerning the poet's ancestral *genus* by exemplifying the tangibility of sorrow. He also bears the most familiar possible relationship to place, a corpse lying on open ground, intimate with dust. Verbally (the sentiments are treated chiastically) *pulvis* and *solo*, dirt and soil, "embrace" limbs and bones (*membra, ossa*). Yet this physical proximity, ironically in view of the poet's special emotional nearness, is actually the least fulfilled in the poem. Bones rest on soil, but the soil, instead of surrounding the corpse and completing its role as burial agent, merely purveys an intangible grief while the body itself is a source only of sadness.

It would seem at first almost a relief from this intense display of feeling when Propertius finally does answer Tullus' initial inquiry. As we have seen, the first and last couplets balance each other. *Me genuit* is the result of *unde genus* ... We would expect, therefore — what symmetry encourages — that Propertius' *amicitia* with Tullus would find its counter-balance in some positive relationship with his native province, *Umbria fertilis*. But the connection of the poet's response to Tullus with the preceding address to Etruria is too vivid and intimate to allow for easy generaliza-

189

tions. We have seen the importance of the tripartite interplay of difference among Propertius, Tullus and the *propinquus*, the first inquiring of birth, the other an immediate example of death. The poet now turns specifically to the subject of place and casts an ironic look on the dramatic association (again threefold, as so often in Propertius) of the writer's immediate, perhaps hypothetical stance, initially with Etruria and then with Umbria.

At first it is the differences between the latter which stand out, as we move away from the harsh occasions of war's ravages to the setting of birth. The ashen dust of Etruria stands in contrast to Umbrian fertility, a land distinguished for tombs and the bones of an unburied corpse contrasts with enriching earths. (There is even the suggestion of a play on the word *uber*, the fruitful land that suckles poets. What nourishment will dusty Etruria gain from limbs and bones?) [17]. But it is this very disparity that puts into bold relief the actual fact of contiguity. As in the case of the first two couplets, we have been led to expect union, not friction, by the enmeshed patterns of sound. *Contegis* heralds *contingens* while *proiecta* and *propinqui* anticipate *proxima*, perhaps the most sharply focussed word in the poem. *Membra* allows easy transition to *uberibus* by means of *Umbria*. Though all appearances be to the contrary, can what is nearest to something else, touching it in fact, remain unaffected by this neighbor's plight? The force of the poem's emotion and the intricacy of its verbal patterning assure the reader that it cannot.

If the sound of lines 7-8 strongly anticipates what follows, the interlocked word order of line 9 in itself allows us to affirm the same notion, that the contiguity of Etruria and Umbria is of far greater moment than their superficial disparity. Synchysis rightly stresses *contingens* but grammatical and verbal ambiguity throws equal emphasis on *supposito campo*, a phrase which should be read closely with both *proxima* and *contingens* [18]. Propertius

---

[17] The plural *terris* stands in open contrast to the previous dust and bones. This sudden broadening out into spaces of earth, types of land, makes it more apparent how impossible it remains to diffuse intense emotion connected with a particular spot by either change of place or enlarged perspective.

[18] Here I cannot agree with either Camps (*op. cit.* n. 4 *supra*) or Rothstein (*Sextus Propertius: Elegien* [repr., Zürich, 1966]), *ad loc.*, that *supposito campo* is

plays with particular dexterity on *supposito*. Given its context the word is not allowed to retain a purely geographical reference (" placed underneath ", i. e. in the plain below Perusia) but gains the added metaphors of " enslaved " and, more pointed still, " buried " [19]. A land subjected to Rome and known for its tombs is indeed a buried land.

The final couplet carries through brilliantly the insistent, paradoxical theme of the poem, that life's essential facts and occurrences must be interpreted through antonyms and synonyms, opposites and unities which interact and somet;mes merge. Propertius studies the notion of nearness — of friend to friend, cousin to cousin, province to province, of corpse to earth. Above all the poet contemplates his own problematical relationships to place and time, as he counterpoises private *amicitia* with general *discordia*, universal and individual suffering with his own birth. It could be said that the notion of *patria*, birthplace of countless diverse selves, is an overriding unity. But under this rubric lurks one irresistible negative force which rules the poem — the pernicious might of Rome in the face of which the strengthening comforts of individual allegiances vanish. The last couplet by itself can be seen as a reply to *unde genus*, Umbria defined by proximity to Etruria. The total poem, however, answers *qualis*, that tense bundle of thoughts and reactions which forms the personality of a poet. This deeper self-definition responds to a hatred of the martial character of Rome which abides with the poet throughout his career. I will return to this theme later. Here it is best to turn for a moment to one more type of relationship significant for a reading of 1. 22, that of the poet and his tradition.

The poem, as noted earlier, is technically a σφραγίς, the author's personal " seal ", detailing something of his life [20]. Since this life

---

an instrumental ablative describing the plain of Umbria underneath Asisium where the poet was born. Butler and Barber (*The Elegies of Propertius*, Oxford, 1933) *ad loc.*, give a correct defense of the grammar (" The dative, *supposito campo*, may equally well depend on *proxima* or *contingens*, either of which may serve to emphasize the other.") but they offer no further critical reasoning for their explanation.

[19] Both voice and tense, passive and past, add to this ominous ambiguity.

[20] For detailed literature on the tradition of the σφραγίς see W. Kranz " Sphragis: Ichform und Namenssiegel als Eingangs- und Schlussmotiv antiker Dichtung ", *Rh. Mus.* 104, 1961, 3-46, 97-124; Schulz-Vanheyden *op. cit.* 37, n. 39.

is defined by another's death, the poem melts easily into another branch of the epigrammatic tradition and also takes on peculiarities of an epitaph, as we have seen. The interplay is brilliant and neither aspect gains the upper hand. As a σφραγίς, the poem should boast of vital accomplishments whereas notions of mortality prevail. It also necessarily remains incomplete as an epitaph. Propertius writes of himself (the epitaph, like the σφραγίς, is regularly in the first person) but concerning himself he can tell explicitly only about birth — *Umbria me genuit.* This is one logical way for an epitaph to begin [21]. The *monobiblos* is sealed finished by a fresh start, but it is the start of a funerary inscription, intimating a life's work partly over.

The poem is a cycle with the beginning carefully balancing the end and a contrasting climax intervening. In another sense the poem is also psychologically unified in an extraordinary manner. The very incompleteness of the end, a life only begun, forces the reader's thoughts back into the central section to emphasize its bitterness afresh. There death is in control, but once again a deliberate, terrifying sense of incompleteness remains [22]. In the

---

[21] One thinks, for instance, of the epitaph of Virgil which appears in the *Vitae* quoted by Donatus and Philargyrius:

> Mantua me genuit, Calabri rapuere, tenet nunc
> Parthenope; cecini pascua rura duces.

If not written by Virgil or immediately upon his death, it is at least as early as the second century. See A. S. Pease, ' Mantua me genuit ', *Class. Philol.* 35, 1940, 180-82.

Such information need not appear at the outset of a poem. See for instance the " epitaph " of Nossis (*A. P.* 7. 718 = Nossis 11 in *The Greek Anthology: Hellenistic Epigrams*, ed. Gow and Page), a poem in which Wilamowitz saw elements also of an *envoi* (*op. cit.* 299). Though the combination would at first seem to parallel that of Propertius 1. 22, Nossis in fact identifies herself by a bow to Sappho. For Propertius, poetic forebears are of less importance as an aid to self-characterization than the present substance of Italy.

For further parallels between *Umbria me genuit* and the *carmina epigraphica*, see Abel *op. cit.* 33, who cites *CE* 479, 1175.

[22] The incompleteness of this " elegiac " central section of the poem was long ago noted by F. Leo (' Das Schlussgedicht des ersten Buches des Properz ' *Nachr. Goett. Ges.* 1898, h. 4, 473: " Wenn aber hier Elegie ist, so ist es der Anfang einer Elegie, und das Ende fehlt "). By viewing the poem itself as a fragment, however, Leo failed to see not only the importance of this stylistic " incompleteness " as complement of subject matter but also the paradox of its incorporation within a most exacting, balanced poetic frame.

case of the poet's *propinquus* life does not lead easily to death. He lies unburied without a funeral monument. His life cannot be properly finalized, nor his interment concluded, by the ritual of engraved words which would allow him to continue thereafter to speak out his deeds to the passerby. There is only the perversion of an epitaph in the poet's third person description of the event in its stark sorrow. Two lyric impulses compete to form a whole as individual projection of self, one instant of time (Tullus' question answered at last, Propertius finally born) is glossed by more universal concerns which it frames. Epic's temporal thrust, the tragic operations of Rome, seem controlled, even avoided by the lyric comedy of a poet suckled by the productive earth.

Yet prospects of neat symmetry are glossed by inconclusion. Two lives are never finished, poetic forms, however classic, never fulfilled. History and the lyric poems that brood in depth on its moments present only a continuing series of destructive incursions which force the reader to view with irony the friendships of men and the fertility of provinces which struggle vainly to circumscribe a world of death.

There is another irony in the choice of form. Elegy was often thought of by Propertius' contemporaries as an essentially melancholy genre (Horace speaks of *miserabilis elegos*, Ovid of *flebilis elegeia*) [23]. Propertius would have sensed, too, that subjective love elegy, of which he was a master, sprang initially from the expansion and elaboration of an erotic epigram's intensity. In two ways then poem 1. 22 returns to origins. The birth of the poet finds its literary parallel in the birth of a form, as epigram and as lament. Because of the heritage of lament, the reader will not be surprised by a paradox that the poem's ultimate position suggests. What initiates also concludes. One's birth already anticipates one's dying. Propertius builds his *envoi* around such inevitability, for while composing a final epigraph to his first book — partially rounded with careful balance — and telling of a cousin's death he has embarked with appropriate incompleteness on his own epitaph as well. A poet's accomplishment is formally sealed in startling directness by a rich glance at mortality.

---

[23] Hor. *c.* 1. 33. 3 (of Tibullus' life); Ovid. *Am.* 3. 9. 3 (of Tibullus' death).

It is logical for a number of reasons to expect and find a deep influence on this poem by Catullus who profoundly affected the development of elegy out of epigram [24]. Clearly Propertius felt the power of Catullus' verses on his dead brother. Poem 101, for instance, an elegy also in five distichs, gains much of its strength from the same chiastic impulse, leading to a core of intense emotion which is calmed by a carefully balanced structure of return to the opening sentiments. The poem is a *munus*, at once a gift and act of love, a funeral offering and a valedictory epigraph.

Still closer, however, is an only scarcely longer segment of poem 68 which details the burial of Catullus' brother at Troy (68. 87-100):

> nam tum Helenae raptu primores Argivorum
>   coeperat ad sese Troia ciere viros,
> Troia (nefas!) commune sepulcrum Asiae Europaeque,
>   Troia virum et virtutum omnium acerba cinis,
> quaene etiam nostro letum miserabile fratri
>   attulit. ei misero frater adempte mihi,
> ei misero fratri iucundum lumen ademptum,
>   tecum una tota est nostra sepulta domus,
> omnia tecum una perierunt gaudia nostra,
>   quae tuus in vita dulcis alebat amor.
> quem nunc tam longe non inter nota sepulcra
>   nec prope cognatos compositum cineres,
> sed Troia obscena, Troia infelice sepultum
>   detinet extremo terra aliena solo.

This poem is one of the most important in the Catullan corpus for those seeking in his writings the origins of subjective erotic

---

[24] It is clearly important to limit the influence of neither tradition in a reading of 1. 22. For a summary of debate on the matter in German scholarship see E. Reitzenstein, ' Wirklichkeitsbild und Gefühlsentwicklung bei Properz ', *Philologus*, Supplementband 29, 1936, esp. ch. 1, "Epigramm oder Elegie?" (pp. 12 ff. deal with Propertius 1. 22). For detailed discussions of the background of Latin love elegy see A. A. Day, *The Origins of Latin Love-Elegy*, Oxford, 1938, and G. Luck, *The Latin Love Elegy*, London, 1969, esp. ch. 2 and 3.

elegy [25]. Here too chiasmus is a crucial device of style, serving through pyramidal structuring to focus attention on this very passage and indeed on the center of the apostrophe itself. A list of parallels between the two poems will plot at once Propertius' debt and his originality. Catullus is mourning a brother, Propertius a cousin. The setting is in one instance Italy, narrowed to Etruria and Perusia, in the other Troy, battleground of Europe and Asia. Grief naturally enough permeates each set of verses. His brother's death is a *letum miserabile* (91) for Catullus while he himself also deserves the pity (*misero mihi*, 92) that Propertius in turn reserves for his kinsman (*miseri*, 9) [26]. But it is over the common question of burial that Propertius scores his special points.

First there is the element of distance. Propertius posits his tombs in his Italian fatherland where they should be known to all (*nota sepulcra*, 3). Catullus must look to a remoter spot where no such kindred sepulchres exist (*non nota sepulcra*, 97) and no ashes of relatives are nearby (98) [27]. Yet for all the remoteness involved, Catullus' brother has at least been placed in a tomb (*compositum*, 98) while Propertius' relative lies thrown out on the ground (*proiecta membra*, 7) [28]. He was entombed in a land far removed (*extremo solo*, 100), in earth belonging to people not his own (*terra aliena*). To a civilized person, however, this treatment would seem far preferable to receiving no covering of soil (*nullo solo*, 8), even if the event occurred nearer to hand and even if his

---

[25] The influence of Catullus 68 on Prop. 1. 22 is also noted by Schulz-Vanheyden, *op. cit.* 35.

On the structure of Catullus 68 see Day (*op. cit.* above n. 24), 108 ff.; on its symbolic aspects see J. P. Elder, ' Notes on Some Conscious and Subconscious Elements in Catullus' Poetry ', *Harv. Stud. Class. Philol.* 60, 1951, 101-36, esp. 126 ff.

[26] There are other possible, minor parallels. For instance, the address to *frater* and *lumen* in lines 92-93, followed in successive lines by *tecum* repeated, may anticipate *pulvis Etrusca* and the reiteration of *tu*.

[27] There is a special richness to the word *nota* — " known " and, more pertinently, " belonging to relatives ". Through one word Propertius elicits both Tullus' ignorance and his own deep concern. On one level Tullus, who is only an *amicus*, need not realize the full implications to Propertius. His implicit indifference to Rome's deadly influence is reason enough for worry.

[28] Rothstein (*op. cit.* n. 10 above) points out the distinction in his comment *ad loc.*

poet cousin can boast with a sharp irony we have analyzed that he was born nearby in lands rich and productive (*terris uberibus*, 10). In Propertius' case literal proximity, whether through geography or kinship, sets off still further the intellectual horror of an event which in one sense surpasses Catullus' own grief, though for him a brother is involved as well as a far greater intervening distance.

In one other way Propertius gains a cogency through irony that the more immediately explicit Catullus lacks. Propertius still possesses Penates, household gods who can be named and, in spite of a kinsman's brutal death, nourish a poet in fertile Umbria[29]. Catullus' whole house, on the other hand, is " buried " (*sepulta domus*, 94). Yet when we turn back to the middle section of Propertius' poem we are forced to see a relative's corpse as symbol for a still more wretched catastrophe — a fatherland, victimized by strife, that no longer can play its creative paternal role over a terrain celebrated for death. Family disaster is emblematic of a larger cataclysm of which it is only a small part.

This larger area of concern — the effect of Rome on the people and places it dominated — became increasingly important to Propertius as his career progressed. Catullus' allusions to Rome as a political entity are rare if forceful. Rather here, as so often, it is Virgil who has the most profound influence on contemporary and later letters. His poetry, especially the extraordinary first *eclogue*, is the other great imaginative force exerted on Propertius' σφραγίς. Once again, to look only at its opening lines, chiasmus is an essential figure of speech, illustrating through grammar two diverse yet juxtaposed worlds (*eclogue* 1. 1-5):

---

[29] The etymology of *Penates* from *penus* helps lead directly into the sense of the final lines. In the meantime the private, sequestered world of natal divinities and a friend's questions has yielded to a public disaster made explicit by *Perusina sepulcra*. (Once more sound abets meaning as the verb of the indirect question, *sint*, leads by another brilliant transfer, to *sunt*, the beginning of the direct answer). It is a mark of Propertius' character in this poem to define his true worth (*qualis*) not by the intimacies of an elegist's notoriously centripetal existence but by a broad reaction to the effects of Rome's unrest.

For the Penates in Propertius as symbol for a stability which contrasts strongly with negative sides of activist Rome (in this instance exemplified in the acquisition of wealth through commerce) cf. 3. 7. 33 and 45.

Tityre, tu patulae recubans sub tegmine fagi
silvestrem tenui Musam meditaris avena;
nos patriae finis et dulcia linquimus arva.
nos patriam fugimus; tu, Tityre, lentus in umbra
formosam resonare doces Amaryllida silvas.

In this dialogue concerning ways of existence, Meliboeus, whose words these are, observes Tityrus, pastoral poet and lover, at ease under a beech's spreading protection while the speaker is suffering exile from his country-side. Anaphora serves to mark the word *patria* in Virgil's third and fourth lines as centrality does in the third verse of Propertius [30]. The explicit evidence of trouble within the fatherland is different in each instance. Meliboeus tells of turmoil omnipresent in the land, of his own sickness and sad withdrawal from this world of song, of misfortune in the flocks. Propertius takes note of harsh times, tombs and unburied corpses — expulsion of another sort. Yet in both cases civil *discordia* is the cause, afflicting for Virgil many *miseri* (72), for Propertius specifically his *propinqui miseri* [31].

In each poem, too, the might of Rome is preeminently felt. Propertius speaks out bluntly: the destructive strife is indeed *Romana*. Virgil is less extreme, more subtle. *Discordia* is mentioned late in the poem (71), far separated from earlier references to Rome with which it has no explicit connection. Propertius' formulation demands direct topographical reference and relies on the immediate challenges of friendship and hate, fertility and dust, life and death. Virgil's dialectic is more philosophical, reality playing but one part in a very intellectual design. Nevertheless

---

[30] The iteration of *patria* in lines 3 and 4 lends special force to *patrios fines* in 67.

[31] Since the phrase *discordia civis* appears at the end of an hexameter line in each poem, it is hard to dismiss the direct influence of Virgil. Rothstein (*op. cit.* above n. 10, *ad loc.*) notes the parallel and Nethercut ('The ΣΦΡΑΓΙΣ of the Monobiblos', 466 f.) comments in greater detail. There are possibly other, more tenuous verbal links between the poems (*flumina nota*, *ecl.* 1. 51, *nota sepulcra*, 1. 22. 3; *longo post tempore*, *ecl.* 1. 67, *duris temporibus*, 1. 22. 4). Certainly the shift in subject between lines 18 and 19 of *eclogue* 1 is as striking as that in 1. 22 between lines 2 and 3. In each case Rome is about to be introduced.

8

for each poet the proximity and clash between two antagonistic spheres of existence project a series of binary oppositions which are resolved only in irony — Umbria is prosperous and Tityrus survives in his idyll to offer rest and nourishment to the departing Meliboeus! We never lose sight either of the literal fact of contiguity or of its spiritual implications. Fertile Umbria neighbors (*contingens*) a buried land. Meliboeus observes that evil contacts (*mala contagia*: *eclogue* 1. 50) with an adjacent flock will not affect Tityrus' sanctuary. Though the reader is allowed to suspect that Meliboeus means his own diseased goats, he knows full well (what need not be stated directly) that such " illness " is merely the factual manifestation of " disease " which from his point of view has stricken Rome and through her the world under her sway.

At first we might believe that for reasons of their apparent happiness Propertius and Tityrus are spiritual kindred. Tityrus makes a happy journey to the city of Rome and its young god, and returns home not only unscathed but with the continuity of his existence assured. His creative vocation is strengthened and a blissful context guaranteed for the continuation of his intellectual idyl. We must beware, however, when dealing with Propertius of falling into the same trap which has caught critics of Virgil: Tityrus must be Virgil, expressing his gratitude to young Octavian for mending his fortunes and securing his poetic future. On the contrary Virgil, one need scarcely now say, is the creator of the whole, viewing from a distance this many-layered fabric intertwining happiness and suffering, poetry and politics, that he has spun out. The chief difference between the two poems is in degree, not kind. As befits the highly personal form in which he writes, Propertius is egocentric, an author forthrightly and intensely involved with his material. It is easy, and initially correct, to see Propertius (and his geographic surrogate, Umbria) as equivalent to Virgil's Tityrus while troubled Etruria is the counterpart of Meliboeus. Yet Propertius too is the unifying mind behind the whole poem, as touched by grief over his cousin's death as the necessarily less explicit Virgil is by the plight of Meliboeus. By the time we reach the end of each poem we are forced to treat both Umbrian richness and Tityran idealism with a certain irony. Both are illusive and remote, perhaps visionary, perhaps sham, depending on how the reader reacts to the context in which they are set [32].

Propertius, as we have seen, sets up another contrast which evokes a still more expressive parallelism with Virgil, namely the contrast between *Tulle* and *pulvis Etrusca*, the two vocatives each introducing a half of the poem. It is easy enough to see in the image of Etruscan dust and a kinsman's bones a more extreme version of Meliboeus' plight which, through sickness and exile, only hints at death in and of landscape. To analyze the negative intensity of Propertius' present feelings about Tullus, and offer reasons why he occupies a similar position in Propertius' thinking to that of Tityrus for Virgil in *eclogue* 1, we must turn back into the body of the *monobiblos*. If for no other fact than that he appears in its first and last poems Tullus is a unifying figure in the book [33]. But his appearances in poems 6 and 14 add further force to a characterization which makes all the more weighty the apostrophe in the book's finale.

The first poem gives no explicit evidence why Tullus is addressed but it is easy to view him simply as a foil — one out of many whose happier lot contrasts with the poet's. The only time Tullus' name is mentioned (line 9) is at the critical moment when Propertius announces that his love is not the ordinary kind in which a suitor's efforts finally prevail (the myth of Milanion details the opposite of his own situation). His mistress is moved neither by prayers nor by good deeds. From this moment on Tullus is absorbed into a more general " you " divided into three categories each carefully distinct from the poet. The first are magicians who might alter Cynthia's mood by witchcraft. The second are friends who propose more practical advice, this time for the poet's own cure. Finally those happy in love are offered grim warning

---

[32] Both Catullus and Virgil, it should be noted, make a distinction between private and public parallel to that which is so significant in Propertius 1. 22. In Catullus Troy's general disaster contrasts with the poet's special, personal grief. Meliboeus speaks for many victims of civil conflicts; Tityrus, one suspects, is more nearly unique in his restored idyl.

[33] For other plausible links between the first and last poems of the *monobiblos* see Davis (*op. cit.* above n. 1), 213; Nethercut, ' The ΣΦΡΑΓΙΣ of the Monobiblos ', 465.

to be steadfast in fidelity. We may cautiously judge that Tullus knows little of love's trials, certainly not those which Propertius must grievously endure [34].

Poem 6 confirms this portrait of someone disinterested in affairs of the heart and at the same time adds another whole dimension (1. 6. 19-22):

> tu patrui meritas conare anteire securis,
>   et vetera oblitis iura refer sociis.
> nam tua non aetas umquam cessavit amori,
>   semper et armatae cura fuit patriae; ...

Tullus is a soldier and politician (it is tempting to assume with most critics that the uncle in question is L. Volcacius Tullus, consul in 33 B. C. and proconsul of Asia for 30-29). His continuing " love " is for his fatherland under arms, a troublesome affection for Propertius if we may rely on the reference to *patria* at 1. 22. 3 (the only other use in book 1). By contrast with the slothful singer of love's " battles ", Tullus is interested in real

---

[34] The fact that both poems are addressed to Tullus is only one of many reasons to connect 1. 1 and 1. 22. Cynthia's absence from the final poem of what at first would seem to be a cycle dedicated to her (" Cynthia prima ...") only suggests the more that the poems are partially foils for each other. Each, for instance, is concerned with *dolor*, but from the self-oriented sorrow of the lovesick poet (*miserum me*) in one we turn in the other to his projection of grief onto a corpse deserving of pity (*propinqui ... miseri*). Instead of Propertius " touched " by lust (bowed down by the constraining feet of *amor*) we find fertility bordering death and a land subdued.

For these and other reasons I cannot subscribe to a trend in recent Propertian scholarship that divines stringent, symmetrical balances in the structure of the *monobiblos*, especially in its first nineteen poems. See, in particular, O. Skutsch, ' The Structure of the Propertian Monobiblos ', *Class. Philol.* 58, 1963, 238-39; B. Otis, ' Propertius ' Single Book ', *Harv. Stud. Class. Philol.* 70, 1965, 1-44, esp. 7 ff.; E. Courtney, ' The Structure of Propertius Book I and some Textual Consequences ', *Phoenix* 22, 1968, 250-58. It is hard, for instance, to understand the designation of the first nineteen elegies as " the Monobiblos in the strict sense " (Otis, p. 7) when the last three poems extend so carefully the theme of immediate and final separation which permeates the other elegies. Moreover the actual (or even intimated) presence of Cynthia is not a common unifying factor in poems 1 through 19. She need have no connection with poem 16, for example.

militia and its concomitant attributes (*securis* [35], *laus, arma*) all of which enforce rights (*iura*) and maintain imperial might (*imperium*, 34). He is also by the necessity of his profession involved in regular travel impossible for a poet unwilling to offend love. Travel has several sides. It could allow a scholar to investigate learned Athens (*doctas cognoscere Athenas*, 13) or a tourist to behold the hoary riches of Asia (*Asiae veteres cernere divitias*, 14) [36]. This latter activity is also connected with Tullus' present occupation, as the beginning of Propertius' final address suggests (31-2):

> at tu seu mollis qua tendit Ionia, seu qua
> Lydia Pactoli tingit arata liquor ...

Tullus, off vying with his uncle in the application of Roman might to Asia, would well know that he was performing his duties in a land tinged richly with gold.

Propertius adumbrates an intimacy between war and wealth which he makes boldly patent on other occasions. The opening of elegy 3. 12 will serve as an example:

> Postume, plorantem potuisti linquere Gallam,
>   miles et Augusti fortia signa sequi?
> tantine ulla fuit spoliati gloria Parthi,
>   ne faceres Galla multa rogante tua?

To some eyes the standards of Augustus offer occasion for pillage as well as renown. The reader has been prepared for such slightly veiled sharpness by the opening of 3. 4:

> Arma deus Caesar dites meditatur ad Indos
>   et freta gemmiferi findere classe maris.
> magna, viri, merces: parat ultima terra triumphos;
>   Tigris et Euphrates sub tua iura fluent; ...[37]

---

[35] For Propertius on the power of *secures*, see 3. 9. 23 (and the comments of Nethercut, *op. cit.* above n. 2, pp. 411-12, n. 2).

[36] This is in part the subject of poem 3. 22 where Tullus (presumably the same Tullus) reappears for the last time in Propertius.

[37] The juxtaposition of poem 3. 5 is all the more telling. It begins:

> Pacis amor deus est, pacem veneramur amantes:
>   sat mihi cum domina proelia dura mea.

Elsewhere he can speak out specifically and generally against the new non-Romulus on the Palatine (2. 16. 19-20) —

> atque utinam Romae nemo esset dives, et ipse
> straminea posset dux habitare casa! —

or against Roman luxury (3. 13. 59-60):

> proloquar: — atque utinam patriae sim verus haruspex! —
> frangitur ipsa suis Roma superba bonis.

These are common enough themes in Augustan poetry (though rarely expressed with such vehemence) and, to be sure, they lie ahead in Propertius' poetic future. But the close reader of poem 1. 6 will not be surprised to find that in the next elegy addressed to Tullus, 1. 14, riches have replaced arms as the main topic. Tullus is now in Rome, drinking wine of Lesbos from a goblet made by Mentor, watching ships pass from the Tiber shore while orchards, grand as forests on the Caucasus, loom behind. The actual apostrophe to Tullus is delayed until the poem has nearly run its course, giving special emphasis to the concluding notion that love is an omnipotent leveller. Love breaks the strength of heroes (and of the warrior Tullus?). It fearlessly crosses thresholds of onyx and mounts couches gaudily dyed. Propertius has already told us (with a knowing nod back to 6. 32) that an abstraction, happy love, surpasses the (golden) streams of the Pactolus (*Pactoli liquores*, 11). He concludes by claiming to despise the wealth of Alcinous (assuming, of course, that love remains happy). A prominent part of this wealth, we recall from Homer, was in orchards, themselves a notable aspect of Tullus' setting.

The portrayal of Tullus that leads up to poem 22 is as unsympathetic for Propertius as it probably was typical of the average upper-class Roman [38]. Propertius proves continually aware of the

---

[38] Tullus is only one exemplar of the shallow ambitions Propertius sensed in contemporary society. To see this side of his genius is one of Ezra Pound's great insights in *Homage to Sextus Propertius*. As J. P. Sullivan has written, " This stress on the relation of the artist to society, the vindication of private poetic morality against public compulsions whether these be the demands of a government or promises of fame and fortune, is what Pound saw as the important element in

profound moral crisis of his contemporary society. Because he is non-Roman by birth, and a poet, he views in broad prospect the literal facts and symbolic qualities of a *patria* whose partially negative influence his friend seems not to realize any more than he does her capability of maiming herself and those enmeshed in the extended web of her feuds. Tullus, active in the processes of Roman political life, remains ambitious for prestige and money, unconcerned with the destructive potential of his superficial goals on deeper values. Above all — and here we must return to the third line of our poem, with its conditional statement — Tullus seems not to realize that death, the other great leveller of humanity, presides over the union of a fatherland and arms. *Sepulcra* and corpses, as well as poets born to sing of mortality, are their offspring.

Death, of course, is a subject that haunted Propertius throughout his career[39]. For illustration one pervasive example must suffice, centered around his use of the word *sepulcrum* itself. Somewhere in the first elegy of his fourth book (the placement is uncertain but the distich appears in the manuscripts at lines 87-88) appears the following couplet[40]:

dicam: " Troia cades, et Troica Roma resurges ";
et maris et terrae longa sepulcra canam.

This is the essential topic the Roman Callimachus will sing for his native Umbria to swell with pride. He holds to his word. We are often assured — and it is a claim also made for Horace at an equivalent moment in his career — that in his last book of elegies Propertius finally absorbed the spirit of the Augustan prin-

---

Propertius and this is the critical burden of the Homage " (*Ezra Pound and Sextus Propertius: A Study in Creative Translation*, Austin, 1964, 28-29. See also p. 58 ff.).

[39] Propertius' entrancement with death and burial, especially his own, pervades all his poetry. For sensitive treatments of the matter see E. H. Haight *Romance in the Latin Elegiac Poets*, New York, 1932, 98-101 (and *ibid.* ' Another Note on Propertius i. 22 ', *Class. Philol.* 35, 1940, 426); J.-P. Boucher *Etudes sur Properce*, Paris, 1965, 65-81; and especially A. K. (Lake) Michels, ' Death and Two Poets ', *Trans. and Proceed. Am. Philol. Assoc.* 86, 1955, 160-79, esp. 171ff.

[40] I tend to agree with the suggestion of Theodorus Marcilius that they follow line 68.

cipate to make a committedly chauvinistic offering to the emperor. Discussion of tombs is a peculiar way to show approval, however, and yet it forms a major motif in the book.

After the initial poem, which is itself a warning to Propertius not to continue on his projected course, the word *sepulcra* appears in the opening distich of three poems (4; 5; 11). The famous seventh poem conjures up the ghost of Cynthia who pronounces her epitaph and predicts her coming sexual union with the poet in death (*mixtis ossibus ossa teram*: 4. 7. 94). The elegies on Vortumnus and the battle of Actium (2 and 6) conclude with allusions to the tombs of the sculptor Mamurius in Oscan territory and of Crassus among the Parthians (now avenged by the battle of Actium) [41]. Poems 8, 9, and 10 deal with a culminative series of violent and vengeful acts beginning mildly with Cynthia's curse against Lygdamus (no intimation of death here), continuing with thirsty Hercules' spiteful requital of a priestess reluctant to give him water [42], and culminating in the aetiology of the *spolia opima* — three triumphant Roman killings. And we would be mistaken to set the third elegy completely apart from its colleagues. Arethusa sends a letter to her soldier lover off fighting the Parthians [43]. May he count it not of too great value to climb the heights of

---

[41] For an apt reappraisal of this difficult poem see the essay of J. P. Sullivan, ' The Politics of Elegy ', *Arethusa* 5, 1972, 17-34 and its critique by F. Sweet, ' Propertius and Political Panegyric ', *Arethusa* 5, 1972, 169-75. It will be apparent even from this brief analysis that I cannot subscribe to the conclusion of P. Grimal that book 4 is " le plus romain et en même temps le plus mystique de ses livres " (' Les intentions de Properce et la composition du livre IV des ' Elegies ' ', *Latomus* 11, 1952, 450).

It is important to note that two of Propertius' most autobiographical poems (concluding the first book and beginning the last) press toward a definition of *patria* by *sepulcra*. The difference lies primarily in breadth of intent.

[42] In his analysis of 4. 9 W. S. Anderson speaks rightly of the poem as an example of " amused sophistication " that is neither gloomy " nor a servile justification of the Augustan Program (' *Hercules Exclusus*: Propertius, IV, 9 ', *Am. Journ. Philol.* 85, 1964, 2). Such detachment is another means of showing less than the strongest commitment to whatever Augustan elements remain in Propertius' treatment of the legend.

[43] On the poet's dread of the " civil " war possible in a campaign against Parthia see 2. 30. 19-22 and the note of W. A. Camps (ed., Propertius *Elegies*, *Book II*, Cambridge 1967) *ad loc.*

Bactria and claim as booty the linen torn from a perfumed chieftain!

Presumably the cleverest way for a poet to avoid repeated refusals to write for his patron on distasteful topics of Rome and Romanness is to confront the topics themselves and leave his individual readers to interpret his tone. It is not suprising that a decade or so earlier than the composition of the fourth book Propertius found the matter more difficult to handle. The *recusatio* that opens the second book is a case in point. Since it bears an intimate relationship with the last poem Propertius can be presumed to have published, 1. 22, it is well to conclude with a brief examination. Though Maecenas replaces Tullus as the addressee [44], a searching question has again been asked by friend of friend — or, more stereotypically, of poet by readers — (*Quaeritis unde ...*). As with 1. 22 the elegy begins and ends with the poet, this time viewing himself specifically in the role of lover. He has a *puella* who is the source of his inspiration (4). He presupposes that in the end she will also be the cause of his death (78), sparking Maecenas' final farewell.

As a *recusatio* this poem, though far grander in scope, is built on the same principle of contrast as 1. 22. This contrast, introduced at line 17 by the first direct naming of the poet's patron, culminates in his refusal to chant the epic deeds of " your Caesar " (*tui Caesaris*, 25). The pronominal adjective thrusts the proposed subject away from Propertius back to Maecenas, and this marked dissociation leads into a catalogue of Roman civil fighting which might (but will not) form the subject of any prospective salley into epic. This list of the mighty accomplishments (*bellaque resque*) of " your Caesar " ends ostentatiously and a trifle sardonically with a vignette of Octavian's triple triumph of 29 B. C. We have the humbled Nile and necks of conquered kings bound with gilded chains (as if plain iron was not sufficiently glistering) [45]. Finally

---

[44] It is well to put the poet's dependence, at least acknowledged dependence, on Maecenas in proper perspective. He appears in only two out of some ninety-two poems in the *corpus*. The other poem is 3. 9.

[45] Gilded objects, for Propertius as for other Roman poets, are a regular symbol of ostentation and luxury (re. 2. 33. 40, *aurato calice*; 3. 2. 12, *auratas trabes*; 3. 13. 57, *auratos lacertos*).

come the beaks of Actian ships which can only mean captured
" enemy " ships — Antony's as well as Cleopatra's.   Later in the
book Propertius will return with greater elaboration to the subject
of warships on the Actian sea, swirling " our bones ", and of
Rome besieged by triumphs over her own kin [46].   But the mood
was already set earlier in 2. 1 by the denotation of Mutina and
Philippi as *civilia busta*, tombs holding citizens slain by citizens,
and by the striking temporal displacement of the Perusine war to
come between the sea battle of Naulochus and the capture of
Egypt.   These are among great Caesar's exploits of which Propertius would (not) sing:

> eversosque focos antiquae gentis Etruscae [47].

The Etruscan race neighbors on that of Propertius.   Near the same
hearth his own genial Penates rested.   The setting of such references to civil war is, to be sure, quite disparate in 1. 22 and 2. 1.
The seriousness of amatory engagements seems far deeper than
inquiries about genealogy.   But the ultimate impetus of the core
sections in each poem is similar.   A feeling of bitterness from the
envoi of the first book spills over into the introductory elegy of
book 2, Propertius' first but by no means unique indictment of
Rome's governing powers.

Though published after the battle of Actium, poem 1. 22 gives
a pre-Actian perspective.   We may assume that Propertius could
not yet face its implications.   Actium, in the poet's initial reaction,
is a culmination of horror, not grace (one can only solve problems
by creative not fraudulent love, his glances at Antony suggest).
In 1. 22 we are forced backward to a previous moment of terror.
In 2. 1 Actium, avoided until now, is placed squarely in the

---

[46] The passage is at 2. 15. 43-46. For a detailed discussion of Propertius' references to Actium in his second book see Nethercut (*op. cit.* above, n. 2), esp. 413 ff.

[47] The chronological disorder is noted by Nethercut (*op. cit.* above n. 2, p. 413).
It is curious that the adjective *Etruscus* occurs only once more in Propertius after
its appearances in 1. 21, 1. 22, and 2. 1, and that is to describe Maecenas *eques
Etrusco de sanguine regum* (3. 9. 1) — Maecenas who lives within his fortune yet
whose fame is next to Caesar's.   Would Maecenas remember his more recent
Etruscan heritage when Propertius later in the poem speaks of the ramparts of
Rome as *caeso moenia firma Remo* (50)?

Perusine tradition. Propertius has been drawn closer to the sources of power yet this increased proximity in no way diminishes his honesty as he takes first, negative stock of the crisis of September, 31 B. C. Though his approach varies in the poems and books that follow, it remains essentially pessimistic, as our reading of 1. 22 would lead us to expect [48].

Brown University
Providence, R. I.

[48] I am deeply grateful to Professors William Nethercut and John Van Sickle for their helpful criticism.

PROPERTIUS' THIRD BOOK:
PATTERNS OF COHESION

M. C. J. PUTNAM

My purpose is to survey certain means by which Propertius unifies his third book, and to examine how this book in turn coheres with the first book to complete a larger unity. I embrace the general proposition that in the elegies of Propertius, as in any great poetry, design and value, medium and feeling constantly reinforce each other.[1] It is my conviction that, at least from the writing of the *Eclogues,* the Roman poets were aware of the power over the reader of a variety of structural designs even within a single book. I will specifically urge that we read the unity of Propertius' third book through two complementary and inseparable patterns, the concentric and the linear, whose diverse energies play in different ways upon individual poems to enrich our understanding.[2]

We presume linearity in any Roman poetry book to which its author manifestly applied his *ultima manus.* A linear frame of reference leads the studious critic in a logical progress from first poem to last. Propertius is ever the master of an allusiveness that links, and distinguishes, contiguous poems. He also relies constantly in book 3 on flexibility of theme and mood to focus as well as startle the reader's attention. These fluctuations involve not only groups of poems from two to five in number, which stand apart as smaller entities within the whole, but also individual elegies whose interaction with adjacent or more distant poems plots a careful dialectic.

The twenty-five poems press toward a central climax in the thirteenth elegy as Propertius, an Augustan Cassandra, indicts the present moral climate of Rome. On either side of this core the book also extends in opposing directions. The immediately adjacent groupings, elegies 6 and 12 and 14 through 20, offer a varied pattern of poetic fare, alternating grand and limited perspectives, the concrete and the abstract, objective and subjective, between poems and on occasion within them. The final poems return to the book's initial concern with the power of poetry and bring matters full circle. Chiasmus, therefore, proves as important an organizing figure for the book as the line's uni- directional inevitability. It forces on the reader an obligation to reappraise constantly what has preceded in the light of what remains before him.

The excitement of Propertius' third book lies in the confirmation for elegy of a new modality. This intellectual novelty can be gauged, baldly and with only partial justice, by comparison with book 2. We find therein poems on Cynthia's greed, fickleness, faithlessness and promiscuity, on the poet's fidelity, enslavement to love, passion for whores, and death. The subject of poetry itself forms an occasional counterpoint to this standard elegiac fare, but Propertius' chief concern remains the elegist's subjective world, not any strength or purpose behind its depiction.

This pattern changes dramatically with the opening poems of book 3 which deal with the inherent potential of the poet and his verses. In the book as a whole we contemplate the assured broadening out of the private elegist not only to formalize his place in inherited poetic tradition but to assume a novel, vatic stance in relation to the present. The self-indulgence of the subjective elegist immersed in his personal feelings, often a retrospective and escapist posture however ironically maintained, yields before the broader critical impulses of the poet commenting on his powers and on means of communication between people. We now contemplate the vivid abstractions that rule our lives, the relationship between style and ethics and, generally, social as much as sexual *mores*. This growth of self-consciousness, which renounces the potentially narcissistic complacency of private elegy, is not gained through the detachment or self-parody which often accompanies the artist reduced to delving into his creativity. Rather it helps raise the potential of elegy to compete with the heroic ode, and proves it capable of embracing ethical issues of deep importance on both a personal and a public level.

Perhaps the greatest accomplishment involves Callimachus whose name heads the first poem.[3] Of Propertius' stylistic devotion to his Alexandrian predecessor the initial books offer continuing evidence. The third book furthers the Romanization of Callimachus by making refined style more fully congruent with a wider moral outlook and applicable more generously to society at large. It is no longer merely a vehicle for a poet's personal proclivity for the precise and the modest. A poetics of careful control now complements an ethics of restraint. Books 1 and 2 often announced the poet's preference of elegy over epic or revealed his abhorrence of a Roman soldier's greedy, itinerant lot. Book 3 sees the two attitudes finely merged. Renunciation of epic demands abandonment of the ambition and warring that are its subjects. This means a looking askance at the present Roman political situation. Poem 9 even suggests to Maecenas that the statesman's humility, when self-aggrandizement in economic or social postures might have been his goal, mirrors the poet's own instinctive circumscription in content and in the representation of meaning. Callimachus may be Romanized, and elegy further objectified in this process, but the composite portrait of Rome itself that emerges from the third book is scarcely a complimentary one. The raising of the elegist's consciousness toward the potentiality of language is accompanied by a sharpened awareness of his duty to criticize both self and society at large. That these grander linguistic and ideological schemata ultimately invoke Callimachean reserve as critique for the rhetoric of expression and for patterns of conduct is only momentarily paradoxical.

Propertius claims at the start the posture of priest that he will adopt again in poem 13 when he becomes the scrutinizing *haruspex* of contemporary life. But the whole book is in fact one large intellectual vaticination, one delving after another, as the poet peers behind and beyond the surface of human activity to expound what might be termed the aetiology of motivations, of inspiration and ethics, of gestures public or private, specific or general. Summary overviews must serve as illustration.

The three initial poems form a triad observing poetry from various angles. The first centers explicitly on the poet himself, boasting of his profession as priest of words. If envy is his lot in life, as *augur* he foresees that honor will befall him in death. His mental wizardry surmounts time for himself and his progeny. The second elegy is concerned with the power and eternity of song itself. The *honores* and *nomen* that before were the poet's are now due his works. It is not its creator but *carmen,* song, which is in the position of authority. The immortality of the elegist and the endurance of his verse yield in the third elegy to the content of poems that should occupy Propertius' attention. He contemplates epic themes only to abandon them by order of Calliope who proclaims the need for limitation at the start of her apostrophe (39):

"Contentus niveis semper vectabere cycnis, . . ."

To adopt elegy over epic as one's expressive vehicle is to cling to the personal over the historical, and to espouse a rhetoric of reticence instead of grandiloquence.

Questions of ideology and utterance contemplated at a poet's mythic source of inspiration are replaced in the fourth and fifth poems by more vivid social truths and renunciations. The fourth projects Caesar's accomplishments in war, and the poet's aloof surveillance of them. The fifth declares the corruption war's riches bring and the twisted quality of contemporary man's mind, unaware that in death rich and poor, conqueror and conquered, are united. Propertius intends at the close of his career to turn not to epic, the intellectual equivalent of avarice and earthly dominion, but to examining the nature of things and the problem of life after death. The interaction is clear. It draws on the preceding three poems and expands their hermetic vision of a poet's pride in order to focus on his consciousness of present Roman realities.

The second poem of the book saw Propertius' girl "touched" as he sings, and the fourth found him leaning against her lap as he viewed Caesar's treasure-laden chariots. The sixth now returns to a more strictly inner elegiac environment, while yet revealing the same spirit of inquiry, on this occasion into the causality of immediate emotion. The poet, wishing to find out his mistress' situation, addresses Lygdamus, Cynthia's slave. But what in book 2 might have remained a poem about mere yearning and the vagaries of emotional commitment becomes a scrutiny of the meaning of words as vehicles for expression. Is Lygdamus telling the truth to the poet or only what he thinks the poet wants to hear? Even if Lygdamus is uttering what he really knows, were Cynthia's complaints lying or veracious? Would Cynthia realize that the poet's previous response had stemmed from anger, not deceit?

The sixth elegy initiates a series of poems self- oriented in nature which yet, unlike the manner of books 1 and 2, continually pry beyond the surface of events to examine the processes whereby emotions are caused or made manifest. A complex inner life stands revealed through a critique of the tone in what is spoken and heard. The seventh elegy, expanding outward more in the manner of poem 5, makes personal response to a private grief a matter of public concern. It is the first of two poems in book 3 to begin *ergo,* as if the poet were only summing up his point and giving his last example to prove a case. Money is the reason that Paetus has drowned at sea. It furnishes cruel fodder to the vices of man with the result that Paetus himself is now food for fish. The sixth elegy's world of verbal indirection is succeeded by a manifestation of the suffering a more universal and, as Propertius now sees it, Augustan fault conveys. Paetus' individual grief is only one symptom of a more general malaise. But even here the poet is watching what lies behind human maneuvers. *Pecunia* initiates a *mortis iter* and is the fountainhead of *vitia* and *curae.* It is the cause of a sea voyage leading to death, not gain, and of a poem about causes.

The eighth poem returns to the poet's amatory predicament, but it too is no mere description of a lover's trials and pleasures. It builds from a standard contradiction (that strife with his girl and her inane cursings are "sweet") to ponder the meaning of the *signa* that lie behind any action. Cynthia's doings exhibit differing evidence of love, and the poet is a *verus haruspex,* a true voyeur into the torments of the mind. This visionary's *exposé* ends brilliantly with one last "sign" to a potential rival. If he has stolen a night of love it is really because Cynthia means to hurt the poet, not to be friendly to any competitor![4]

Like elegy 7, poem 9 merges the public and the private. Propertius' probing here consists in seeing his writing of poetry and Maecenas' ethics of personal behavior in complementary terms. Maecenas' economic and political standards serve as model for the poet's life of the mind. For Maecenas to surrender to the temptation of using his fortune and standing with Augustus for opportunistic purposes would be as if the poet were to undertake the writing of epic, the imaginative equivalent of a life of ambition. But the poet, generically and stylistically refined, eschews epic for elegy and Callimachus. Propertius controls his verbal expansiveness, Maecenas marshalls his habits of conduct. The *signa* (58) his patron finally gives the poet "racing" toward political themes are that he follow his own example which we

211

have already learned was one of moderation. Praise is assumed for the internally heroic espousal of an externally non-heroic role.[5]

Poem 10 leaves behind these heady thoughts and peers once more into the poet's personal world as he celebrates Cynthia's birthday. We begin here with a *signum* (3) as Propertius interprets the appearance of the Camenae at dawn before his bed, a seer imagining his inspiring prophetesses, enliveners of memory and viewers of time to come. The elegy is centered on ritual and prayer, detailing a texture of omens and events to lift the reader out of historical time into elegiac make-believe. After the initial happy sign, the poem prays the day through its wish-fulfilling course with a series of commands and entreaties. Unlike the lover's analysis in poem 8 of yesterday's gestures that often said one thing and meant another, we watch here only the future of a day and of a life. This happy temporal round, a purely symbolic "journey," extends from the reddening sun to the fall of night and a final prayer: *peragamus iter* (32). His hope is that *annua sollemnia* (31), if repeated properly, will assure to Cynthia a *forma perennis* (17), that daily and annual will be fused with eternal time. Since his ceremony of words proposes a stability untouched by temporality, this is the most explicit statement yet of the poet's visionary power and of the potency of his words.

As we continue to follow two parallel and complementary expositions, even in this linear survey, the eleventh elegy again makes a transition from private to public. The theme is the domination of women. Examples of physical, sexual and political might culminate and combine in Cleopatra, the consummate female warrior-politician who is also libidinous enough to seek intercourse with her slaves. As the poem progresses Augustus receives praise as the liberator of Rome from this curse. But there is a counteracting irony. The liberator is at the same time the conqueror. Augustus, on whose safety Rome depends, is the final secure example of power in the poem.

There seems at first a notable differentiation between the emperor and those other possessors of power that the poem has already registered. His girl dominates the elegist's inner life. Cleopatra's sway is both sexual over Antony and political over Rome. Augustus' strength is purely social and historical. But the poem's evolution speaks only a change from figurative to literal bondage, from Cynthia's chains that the poet is unable to break on the one hand, to the fetters that Augustus places on Cleopatra and to the grander dominion of the *pax Augusti* on the other. For Propertius it is not only that Cleopatra is dishonored but that Augustus is brought poetically to the same level as the queen he has subdued. In the hierarchy of strength the poem unfolds, Augustus is at the summit. In the line of *exempla* that evolve at the same time, Augustus is only a further representation of Cynthia.

The shroud of eulogy is brusquely torn aside in poem 12, which forms a doublet with its predecessor. We now observe patently the ruinous effects Augustus' immoral public strategies have on the vulnerable individual lives of those drawn into his orbit. Although in both poems the force of Caesar's arms touches a woman, otherwise the distinction between Cleopatra and Galla, heroine of 12, is clear. The first is an unprincipled creature bent on enslaving Rome. The second is a symbol of family, and Roman, continuity. In poem 11 Augustus has saved Rome from the unseemly yoke of a degraded nymphomaniac. In its companion piece, by fostering avarice and war abroad he is eroding the moral fabric of the civilization which in historical terms he would seem to have saved. Militarism and love's constancy are ever at odds, but in this Rome-centered world it is a woman who signifies steadfastness. Galla is a Penelope waiting for her wandering Ulysses. Destructive woman and saving man reverse roles into redeeming woman and injurious man. We are drawn to ask what good comes from political salvation through arms if they are then turned (and these poems tell a chronological tale) to the undoing of the society that they supposedly have bolstered.

Once more journey is an important motif. The detailed allusions to Ulysses prove Postumus also a follower of informing sign-posts in search of the final signs -- home and wife. These posit the end of wandering and of "fidelity" to Augustus, which is only a type of faithlessness to life's essential stabilities. The gaining of *modus* comes by reevaluation of past, composite *error* (36). Allegiance to the *signa* (2) of Augustus means Parthia and the Araxes, a soldier's reference points. When poem 12, as poem 22 to come, brings the adventuring warrior back to Rome, it does so through a universal myth of husband returning to wife, not of a spoil-laden victor honored at a center of power. For Postumus to emulate Ulysses' course from Troy to Ithaca suggests not merely the topographical change from Parthia to Rome but a metamorphosis from soldier to spouse, from an acquirer of wealth through might to a devotee of a more enduring *fides*.

Propertius makes his prophecy with a secure voice: no other love will entice Galla in Postumus' absence; she will not remember his harshness but will remain steadfast. Poem 12 therefore fits into the sequence of 6, 8, and 10 not only because it deals in part with personal concerns but also because the poet speaks out with an assurance now supported by a strength at interpretation we saw growing in the earlier poems. The poet, who previously has sought to understand, interpret and confirm the meaning of signs, now himself adopts a vatic stance to instruct by direct address. But the poem also follows in the line from elegies 7 and 9 which had dealt with the interrelationships between public ambitions and private needs and limitations. Postumus is a Paetus who will be saved. He likewise serves to remind Maecenas why Propertius accepts the limitations of elegy instead of the expansive pretensions of epic and why, to glance still further back, Propertius will stand on the sidelines at some future Augustan triumph because love is a god of peace.

The poet's posture as instructor in matters that blend public and private concerns from a Roman vantage-point leads climactically to poem 13 as he surveys the city itself and what is rotten at its core.[6] Postumus' Galla, in spite of her exposure to the tutelage of *luxuriae Roma magistra* (18), remained loyal to her absent wanderer. But luxury is a potent ally of immorality. The evil that flows back into Rome becomes the "arms" that overwhelm propriety. Private licentiousness becomes a matter of universal concern. In Rome there is neither a *fida* Evadne nor a *pia* Penelope, perhaps even, as the juxtaposition hints, no longer a steadfast Galla. Matters were not always thus. At the center of the poem and of Roman myths about its heritage lies a simpler past when youth was at peace and men mingled with gods. But Rome must now be prepared for a divine vendetta aimed against present corruption (59-60):

> proloquar: – atque utinam patriae sim verus haruspex!
> frangitur ipsa suis Roma superba bonis.

The credentials marshalled and inspiration proclaimed from the book's first poems build toward this moment. As *sacerdos* of the Muses become Cassandra *rediviva,* predicting unchastity and avarice as Rome's wooden horse, Propertius becomes an outspoken seer, analyzing not only the signs, gestures and apparitions by which individuals communicate but the ethical foundations on which larger cultural edifices are reared. Rome is made up of many Paetuses who set up mammon as their goal and fail to practice the restraint of a Propertius or a Maecenas. Rome's dominion brings *bona* which prove the greatest bane. Literal acquisitiveness undermines the abstractions on which a principled society must rely. The elegist who voices such truths becomes at last a spokesman for public anger and not merely for private distraction.

It is a brilliant occasion, the most conspicuous example of the new Propertius that emerges completely in the third book. He is now a poet fully conscious of his vatic powers and aware of his importance as critic of public attitudes. Both style and ideology, confirmed by the potency of the writer and his words, merge in this wise scrutiny, more subjective toward those individuals whose emotional lot casts them together with the poet, more objective toward that grander entity called Rome.[7]

After this tirade the poems become more strictly inward, concerned with private feelings but always reaching beyond mere subjective meditation. The idea of journeying, whether literal or figurative, continues to play a prominent part. The fourteenth elegy orients the reader toward Greece by contrasting Spartan discipline and display with Roman deviousness and darkness. The contrast is partly ethical, partly erotic. No luxurious colors and scents corrupt Sparta as the preceding poem shows they have beguiled Rome. Besides, at Rome "the lover turns a darkened road," blind toward the means of eliciting a true response in love.[8] This elegiac truism projects us into the subsequent poem which is also concerned with an *iter amoris*. The immediate subject is Cynthia's potential jealousy of Lycinna. The poem in fact examines the turmoil which abstractions, *ira* and *saevitia*, cause, and fleshes this out mythically with the tale of Dirce. This expounds a phantasmagoria of violence, of bondage and torture, escape into night's uncertainties, relief from hurt and physical vengeance. The simile remains an elaborate metaphoric proof, in the semblance of myth, of the varying inner torments that love's unease can foster.

Poem 16 transforms a mythic movement illustrating states of mind into another journey to love that starts literally. Cynthia calls Propertius from Rome to Tibur. But the process of the poem documents the sacrosanctity of the poet's person as part of the poet's extended worry over his tomb and the *nomen* it presumes, when he is no longer actively travelling but passively enduring the potential defamation of others skirting past him. No poem of Propertius uses the motif of travel as intensely to demonstrate both the evidential and the figurative. The path of love ends in Tibur. The more distant wayside sepulchre, away from the throng in good Callimachean fashion, posits the end of a more final *via* from life to death to, presumably, immortality.[9]

Elegy 17, by contrast, details a purely symbolic itinerary, away from the sufferings of love and into wine of release and the intellectual effort of singing Bacchus' praises. As with poems 5 and 21 (in this segment of the book three elegies often intervene between parallel poems), journey metaphorizes variations of absorption into differing mental territories. But whereas the fifth poem of the book only documents the chronology of the poet's mental development, elegy 17 evolves from an essential subjective context into concern for a special divinity's *aristeia*. The eighteenth elegy starts more referentially. Poems 14 and 16 use Rome as object of comparison or topographical place of origin but lead us in due course to matters of ethics or poetic style. Pome 18 transports us to Baiae and the dead Marcellus, but Rome stands behind the poem whose theme is one of considerable daring. Propertius first draws our eye to the famous resort and the mortal or divine heroes intimate with it. At the end, separating the youth's body and soul, he divides our attention between Rome (where the body returns) and the stars where his immortal side will join his illustrious ancestors. But the core of the poem not only pronounces the universality of death but indicts the meaninglessness of the trappings that substance and rank assume by offering Marcellus as a highly public example of the vanity of human wishes.

Poem 18 surveys the responsibility of a Caesar's nephew to the ethics of ambition and to death. Its successor, more stringently abstract like 15 and to a degree 17, turns inward to examine the power of *libido* in a woman. The abstract is visualized as an uncontrolled animal, heedless of shame's bridle and goaded by *nequitia*. Its guilt is proved by a list of examples. It animalizes

215

(Pasiphae) and elementalizes (Tyro). It perverts family relationships to the point where humans become inanimate (Myrrha). Scylla, Propertius' final witness, suffered in retribution a physical tearing apart which, like the fate of Dirce in poem 15, is only the external result of the disruptions her passion had caused.

Poem 19 deals with an aspect of *phusis* that embraces many levels of bestiality. Poem 20 offers a form of *nomos* in counterpoint. From mythic *exempla* of love's perversions, Propertius turns to himself and to what he can offer fresh love. Lust rends those possessed by it. At the start of an affair the poet, by contrast, can manifest the *fides* that restrains and binds instead of the passion that releases all bonds. Following the pattern of much in book 3, the poem is not about love *per se* but about its appurtenances. The poet sees his new intimacy in terms of a house, symbol of family stability blessed by fortune, and of the *iura, pignora* and, above all, *foedera* that assure its functioning. The preceding elegy had been couched in terms of a legal argument which worked out its form as accusation and riposte. Elegy 20, by documenting the socialization of love and bringing it under civilization's constraints, is built around commitment to a pact. It stands as holistic metaphor for the power of its parts -- an answer to the disjunction posited in the manner and matter of its predecessor.

The twenty-first poem, varying more literally the spiritual escape poem 17 posited, finds Propertius compelled to travel the long way to Athens for retreat from love's tortures. No shallow ambition drives the poet, only the wish "to emend the mind" by topographical displacement equivalent to an intellectual change from elegy to philosophy and aesthetics. Elegy 22, its careful companion piece yet close in spirit to 20 as well, reverses perspective to redefine Rome. Propertius' friend Tullus is off in Cyzicus contemplating what the poet sees as exotic forms of mythic heroism and of artistry used or misused for bizarre purposes. By comparison, arms and weapons, crime, *pietas,* anger and restraint all bubble in the complex historical melting-pot that Propertius sees as Rome. Rome eschews the abuses of human dignity familiar from Greek myths depicting the relationships of parents and children, mortals and gods, guests and hosts. Yet for Tullus to return home suggests a change not only in the Roman enterprise but in the individual lives it affects. The poet's proposition is that distant warring and the wrath or self-control which humans exercise in its pursuit be altered into less awesome patterns of behavior. Tullus should devote himself to urban and familial endeavors, to rhetoric for the good of his fellow citizens, to *honor* (owed to the *dignitas* of his *gens*) and to *amor* lavished on his future wife, for the continuance of his *gens.* Such a Rome, achieved once again by a leap from one mental topography to another, is neither the ambitious, aggressive wielder of *imperium* in wars foreign or civil, nor is it the implicit setting for the special imaginative workings of an elegiac poet, bent on varying his conventions of amatory distress. It stands as something of a compromise, not totally political, not totally of the mind, but realistically promoting in the individual virtues operative in any state and essential for its permanence.

Poem 23 finds us established in the elegist's Rome as he worries about the loss of his writing tablets to some covetous soul who uses them to record his monetary transactions. Imaginative creations are replaced by the most prosaic material, as a poet's concern for words and love defers to a miser's inclination for money, and greed. These two protagonists share a concern for time that furthers their differentiation. The miser jots down his literal *rationem* -- a concern unimportant to the "seductive wiliness" of the elegist -- and his cotidian reckonings, *ephemeridas.* The poet is also interested in days, but from an imaginative, emotional point of view. He is obsessed with yesterday, when his girl delayed, and with today, tonight and the trysting hour. The poem's close finds Propertius ironically playing into the hands of greed. Since money, not mental brilliance, speaks to the *avarus,* the poet offers gold for what is only cheap wax and boxwood. He even proposes a third means of communication, the most public of all, by commanding his slave to post a billboard that he dwells on the Esquiline. Such display someone devoted to the superficial might understand.

There is a special sadness to the poem. His tablets are a visible extension of the poet. Even unsigned they bear his mark. They have now died (*periere* twice over), as if, like their master, they had suffered an appropriately elegiac finale. In life they were always faithful as was the poet. Both learned and enticing, they served as the perfect go-between, tangibly stating the intangible. But decisions about what to write are now of little importance when the means of transmitting information is lost or perversely misused. Abstractly poetry may be immortal and a guarantee of immortality, but words are also signs and in a literate society primarily depend for understanding on being read. Poetry, therefore, has its vulnerable side because its notations must be published on evanescent material, enslaved to the vicissitudes of fortune. Without the written *signa*, author, his inspiration and ideas, the act of composition and audience are all meaningless terms.

Sad notions of farewell and of the passage of time lead us directly into the two brief concluding elegies of the book which form a close-knit duet. We end with stringent, forceful analyses of suffering endured now by the poet, or to be experienced later by his chief figure, Cynthia, as their affair diminishes to the accompaniment of final words.

Propertius' ultimate concern is with *forma,* feminine beauty. Yet, though the word appears in the first line of poem 24 and the last of 25, the two poems offer more than cyclic meditation. The first looks specifically to effects of womanly charm on the poet. We follow his progress from early bouts of praise, when love's passion ignored Cynthia's manifest deceitfulness, to realization of the physical bitterness of his *servitium,* and finally to escape from the horrors of this voyage into insanity. The second poem makes the transition from eulogy to curse, from Propertius to Cynthia, from Cynthia once upon a time too exalted in the poet's eyes to Cynthia in the future, now *exclusa,* in the place where her lovers had been heretofore, soon to experience the disdain of others. We abandon the poet's own self-critical progress from deception to torture and release, and face not only the emotion of his withdrawal but the metamorphic potency of time's passage and of a poem's power to demean its subject. The poet's final, appropriate pose is as seer and defamer at once.

It is a poem about change, from past to present and future, and hence above all about temporality. We move from the specific five years of Propertius' faithfulness to the "hidden years" by which age presses on Cynthia, wrinkling her features and whitening her hair. She had once been ennobled by his eyes. She is now made old by his words. The poet in his love had once praised her in verse. It is now his page that in the end sings her damnation at the hands of fate.[10]

Though his material is more subjective, Propertius has returned for his finale to essential themes from the book's first two poems, balancing the four elegies in parallel order. In the initial elegy Propertius deals with the stance of the poet, measured against his inheritance and anticipating his worship as Roman hero of the mind. The second sets forth the claims of poetry to lure its contents from the clutches of mortality. The penultimate of the final poems turns this *biographia litteraria* of the mind's life into the poet's personal itinerary of love sought and evaded. The last returns again to the power and intentions of time, surmounted in the second poem but in conclusion exerted explicitly against Cynthia, the foremost character of Propertius' invention.

Verbal echoes draw attention to the parallelisms.[11] Poems 1 and 24, for instance, share the communality of praise. In the first poem the eulogy given by others to Roman *annales* (15) becomes by the poem's end praise that will finally be given the poet by Rome (35). Poem 24 sees laudation twice bestowed by the poet on Cynthia (3, 5). But it is the Propertian addiction to the metaphor of journey that most strengthens unity.[12] The first poem of the book is built around the poetic general's conquering arrival "with horses crowned" (*coronatis equis,* 10). Poem 24 sees Propertius safely landed from the voyage of turbulent love, pointing out his duly garlanded ships *(coronatae carinae,* 15). Each elegy ends with prayers *(vota)*. The one set is addressed to Apollo in the hope that his tomb will be honored with glory. The other was once offered vainly to deaf Jupiter, whereas the poet can now dedicate himself to *Mens Bona,* goddess of clear thought. Apollo senses Propertius' proper place in the canon of his art. *Mens Bona* salvages him, in a more physical sense, from love's wrecking cares.

An exclamation central to poem 2 presses its connection with poem 25:

fortunata, meo si qua es celebrata libello!
   carmina erunt formae tot monumenta tuae. (3. 2. 17-18)

As the final lines reassure us, both *nomen* and *decus* survive time with the help of *ingenium*. The poet's songs are the eternal "monuments" of his girl's loveliness.[13] Enduring assurance of reputation and true continuance of "grace" are dependent on the benediction of a poet's wit which whisks itself and its subject out of death's precinct. The parallelism exposes poem 25 as bitter and ironic. The valedictory elegy does indeed establish the *nomen* of Cynthia and secure the power of song to immortalize. But what poetic *decus* now freezes in deathless record is the evolving loss of personal *decus*. From a timeless perspective we watch the inroads of human time on a woman's *forma*. Wizened Cynthia's enslavement to mortality is celebrated in immortal words as one "grace" forever preserves the loss of another.

The second poem begins with the hope that the poet's girl, and no doubt his reader, will rejoice in the touch of his verses' wonted music, but the sounds of the final poem are not pleasant. Ribald laughter, mourning, weeping, chiding could not bring much joy. But the harshest alteration takes us from the Orphic voice, bending formidable nature, even the nature of death, through charm heard, to the page singing its creative curse against a piteous creature whose comeliness, like the tenuous substantiality of some elegiac Sibyl, now forever fades. Both the poet and his imagination's most prominent theme are objects of ridicule, the first by the world at large, the second in his mind's eye.

To read linearly is therefore to complete a poetic circle whose center is three poems dealing specifically with Rome. There is reason to see this structuring chiasmus extending inward from the framing poems still further. Poems 3 and 23 deal in diverse ways with the writing of poetry, the first more concerned with the content, the second with the communication, of song. Poems 4 and 22, 5 and 21, all deal with a variety of comings and goings from Rome.[14] The intimacy between the last two is particularly impressive. The first is a spiritual *recusatio*. As age, and a heightening of genre, comes upon the poet, his deeper thought will turn from elegy not to epic and Homer's tradition at Rome but to Hesiod and Lucretius and the problems of physiology and eschatology. The second is a more literal leave-taking, renouncing the torture of passion unrequited for the setting of Plato and Menander. Poems 6 and 20 turn inward and initiate a series of poems which alternate or combine subjective and objective, private and public, personal and historical until we reach Rome at the center. The abstractions that rule our lives, the signs by which we communicate our feelings, and the mental and physical journeyings that symbolize the progressions of our emotional and intellectual lives are salient themes here and throughout the book.

The twenty-fourth poem, however, helps open out a still grander structural pattern of which the third book becomes only the final segment. Elegy 24 not only varies the autobiographical impulse of the book's first poem, it also carefully alludes to the initial elegies of the first book. The eyes of Cynthia that first seized the poet become now his admiring eyes by which she had been made too haughty. They glance back at time past, first to her, then to himself. Key references in 3. 24 to *forma, amor, figura, color* and *candor* are likewise focal in the second elegy of the *Monobiblos* which is concerned with the difference between what is natural and artifical in human beauty. Culture falsifies natural attractiveness, warns the poet, worried especially when a third party may be involved. The later poem turns presentiment feared into truth experienced. But in 3. 24 we are not merely beholding the distinction between seeming and being or superficiality and depth. What is truly false about Cynthia is not that her beauty is fraudulent enough to dupe the poet, as he now admits that it had, but that her trust in it is misplaced. As the last poem makes clear, the poet too had lived by a form of *fides,* fidelity toward his love and allegiance to the "forms" of elegy. For Cynthia to rely on *forma,* whether spontaneous or not, is to forget where true affection lies.

The suffering and survival of the poet himself are central to what follows (3. 24. 9-14):

> quod mihi non patrii poterant avertere amici,
>   eluere aut vasto Thessala saga mari,
> hoc ego non ferro, non igne coactus, et ipsa
>   naufragus Aegaea -- vera fatebor -- aqua:
> correptus saevo Veneris torrebar aeno;
>   vinctus eram versas in mea terga manus.

Propertius makes a clear allusion to the prayer for aid in the expanded outburst which begins his collection (1. 1. 25-8):

> et vos, qui sero lapsum revocatis, amici,
>   quaerite non sani pectoris auxilia.
> fortiter et ferrum saevos patiemur et ignis,
>   sit modo libertas quae velit ira loqui.

In the opening elegy sorcerers or friends are beseeched to intercede with help to gain the lover his liberty. Poem 3. 24 still admits that although successful help from witchcraft or from a father's friends was then impossible, now he can at least voice the truth under no form of compulsion. There is no need for instruments of torture. In at last speaking out what was and is, the poet projects his cure. The first poem ends with advice to those unlike the poet "to whom the god has bowed with easy ear." They should remain steadfast. If they offer "slow ears" to the poet's commendation of stability, much sorrow will be their lot. At the conclusion of 3. 24 the poet in his own person, rejected by deaf Jupiter, offers himself to the shrine of Sanity to complete his escape from the agony that his former constancy ultimately brought. The verbal cycle completed means not the renewal of love's chains but the end of a complex linear strand that began in madness and the "taints of lust" and ends at last in wisdom and a return to health.

It is the penultimate, not the final elegy of the third book that looks back to the initial poems of books 1 and 3. The last poem, though intimate with the second elegy of its book, therefore stands more nearly alone. It receives special stress as a poetic seal. Propertius' initiation of book 3 spoke pridefully of poetry's inheritance and power. His conclusion, a melancholy, bitter vision of life's enchantment withering away, is a more traditional elegy. It bears comparison with the sad specificity of the *sphragis* of book 1 in which the poet defines himself and his birthplace through a cousin's death and the sepulchres of a neighboring land.[15] Elegy 3. 25 is also a petering out, but we have added interest from the poet's patent awareness of his art. Cynthia is the beginning and the end. At the start she rules the poet who smarts under her wiles. At the finale the further dimension of a poet's assured artistry, clinical for all its emotionalism, gains its revenge by cursing with immortality her subjection to time's ravages.

Life and death, imagination and corporeality, are intertwined in the poems that begin and end book three and, in different guises, book one as well. This pattern of concentric balances constructs for the reader a design of mental space which holistically counteracts any linear dwindling. Thematic variety in a series of poems nourished by alternatives or the familiar elegiac pattern of emotions roused and spent are aesthetic servants of a grandly united design.

Several aspects of this balanced structure are confirmed by reference to the patterning of his first three books of *Odes* by Horace, a poet who also lays studied claim to a priestly vocation as he becomes assured of the magnitude of his accomplishment.[16] Meter and careful frame of reference link *Maecenas atavis* (*Odes* 1. 1) with *Exegi monumentum* (3. 30). The latter poem also deliberately echoes the solipsistic assertiveness of *Odi profanum vulgus* which opens a third book of poems as intricate in arrangement as Propertius' parallel accomplishment. Yet *Exegi monumentum* also stands apart. *Odes* 1. 1 and 2. 29, like *Epistles* 1. 1 and 1. 19, are addressed to Maecenas. The last poem no longer offers apostrophe as a pretense at dependence but lays claim to a unique accomplishment through which the poet also stands alone.[17]

In certain respects Propertius' generic accomplishment is also parallel to that of his great contemporary. Horace not only had his models in Sappho and Alcaeus, but could also follow the heritage of Pindar and raise the stature of the ode to the point where lyric could unflinchingly embrace themes of a public and heroic nature. Propertius in his turn reasserts his inheritance from Greek political elegy to combine a persona which speaks out on ethical and emotional matters with a style of reserve. Unless in the lost poetry of Gallus, the Latin elegy had not before this crucial moment found a voice with which to address society at large on consequential matters. After the publication of Propertius' fourth book it would not discover it again, for the *Amores* of Ovid kills by reversion. Where Propertius desexualizes, moving away from tactile realities to more objective analysis of Roman ideology and its paradoxes, Ovid merely ironizes the genre and its contents out of existence. Fascination with entertainment for its own sake bespeaks a measure of vapidity. In his terms Ovid stops where Propertius also concludes, with the end of love and with bitter renunciation. But whereas Ovid rounds off subjective elegy by leading his reader to the emptiness of erotic play as generic exhaustion, Propertius shifts his emphasis into other spheres, but without losing the contemplative bias that the third book so clearly asserts.

Restricted to the elegiac couplet, Propertius lacks one of Horace's major weapons for diversifying poetic expression. That he succeeds in challenging the reader by a wide-ranging stylistic and ideological breadth is a measure of his triumph. Loyal to his poetic heritage but also to a grander idiosyncratic vocation, he lifts elegy to a level of intent hitherto unexplored. His third book is a worthy companion to those contemporary masterpieces of Augustan Rome, the *Odes* of Horace and Virgil's *Aeneid*. Each has its deeply subjective side, yet at the same time each casts a cautious, not totally dissimilar eye on modern Roman man and his ambiguous success.[18]

Brown University

NOTES

[1] Book 3 has not been much admired of late. Miss Hubbard, sensing a tentative tone in the writing, speaks of the loss "of the dramatic power of the love poem in his earlier manner" (1975.89), of "an exhaustion of the genre" *(ibid.)* in the middle poems, and of "the tedium inescapable in the spectacle of a good poet in an impasse" *(ibid.)*. J. P. Sullivan, failing to discover the first book's immediacy in the third, considers poem 15 "the poetic heart of the book" (1976.39) because of its committed eroticism. Though he finds the opening of the third book is "solid and well arranged," he feels "the disposition of the closing poems, uneven in quality, is most disappointing" *(ibid.,* 40).

[2] For a brief summary of recent views on the structure of book 3 see Putnam 1977.253.n.19. Though our interpretations differ over details, I agree with Courtney (1970.48ff.) that linearity is essential to the book's composition. Camps (1966.4) confirms the established view that

the beginning and end of the book are made up of two groupings of five poems but does not press any intimacy, chiastic or otherwise, between them.

The possibility of utilizing chiastic balances among poems within individual books as a poetic tool is dismissed by Williams (1968.480). He writes: ". . . if a book consists of a roll of paper, how can it reasonably occur to a poet to create a significant balance between poems at the beginning and at the end of the same book?" This, one of "the hard realities of the ancient world," would presumably mean that an ancient reader, because he unfolds a roll rather than turns a page, felt no sense of climax or balance as a book progressed other than that engendered by the straightforward movement from one poem to the next (of which Propertius is a brilliant master). I suspect that this *dictum* underestimates the mnemonic aptitude of the Roman mind and the readiness of an author of any age to take multifaceted advantage of his reader's competence.

[3] For precise surveys of the influence of Callimachean aesthetics on Roman poetry from the neoterics on, see Clausen (1964.181ff.) and Ross (1975.5f). Ross (120f.) also discusses the special importance of Callimachus in the third book and (125ff.) Propertius' altering goals therein. He finds the change from the first two books of elegies primarily in terms of a greater historical, more explicitly Roman emphasis in the poet's themes and concerns.

[4] I cannot agree with those commentators (e.g., Camps 1966, *ad loc.*) who interpret lines 35-40 as a separate elegy.

[5] Miss Hubbard (1974.114f.) sees Propertius yielding in poem 9 to pressure from Maecenas that he now write Roman *aitia* (cf. also Ross 1975.126f.). Since the poetic course is already embarked upon (*coeptae,* 57), not merely contemplated, I would urge a different emphasis. Since there is little to praise in Rome, there is, here at least, small reason to write about it -- and only then if Maecenas leads the way. The poem reconciles Maecenas to Propertius and offers good reason why he should not take such a stand. It is a *recusatio,* not a preliminary to the fourth book. For a further alternative view cf. Bennett 1968.335ff.

[6] Further connections between poem 13 and its neighbors are enumerated by Nethercut 1970b and Jacobson 1976. Michelfeit also sees poem 13 as the axis of concentric balances but his labelling (poems 9 and 17 are concerned with "poetry"; poems 10 and 16 are "elegies") betrays a certain facility.

For a discussion of the meaning and use of the term *vates* by Propertius with important bearing on his stance as seer in the third book, see Van Sickle 1975.117ff.

[7] In his important article on "Horace and the Elegists" Otis (1945) comes to an opposite con- clusion. Though Otis' view of elegy's neoteric inheritance is well taken, my own thesis is otherwise at variance to his. For the very reason that his exposure of contemporary ethical problems is in no way veiled, an exposure initiated in book 1, carried through more openly in book 2 and brought to high polish in the third book, Propertius is securing the Romanization of elegy. To be anti-governmental is of itself to be neither apolitical nor truly anti-Roman.

For perceptive reappraisal of the relationship between Augustus and his poets see Johnson 1974.171ff.

[8] The repetitions of *iura* and *bona* (1-2) in the concluding couplet (33-4) unify the poem while *bona* itself is a careful link with the preceding elegy (3. 13. 60).

[9] The words *via* and *iter* appear five times in the poem, on three occasions ending lines. The participle *amans* ends lines 11, 19 and 27. The "literal" bow to Callimachus' metaphor of poetic fineness (re. *Aetia* 1. 25-28Pf.) may not be unintentional, especially as it follows on the more abstract typology of a poet's invulnerability.

[10] For another interpretation which sees these final poems as Propertius' farewell to his mistress and to the writing of love elegy, see Burck 1959. His interpretation is challenged by Bennett (1969) whose assumptions are in turn questioned by Koniaris (1971).

[11] Flach 1967.113-4 correctly sees the relationship of 1. 1. 1 and 3. 24. 2 and the cycle thus formed by the echo. In order to make his pattern of reverberation fit stringently, poems 3. 24 and 3. 25 must be seen as one. But reasons against such a merger carry greater weight than arguments in favor of union. For the latter it must be said that the combined line numbers of poems 24 and 25 equal the length of 3. 1. But the groupings of five and the pronounced ideological break after what would become line 20 of the poem argue tellingly against unification. The Neapolitanus separates the poems as do the majority of critics, among them Barber, Shackleton Bailey, and Camps..

[12] The appearance of *versus* in book 3 only at 3. 1. 8 and 3. 24. 4 is another small connection between the two poems.

[13] Propertius' only other mentions of *decus* concern strictly physical beauty and occur early in book 1 (1. 2. 5; 1. 4. 13 and, in conjecture, 26). The use of *decus* in 3. 2 seems to imply that sexual "grace" lives on in the "glory" a poet's genius can bestow.

[14] On the interconnection between the first five elegies see Nethercut 1961.389ff. and 1970a *passim;* also Baker 1968.35ff.

For a differing attempt to link poems 3 and 23 see Juhnke 1971.118. Baker 1969.333ff. sees the loss of the tablets as metaphoric for the loss of the elegiac world.

For an alternative interpretation of poem 23 which also places it carefully in the sequence of the final poems see Jacobson 1976.171f.

[15] On 1. 22 and its relationship to book 1 as a whole see Putnam 1976 *passim.*

[16] For various views on the relationship between Propertius and Horace see Flach 1967; Nethercut 1970a; Jozefowicz 1974; Sullivan 1976.12-31. Solmsen (1948) surveys the influence of *Odes* 3. 30 on the initial elegies of book 3.

It is a received assumption in histories of Latin literature that Horace, the older and presumably superior writer, must be the leader and Propertius, the younger, lesser genius, the follower. That influence could in fact run the other way is a thesis rarely, if ever, proposed.

[17] *Epistles* 1. 19, largely an autobiography of the spirit, looks backward to embrace the *Odes* and *Epodes* in its meditation on originality. *Epistles* 1. 20, with its factual reminiscence back to *Satires* 1. 6, seeks to embrace the poet's whole production.

[18] I would like to thank Professors William Nethercut, John Van Sickle and James Zetzel for their helpful criticism.

Propertius 3.22: Tullus' Return

MICHAEL C. J. PUTNAM

Propertius' friend Tullus is the recipient of five poems, four from the
Monobiblos, which tell us as much about the poet as about his interlocutor. The first poem, initiating the collection, announces the taut
suffering of Propertius' affair with Cynthia, and the envoi of the book
expands self-scrutiny into the wider scope of a land maimed by civic
hostility. Two intervening elegies, 6 and 14, look to specific differences
between poet and acquaintance. Tullus is richer and loveless, Propertius
caught in passion's toils (and Tullus should be wary!). Tullus also is a
servant of the state. and is associated with Ionia and Lydia, with the
Pactolus as well as the Tiber. Engrossed by his allegiance to *armata
patria* (1.6.22), to his fatherland under arms, he has no time for love or
marriage.

Finally, with one book of poems and presumably some time intervening, Propertius imagines Tullus' reorientation toward Rome and
amor in the extraordinary twenty-second poem of book 3.[1] Thought of
this literal return to the mother city from Cyzicus, where Tullus has
apparently been stationed on the Propontis, sparks a meditation not
only on what this means for Tullus' life but also on differing concepts of
public and private ethics, of heroism and individual dignity, and the
landscape backgrounds which embody their continuity. There can be
little doubt that Propertius measured his thoughts against Virgil's famous
laudes Italiae of *georgic* 2, and the challenging moral dilemmas of the

---

[1] The most valuable critical discussion of 3.22 is by W. R. Nethercut "The Ironic
Priest: Propertius' 'Roman Elegies' III, 1–5: Imitations of Horace and Vergil," *AJP*
91 (1970), 385–407, esp. 403 ff. He does much to counter the strictures of E. Paratore
in "Virgilio georgico e Properzio," *A&R* 10 (1942), 49–58 ("pedisequa imitazione," 53).

It is surely no accident that 3.22 bears the same number in its book as the last preceding apostrophe to Tullus, 1.22 (on which see M. C. J. Putnam, "Propertius 1.22: A
Poet's Self-definition" forthcoming in *Quaderni Urbinati*).

Aeneid may also have been his concern. In each instance comparison instructs us in Propertian intellectual modes.

The poem divides neatly in half, its central focus resting on a concise but tonally ambiguous definition of contemporary Roman political ideology (21–22):

> nam quantum ferro tantum pietate potentes
> stamus: victrices temperat ira manus.

Immediately to either side of this fulcrum of abstraction we find (preceding it) four lines on the omni-productive quality of *Romana terra*, and, following, four verses on Rome-centered rivers, lakes and a spring. Working chiastically from this core, Propertius devotes twelve lines to detailing Tullus' putative travels in the Mediterranean basin (5–16) and a counter-balancing, equal number to monsters and monstrous doings on the part of human and divine culled primarily from Greek myth. Framing these segments, and thus also the poem, are two pairs of couplets devoted to Tullus, the one outlining his situation in chill Cyzicus, the other cataloguing the duties and rewards that should await a Tullus newly returned to accept a citizen's allegiance toward Rome as land and city, and an individual's responsibility to *gens* and married life (39–42). The journey toward Rome leads from *frigida Cyzicus* to *amor*, from present to future, from visual excitement to a deeper stability based on deeper commitments.[2] This future destiny, paradoxically, would seem to renounce a teleology of empire for more intimate, yet more universal cycles of human regeneration. Rome and her servant suffer a critical evolution as the mythic pretensions of Augustan Rome diminish before more realistic ends.

The initial segments define Tullus principally as sightseer, following out the exploits of errant Greek warriors. His own domain features a famous isthmus built by Alexander the Great, which strangely "flows" like the water it intersects, and a statue of Cybele with Argonautic associations, made from a vine stalk.[3] It also contains one of the "ways" which carried the horses of Dis during the rape of Persephone. This is an excitable, poetically energized landscape, lively with event and doubly studded with the effects of human artisanship and divine amatory exploit. This vitality carries over into Propertius' musings on Tullus' vicarious adventuring which divides itself between east and west, between the

---

[2] Cf. Nethercut, *op. cit.*, 405.

[3] On the peculiar use of *fluo*, see H. Tränkle *Die Sprachkunst des Properz und die Tradition der lateinischen Dichtersprache* (*Hermes* Einzelschrift 15: Wiesbaden, 1960), 51. Pliny (*H.N.* 5.142) discusses the construction of the isthmus. I agree with the defense of the reading *vite* by W. A. Camps (ed., Propertius *Elegies* Book III [Cambridge, 1966]) *ad loc.*

more individualistic hazards of Theseus and Hercules and the communal heroism of the Argonauts whose leader is not named.

Here too there are hints first at metamorphosis, then of the hero as craftsman. Tullus might behold Atlas, once giant, now a mountain. He might see the head of Medusa (with the power to alter man to stone) which Propertius treats metaphorically as if Perseus' brave act were one of careful facial sculpting, not violent decapitation (*secta . . . Persea Phorcidos ora manu*). Other labors of Hercules are defined not by deed but by nominal remnant—*stabula, signa, choros*, marks of event but statuary as well, choral dances but also dancing floors, former deeds frozen into present artifact to be contemplated by a spectator. Propertius chooses to see Tullus' emulation of the Argonauts in more physical terms. He must urge on the river Phasis itself, and not merely his boat, toward its Colchian mouth.[4] The *Argo* furnishes elaborate evidence of the object crafted as the poet turns from synecdoche to accomplished fact, from the poetic part (*trabs*) to the reality of the ship's construction (*in faciem prorae pinus adacta novae*). The formative act, the moulding of the first boat's features, appears a violence offered to nature, a pine forced to take novel shape.

Propertius had begun his catalogue of Tullus' foreign doings with allusion to Sestos and Abydos, the cities of Helle, daughter of Athamas (another piece of Argonautica). He concludes by reference to the Cayster mouth, with Ortygie its neighboring grove, and to the spreading Nile delta. On an immediate level the list supplements previous references to the Mediterranean's impressive tributaries, Propontic waters or the Phasis. An ancient reader would also have foreseen these estuaries as marks for the famous temple to Diana at Ephesus or the pyramids, magnets on the grand tour but also striking natural settings, the ultimate in tangible reminders of vainglorious man's achievements as monumental artist.[5] As such they would typify another, still more political aspect of the hero as artisan, and serve as climax to a list which began with the Argonauts' manufacture of Cybele's statue and extended to the strange creation of the *Argo* itself.

It is an effective moment at which to face Rome (17–20):

> omnia Romanae cedent miracula terrae:
>   natura hic posuit, quidquid ubique fuit.
> armis apta magis tellus quam commoda noxae:
>   Famam, Roma, tuae non pudet historiae.

---

[4] On *propello*, re. Tränkle *op. cit.* 84 f.

[5] M. E. Hubbard ("Propertiana," *CQ* 18 [1968], 319), unwilling to see a visit to Egypt possible for Tullus, would change *septenae* to *serpentes* and see the Meander, not the Nile, as the river in question.

We have seen many *miracula*, much grandeur in landscape and human-kind, but all are surpassed, so the poet hyperbolically claims, by a land whose chief accomplishment (we are no longer dealing with things tangible) is the combination of mental and physical prowess to pattern a world under sway, force of arms at the service of consequential abstractions: "for we stand mighty as much from weaponry as from piety; our anger restrains its conquering hands."[6] This apothegm first appears a precis of that particular Roman humanistic heroism, displayed in her surpassing organizational talent, with force applied to create and maintain peace and order. Nevertheless there are ambiguities to the sentiment already adumbrated in the preceding couplets. Propertius uses the future, not the present tense, to predict, not preserve, the Roman miracle. If nature placed here whatever existed anywhere, nature created thereby a motley product embracing all levels of the moral spectrum. This is a land more fitting for arms than suitable to fault, but the situation, as Propertius phrases it, is relative. There is more emphasis on war than criminality but the latter is not totally absent. When Rome is addressed it is only to give assurance that *Fama* will not be ashamed of her history. This is an equivocal utterance at best. Propertius could simply have claimed that the Roman past was reputable. But he complicates his statement by adding the dubious figure of *Fama* who can dispense propagandistic report as well as an honest renown. This convoluted phraseology, with the challenge of sensing *pudor* arrogated to such a creature, raises doubts about the poet's tone which are sustained in the next and culminative couplet.

A proper balance between *ferrum* and *pietas*, supplementing and correcting the previous distinction between *armis* and *noxa*, is at the core of the Augustan ideology—piety toward state and family based on restrained martial strength. Augustus' self-control had at an earlier time elicited one of the poet's rare moments of apparent praise (2.16.41–42):

> Caesaris haec virtus et gloria Caesaris haec est:
> illa, qua vicit, condidit arma manu.

But the present utterance is less straightforward. Anger and temperance provoke antagonistic not cumulative reactions. A victor who relies on wrath for moderation bases his actions on a moral paradox.

We may survey this friction between *temperat* and *ira*, toward which *armis*, *noxa*, *ferro* and *pietate* aim, expanded still more generously in the

---

[6] The different contexts in which *manus* and *temperat* have already been used (8 and 16) point up this change from literal to ideological in its several guises.

ethical world of the *Aeneid* and its hero.[7] Virgil's song deals with the interrelationship between *arma virumque*, between arms and a man who is, we soon learn, *insignem pietate* (*Aen.* 1.10) and the victim of a goddess' anger (*iram*, 1.4). The end of the epic finds him, fierce in his arms (*acer in armis*, 12.938), watching the beaten Turnus and for a moment restraining his hand (*dextram repressit*, 939). The sight of Pallas' belt provokes an outburst of anger (he is *ira terribilis*, 946–947) during which he kills the suppliant (*ferrum adverso sub pectore condit*, 950).

I have quoted the Latin in detail to show the similarity in Virgil's treatment of his hero's final deed to the tensions in the Roman programme as defined by Propertius. Momentary restraint yields to a furious anger. Each characteristic of Aeneas, his *temperantia* and his *ira*, can be defended as an act of *pietas*, either toward his father, who had urged clemency for the prideful subdued, or toward Pallas and Evander, his protege and befriender. But Anchises' famous words—*parcere subiectis et debellare superbos*—should also be weighty. Their continued vitality is illustrated in Horace's near-contemporary portrait of Augustus in a poem where he is specifically given the pedigree of Aeneas, scion of Anchises and Venus:

> . . . bellante prior, iacentem
> lenis in hostem. (*c.s.* 51–52)

Here battling comes first, moderation afterwards, a clear reversal of Aeneas' procedure. Virgil regularly pits the intimate cycles of human suffering or the grander swirls of civilization in history against the linear vision of Rome's imperial apocalypse. Propertius, without direct allusion, sensed the conflict between the morality of a model Roman, living out his ideal role as a gentle conqueror, and the dictates of human emotion which rely more on passion than control. This is a dilemma at the core

[7] That Propertius knew the gist, if not the scope, of the *Aeneid* as early as 25 is clear from the grandiloquent, perhaps condescending, maybe even deprecatory reference to the epic in 2.34.66 (*nescio quid maius nascitur Iliade*). Since the third book was published after the death of Marcellus in 23 or 22, presumably some further time elapsed before the writing of 3.22 during which his knowledge of the epic would have expanded. For the death of Marcellus in the chronology of Virgil's readings from the *Aeneid*, see *vita Donati* 32 (Hardie).

For more general, recent examinations of the poetic interplay between Propertius and Virgil, see A. La Penna "Properzio e i poeti latini dell'età aurea," *Maia* 3 (1950), 209–236 and 4 (1951), 43–69; F. Solmsen "Propertius in his Literary Relations with Tibullus and Vergil," *Philologus* 105 (1961), 273–289 = *Kleine Schriften* II (Hildesheim, 1965), 299–315; J. Van Sickle "Propertius (vates): Augustan Ideology, Topography, and Poetics in Eleg. IV, 1," *Dialoghi di Archeologia* VIII–IX, fasc. 1 (1974–1975), 104–133, esp. 104 ff.

of the Augustan dream with manifest bearing on Tullus or anyone in service to an *armata patria*, who must support pietistic allegiance through force of arms.

It is reasonable that the center, though not the climax, of a poem luring Tullus back to Rome should scrutinize Rome's unquestioned devotion to the state, in all its guises, over self and family. In Cicero, for example, the importance of fidelity to republic instead of individual can be seen in his strictures to the hedonistic Caelius who changed his ways after a period of pleasure: "revocet se aliquando ad curam rei domesticae, rei forensis reique publicae . . ." (*pro Cael.* 42).[8] But this last needs to be qualified by a more elaborate breakdown in *de Officiis* (1.74): "Sed cum plerique arbitrentur res bellicas maiores esse quam urbanas, minuenda est haec opinio . . . vere autem si volumus iudicare, multae res exstiterunt urbanae maiores clarioresque quam bellicae."

In suggesting to Tullus a similar reordering of priorities, Propertius suitably enough begins with one sempiternal aspect of what "nature" gave the Roman earth, namely the landscape background of these multifarious patterns of organization (23–26):

> hic Anio Tiburne fluis, Clitumnus ab Umbro
>   tramite, et aeternum Marcius umor opus,
> Albanus lacus et socia Nemorensis ab unda,
>   potaque Pollucis nympha salubris equo.

By contrast to the exotic waters now Tullus' wandering lot Propertius sets his vision on Rome and catalogues first rivers, then lakes that decorate her setting. The reader's eye is always directed on the city. It first follows the Anio, then the Clitumnus from its Umbrian course, each tributaries to Rome's great river. And the *aqua Marcia*, splendid example of man's technology used for civic benefit, coursed in the only aqueduct that led directly to the Capitolium.[9] The same orientation holds for the stationary waters, the lakes of Albanus and Nemorensis and the *fons Iuturnae*. The first are in the distant hills (and fed from an allied further source, *socia ab unda*). The last takes us directly to the Roman forum and to a moment in history long past when the Dioscuri were said to refresh their horses at the spring of Juturna after the battle of Lake Regillus. This spot is a far cry, literally and figuratively, from the path which Tullus at present admires where the steeds of Dis carried off Persephone. It might serve as a positive reminder to him not only of Rome's essence but

[8] Quoted by S. Commager in his excellent survey of Propertius' "anti-political legacy" (*A Prolegomenon to Propertius* [Cincinnati, 1974], 37 ff.).

[9] Re. Front. *de Aquaeductu* 7.4–5. A union of *aeternum opus*, the Capitoline, and Roman imperial continuity was a congenial subject of speculation for Horace and Virgil as well.

of a former moment when battling in the hills near Rome was over and horses were watered at peace in the midst of *res urbanae*.[10]

With landscape established, Propertius turns back to Greece to show by contrast with Italy first what natural enormities, then, more expansively, what human oddities fail to exist on Italian soil. These lines (27–38) serve as counterpoise to the earlier outline of Tullus' supposed itineraries and the aspects of vivid heroism they conveyed. We relinquish the public for the private sphere of action, exchanging emphasis on physical prowess, craftsmanship or mere visual persistence for scrutiny of myths involving the ethics of individual human conduct. These emphasize heavily but not exclusively the perversion of *pietas* between parents and offspring, the burden of guilt resting largely with the former. We begin with Andromeda who suffered for her mother's pride and with an allusion to the banquet of Thyestes, engorging his own children. The first part of the list concludes with reference to another mother, Althea, who killed her son Meleager by burning a log on whose preservation his life depended.

Mention of Pentheus, torn apart by his mother Agave and her sisters, introduces a new variable (33–36):

> Penthea non saevae venantur in arbore Bacchae,
>   nec solvit Danaas subdita cerva ratis;
> cornua nec valuit curvare in paelice Iuno
>   aut faciem turpi dedecorare bove; . . .

Not only does parent do violence to child but the poet treats Pentheus, seen by his mother, as prey, herself as predator. The same notion of human envisioned as beast, reflecting metaphorically back on the protagonist's behavior, is extended in the next episode to Agamemnon who would have sacrificed his daughter had not an animal been substituted in her place. The point becomes most explicit in the episode of Juno and Io. We move from a level of parental misdeeds to divine mistreatment of human in an action which at once makes a mockery of *pietas* and eliminates human dignity by forcing the victim to suffer direct metamorphosis into an animal. In a parallel passage earlier in the poem Propertius planned the construction of the *Argo* as in part a forced twisting of the natural into the unnatural (*in faciem prorae pinus adacta novae*, 14), a novel monster that would not rage, we assume, in Italian waters (*Itala portentis nec furit unda novis*, 28). We now watch *decus* withdrawn from a human being by a similarly degrading alteration, this time

---

[10] The Greek mythic-heroic world thus finds a creative resolution in Roman civic peace.

totally within the realm of the animate and of supposedly rational beings.

Sinis, Sciron and Procrustes figure with enigmatic briskness in the final couplet of perversities (37–38):

> arboreasque cruces Sinis, et non hospita Grais
> saxa, et curvatas in sua fata trabes. [11]

Abuse here extends from human to inanimate. Not only do these three uncivilized denizens of the Saronic coast destroy the traditionally sacred relationship between host and guest, they corrupt nature and landscape in the process. Trees are transformed into instruments of torture, timbers are curved against their own instinct for the undoing of others. The verb *curvare* is deliberately repeated from line 35: Juno's disfigurement of her rival is only varied in a robber's misuse of land for the destruction of mankind. It remained for Theseus to remove these hybrid menaces from the path of those travelling toward Athens. The two basic subjects called to Tullus' attention, aspects of public heroism and personal morality, thus converge at the end. And while Theseus recalls Athens, Tullus, and Propertius' readers would think of Rome by analogy.

It is surely no accident that Propertius urges Italy on her errant son by a pejorative register of what she does not possess in tangible monuments to former heroic prowess or in unenviable standards of personal conduct. He singles out for praise neither specific deeds in the Roman past nor personalities embodying virtues of consequence. Italy could be said to gain by comparison with the Hellenic past, yet the poet's avoidance of open praise, save in his treatment of landscape setting, strengthens its negative opposite. Tullus, though his potential change of heart is treated positively, is the only Roman named, whether public or private ethics, imperial or civic virtue is Propertius' concern.

Certainly the new relationship between Tullus and the metropolis to which Propertius devotes his final, climactic lines, appears the more productive by comparison with what has gone before (39–42):

> haec, tibi, Tulle, parens, haec est pulcherrima sedes,
> hic tibi pro digna gente petendus honos,
> hic tibi ad eloquium cives, hic ampla nepotum
> spes et venturae coniugis aptus amor.

---

[11] Though absence of a verb has led most critics to postulate a *lacuna* before line 37, the exacting symmetry of the poem tells against such a view (such a syntactic disjunction is by no means unique in Propertius). More troublesome is the distribution of *arboreas cruces*, *saxa* and *trabes* among Sinis, Sciron and Procrustes. My own view is that Propertius, for his own purposes, has exchanged Sinis and Procrustes. See the detailed discussion of both problems by Camps, *op. cit.*, *ad loc.*

Suddenly the complexities of the Propertian style disappear, and therewith much of the problematics the poem had posed to highlight this very moment.[12] Nurturing landscape and the intense beauty of a stable spot affirm an important reformation of Tullus' values, a turning away from heroism based on strength or itinerant hedonism, from propagandistic representations of Roman imperialism combining virtue and force, from ethical values corrupting family life and personal *dignitas*. Their replacements, which take eternal abstractions and posit them in Tullus' putative future, conjoin the urban and the familial. To lure Tullus out of distant service to arms Propertius formulates a union of devotion to one's immediate household, to tribe and to state that assumes a continuous responsibility. Art lies in the use of words, not deeds, not in reinforcing Roman rule over Asian allies but in rhetoric before citizens (it is not long since our inner eye has rested on the forum's grace). Embarking on the *cursus honorum* will reassert the quality of *gens*. Above all *nepotes* and *amor* will assure not only domestic happiness but family continuity as well.

I will return to the intimations of immortality that children bring by assuring endurance of *nomen*, and to an inherent contrast with Propertius' own grasping at eternity. Suffice it to point out here the wide difference between this ending and Virgil's thoughts on Roman spiritual objectives, first because they conclude where Propertius has only reached midpoint, second because of an added pessimism constantly tempering Virgil's projection of future Roman glory.

Throughout his speeches in *Aeneid* 6, Anchises makes clear the tight interdependence of "name" and *nepotes*. Yet the latter word recurs emphatically in his final obituary of Marcellus whose human mortality obliterates genetic future and makes meaningless the combination of *pietas* with *invicta bello dextera* that links him with the Augustan credo as detailed by Virgil and summarized by Propertius.[13] Virgil undermines this

---

[12] These lines seem particularly inept to G. Williams who speaks of "empty and unconvincing talk of magisterial office, eloquence, hope of descendants" (*Tradition and Originality in Roman Poetry* [Oxford, 1968], 425). His complaints have been in part answered by R. J. Baker "*Duplices Tabellae*: Propertius 3.23 and Ovid *Amores* 1.12," *CP* 68 (1973), 109–113, esp. 110.

[13] *Aen.* 6.878–879. Virgil's gloom in forecasting continued reputation in historical time after death takes many guises. In one form we ponder Priam *truncus* (*Aen.* 2.557) and Aeneas himself *inhumatus* (*Aen.* 4.620). Lesser characters like Palinurus, Misenus or Caieta, give their names to features of topography, a dubious distinction Virgil makes clear in the case of the last (*si qua est ea gloria*, *Aen.* 7.4). The reputation of Nisus and Euryalus will endure as long as the house of Aeneas dwells on the Capitoline (*Aen.* 9.448–449), but the fallibility inherent in such a prediction is magnified in Virgil's irony at the greed of their blood-thirsty progress.

ideology most succinctly at the end of his epic, allowing his hero to be victimized by an aspect of that *furor* which had guided his opponents and challenged his own goals. Propertius strides forward in a direction Anchises might have considered mediocre. *Alii . . . orabunt causas melius* Aeneas' father had said just before his famous dictum on sparing suppliants and warring down the prideful. In spite of a Cicero in Rome's future, others will be better rhetors. For Propertius, however, such prowess is an essential part of civic duty, of the *res urbanae* that, as a good elegist, he urges for antidote to the martial activism of Rome found incorporated most expansively in the paradoxes of Virgilian epic.

Virgil also forces us, again by internal means, to question the tone of his *laudes Italiae* from the second *georgic*, the single strongest influence on Propertius' ideas in 3.22 and their ordering (*geo.* 2.136–176).[14] Here too the elegist, with his own special difficulties of modulation, has proposed an alternative to Virgil's didactic awareness of nature's combined violence and productivity, and of man the warrior, Italy's strangest crop. In pieces of virtually the same length (the Virgilian excerpt measures forty-one lines), each poet deals with the land as *parens*, though Virgil's concluding apostrophe is more fulsome (173–174):

> salve, magna parens frugum, Saturnia tellus,
> magna virum: . . .

Allusion to a once golden age, *Saturnia tellus*, becomes for Propertius acknowledgement of actual Rome's universality, first through *Romana terra*, to which a generously ambiguous nature gave everything that had been created, then by the more directly worrisome *armis apta tellus*.

Propertius has little concern with nature's beneficence and Virgil leaves reference to her constant spring and double creativity to only a few lines. Even the products of a presumably Saturnian age, when the land flowed with silver, bronze, and gold, contemporary man, artificer of competition, has hardened for his destructive ends, Virgil tells us elsewhere in the same book. But the poets overlap in dealing with the realms

---

[14] The relationship between 3.22 and Virgil's *laudes* has recently been treated in detail by Tränkle, *op. cit.*, 101 f., and G. Williams, *op. cit.*, 421–426, with Virgil winning the prize in each case. Tränkle finds the Propertius poem disjointed by comparison: "Bei Virgil fügt sich alles zusammen, . . ." (101). In Propertius "haben wir kein einheitliches, sich rundendes Gesamtbild, da die einzelnen Beispiele nicht angekündigt und vorbereitet heraustreten, sondern überraschend und stossweise, aber reiche, ja verwirrende Fülle und bunte Vielfalt" (102). Williams (425) speaks of the "verbal posturings and erudite elegances" as well as "the tasteless ineptitude of style and content in Propertius." Cf. also C. Becker "Die späten Elegien des Properz," *Hermes* 99 (1971), 449–480, esp. 461 f.

of landscape and of myth. Virgil singles out large bodies of water, the northern lakes Larius and Benacus, and the Lucrine harbor constructed by Agrippa, and comments primarily on their energy—Benacus rising with the roar of the sea, the Lucrine chafing with loud thunderings against its man-made barriers. Propertius, as we have seen, has none of this, offering instead a catalogue of specifically Roman waters remarkable for its simplicity and restraint, to enhance his turning of Tullus away from arms, distant or near, to Roman civilities, from *armis apta tellus* to *aptus amor*, from *noxa* to a *nympha salubris*. Unlike Agrippa's forced control of nature for military purposes, Propertius' *aqua Marcia* orders nature for civic ends.

The one topographical spot both poets share illustrates graphically their divergence. For Propertius mention of the Clitumnus merely draws the eye along its stream from his native Umbria (*ab Umbro tramite*) toward the Tiber and Rome. For Virgil it serves the same purpose but with an additional fillip (146–148):

> hinc albi, Clitumne, greges et maxima taurus
> victima, saepe tuo perfusi flumine sacro,
> Romanos ad templa deum duxere triumphos.

The eye again leaps to Rome but only to see Clitumnus' white bulls partaking in Roman ceremonies of triumph and then immolated, the final amalgamation of military glory and Rome.

The poets' use of myth also provides an object lesson in their differences. Propertius analogizes through myth what Tullus now is and what his Rome should not be. Tullus, in his patriotic journeying, is viewed as a Herculean or Argonautic wanderer, not necessarily fully committed to the Roman heroic fusion of *pietas* and *ferrum*, the "here" of Rome's miraculous, volatile, abstractions. This "here," as we have noted, is also scrutinized by Propertius for its private ethics, this time using Hellenic tales to mirror what Italy is not. In watching Greek models for the relationships of parents and children, gods and mortals, hosts and strangers, we substituted torture, annihilation, de-personalization, even the rending apart of the human body, for sustained affection and respect for personal integrity. In finally embracing as his goals civic *honos* and familial *amor*, Tullus would suffer dual metamorphosis away from his chill Cyzicus, not only from Greek heroics and Roman arms guided by piety instead of evil, but also from the private improprieties of Hellenic legend. In the process Propertius' Rome would seem to change for the better as well.

Virgil by contrast treats myth with a more pervasive irony. His one bow to the Greek past comes at the start of his aretology and also is meant to urge contemplation of what Italy does not offer (140–142):

haec loca non tauri spirantes naribus ignem
invertere satis immanis dentibus hydri,
nec galeis densisque virum seges horruit hastis; . . .

Virgil also disclaims any Argonautic influence on Italy's growth. Literally there are no fire-breathing bulls, no dragon's teeth to sow, no crops of men armed with helmets and spears, springing from Italian soil. By the end of his hymn, however, Virgil has enticed his reader to perceive the symbolic aptness of the same tale of Jason. The developing "myth" of an historical Rome, that uses bulls for sacrifice at triumphs and encloses a seaside bay as an arena for naval maneuvers, is in fact engendered by its crop of armed men, the *genus acre virum* that Italy has borne. This harvest begins with general reference to peninsular tribes—Marsi and Volsci equipped with darts—extends to pluralities of Republican Roman notables—Decii, Camilli, sons of Scipio hard in war—and culminates in a unique Caesar, mightiest of them all upon whom Virgil casts a particularly detached glance. This apex of the Italian martial heritage is off in the farthest reaches of Asia, making war against the unwarlike Indi, preserving the fortresses of Rome from her onslaughts. It is no wonder that the art of Virgil's praises is based on Hesiod's *Ascraeum carmen*, for both have full, if idiosyncratic, awareness of the many levels of *labor* in human existence.

Virgil, treating landscape and people in one ontological expression, thrusts against his formal thesis from within by imaginative means.[15] Propertius, while he unfolds a linear development of heroism and of Rome itself as backdrop for Tullus' own growth, senses alternatives both in the literal placement and in the spiritual outlook of his protagonist. Virgil offers no relieving modification. There was, to be sure, a time past (the second *georgic* concludes) when families were stable and man's competitiveness found easy release in gaming at festival time. The present, by contrast, finds Saturn yielding to Jupiter as men banquet on cattle they have slaughtered and forge swords. The contemporary stance which Propertius and Tullus share (*stamus*) objectifies much the same ethical pattern.[16] But the elegist's personal involvement ultimately directs itself toward a future for which Rome is centripetal. This future moment of Tullus' return would fulfill the poet's desire. It would also

[15] For a more detailed re-evaluation of *georgic* 2.136–176 see M. C. J. Putnam "Italian Virgil and the Idea of Rome," forthcoming in *Janus*.

[16] The ideological significance of *statio* is discussed by G. Binder *Aeneas und Augustus* (Meisenheim, 1972), 15 f. and n. 37 for further bibliography.

assure Tullus of a continued existence based on his progeny. The final emotion is *amor* but the operative virtue is *spes*. Each challenges war's destructive feuding in a Rome which can now promise a setting for the peaceful execution of civil and familial trust.

Propertius' meaning is often sharpened by friction with adjacent poems, and 3.22, as recent critics have well noted, is no exception. The preceding poem outlines a trip to Athens and its intellectual attractions as a *remedium amoris*. Where Tullus at Cyzicus had avoided love and city through Roman adventuring, Propertius urges on his boat toward a different isthmus, away from Rome and the bitterness of an unresponsive Cynthia. The elegy that succeeds 3.22 finds Propertius again in Rome but now with his *tabellae* lost.[17] This is thought, with some reason, to define a lack of inspiration or productivity concomitant with the cooling of the Cynthia affair. The last two poems of the book, bitter leave-takings, are climax and conclusion of the series. It is natural that the linear directness of this grouping should find its balance in the opening five elegies which have long been recognized to coalesce around the theme of a poet's response to his craft and to its relationship with present Roman society.[18]

There is elaborate poetic interaction between the two segments. If this parallelism is viewed chiastically, the fourth and the twenty-second poems are complements. In each the poet is at Rome, voicing his concern for the attitudes of those in power. The first word *arma* sets the tone for an appraisal more rich with irony than the exhortation to Tullus. Roman *historia* (the word appears prominently in each poem) at the moment could be seen as idealistically based on the piety of revenge (*Crassos clademque piate!*). The immediate results of this plea, however, are victories and booty, not moral uplift. The arms godlike Caesar is pondering are against the wealthy Indi as he prepares to cleave a gem-rich sea. A great reward, the poet exclaims, to achieve a triumph from the farthest land (and from a people Virgil called unwarlike). But Propertius expresses his final disdain by surveying the procession pass by from the lap of his girl. The aloof elegist observes, and that is all, the celebration of background facts for an epic he could never write.

[17] The relationship between 3.22 and 3.23 is treated in detail by R. J. Baker "Propertius' lost *Bona*," *AJP* 90 (1969), 333–337.

[18] The linear interrelationship of the last poems is discussed by R. J. Baker "*Miles annosus*: the Military Motif in Propertius," *Latomus* 27 (1968), 322–349, esp. 339 f.; J. A. Barsby "The Composition and Publication of the first three books of Propertius," *G&R* 21 (1974), 128–137, esp. 135 ff. Cf. the words of W. A. Camps, *op. cit.* 154, in his introduction to 3.22: "His [Tullus'] reappearance here may be significant, for the neighboring Elegies xxi, xxiv and xxv suggest that a new phase is about to begin for the poet."

Juxtaposition again sharpens intellectual design since the subsequent poem reviews similar arguments. Propertius is a poet of peace and needs no rich crystal from which to slake his thirst nor bronzes from the sack of Corinth. What good reliance on externals since death, the great equalizer, mixes conquered and conqueror, poor and rich. In his life of the mind, when old age interrupts elegiac powers, he will turn to larger realms of nature, to didactic physiology, certainly not to the epic of those who care for arms and for vengeance over the standards of Crassus.

The number of such correlations in Propertius' third book argues for a pattern of organization extending beyond the linear stretches of the beginning and the end. These correlations rely as much on alternation as on unity of theme for their potential. Divergence between what might be called public and private topics becomes a frequent principle of fusion. Taking up after poem 5 we have a poem on the depth of Cynthia's affection next to an indictment of the avarice that drove Paetus to his maritime death. Praise for the advantages of lovers' squabbles (8) neighbors one of Propertius' two addresses to Maecenas: his restraint in matters of politics should serve as warning against any generic overreaching on the poet's part (9). The tenth poem is a birthday hymn to Cynthia while the eleventh, announcing the dictatorial power of woman, ends pointedly with praises of Caesar for extricating Rome from Cleopatra's threatening coils. But the ring of this laudation is immediately dulled with a poem that shows the devastating results of public intrusion on the private sphere (3.12.1–2):

> Postume, plorantem potuisti linquere Gallam,
> miles et Augusti fortia signa sequi?

Postumus and Augustus, warring, journeying and greed are on one side, Galla and Rome, stability and fidelity remain on the other.

But whether one traces patterns of sequence or alternation or their combination, there are certain topics that permeate the book as a whole.[19] The chief of these, which in some way marks each poem, is the idea of time and the artist's desperate postures between death and life. We contemplate this struggle in the most intimate as well as the most expansive poems. In poem 16, for instance, as he faces the danger of a

---

[19] For recent views of the structure of the third book see A. Woolley "The Structure of Propertius Book III," *BICS* 14 (1967), 80–83; E. Courtney "The Structure of Propertius Book III," *Phoenix* 24 (1970), 48–53; H. Juhnke "Zum Aufbau des zweiten und dritten Buches des Properz," *Hermes* 99 (1971), 91–125, esp. 113 ff.; J. A. Barsby, *op. cit. passim.* Woolley (81) sees poem 22 balancing 14. Juhnke summarizes 3.22 as "Römische Land und Leben als Überhöhung der elegischen Welt." But one of the curious facts of 3.22 is the presence of only slight relatedness to the poet's inner elegiac world.

nocturnal venture to his mistress in Tibur, Propertius concludes with a meditation on the proper status of a poet's tomb. Cynthia's genethliacon prays for frozen time: may her beauty (*forma*) be everlasting (*perennis*), her reign over the poet eternal and these rituals annual. But *forma*, as the last duet of poems proves, is a highly evanescent endowment. Its disappearance should strike fear into Cynthia as it does final scorn in the poet (3.25.17–18):

> has tibi fatalis cecinit mea pagina diras:
> eventum formae disce timere tuae!

The road to immortality, that ultimate illusion of genius, lies through poetry for his material and for its creator (3.1.23–24):

> omnia post obitum fingit maiora vetustas:
> maius ab exsequiis nomen in ora venit.

Propertius' page is from the muses, whatever its contents, and as a *vatis* he can predict its endurance as well as Rome's moral breakdown or Cynthia's withering age (3.1.35–36):

> meque inter seros laudabit Roma nepotes:
> illum post cineres auguror ipse diem.[20]

The defiance time's variousness presents human goals is a theme that unifies Propertius and Tullus, each in his different sphere. For Tullus, return to Rome betokens espousal on the ethical level of what Propertius lays claim to on the aesthetic. The autonomous purposes of history and poetry, fact and imagination for once supplement each other. Propertius' renunciation of epic to maintain his stand as an elegist of breadth parallels Tullus' foregoing of an imperial Rome bolstered by dogmatic arms to accept the urban civilities of political and familial life. Each will have his *nepotes*—those who in a later time will sing the praises of Propertius' poetic accomplishment or those more literal creatures who will carry on Tullus' name into the future. Tullus is more fortunate than Augustus who loses his Marcellus (genealogy, the poet matter-of-factly observes in elegy 18, gave him little help in the face of death). He is more felicitous still in that, like Cynthia, he was befriended by a poet. In spite of Propertius' yearning for the one and seeming repulsion of the other, it is the strange excellence of his verse that has earned for them both, as well as for himself, their fragile yet continued triumph over mortality.

Brown University

20 R. J. Baker, among others, has discussed in detail Propertius' grasping at eternity in "Propertius III, i, 1–6 again. Intimations of Immortality?" *Mnemosyne* 21 (1968), 35–39. See also Nethercut, *op. cit. passim.*

Virgil

VIRGIL'S FIRST ECLOGUE: POETICS OF ENCLOSURE

Michael C. J. Putnam

Tityre, tu patulae recubans sub tegmine fagi
silvestrem tenui Musam meditaris avena;
nos patriae finis et dulcia linquimus arva.
nos patriam fugimus; tu, Tityre, lentus in umbra
formosam resonare doces Amaryllida silvas.

Tityrus, you reclining under the protection of a spreading beech, you ponder the sylvan muse on slender reed.
We are leaving the bounds of our fatherland and our
sweet fields, we are in flight from our fatherland. You,
Tityrus, at ease in the shade, teach the woods to resound 'beautiful Amaryllis'.

The literary historian must value the opening lines of the first *eclogue*
for many reasons but their role in the development of the rhetoric of
pastoralism is especially significant.[1] For the first time in ancient pastoral
poetry two intellectual worlds are in collision, seen in the characteriza-
tions of two shepherds only one of whom is finally settled in a landscape
of permanence and continuity. Tityrus remains and Meliboeus is forced
to depart. It is the elaboration and significance of Tityrus' setting that I
wish to consider here. In a few deft strokes Virgil's Meliboeus creates a
landscape of the mind, intellectualizing what Theocritus had left as
enticing framework for song and establishing a stylistic principle that
proves a powerful influence on all the poet's subsequent creative efforts.

The physical framework enclosing Tityrus is briefly told. The vertical
dimension is defined by *sub tegmine*, Tityrus under, the protection above.
The horizontal is twice seen in *patulae* and *recubans* — the tree extended
over, the shepherd stretched out below. This environment is then shaped
by *umbra*, the actual shadow cast by the beech tree upon the reclining
singer and expanded by *resonare*.[2] Through echo this extended area of
landscape becomes both bounded by and filled with sound. The poet's
presence is crucial to create and recreate the *locus*. His imagination
bodies forth his context through song, and without him it loses
that beauty which develops with his thoughts. This forming of literal
and intellectual space complements the process of the poet's own intellectual development from *meditaris* to *doces*, from mental pondering to
physical voicing. This change itself is visualized in the metamorphosis
of a rustic singer's abstract inspiration, *silvestrem Musam*, into a shaped

result, tangible to eye and ear, *formosam Amaryllida*. The singer is appropriately *lentus*, verbally reflecting his bifold setting, 'bending' with his self-engendered context, at ease and unconcerned.[3]

Masterful use of figures of sound, enhanced by the symmetrical melody of Greek names, unifies the five line portrait of Tityrus while chiasmus strengthened at the center by anaphora both sets Meliboeus apart and yet for a moment adds a further dimension to Tityrus' enclosure. In the midst of an idyll where shaded leisure enhances music we find an intense verbal pocket of repetitions, non-tactile save for the one embellishment of *dulcia* ('sweet'). Meliboeus, in fact, makes his own desperate echo, a seeming parody of Tityrus' iterations because for him they are created by words alone, not sprung from a relationship with landscape. Virgil will tell us more of Meliboeus' realm of bounded plots and ploughlands, part of a fatherland in turmoil. At the moment he merely sets forth the irony that Meliboeus neither enhances Tityrus' preserve beyond his momentary presence nor does he learn of himself as he suggests the multitude of distinctions between them. If in pastoral poetry complexity is seen simply and experience is often gained by a passing identification with innocence, this is no ordinary exemplar. Meliboeus' contemplation of the ideal while suffering the real, watching the timeless and spatially controlled while suffering the presence of time and distance, fosters a broader definition.

The practical Meliboeus gives two further portraits of Tityrus' enclosure. The first, as Perret has noted,[4] has a legalistic ring (46-48):

> Fortunate senex, ergo tua rura manebunt
> et tibi magna satis, quamvis lapis omnia nudus
> limosoque palus obducat pascua iunco: . . .

> Fortunate old man, and so your acres will remain, and
> they are large enough for you, though naked rock and
> swamp with muddy reed cover all your pasture land . . .

These signposts are a surveyor's measure for possession. But Servius sees *lapis* and *palus*, rock and swamp (the latter supplemented by mud and reed), with equal justice as a synecdochic representation of that broader sweep of the pastoral domain that embraces on the one side mountains, on the other lakes bordered by beeches.[5] This is the land in the ninth *eclogue* that Menalcas might save, extending from the hills up to the water and the old beeches. It is Corydon's purview in the second poem as he takes his stand amid thick beeches chanting his woes to woods and mountains (with no intimation of their loss, only his suffering). Meliboeus, with the practised, georgic eye of one with his own *novalia*, who

244

knows the fortunes of growing crops, who grafted trees and worked his vines, merely pinpoints dry and wet problem areas within Tityrus' pasture. Assuming the difficulties swamp presents those who live on the land, Virgil in the *Georgics* would ask his farmer (1. 113-116):

> . . . cum primum sulcos aequant sata, quique paludis
> collectum umorem bibula deducit harena?
> praesertim incertis si mensibus amnis abundans
> exit et obducto late tenet omnia limo, . . .

> . . . what of him who, when first the seedlings are level with their furrows, leads off the swamp's gathered moisture with soaking sand? — especially if during changeful months a stream in spate overflows and holds everything far and wide with covering mud, . . .

Unlike Meliboeus, who is now to be exiled by man's martial importunity, Tityrus is subject to the vicissitudes of nature which are counteracted by man's effortful awareness. Nature's difficulties are as continuous as the landscape, but, though recurrent, they are seasonal and as such both limited and temporary.

Meliboeus' second detailed look at Tityrus' enclosure is more easeful (51-58):

> fortunate senex, hic inter flumina nota
> et fontis sacros frigus captabis opacum;
> hinc tibi, quae semper, vicino ab limite saepes
> Hyblaeis apibus florem depasta salicti
> saepe levi somnum suadebit inire susurro;
> hinc alta sub rupe canet frondator ad auras,
> nec tamen interea raucae, tua cura, palumbes
> nec gemere aeria cessabit turtur ab ulmo.

> Fortunate old man, here amid well-known rivers and holy springs you will grasp shady coolness. From here, as always, the hedge on the neighbouring bound, whose willow flower is sipped by bees of Hybla, will often persuade you to fall asleep by its gentle buzzing. From here the pruner under his lofty rock will sing to the breezes, nor meanwhile will the cooing pigeons, your pets, nor the turtle-doves yet cease to moan from the lofty elm.

It too postulates moments of labor. There is a *frondator* and any reader of the *Georgics* would appreciate the exigencies of bee-keeping. But the pruner is at leisure and the bees induce more the sonorous otiosity of pastoral than worries over more practical, pressing concerns. Here again the two dimensions which define space are carefully wrought. We sense the horizontal by mention of proximate flock, known streams, neighbouring bounds, but the linear dimension comes most vividly alive in the hedge which separates the shepherd from contagion beyond. Its magic sets us apart in a place of musical quiet. Line 54, which could be omitted without any break in grammatical order, reflects this verbally. Syntactic disjunction — bees, flower, willow clump — increases a sense of removal from what is beyond, while allusion to Hybla lures the reader into thoughts of Sicily and the Theocritean inheritance. This persuasive hedge, enticing sleep outside its regular time, is another muse, forwarding the intellectual sphere bounded by Tityrus and Amaryllis in the opening lines.

Three lines describe this phenomenon, and an equal three, also introduced by *hinc,* are dedicated to the pruner and doves which serve as a vertical counterpoise. Our inner eye, focussed on the *frondator*, goes first up — the rock is lofty — then down, since he is underneath it, then up again as he sings to the breezes. The doves stress the opposite direction. Instead of watching an earthbound object facing heavenward we now catch their song sent back down to us from an airy elm. Here, too, through song and moan music fills up space and assures its continuity.

This interdependence of setting and sound qualifies more briefly Meliboeus' final view of his past life (75-78):

> non ego vos posthac viridi proiectus in antro
> dumosa pendere procul de rupe videbo;
> carmina nulla canam; non me pascente, capellae,
> florentem cytisum et salices carpetis amaras.

> Not after this will I, stretched out in a green cave, see you afar hanging from a bushy rock. I will sing no songs. Nor as I pasture you, goats, will you crop flowering clover and bitter willows.

Like Tityrus he was stretched out, but from his green cave he looked across a more extensive vista to his distant flock which, in turn, because they are hanging from a thickety rock, again force our vision up and down as well as across. Since they fed on lowland willows as well as hung from rocks, we also redefine the pastoral enclosure of mountain and lake. And as they fed, Meliboeus sang, which, as Tityrus has long since told us, is the same thing seen metaphorically. Tityrus' cattle, with a god's benediction, now still wander as he plays what he will on rustic pipe.

Specifically, however, this last remembrance of Meliboeus points directly into the final lines of the poem which immediately follow (79-83):

> Hic tamen hanc mecum poteras requiescere noctem
> fronde super viridi: sunt nobis mitia poma,
> castaneae molles et pressi copia lactis,
> et iam summa procul villarum culmina fumant
> maioresque cadant altis de montibus umbrae.

> Here nevertheless you could rest this night with me on green foliage. I have ripe apples, soft chestnuts and a supply of cheese, and now the roof peaks of the houses are smoking afar off and larger shadows are falling from the lofty mountains.

Tityrus' invitation varies subtly the preceding details of Meliboeus' farewell. His green leaves gently recall Meliboeus' green grotto and his prospect, also over a distance, alters that of his interlocutor. But much else besides is drawn in here from the body of the poem. The soft fruit now readily available remind the reader of the ripening fruit that Amaryllis suffered to hang unplucked on their boughs because of Tityrus' former absence. Mention of a ready supply of cheese conjures up an earlier day when the same product was pressed and sold to an unresponsive town nearby. The diurnal smoking of farm houses at nightfall complements the monthly smoking of the sacrifice to the young god who now assures the maintenance of Tityrus' idyll. The victims he once sold to bring small increment for his savings he now sacrifices himself for grander ends. In particular the mention of *culmina* following closely on Meliboeus' hope some day to see again the rooftop of his poor hut (*pauperis tuguris culmen*) is further acknowledgment that Tityrus' bliss and Meliboeus' yearning often rest on the same objects.

The poet's methodology in sketching his final vista of pastoral enclosure is by now predictable. Once again the eye works in two directions to control the prospect. It is cast outward into the distance, first to the smoking chimneys nearer by, then to the mountains further removed. At the same time the eye turns upward following the rising smoke and the height of the hills, then accompanies the downward fall of greater shadows. The mountains, though lofty and afar, effect the final horizontal boundary, and shadows fill the intervening space.

247

I will return later to the negative implications of these greater shadows cast for Meliboeus by specific comparison with Tityrus' stability of time and place. Here it is important to see them simply as a grander vision of the opening lines — the near tree and smaller shade expanded into distant hills and a larger darkening that encompasses a wider vista. Though much of the poem's matter leads pointedly to the final five lines, these in turn refer cyclically back to the initial quintet. The operative rhetorical figure there and in other smaller segments of the poem, chiasmus, dominates the poem as a whole.[6] The miniature interplay of Tityrus and Meliboeus, the latter briefly stopping in Tityrus' ideal preserve, is magnified into a grander dialogue which develops in intensity as the vistas themselves grow. The spatial vision of a Tityran literal and symbolic mode of life and mind is thus complemented by a poetics of ordering which verbally also embraces balancing objects within a frame.

The search for putative models of this enclosed landscape of the mind can tell us something of Virgil's purpose as well as his originality. We expect but do not find anything beyond remote parallelisms in Theocritus. In Theocritus pine and springs, sloping banks, tamarisks, elms, oaks, statues of Priapus and fountain goddesses, a shepherd's seat (I choose details from the opening of the first *idyll*) draw attention to individual excellences of setting, offering proper opportunity for rest and occasions for song. The singer often sits under or near a tree (elm, pine, or olive). In *idyll* 5 there is a grassy resting-place, and in several poems water, whether springs or a fall, is essential. The fifth *idyll* finds Comatas capping Lacon's earlier boasts by claiming for himself two springs of cold water, twittering birds, better shade, a pine with cones. These are luxuriant spots bursting with excitement. In Theocritus nature provides an appropriate ambience for song, relieving some of her ordinary oppression for the sake of inspiration. Virgil in the first *eclogue* by contrast will be seen to outline and fill a green oasis of the mind, an echoing landscape vivified by the poet and as vulnerable as his thoughts.

We may take as one example in Theocritus with direct bearing on Virgil a segment of the harvest-home of Phrasidamus which concludes *idyll* 7 on a note of opulence (135-142):

> Many a poplar and elm murmured above our heads,
> and near at hand the sacred water from the cave of the
> Nymphs fell plashing. On the shady boughs the dusky
> cicadas were busy with their chatter, and the tree-frog
> far off cried in the dense thornbrake. Larks and finches
> sang, the dove made moan, and bees flitted humming
> about the springs. (Gow)

This lush spot is as alive with sound as Tityrus' *locus amoenus* which it inspired. But, aside from the basic fact that for Virgil nature conspires with man to create song while Theocritus seems caught up in lushness for its own joyous sake — this is the end of the *idyll*, not even a setting for singing — the variations in detail are instructive. Most changes reflect Virgil's need to protect his spot as a retreat for creativity. Theocritus has a specific bubbling fountain, sacred to the Nymphs; Virgil mentions vaguer streams and holy springs which will soon serve to distinguish Tityrus' bounded lot from the distant Oaxes in readiness for exiled Meliboeus. In Theocritus the dove moans, and larks and finches sing. Virgil's dove, we remember, coos from a lofty elm. Virgil replaces tree-frog (in the thornbush) and crickets chirping (on shady boughs) with the singing pruner whose careful placement we have already noted. Finally Theocritus has bees humming around springs, while for Virgil they are essential creators of the hedge cloistering known from unknown, poetry from disease. In brief, both authors share a common respect for the importance of sound and other seductive details in an inspiring setting. In Theocritus they regularly form a complement to singing. In Virgil they are as much inspired as inspiring, defined by the poet and filled out by his singer's voice.

Several poets among Theocritus' contemporaries furnish examples of similarly rich landscapes. Moschus contrasts a seafarer's lot with the landsman's shade, singing pine, sweet sleep, a bubbling spring, and the Arcadian poetess Anyte has several epigrams inscribing the virtues of fountains whose restful shade and cooling waters seduce the stranger from heat and effort.[7] Such details hark back to two moments in the *Odyssey*, Homer's description of the cave of Calypso in book 5 and of Alcinous' demesne in the seventh book. Trees, birds, a wild vine, fountains and a meadow enhance the first, while the Phaeacian king's orchard, surrounded by a hedge, contains varied trees, vineyards in different stages of ripening, gardens and twin fountains.

Homer as always celebrates his world but has no interest in landscape, whether literal or symbolic, save for its enrichment of narrative flow. Hesiod, however, points the way through which landscape will finally evolve from literal to figurative. In *Works and Days* the month of May is the time one labors with the sickle and brings home fruit. Orion's first appearance in July occasions the winnowing and storage of grain. In between, during June, as the artichoke flowers, when goats are plumpest, women most wanton and wine at its sweetest, Hesiod asks for a shady rock and wine of Biblis (592-596):

> . . . let me drink bright wine, sitting in the shade, when
> my heart is satisfied with food, and so, turning my head

to face the fresh Zephyr, from the everflowing spring
which pours down unfouled thrice pour an offering
of water, but make a fourth libation of wine. (Evelyn-
White)

Within the space of fifteen lines there are four mentions of wine as well
as shade, the Zephyr and a spring — regular concomitants of the later
pastoral singer's retreat. Poetically, topographically and temporally it is
a world apart, a break from what follows and precedes, but there is no
ideological distinction between outer and inner. Wine and shade only
lessen the pressures of the georgic life, from which they betoken a
momentary stepping aside.[8]

In the famous opening to the *Phaedrus* Plato hints at the deeper distinction. Socrates allows himself to be seduced out of the city along the
Ilissus to a country spot whose individual features only gradually evolve
— plane tree, shade, breeze, agnus castus, a spring, cicadas.[9] Phaedrus'
hope is that this gracious retreat will inspire the philosopher to greater
insights much as it will be a necessity for later pastoral singers. What it
could become is made clear by Socrates' pronouncement of non-involvement. People have more to teach him than country things. The next logical
step would have been to expand the distinction of city and country
beyond questions of mere content to embrace a deeper philosophical
dialectic of retreat or involvement with life which any challenge between
urban and pastoral only adumbrates. It remains for the philosopher-poet
Lucretius to accomplish the intellectualization of the *locus amoenus* by
changing it from a quickening place to sing into a metaphor for living
and thinking. It is Virgil's genius to fuse the two, merging poetry and
landscape in a composite vision.

The most pertinent example in Lucretius of country setting as symbol
occurs in the middle of the *prooemium* to the second book. The body
needs few things to survive in comfort, says the poet, certainly not golden
statues to carry torches for banquets or fretted ceilings reverberating to
the lute (29-33):

> cum tamen inter se prostrati in gramine molli
> propter aquae rivum sub ramis arboris altae
> non magnis opibus iucunde corpora curant,
> praesertim cum tempestas arridet et anni
> tempora conspergunt viridantis floribus herbas.

> but yet men lie in friendly groups on the soft grass near
> some stream of water under the branches of a tall tree,
> and at no great cost delightfully refresh their bodies,

above all when the weather smiles on them, and the
season of the year bestrews the green grass with flowers.

(Bailey)

This is no literal landscape. Lucretius makes clear elsewhere how oppressive for him would be a life eked from the earth. It is a model of mind, a conscious metamorphosis of the Theocritean landscape into a symbol of philosophical stance, that is, in Lucretius' thinking, of a life free from pain and fear, unambitious yet self-contained, intent on that spiritual calm which comes from deep scrutiny of the *naturae species ratioque,* the external and internal patternings of nature. This is the famous Epicurean *hortus conclusus* out of which the philosopher made an emblem for his way of life. Cicero visualizes it as follows (*de Or.* 3. 63): . . . *in hortulis quiescet suis, ubi volt, ubi etiam recubans molliter et delicate nos avocat a Rostris, a iudiciis, a curia, fortasse sapienter, hac praesertim re publica* ('But it [i.e. Epicurean philosophy] will rest in its own gardens, where it desires to be, where moreover as it reclines it seduces us softly and gently from public speaking, from the courts, from government, perhaps wisely especially given the present state of public affairs').[10] But this garden is more than an escape from politics and the realities of history. More positively it incorporates an ethical state of spirit that prefers simplicity to luxury, restraint to grandiosity, inner tranquillity to the turmoil of competition. It is no accident that Lucretius' anonymous landscape peopled by men at ease, bounded by water and tree, blessed by the seasons, comes at the center of the proem, hedged in by addicts of self-interest and dependency on the superficial. At the outer extremes of this splendid passage we find the philosopher who views the intervening battlings of men from his eminence of unconcern, aware that terrors and darkness of the mind are dispelled by a mental calm symbolized by the garden at the core of his thoughts.[11]

These lines are repeated with minor variants for a similar ideological purpose during the anthropology of the fifth book (1392-96).[12] They are central to Lucretius' overview of the development of music and ritual dance at a moment in mankind's evolution between primitive and sophisticated just as, more immediately, the farmer yields to the song and rhythm of rustic music at moments interposed among seasonal pressures.[13] It is the whistling of the Zephyr which teaches, the *agrestis* who learns in a setting (1386-87):

> avia per nemora ac silvas saltusque . . .,
> per loca pastorum deserta atque otia dia.

amid the pathless woods and forests and glades, among
the desolate haunts of shepherds, and the lonely places
of their rest. (Bailey)

This is a place and time for an instant outside of human temporal
development and its accompanying ambitions which range, as Lucretius
soon puts it, from rude skins to hyper-civilized gold and purples. Goals
and methodology of acquisition may differ but in each case greed and
vengeance are operative in the pursuit. A pastoral haven wherein the
rural muse surrounds the leisured rustic with rhythmic song forms both
a physical and an intellectual contrast, offering a further specification
of that mental attitude free from pain and fear by which Lucretius in
the second book already expands upon Theocritus.

Virgil may have had these very *otia dia*, these divine moments of
repose in his mind when he has Tityrus speak of the leisure his god has
fashioned (*deus nobis haec otia fecit*). In fact the presence of Lucretius
is strongly felt behind these lines, for the resonance through his five verse
eulogy of Tityrus' youthful divinity we soon learn about at Rome —
deus . . . ille . . . deus, illius . . . ille — clearly resembles Lucretius' apostrophe of Epicurus at the opening of book 5: *deus ille fuit, deus, inclute
Memmi* ('he was a god, a god, renowned Memmius', 8).[14] The phrase
silvestrem musam, the object of Tityrus' present pondering, is drawn
from the fourth book of *de rerum natura* where music also plays a part
(589).[15] Yet since there it forms one feature in a lonely, echoic countryside peopled by its dwellers with figures of make-believe, with nymphs
and satyrs and Pan with his reeds, Virgil may mean us to scrutinize both
the reality and, by corollary, any potential Epicureanism of Tityrus.

Lucretius in his fourth book questions the existence of pastoral landscape and in the fifth treats it as a thing of the past. The symbolism of
the *locus amoenus*, however, remains true because it denotes an ethical
state of being contrasted with more intense, grasping attitudes. For
Virgil pastoral living, indolent shepherding and singing, and *locus
amoenus* are merged in imagination as a musical retreat placed against
agricultural and Roman realities from which Meliboeus is soon to be
thrust into still broader and more bitter versions of history. But his protagonists, viewed in the light of Epicurean tenets, must each to a certain
measure be considered a failure as Epicurean 'spectators' of the world's
march past. Meliboeus first looks back into the paradise of Tityrus, then
contemplates the remote possibility of a later return to observe the
kingdom of his small acreage. On the edge of the abyss he reviews a
confined world of beauty to which he no longer belongs, as an Epicurean
by definition must. Tityrus on the contrary must be judged a failure as
spectator because he makes no attempt to broaden his intellectual bounds

to learn of himself. The journey to Rome, a withdrawal from hard pastoral in the pursuit of *libertas* gained, leads not to a deepened self-knowledge sparked by the friction of opposing values but into a smoother perfection, assured not by analogy with some remote, Epicurean god but by a politically active divinity present at the center of power. Meliboeus is a failed Epicurean *malgré lui* because he is swept by conditions he cannot control out of simple into complex, out of dream into history. Tityrus may for an instant enclose Meliboean complexity inside his more easeful lot but he lapses intellectually, and the Lucretian allusions with which Virgil touches him betoken limitation, not expansion of human response.[16]

The pastoral vision or indeed any work of literature that touches on pastoral notions is rarely filled with the unresolved ambiguities and tensions rife in *eclogue* 1. Seen by itself, the posture of Tityrus may be deemed to sketch perfected *otium* but the poem as a whole dwells on fraction, not resolution. Here too we may draw on the categories of time and space to help clarify Virgil's distinctions. Tityrus, it is clear, has once been subject to time. He is now a *senex*, an old man, and his beard fell white beneath the barber's shears even before he went in search of liberty.[17] The passage of time from youth to age had been accompanied by regular servile trips to answer the demands of the nearby town. Now by contrast the shepherd makes a greater leap in space from countryside to Rome. But such action, appropriately enough accomplished by the instance of a creature both young and in some eyes eternal, confirms the change from slavery to freedom and restores a landscape now stable and uninterrupted.

Temporally too there is process within this idyll. Amaryllis we assume need no longer impede ripening of fruit now that Tityrus is happily returned. The presence of a pruner suggests the need for seasonal labor, trimming vines in the spring or culling leaves for winter must. But he is at leisure, singing, controlling his life just as Tityrus' cheese and animals are now his own to distribute. Seasonal change, if we are meant to see it as such, is not for Tityrus an aspect of Adam's curse[18] but part of daily, monthly, or annual continuity which the poet twice stipulates as occurring 'often' and 'always'. The youth to whom Tityrus sacrifices twelve times a year is to him as immortal as the enclosure he assures (7-8):

> namque erit ille mihi semper deus, illius aram
> saepe tener nostris ab ovilibus imbuet agnus.

> for he will always be a god to me. Often a tender lamb
> from our folds will dye his altar.

These same temporal adverbs purposefully qualify one aspect of the musical hedge that, as we have seen, serves for a bastion against outer trouble and disease (53-55):

> hinc tibi, quae semper, vicino ab limite saepes
> Hyblaeis apibus florem depasta salicti
> saepe levi somnum suadebit inire susurro; . . .

For Tityrus the mensual smoking of altars, characterizing orderly liaison between man and god, is a grander version of the smoking chimneys that locate the countryman's daily awareness of nightfall.[19]

Tityrus acknowledges that liberty came to him after a long time (*longo post tempore*, 29), and Meliboeus uses the same phrase in his prayer that one day he may renew his acquaintance with his land (67). In between lies the void that differentiates the two shepherds. Naked rock for Tityrus means a boundary stone that alludes to a shepherd's efforts at pasturing. For Meliboeus it means disintegration and death. The flint on which his mother ewe bears and abandons her twins is precursor of unlimited motion in space and time that now has fallen his lot. The presence of suffering is universal (*undique*), in all the fields (*totis agris*), continuous and unrelenting (*usque adeo*). From Tityrus' cyclical time Meliboeus plunges into the linearity of history, and from an enclosed space he turns in future toward geography's farthest reaches. Tityrus has left the land to experience an ideal urbanism which restores him to a nearly ideal setting. Meliboeus relies only on hope as he plunges into the realities of exile forced by equally realistic politics. This pressure is epitomized not in the person of a young god who fosters uplifting abstractions and commands pastoral to endure but in the guise of a soldier, barbarian though Roman, impious though (we are never directly told) the minion of the same Roman god.

Meliboeus' is a verbal world where dualities reinforce each other. The more general *linquimus . . . fugimus* ('are leaving . . . are in flight') of the opening lines is soon taken up by *ago . . . duco* ('drive . . . lead'), activity forced upon him in his illness and upon his sick flock. This expands into his later prophecy of arrival at great distances — *ibimus . . . venemus* ('will go . . . will come') — into places specified because unknown, Africa and Scythia, Britain and the Oaxes. These are the geographical counterparts of Rome in Tityrus' life just as Meliboeus' soldier contrasts with the latter's god. Idealized intellectual retreat is a foil for extreme impositions of time and place. The reader does not miss the irony of the final doublets, *insere . . . pone* ('graft . . . put'), *ite . . . ite* ('on . . . on'). Futile commands to restore a lost order of grafting and viticulture yield to a still simpler, iterated farewell. Tityrus returns from Rome to an enhanced dream. Meliboeus loses his land entirely, The line is his symbol, not the circle. The sharp contours with which he etches Tityrus' regained and his lost paradise are drawn from the spectator's astonished, final vision for remembrance in the mind's eye alone.

Rarely does Virgil allow himself the luxury of picturing a worked landscape verging on freedom from the concerns of those who people it, but there is one moment in the third book of the *Georgics* which both offers another verbal definition of the *locus amoenus* and comments on the plight of Meliboeus. It is a seventeen line sketch of a shepherd's summer day which deserves quotation in full (322-338):

> At vero Zephyris cum laeta vocantibus aestas
> in saltus utrumque gregem atque in pascua mittet,
> Luciferi primo cum sidere frigida rura
> carpamus, dum mane novum, dum gramina canent,
> et ros tenera pecori gratissimus herba.
> inde ubi quarta sitim caeli collegerit hora
> et cantu querulae rumpent arbusta cicadae,
> ad puteos aut alta greges ad stagna iubebo
> currentem ilignis potare canalibus undam;
> aestibus at mediis umbrosam exquirere vallem,
> sicubi magna Iovis antiquo robore quercus
> ingentis tendat ramos, aut sicubi nigrum
> ilicibus crebris sacra nemus accubet umbra;
> tum tenuis dare rursus aquas et pascere rursus
> solis ad occasum, cum frigidus aera Vesper
> temperat, et saltus reficit iam roscida luna,
> litoraque alcyonen resonant, acalanthida dumi.

> But when, at the Zephyrs' call, joyous summer sends both sheep and goats to the glades and pastures, let us haste to the cool fields, as the morning-star begins to rise, while the day is young, while the grass is hoar, and the dew on the tender blade most sweet to the cattle. Then, when heaven's fourth hour has brought thirst to all, and the plaintive cicadas rend the thickets with song, I will bid the flocks at the side of the wells or deep pools drink of the water that runs in oaken channels. But in midday heat let them seek out a shady dell, where haply Jove's mighty oak with its ancient trunk stretches out giant branches, or where the grove, black with many holms, lies brooding with hallowed

shade. Then give them once more the trickling stream, and once more feed them till sunset, when the cool evening-star allays the air, and the moon, now dropping dew, gives strength to the glades, when the shores ring with the halcyon, and the copses with the finch. (Fairclough)

In this gloomy book which dwells so broodingly on the destructive aspects of passion and death such a moment comes as a welcome relief.[20] We will return shortly to its particular context, but first we should observe the artistic unity of the passage, the cycle of daily round achieved in words. There is of course the linear passage of time seen in four divisions, dawn, mid-morning, high-noon and evening. Yet within each group there are alternatives which relieve the pressures of temporality. In early morning warmth urges the flocks into glades (*in saltus*) or pastureland (*in pascua*), while the day is fresh (*dum*), while grass is still dewy (*dum*). At the fourth hour we have the choice of wells (*ad puteos*) or lakes (*ad stagna*) at which to water the animals. When the sun is at its highest, nature and her poet offer a miniature cycle of enclosing shade from *umbrosam vallem* to *umbra*, with the most extensive possibilities of recourse, either to where the oak stretches its branches (*sicubi*) or where there is a grove rich with ilex (*sicubi*). Finally toward evening we have the opportunity of offering water again (*rursus*) or pasture (*rursus*) until sunset.

These last lines draw together the practical intent of the early episodes, pasture at dawn, water at ten. Yet they also frame the whole into a cycle which endures from dawn to dusk, Lucifer to evening-star, and beyond. *Frigidus Vesper* ('cool evening-star') anticipates renewal of *frigida rura* ('cool fields') for the early morning, and the dewy moon (*roscida luna*) refreshes the same glades with dew to tempt the flock again when night has run its course. The daily time of aestival herding is in fact timeless here through nature's constant self-revival. But there is a still more important outer layer that envelops this pastoral cycle. Water, coolness and sanctity stand at the core of the pastoral retreat, both here and for Tityrus. Jupiter's oak and the sacred shade of the ilex are at the center of day and of life. But, if, for Tityrus, inspiration's music lends third dimensional shape to what is already bounded, here sound itself defines the outer reaches. We begin with the Zephyr's call, summer's harbinger, and end as shore resounds with halcyon and thicket with finch.[21] Shore and thicket, water and land, perhaps even high and low, touch on those limnings of the inner landscape which we saw so frequently in the first *eclogue*, but sound is what forms its special loveliness.[22]

It is with every reason that Virgil draws on the eighth *eclogue* for one of his most joyous lines here. This is the time when Damon begins to sing (14-15):

> frigida vix caelo noctis decesserat umbra,
> cum ros in tenera pecori gratissimus herba: . . .

> Scarcely had the cool shade of night left the heavens,
> when dew on the tender grass is most pleasant to the
> flock . . .

The same occasion is seductive for beast and inspirational for his singer-keeper. But the last line—

> litoraque alcyonen resonant acalanthida dumi

> when the shores ring with the halcyon, and the copses
> with the finch—

has the richest ring. It takes our ear back to the culminative moment in Meliboeus' portrait of Tityrus at his ease (5):

> formosam resonare doces Amaryllida silvas.

> you teach the woods to resound 'beautiful Amaryllis'.

Music is conceived by sounded word but the harmony of the whole is in each instance evoked by the use of Greek, the name of Amaryllis which Tityrus teaches his woods, the halcyon and *acalanthis* that fulfill the shores and bushes. In each instance there is a sense of romanticism that warns how fragile, brief and remote this beauty remains and how untouched by the persistence of our mortal cares.[23]

Once again it is context that verbally sets apart and defines Virgil's intellectual design. What precedes in the third *georgic* concerns the difficulties of raising sheep and goats, giving proper care to their wool and milk especially when nature puts the obstacles of chilling ice and winter wind in the path of the husbandman. What follows is a disquisition on Libya and Scythia, realms which the poet has told us in the first *georgic* border on and therefore outline one of the two temperate zones which have been granted for subsistence by the gods to mortals (237-38). It is not only that these spots define north and south and therefore stand for the elementally cold and hot. We suddenly pass from a utopia where life is so regular that no names matter to places named and scrutinized as being far beyond the ordinary, where efforts are strangely unceasing and unvaried or fitful and abrupt.

For the Libyans space is viewed only in horizontal terms. Existence consists of continuous motion and time is never stopped or changed: 'often the flock pastures day and night and a whole month in a row'. There is no distinction between day and night, or day and day. The very expanse of space — *tantum campi iacet* ('so vast a plain lies outstretched') — helps further to blur calendar distinctions. Virgil compares the weapon-bearing African to a Roman soldier, 'sharp' in the arms of his fatherland, and the simile is not unjustified. This linear world of constantly 'seizing the road' stops only for the moment of a surprise attack against the enemy.

The Scythians on the other hand offer different though equally extreme variants of the same categories. Time now is not only undifferentiated but nearly stopped (356):

> semper hiems, semper spirantes frigora Cauri; . . .

> It is always winter, always the north winds breathe
> chill . . .

It is always one season, winter, and its chill winds are ever blowing. Here Virgil sees space mostly in vertical terms (354-55):

> sed iacet aggeribus niveis informis et alto
> terra gelu late septemque adsurgit in ulnas.

> But far and wide earth lies shapeless under ramparts of
> snow and deep ice, and is piled up seven cubits in
> height.

We see snow through its mass, and ice is measured by depth and height. Not surprisingly in this world where space is abruptly limited there is scarcely any motion. Life is frozen to a virtual standstill from numbness, the only action being the pre-pastoral hunting of the primitive inhabitants who slaughter animals immobilized by the stiffening chill. By direct contrast with the nomadic natives of north Africa, and fittingly enough for those whose world is delineated by up and down, they live underground. There they while away enforced leisure hours with drinking and gaming, meanwhile mollifying nature's perpetual cold with a fire as different from the natural temperature variations of ordinary pastoral life as the Libyans' perpetual moving is a destructive variant of pastoral's gentle balance between ease and effort.

Hence, as in Lucretius, the preceding idyll of a shepherd's day is defined by its context. It is no wonder that two of the names Meliboeus mentions as possible distant receivers of his exile are the Afri and Scythia. Ideologically speaking they are as remote on one side from Meliboeus' *dulcia arva* ('sweet fields') and the grain ears that form his georgic kingdom as Tityrus' musical retreat is on the other. In their oppressive one-dimensionality they pervert spatial and temporal cycles we have seen necessary to frame off pastoral landscape from outside demands.

I would like to offer one example drawn from more recent literature where parallel definitions of space are reflections in topography of a state of mind. I draw on the first and last of the so-called 'desolation' sonnets of Gerard Manley Hopkins, numbered 65 and 71 by Robert Bridges. He begins 'No worst, there is none. Pitched past pitch of grief . . .' The poet conceives himself thrown, heaved past grief's black incline – down, down, one imagines, where the Spirit brings no comfort and the Virgin no relief. 'My cries heave, herds-long; huddle . . .' His shouts are like sheep, his mental posture as 'mountains; cliffs of fall'. Everything is vertical, visible correlative to the terrifying ambiguity of Fury's prayer: 'Let me be fell'. The cliffs are 'frightful, sheer, no-man-fathomed'. The speaker has little strength against their steep or deep. One thought alone offers refuge toward which to creep from the exposed whirlwind: 'all / life death does end and each day dies with sleep'.

Nothing horizontal smooths this sheerness, certainly nothing like that ideal aspect of pastoral which orders time in measured space. The mind's comfortless grief is abrupt, interrupted only by the invitation to creep, the one escape from total drop. Such tenuous relief is bleakly distinguished by sleep and death, ways of time that are final, not cyclical, devastating all feeling, not renewing. However, immediately at the start of the final sonnet – 'My own heart let me more have pity on . . .' – a sense of otherness is established in the dialogue between 'heart' and 'me' and, immediately thereafter, 'me' and 'self'. This colloquy divides what had been unified before—

> . . . not live this tormented mind
> with this tormented mind tormenting yet –

and establishes a spatial distance in the mind eliciting hope for comfort which the former, congealed sorrow could not allow. The sestet expands upon this purview:

> Soul, self; come, poor Jackself. I do advise
> You, jaded, let be; call off thoughts awhile
> Elsewhere; leave comfort root-room; let joy size

> At God knows when to God knows what; whose smile
> 's not wrung, see you; unforeseen time rather — as skies
> Betweenpie mountains — lights a lovely mile.

In the scope established between the poet and his soul he has gained strength to banish gloom and allow for the growth of joy that sizes into God's time and space. This spot which fosters comfort's tree is further caught through God's smile which frames a much more pastoral outlook in every sense. Instead of the one sheer cliff of steep despair we now have two intervening ridges which serve to outline 'a lovely mile', completing the necessary horizontal bound. This space is further watched by the splendid phrase 'as skies betweenpie mountains'. God's smile not only lights a forward beam, answering to suffering's dark downward depths. It urges the eye up to 'skies' and then out to the variegated shimmerings cast between the far-off risings — a larger analogy of the space into which comfort's growth can burgeon.

Hopkins' perhaps most famous poem, 'Pied Beauty', begins

> Glory be to God for dappled things —
> For skies of couple-colour as a brinded cow; . . .

Love is the center of Hopkins' world just as for Virgil sacredness is essential in nature's center. When Hopkins chose to 'praise him', to recognize comfort from the joy that lights a lovely mile, it is through country details —

> landscape plotted and pierced — fold, fallow, and
>   plough; —

which can now manage to enclose and control those many seen contradictions in our world that are but segments of one whose beauty is past change.

There is something of the same ordering unity in the setting which Tityrus surveys at the end of the first *eclogue*. In the foreground are the two shepherds, the one inviting the other to share for the night his verdant, productive repose. The middle distance of smoking rooftops associates itself aptly with Meliboeus' georgic preoccupations, herding, ploughing, grafting, viticulture. Mountains are the final boundary at the farthest range. Yet the presence of Meliboeus soon to be exiled is a foil to the validity of Tityrus' time and place. Smoke can be evanescent as well as warming, destructive as well as recreative, and it has been often said that the greater shadows cast as much melancholy as quiescence. Nightfall and the bounty of cheese and fruit connote the daily and seasonal time that remains for Tityrus. Meliboeus is cast into historical time. Tityrus' vista, therefore, in Virgil's ideological survey, extends from pastoral, over georgic to what we might call the prospects of epic. Those distant hills, instead of enclosing, induce the ranging eye toward Rome, the source of barbarous soldiery as well as of pastoral make-believe, of the power that exiles into the most brutal reality as well as consolidates the ideal of imaginative retreat through a politics of conservation. Darkness either refreshes or obliterates depending on one's stance.

As we look back in summary on the whole, the ambiguous aura that surrounds the ending reflects on the pastoralism of the protagonists. Modern criticism generally views pastoral enlightenment as that central though often sequestered moment of discovery that follows after a time of literal or psychic uncertainty and precedes a return to a former regularity with newly heightened realization of identity and self-aware-ness.[24] Innocence can clarify experience, primitivism help discern quality in so-called civilization. Through the metaphor of pastoral the prophetic or imaginative can counterbalance or set in relief the mundane or realistic. An inner moment away often brings outer challenges into proper per-spective. Tityrus' journey from country to city and back to country proffers only a superficial elevation in individual social status from slavery to private, leisured freedom which contrasts with the public confusion rampant elsewhere. Because the source of power, the city and its god, confirms rather than disrupts the idealistic aspects of the inner world, ordinary existence, in this singular instance, is unerringly appreciative of the world apart. Hence we have a double departure from the accepted pastoral canon. Tityrus' experience is innocent, and his renewed 'inno-cence' by being untested lacks any deepened sense of understanding.

For Meliboeus, who already lives a georgic existence, relegation is as much a question of degree as of kind. He confronts a suddenly harshened *patria* displaying its most unsympathetic, oppressive side and needs no pastoral escape, no idyllic fiction contingent to reality, to scrutinize him-self.[25] With beautiful Amaryllis restored to his colleague and his own sweet fields lost, Meliboeus is already aware of what distinguishes himself from Tityrus and there is nothing to be gained save suffering from the comparison.[26] Contingency comes only on the most literal level. Two people remain momentarily near each other on the verge of a scenario landscape which continues for one and is relinquished by the other. Tityrus is shielded while Meliboeus is exposed, victim of political and ethical importunities which his fortunate colleague escapes.

What therefore to some critics might seem the unsatisfactory pastor-alism of the poem may from another viewpoint be its greatest achieve-ment. There is change but no spiritual or intellectual development in the protagonists, no route of self-discovery through a land apart. Differing worlds meet but no one mediates between them or is reshaped by their collision. Rather it is the reader who gains from this collocation and who makes the pastoral pilgrimage himself by bridging the gap between ideal and real, poetry and power, timeless, imaginative retreat and timeful history which separates the two players. We may think of Tityrus' preserve as the precursor of the forest of Arden, or Prospero's magic isle, or even Walden pond, but we also are the ones who in our minds mark off its distinction from Meliboeus and in so doing make an intellectual act of comparison that is at the basis of any version of pastoral.

I do not want to end with the impression that Virgil's use of chiasmus or verbal cycles always has a positive result. One of the chief unifying factors in his poetry is his use of shade. We have seen it in the first *eclogue* as the shade of Tityrus, *lentus in umbra,* is metamorphosed into the larger, in some ways more menacing *umbrae* that descend on the landscape at dusk. Since shade is also an essential subject at the end of the tenth *eclogue* its presence is a coalescing factor for the book as a whole. But there is a difference between these two appearances and the reader is left with a more totally negative impression at the end. Tityrus' shade in part surrounds the troubled Meliboeus. In the last poem Gallus' dream of his mistress Lycoris happily ensconced within the *locus amoenus* is framed by a double circle of reality, first that of Gallus, then the poet's own. For the lovesick soldier-elegist Arcadian roughness could serve as purgative but will not. The truth of his military activism is complemented by the actuality of her unfaithfulness. Beyond this, in the outermost concentric ring, we have Virgil first contemplating his final *labor* (strange word for a singer of pastorals!), then leaping to his feet with the announcement that shade is bad for singers and for crops. With one anti-pastoral gesture he proclaims the end of the *Eclogues* and hints at *Georgics* to come. Shade signifies both. Finally, in a still grander suggestion of unity for all Virgil's works, the word *umbra* recurs at the end of the last line of the *Aeneid* as the life of Turnus, chafing at its lot, makes reluctant way under the shades below, those *umbrae silentes* among which Aeneas, alive in the kingdom of death, had once furthered his own peculiar destiny. It forms an ambiguous but not atypically darkening way for Virgil to conclude his melancholy overview of the relationship of men and arms in the establishment of empire.[27]

There is one moment earlier in the last book of the epic that has more direct bearing on the end of the first *eclogue* and registers further intellectual balance between the beginning and end of his career. In a moment of rage against the Latins Aeneas shouts out to his men that unless their city yields forthwith he will raze it to the ground that very day. His words are instructive (*Aen.* 12. 569):

eruam et aequa solo fumantia culmina ponam.

I will overthrow [the city] and place its smoking rooftops level with the ground.

We have analyzed the only other occasion in his work where Virgil uses
culmen and *fumo* in conjunction as Tityrus looks out over the roofs of
the houses smoking in the distance:

et iam summa procul villarum culmina fumant.

These passages bear on each other, if only through their symbolism. The
whole first *eclogue,* as we have seen, focusses on these lines which for
Tityrus expand and solidify a portrait of rural contentment. We never
hear Meliboeus' final thoughts but it is possible that just as the poem's
readers sense an ambiguity in those larger shades so he, the dispossessed,
might in his mind's eye merge those smoking housetops with the smouldering ruins that a victorious army leaves in its wake. It is he who suffers
the incursion of Rome through a soldier styled *impius* and *barbarus.*[28]
It is through him that we contemplate for the first but far from the last
time that tension between individual human suffering and the composed
achievement of empire which supersedes any rhetorical ideas of order,
yet constantly charges the imagination of Rome's greatest poet.

Brown University.

NOTES

1. The first *eclogue* has been most recently analyzed by E. W. Leach *Vergil's
Eclogues: Landscapes of Experience* (Cornell, 1974), ch. 4 ('Roman Realities and
Poetic Symbolism in *Eclogue* 1') who, as her title intimates, lays particular stress on
the Roman specifics of the poem. I am particularly indebted to John Van Sickle for
many conversations on pastoralism over many years and above all for the opportunity
to read in manuscript those portions devoted to the first *eclogue* in his general
critique of Vergil *Arcadia and Orpheus in the Poetics of Virgil.* It is to be hoped
that his detailed analysis of the dialectic of the poem's opening lines, the most
percipient yet to be written, will soon be published.

2. On the importance of shade see P. L. Smith '*Lentus in umbra*', *Phoenix* 19
(1965), 298-304. On echo as a fulfilling motif see P. Damon 'Modes of Analogy in
Ancient and Medieval Verse', *UCalPClPh* 15 (1961), 261-334, esp. 281ff., for Virgil's
differences with Theocritus. Ancient concepts of shade are surveyed by J. Nováková
Umbra: Ein Beitrag zür dichterischen Semantik (Berlin, 1964). She deals with the
end of *ecl.* 1 on p. 35 ('der älteste sichere Beleg' of a mountain's shadow in western
literature).

3. J. Barrell, *The Idea of Landscape and the Sense of Place* (Cambridge, 1972),
17ff., discusses in detail poetic techniques used to 'compose' landscape. Especially important for readers of the first *eclogue* is his treatment of the 'high viewpoint'

which Thomson purposefully takes in *The Seasons* (pp. 15f., 24ff.). Differing land-scapes are treated as metaphors for modes of thought by E. Wasserman *The Subtler Language* (Baltimore, 1959), *passim* (esp. ch. 3 and 4 on *Cooper's Hill* and *Windsor Forest*).

4. J. Perret *Virgile: Les Bucoliques* (Paris, 1961), p. 23 *ad loc.*

5. John Van Sickle has called to my attention the time-honored association noted by Servius of beech trees and soft primitivism, a quasi-pastoral existence wherein nature's productiveness fosters more leisure than labor for mankind. It is thus particularly apt that Tityrus, *otiosus*, should be shaded by a beech while Meliboeus, *laboriosus* in every sense, exposed to life's glare, sees *dulcia arva* ('sweet fields') as his representative in landscape.

6. The second five line group, 6-10, also is based on a chiastic structure. *Fecit* ('created', 6) anticipates *permisit* ('allowed', 10) and *ille mihi* ('he . . . for me', 7) looks to *ille meas* ('he . . . my', 9). The center of this narcissism is the tender lamb often staining the altar dedicated to Tityrus' young god, paralleling (ironically?) the position of exiled Meliboeus in the first lines.

7. Cf. Moschus 5. 11ff., Anyte *A.P.* 9. 313 = Anyte 16 (Gow-Page *Hellenistic Epigrams*), *A.Pl.* 228 = Anyte 18 (Gow-Page) as well as details of *A.P.* 9. 314 (= 17 Gow-Page) and *A.Pl.* 291 (= 3 Gow-Page).

8. The Hesiod passage is imitated with curious directness by Alcaeus (frag. 347 L-P = 162P), as D. Page, *Sappho and Alcaeus* (Oxford, 1955), 303ff., has shown. Didactic is absorbed into lyric by the translation of georgic labor into symposiastic relaxation, but much remains the same.

9. On the *Phaedrus* and pastoral landscape see M. Putnam *Virgil's Pastoral Art* (Princeton, 1970), p. 10 and n. 11, for further bibliography.

10. The only use of *recubo* in the *Eclogues* and *Georgics* is at *ecl.* 1. 1. The unique instance in Lucretius is 1. 38 where Mars is 'reclining', surrounded by calming Venus, a 'mythical' conjunction personifying those abstractions which govern the relationship of the Epicurean 'garden' to the world at large.

11. It is possible to adduce other examples in Latin letters of escape into the *locus amoenus* placed centrally. Perhaps the most *á propos* is found at lines 19-22 of Horace *Odes* 1. 1:

> est qui nec veteris pocula Massici
> nec partem solido demere de die
> spernit, nunc viridi membra sub arbuto
> stratus, nunc ad aquae lene caput sacrae.

> There is one who does not scorn goblets of old Massic nor to take a portion from the whole day, now with his limbs stretched under a green arbute, now at the gentle source of a holy fountain.

Here too a stance of literal leisure is ideologically surrounded by more activist, competitive styles of life. There are verbal echoes of Lucretius 2. 29-33, though the presence of wine harks back to the Hesiodic tradition while sacredness is Theocritean and Virgilian as well. Stylistically the doublets 'break up' the poem as much as does the content, offering a choice of alternatives by contrast with the surrounding oppressively unidirectional existences. The passage shares much in tone and expression with *georgic* 3. 322-38 to be examined below.

12. For a detailed look at the changes see C. Bailey, ed., Titi Lucreti Cari *de Rerum Natura* (Oxford, 1947), *ad loc.*

13. I am grateful to Mr John Tulp for sharing with me his insights into Lucretius' fifth book.

14. The context of this line also deals with Epicurean aloofness. Life is taken from enormous difficulties into quiet (5. 11-12):

fluctibus e tantis vitam tantisque tenebris
in tam tranquillo et tam clara luce locavit.

From such great floods and such darkness he placed life in so
untroubled and clear a light.

15. If we accept Lachmann's emendation of *dicta* to *docta*, there may also be a
direct influence of Lucr. 4. 579 (*verba . . . docta referre*) on *ecl.* 1. 5 (*formosam
resonare doces*). See P. Damon 'Modes of Analogy', 286.

16. On Epicureanism as the philosophy which most complements and reflects
ancient notions of pastoralism, see T. Rosenmeyer *The Green Cabinet* (Berkeley,
1969), *passim* (e.g. 11f., 42ff.). A. Traina has treated in general the Epicureanism of
the *Eclogues* ('Si numquam fallit imago: Reflessioni sulle Bucoliche e l'epicureismo',
Atene e Roma 10 (1965), 72-78. For different and differing views on the specific
philosophy behind the first *eclogue cf.* V. Pöschl *Die Hirtendichtung Virgils*
(Heidelberg, 1964), 29f.,; G. K. Galinsky 'Vergil's second Eclogue', *C & M* 26 (1965),
172ff.; E. W. Leach, *op. cit.*, 126f., 139 and n. 37.

17. Is the young god at Rome, when he addresses Tityrus (45) —

pascite ut ante boves, pueri; summittite tauros.

Feed your cattle as before, youths; breed your bulls —

being unobservant, ironic, or, stranger still, deliberately anachronistic? Certainly the
reader is forced to question Meliboeus' apostrophe, *fortunate senex*, which immediately follows.

18. '. . . the penalty of Adam / the seasons' difference' (*As You Like It* 2.1.5-6).

19. In dealing with the notion of sacrifice Tityrus visualizes only one side of an
ambiguous situation. For him sacrifice confirms the continuity of a new historical
dispensation. His new stability reflects an ideal ordering, the result of the young
god's actions. Occasional loss of animal nature is facile counterbalance for grander
societal ease and restructuring. But Virgil elsewhere marks banqueting on slaughtered
cattle as a symbol of decline from a peaceful Saturnian to a bellicose Jovian age
(*caesis iuvencis, geo.* 2. 537). It is no mischance that *caesi iuvenci* ('slaughtered bullocks') figure in the ceremony for Octavian that opens the third book of the *Georgics*
(3. 23), and that Virgil likewise sees them as an essential concomitant of the festivities for Octavian's triple triumph of 29 (*Aen.* 8. 719). And while Rome's conquered
world passes in detail before the *triumphator* the poet makes his own easy transition
from animal sacrifice to human slavery.

20. The passage has much in common with Varro *De re rustica* 2. 2. 10-11 and
comparison offers instructive illustration of Virgil's originality. Re. L. P. Wilkinson
The Georgics of Virgil (Cambridge, 1969), 11ff.

21. The cicada supplies its vital music in the middle part of this tuneful day (328).
On the beauty of its song see Theo. *id.* 1. 148; 5. 29 *et al.*, and for its importance to
the pastoral setting see Rosenmeyer, *op cit.*, 134f.

22. One of the other rare mentions of the *acalanthis* is at Theo. *id.* 7. 141 quoted
above, a passage Virgil may well have had again in mind.

23. I do not wish to imply that there is no difficulty, much less practicality, in
Virgil's view of nature here, but the voices are only gently disturbing. We are
offered a realistic, georgic idyll rather than a more idealistic, pastoral sequestered
vale. The most disruptive elements are the poet's regular need to command, the
occasional violence (*rumpent arbusta cicadae*, 'cicadas rend the thickets'), the personification of mid-morning 'collecting' thirst, the implied presence of effort (*ilignis
canalibus*, 'oaken channels'). The last three are clustered as if to focus the day's
chief difficulties between dawn and noon.

24. For recent definitions of pastoral, see A. Lindenberger 'The Idyllic Moment:
On Pastoral and Romanticism', *College English* 34 (1972), 335-51, esp. 338, and Leo

Marx 'Susan Sontag's "New Left" Pastoral: notes on revolutionary pastoralism in America', *TriQuarterly* 23/24 (1972), 552-75, esp. 562ff. From his title on I am indebted to the study of aspects of Renaissance pastoralism by R. Cody *The Landscape of the Mind* (Oxford, 1969).

25. P. Alpers develops the notion of contingency in the *Eclogues* in 'The Eclogue Tradition and the Nature of Pastoralism', *College English* 34 (1972), 355ff.

26. The lines in which Meliboeus describes himself have much in common with *geo*. 2. 510ff. save that there exile is chosen, not imposed. Servius comments on *exsilio* (511): 'Voluntary, doubtlessly because of avarice'.

27. The interrelationship of these endings is sensitively discussed by A. Traina 'La chiusa de la prima egloga virgiliana,' *Lingua e Stile* 3 (1968), 45-53, esp. 52f.

28. Those viewing with dispassion the negative side of Aeneas' final act of killing Turnus could see him in part as *impius* and *barbarus, impius* because, in substituting private hatred for a broader *clementia*, he forgets his father's behest to beat down the proud but spare the suppliant, *barbarus* because, whatever the fates propose, he is still the foreigner displacing or upsetting the native element.

THE THIRD BOOK OF THE AENEID: FROM HOMER TO ROME

Michael C. J. Putnam

FOR BERNARD KNOX ON HIS SIXTY-FIFTH BIRTHDAY

By comparison with the acclaim they have lavished on its neighbors, critics have devoted minimal attention to the *Aeneid's* third book.[1] Though a continuation of Aeneas' narrative to Dido, dealing now with events subsequent to his retreat from Troy, it appears to lack the emotional intensity of the second book's focussed account of the collapse of the hero's homeland. The initial segment of his tale is a study in concentration, centered on one time and place. The conclusion seems diffuse by comparison. The most Iliadic book of the *Aeneid,* topographically organized around the breaching and destruction of Troy, is followed by the most Odyssean.[2] We can easily dismiss such a string of episodes, bridging the considerable distance from Ilium to Carthage, as Virgil's attempt to enliven geographical inevitability with the hero's exposure to incipient history. Aeneas must reach Dido during the book's course, but he must also learn more of Italy and Rome.

Advances in knowledge alternate with setbacks throughout the hero's continuing tale. After their ill-omened settlement on Thrace, the Trojans find comfort in the command from Delos to seek their ancient mother. Subsequent plague on Crete is counterbalanced by the Penates' clearer look forward to a true settlement. Misadventure with the Harpies is followed by the potential stability proclaimed by dedication and games at Actium. After the central episode at Buthrotum, in which Helenus details the events Aeneas will endure until the Sibyl at Cumae resumes and magnifies the prophecy of Rome, the hero assumes a less active role before events, avoiding Scylla and Charybdis and watching Etna and the Cyclopes from whom he rescues Achaemenides. A brief reference to Arethusa and scant mention of Anchises' death end Aeneas' tale, at which point we are reminded that all this time we have been at Carthage, with Dido listening.

But there is more to the book than gradual revelation spread out to cover an embarrassingly large itinerary. Virgil has taken careful liberties with his literary heritage and initiated much that is novel. It is on this originality and specifically on its poetic structuring and elaboration that I would like to concentrate in this essay. The sources against which to judge Virgil's originality have often been traced.[3] The results of the poet's handling of his inherited material have not been so thoroughly studied. Sources are primarily twofold, the literary background and the previous renditions of Aeneas' adventures. The two often interact. From Homer the poet has drawn the Polyphemus episode which, however, he places virtually at the end of Aeneas' narrative whereas in the tale of Odysseus it comes early. The events on the Strophades combine matter in Homer and Apollonius Rhodius. From the latter come certain aspects of the Harpies' mien and

[1]

267

action, while Odysseus' dealings with the cattle of Helios provide the model of an attack against animals that proves unfortunate. Again Virgil's placement is important. Because of their disobedience Odysseus loses all his remaining companions after they ravage the sun's herd. Therefore it is the last of his adventures before Calypso, Phaeacia and his return home. The parallel episode is the second major event in Aeneas' journey. It is so placed for a purpose, as we will see.

If we turn to the tradition of Aeneas' wandering we find that although he regularly lands on the Thracian coast Virgil invents his encounter with the ghost of Polydorus. Virgil would also have known the tradition of Aeneas' crucial meeting with Helenus but he devises for the first time and elaborates at length the emotional encounter with Andromache, now Helenus' wife. Likewise, though Aeneas' sojourn on Sicily is well attested, Virgil has added his saving acceptance of Achaemenides as well as his escape from Polyphemus. To discover meaning behind these alterations and additions to the Aeneas legend we must return to the commencement of the book and watch the story unfold as Virgil would have it.

In spite of the fact that Aeneas continues as speaker, there is a sharp stylistic disjunction between the end of book 2 and the start of 3, as if break in narrative complemented the rupture of withdrawal from Troy. Aeneas pauses to announce what we already well know — that proud Ilium has fallen into smouldering ruins. What remains is a series of exiles, *diversa exilia* (4), for the Trojan remnants and specifically for Aeneas himself (*exul,* 11). The word-play is significant. They are 'soil-less' as they make their way onto the deep and as they search out 'deserted lands' (*desertas terras*), one of which might prove the fixed abode of future dispensation.[4] Active and passive compete in the way Virgil has the hero visualize his lot. To paraphrase Aeneas' words: we build a fleet and collect colleagues, Anchises gives the order and I leave the port, yet we are driven by divine augury and I am borne off into exile. It is an alternation that well accompanies the interweaving of knowledge and ignorance, revelation and uncertainty, gain and loss, in the events that loom ahead. Only when his destined land is reached and the future is fully divulged will Virgil have Aeneas adopt a pronouncedly forward stance, and in the process create a different series of more internal dilemmas.

The first major episode, which as often in books of the *Aeneid* sets the tone for much of what follows, results from Aeneas' attempt to establish a foundation on the Thracian coast. Wishing to decorate an altar to his mother with myrtle boughs, Aeneas tugs at a nearby clump.[5] When blood spurts from the broken roots, Aeneas pulls again and then again until the groaning voice of Polydorus speaks out from his tomb warning him away (24):

'heu fuge crudelis terras, fuge litus avarum.'

'Ah, flee the cruel land, flee the greedy shore.'

Aeneas expounds the reasons for this cruelty and greed, pronouncing in his own person against the 'cursed hunger for gold' (*auri sacra fames,* 57) that drove a host to kill his guest. The land is crime-ridden (*scelerata*), hospitality has been polluted (*pollutum*) and the Trojans must leave.[6]

But the phrase *scelerata terra* returns our attention to one of Polydorus' pleas to Aeneas:

> '. . . iam parce sepulto,
> parce pias scelerare manus.'

'Spare me, now that I am buried; spare the tainting of your holy hands.'

Aeneas also must be asked, twice, to spare, He is guilty of disturbing the dead and of a different form of *scelus* based on a different form of greed. Under his revealing touch what had seemed to be shafts of myrtle prove in fact to be murder weapons piercing a corpse. Aeneas pulls out what before had been thrown, to become the second letter of blood from the same body. But what strikes the reader is the persistence of his violence, even after the appearance of blood.[7] Greed, already associated with Polydorus, now centers not on money but on knowledge. 'To make trial of causes hidden deep within' drives Aeneas three times to rend the foliage at its roots, as if the preliminary sight of blood aroused in the perpetrator a desperate need for understanding, even at the cost of further hurt.

The broader importance of the imagery of breaking and tearing that accompanies this intellectual greed and its physical manifestation will only become clear as the book progresses. Suffice it to acknowledge here that Aeneas engenders and magnifies the very *monstrum* he yearns to comprehend.[8] He is the symbolic cannibal who wrenches the body beneath the ground and as such becomes himself a form of corruptor.[9] He exemplifies the banished hero at his most unsure, the wanderer desirous of steadying knowledge acquired even through violence, the sacrificer who pollutes, the would-be recreator of his people whose act of disturbance only reveals murder and death. It is not the last time in the epic where the physical vehemence and impetuosity that compensate for ignorance and insecurity bring a late learning either unpleasant or dubious at best. Aeneas' spiritual hunger, as Virgil portrays it, is often understandable, especially here at a moment when extreme deprivation and loss of direction would expectedly bring heightened instability. A monstral landscape, where myrtles of love and settlement prove to be instruments for the greed-inspired death of another Trojan who left Troy, where the search for enlightenment draws blood and ends only in the sepulchral revelation of past crimes, not future permanence, is suitable accompaniment for the hero's intemperate mood. What remains prominent in the reader's thoughts is the form and irrational intensity of his action, as Aeneas yields to the landscape and becomes a continuator and parodist of the dark myth whose outrage he reveals by further outrage.

After a ceremony to the dead, the Trojans depart for the island of Delos, once wandering, now secure, where king Anius offers the book's first prophecy of fixed land and dominion.[10] Anchises' misinterpretation of the oracle leads the group to Crete where Pergamea proves as ill-omened a name as Aeneia, title given to the foundation in Thrace. Attempted renewal of the Trojan past again brings with it a type of pollution, this time elemental and celestial, not human in origin. The sky is torn open (*corrupto caeli tractu,* 138 — a Virgilian play on tearing as tainting) and dripping plague *(tabida lues)* descends on bodies, trees and crops. Compensation for withdrawal comes here in the form of a more extended prophecy given to the sleeping Aeneas by the Penates who appear in vivid light, as if to confirm the clear truth of their words. They offer chronologically the first mention of Italy in the poem, and Anchises confirms that Troy claimed ancestry in Hesperia and that Cassandra foretold that Trojans would later return there.

But, for the third and most challenging time in the first half of book three, the movement forward in space, which also furthers our knowledge of a stable, future Rome, is obstructed by the presence of the monstrous and the irrational, whether provoked or endured. This in turn begets personal hurt and death. Such is Virgil's present way of viewing the distinction between history and the individual, between public advantage and private suffering, that is one of the *Aeneid's* main themes. Here nature is the chief prognosticator. The luminosity of the Penates' epiphany is exchanged for a stormy siege of black wandering and loss of detail, obscuring even the distinction between night and day.[11] It is fitting that after such a twisting bout of darkness the Aeneadae should land on the Strophades, the Turning Islands, home of the Harpies, the Grabbers, dripping foul ooze from their bellies and pale with hunger.[12] They form the second great *monstrum* in the book that Aeneas not only confronts but activates.

The Trojans find themselves in a setting with at least one reminiscence of a golden age. Rich cattle are everywhere about with no guardian (220-22):

> laeta boum passim campis armenta videmus
> caprigenumque pecus nullo custode per herbas.
> inruimus ferro . . .
>
> We see prosperous herds of cattle everywhere about in
> the fields and an untended flock of goats on the grass.
> We rush on them with the sword . . .

Without hesitation or hint of concern over the legality of their act, the Trojans rush upon the animals with swords drawn, seize their booty and prepare for a banquet. After the Harpies twice foul the feast, Aeneas orders his men to wage a war that not only proves unfeasible but elicits first a question, then a curse, from Celaeno (247-49):

'bellum etiam pro caede boum stratisque iuvencis,
Laomedontiadae, bellumne inferre paratis
et patrio Harpyias insontis pellere regno? . . .'

'Sons of Laomedon, is it even war in return for the
slaughter of cattle and slain bullocks, is it war you are
preparing to offer and to drive the guiltless Harpies from
their ancestral kingdom? . . .'

A moral dimension is added after the fact by the sufferers, a dimension not
perceived by the perpetrator Aeneas who kills cattle and prepares instinctively to behave like a marauding Greek against the hapless city of Troy and
its defeated. Celaeno, who is both Harpy and Fury at once, reveals more of
the future but in the form of a malediction: the Trojans will reach Italy but
will be compelled to eat their tables out of hunger, in recompense for the
slaughter they have just inflicted.

Once more, in his search for truth, self-identity and wholeness after a
period of upheaval, Aeneas enters the territory of the monstral and yields to
its negative enticements. The Harpies externalize the monster within us. They
objectify grabbers who make us grab, living in a landscape that turns us
around or away from some more steadfast pattern of living.[13] They literally
pollute the sustenance of those invaders who have without thought already
engendered a deeper pollution and have perpetrated an injustice *(iniuria)*
that hazards unnecessary warfare and exiles the guiltless. More explicitly
than in the Polydorus episode, hunger is a major motif. At the beginning
of the episode the Harpies appear with 'faces ever pale from starvation'
(pallida semper/ora fame, 217-18). They end it with the curse of future
want *(dira fames,* 256) against the Trojans. In between, the episode recounts
the working out of physical appetite for food and for violence that succeeds
in neither of its dubious goals. If the Polydorus adventure demonstrated
physical energy misused and blood shed in the service of a headstrong desire
for knowledge, the encounter with the Harpies finds literal and figurative
hunger intertwined. Late learning results, to be sure, and repentance,[14] but
there is the appropriate reversal that hunger inflicted will later be endured,
if only symbolically.

Dante sensed the communion between the two episodes of potential mis-
spent that open *Aeneid* 3. In the thirteenth canto of the *Inferno* he integrates
what Virgil leaves separate. Dante is expounding the vice of the suicides
whom he imagines suffering punishment under the semblance of shrubs.
The symbolism seems as follows. To dissociate self from body elicits the tor-
ment of permanent rooting, of the eternal weightiness of physicality alone.
Suicides persist as unthinking objects, brute and largely inanimate, suffering suitable recompense for the undivine decision to take one's life, and
death, into one's own hands. The conscious decision in life to separate by
force what should remain together brings in death the eternal torture of survival only as vegetation. Harpies feed on the leaves of the bushes, and even

a troubled Dante follows Virgil's command and breaks off the top of a shoot in order to learn what meaning the plant conveys.[15]

Dante's appalled reluctance to follow his guide's instruction, and his single gesture of rending, contrast with Aeneas' eager triple tugging at the whole plant sprouting from the corpse of Polydorus, roots and all, even when blood gushes out. Dante replaces Aeneas' physical prelude to learning with a token gesture leading to a dialogue of discovery. The harsh attitude of the living creature bent on suicide is adopted briefly and without enthusiasm by the pilgrim through hell, but the differentiation from Aeneas' compulsiveness is noteworthy. Already in the first episode of book 3 Aeneas is a type of harpy, seizing and, even as the process of action promotes comprehension from uncertainty, verging near pollution from the criminal shedding of blood. Dante devotes most space in his exposition to the *monstrum* itself, explaining why suicides receive their final unalterable punishment in the guise of trees. Aeneas becomes part of the *monstrum* and further hurts what had already been maimed. The quest for permanence begins ominously as myrtles are discovered to be spear shafts by the hero's fierce touch, and a landscape of apparent innocence is converted into a battleground as the Trojans adopt the attitude that by inheritance and nomenclature should be the Harpies' own.

The Trojans now sail north past Ithaca, seizing the opportunity to curse the land that nourished 'fierce Ulysses' *(saevi Ulixi,* 273), and arrive at the shores of Actium. There they sacrifice to Jupiter and celebrate games. Aeneas dedicates the shield of Abas (288):

> Aeneas haec de Danais victoribus arma.

> Aeneas [dedicates] these arms from the victorious Greeks.

The event is brief but significant. Instead of apprehending their settlement of Italy through prophecy, negative or positive, the Trojans now become prototypes for modern Romans, proclaiming a more immediate victory over a singularly divisive enemy in September of 31 B.C. This leap into the future accounts for a reversal of stance which helps alter the insecure tone of Trojan actions hitherto in the book. To dedicate is to assert control. When Aeneas writes his own *carmen* attached to the offering of a Greek shield, he posits the dominance of conquered over conquerors.[16] His deed presumes a victory which the end of the book will expound in greater detail. It also fosters a new spirit of independence based on the security which suggestion of later history provides. The Trojans reach out to a known event that would ultimately be crucial to Rome's stability. In anticipation they condone its permanence by initiating the custom of festive game. Power over Greece, formalized in written words, follows easily after a ritual performance that posits continuity of Roman procedure, not dictated from elsewhere but begun instinctively by the Trojans themselves.

Virgil anticipates a major strand of thought in what follows, the book's pivotal and most lengthy episode as the Trojans meet first Andromache and then Helenus at Buthrotum. The encounter with Andromache provides the major emotional interest in the book, of particular importance to students of Virgil's originality because it is his most expansive addition to the legends of Aeneas' wandering.[17] Andromache has established for herself a fake Troy replete with memories of the past — a cenotaph for Hector, streams modelled after the Simois and Xanthus, Scaean gates and an imitation Pergamum. Her spirit matches the outward setting she has manufactured. Her thoughts center primarily on her former, not her present, spouse and are noteworthy for a pronounced disjointedness of expression that reflects her wilful withdrawal from reality. Aeneas sees her as *furens,* yet the allure of her escapism comes at a critical moment in the book and in Aeneas' own development.

In its idiosyncratic way, her world is as monstral to Aeneas as his nightmare adventures with Polydorus and the Harpies. Whereas in the latter episodes Aeneas had been the fervid inflicter of physical hurt, Andromache's posture preaches a subtle, deadening passivity which the reader of the first book already knows would have appeal to Aeneas. When Aeneas asks of her present situation, she initates her reply with an apostrophe (321-23):

> 'o felix una ante alias Priameia virgo,
> hostilem ad tumulum Troiae sub moenibus altis
> iussa mori, . . .'

> 'O happy alone beyond the others, virgin daughter of
> Priam, ordered to die at the enemy's tomb under the lofty
> walls of Troy, . . .'

It is a locution that Aeneas himself would imitate at a later moment which nevertheless we have already marked as the first words he utters in the epic (1. 94-6):

> 'o terque quaterque beati,
> quis ante ora patrum Troiae sub moenibus altis
> contigit oppetere!'

> 'O three and four times blessed whose fate it was to die
> before the faces of their fathers under the lofty walls of
> Troy!'

The last great temptation to Aeneas in book 3 is to avoid the demands of history and yield to a life of withdrawal which focusses on the illusory, if agitated, recreation of past feelings in a temporal scheme already known and experienced, and shuns a more demanding commitment to the unknown, even if such a credo also enforces on occasion a seemingly unheroic acceptance of fate.

Almost exactly at the center of the book, however, Aeneas turns to Helenus and the prophet's reply reorients Aeneas and his listeners toward the immediate future and the tangibility of a hitherto evanescent Italy. Like the first half of the book, his speech is built on a series of alternatives and contrasts, now of a more strictly positive quality. He begins with a precis of the impending voyage as far as the settlement in Latium (374-87). Stability is assured by means of a token (388):

> 'signa tibi dicam, tu condita mente teneto: . . .'

> 'I will tell you of signs, do you keep them fast in your mind: . . .'

The *monstrum* of a white sow with thirty white piglets by a stream under an ilex portends a settled future as the founders of Rome become intimate with a landscape of opulence, not penury. As for the voyage immediately ahead, flee (*effuge*), says Helenus, the southern areas of Italy they will first approach (396-402).

Taking our thoughts away from immediate difficulties while at the same time suggesting a further definition of stability, Helenus next explains the proper method of dress at a ceremony in which vows (*vota*) are paid (408-9):

> 'hunc socii morem sacrorum, hunc ipse teneto;
> hac casti maneant in religione nepotes.'

> 'Do your allies, do you yourself keep this manner of sacrifice; let your chaste descendants persevere in this mode of worship.'

Then, returning to present necessities, Helenus follows the pattern of Circe in *Odyssey* 12 and outlines the dangers the Aeneadae must confront as they near the strait separating Italy and Sicily. Once more flight is in order *(fuge),* now from a landscape rent apart by natural catastrophe and appropriately housing Charybdis and Scylla. The first creature swallows and spews forth the ships she has lured into her whirlpool. Scylla, from the hidden security of her dark cave, sticks out her mouths and draws ships against her rocks. Virgil will soon expand further upon this paradigm of intemperate energy confined and released. The detail here is essential to show a landscape of grabbing, rending and swallowing from which Aeneas now distances himself. He will now knowledgeably avoid a course of action involving physical hurt which earlier in the book he might have maintained through ignorance or impetuosity.

In another purposefully abrupt change Helenus next urges on Aeneas the specific need to sacrifice to Juno (437-38):

> 'Iunonis magnae primum prece numen adora,
> Iunoni cane vota libens . . .'

> 'First worship the power of mighty Juno in prayer, willingly pledge vows to Juno . . .'

Then, with a final glance at matters to come, he projects Aeneas' vision toward the Sibyl at Cumae, his next and foremost prophet who writes her sayings on leaves, combining omniscience with fickleness and presenting the hero with the challenge of extracting from the world of the dead the affirmation of an ordered future.

The contrasts in Helenus' segmented rhetoric thus differ markedly from the book's earlier jolting antinomies of clarity and dimness, revelation and setback, dramatic action, repentance or wistful endurance in a context of changing topography. Advances forward in time, place or knowledge have for the Trojans always elicited obstacles from the irrational, whether activated or suffered by them. Helenus now varies the exposition of historical and geographical change, however inexorable, with the steadyings that landscape and above all religion can bring. These will affect Aeneas for the remainder of the epic. In book 8, for instance, he will combine elements of Helenus' first and third interludes when he sacrifices the pig directly to Juno.[18] It is Helenus' role in book 3 to anchor history's relentless pace with the continuities of civilization, by establishing in his hearer's thinking those ritual customs and precedents that mark the behavior of an ordered people. Such procedures bolster society in its constant debate with the novel or the moribund as times change. They offer to Aeneas the necessary combination of firm topographical, historical and ethical focus on an Italy soon at last to materialize. In both these last respects, and of course in geographical detail as well, Helenus distinguishes himself in profundity of ideas from Circe who, in her narrative to Odysseus in *Odyssey* 12, limits her purview to the portentous happenings soon to engage the wits of her wily guest.

The episode ends with the usual presentation of gifts, among which are the weapons of Achilles' son *(arma Neoptolemi,* 469), as if the passing on of a former enemy's relics further consolidated the transfer of power from victorious Greeks to defeated Trojans at the moment when they begin their metamorphosis from weak to strong. In the act of parting, Andromache still thinks of Hector and Astyanax, not of the present, much less the future, as she offers gifts to Iulus, and Aeneas dwells on the happiness of those whose past 'fortune' remains their only present. Yet now he is capable of peering ahead in time to posit enduring friendship between Epirus and those who will dwell along the Tiber.[19] *Maneat nostros ea cura nepotes* (505): Aeneas has adopted an historical role which is as important as the custom of veiling one's head during the performance of ritual. Each detail must last into the future, but in mimicking Helenus' phraseology Aeneas takes to himself the union of steadfast custom and historical movement, to Italy and beyond, that the priest sees in Aeneas' and Rome's career.

As if to reinforce a newfound lucidity of mind and intent, Virgil next has Aenaes describe a landfall at Acroceraunia which has special interest because of the behavior of Palinurus. At a parallel moment earlier in the book the helmsman had lost his way, a victim of blinding waves and blackness that offered a literal prefiguration of Aeneas' impending mental darkness in yielding to the spell of the Harpies.[20] Everything now is clarity.

Palinurus sees all the stars gliding in a silent heaven, all in place with sky serene. As a devoted guide Palinurus neither here nor at his mysterious demise in the fifth book peers beyond the constellations to reality. Yet to the reader his new posture as keen-eyed observer and the generous cooperation of the elements are metaphoric for a similar change on Aeneas' part toward greater penetration of thought. It is no accident that the Helenus episode intervenes.

This profundity of vision is tested when the Trojans first touch on Italian soil, spied, appropriately for a new beginning confirmed again at the Tiber mouth, when dawn first gleams.[21] An authority he had up to now lacked is granted father Anchises (a dubious leader at best earlier in the book), *stans celsa in puppi* (527). Virgil attaches the phrase elsewhere in the epic to Augustus Caesar on Vulcan's shield (8. 680), driving the Itali into battle at Actium, or to Aeneas arriving, with the same shield now likened to comets red with blood or burning Sirius, for battle against the Latins (10. 261). It is a posture of power and a rhetorical prognostication of wars near and far, fought on Italian soil or by Italians. Even the coming of dawn, red, with stars put to flight, intimates through metaphor an innate bellicosity which the landscape also metaphorically bears out. There is a natural *arx* on which Minerva's temple is perched. The port is 'curved into a bow' (*curvatus in arcum,* 533). Turreted crags send 'arms' as outworks along twin walls.[22] The temple itself 'flees back' (*refugit,* 536), as if apprehensive of attack.[23]

Metaphor is soon strengthened by symbol. Anchises interprets the meaning of an omen of four white horses (539-43):

> 'bellum, o terra hospita, portas:
> bello armantur equi, bellum haec armenta minantur.
> sed tamen idem olim curru succedere sueti
> quadripedes et frena iugo concordia ferre:
> spes et pacis' ait.

> 'O land receiving us, you bring war: horses are armed for
> war, these herds threaten war. But nevertheless the same
> animals are wont at times to come under the chariot and
> to carry reins in concord with the yoke: there is even hope
> of peace,' he cries.

Aeneas the narrator repeats *Italia* three times in two lines when land is first sighted (523-4). It is war that Anchises now thricefold pronounces visible on her soil. But there is also hope of peace — though the rhetoric dwells on doubt rather than on the reality of peace itself — if the horses are tamed under harmonious reins.

R. D. Williams comments as follows on Anchises' words: 'The whole concept of the Roman mission is symbolized here — first war against the proud, then civilization for the subdued peoples.'[24] In other words the old man's interpretation of the omen could be said to anticipate his own famous final command to his son in the underworld (6. 853):

'parcere subiectis et debellare superbos.'

'To spare the defeated and war down the proud.'

There may be a still more universal validity to Anchises' precision. Any civilizing act, not just that accomplished by Roman genius, depends on the taming of the bestial by the spiritual, on the moulding of energy to form, in a proper union of order and adventure. Yet Rome, especially the *Roma triumphans* which four horses suggest, can on occasion lose sight of standards which she herself might set. The only other use of the adjective *concors* in the *Aeneid* comes earlier in Anchises' farewell speech in the sixth book. He uses it to compliment the spirits of Pompey and Caesar, harmonious in the underworld but ready to turn their strength against the body of their fatherland in the civil wars their reincarnation will abet.[25] Italy works her negative potentiality on many of those who come in contact with her, and Anchises leaves his sentiments suitably general.

The episode again betokens a change of spirit in the titular hero from that he had displayed in the book's opening scene. Aeneas caused bloodshed in the vehemence of his zeal to know. Anchises needs only words for wise scrutiny of an imposing *monstrum*. The aura of Helenus continues to brood over the action. Immediately after the conclusion of Anchises' interpretation and after prayer to Pallas *armisona,* 'sounding in arms,'[26] the Trojans veil their heads and offer sacrifice to Juno. They thus fulfill at once two of the ritual strictures that the priest had urged on his departing guests. As if to lend further credence to Helenus' words, the Trojans next safely withstand the hazard of Scylla and Charybdis, properly sighted by Anchises and skirted by Palinurus. A new passivity, with incident suffered rather than provoked, allows the Trojans to endure without mishap the most formidable absorbers and breakers of ships in the Homeric legacy.

The experience is one that Virgil will elaborate and vary in the last expansive episode of the book. Scylla and Charybdis were new to the Aeneas legend. So too is the splendid series of events that now follows, as the Trojans experience Etna and save the castaway Achaemenides, himself a Virgilian invention, from the clutches of Polyphemus and his fellow Cyclopes. Etna and Polyphemus are kindred entities as Virgil's imagination envisions them. His graphic personification of Etna finds it breaking forth a black cloud to the heavens, licking the stars, vomiting out, in belches, torn up inwards (*avulsa viscera*) of the mountain.[27] Its groaning (577) links it with Scylla (555), Polyphemus (664) and especially Polydorus,[28] for it too harbors an unquiet grave, this time of the giant Enceladus. The thunderbolts of Jupiter's vengeance piercing his body, whose ferocious burning the furnaces of Etna cannot contain, have their similarity with the deadly *hastilia* which sprout from the mound of Polydorus.

No longer imitating his action in the book's earlier segment, Aeneas only endures the sight and sound of Etna. He at first merely hears tell of Polyphemus from the mouth of Achaemenides whose imagery underscores the similarities between Etna and the monster harbored on its slopes. After a mountain that rends itself in concert with a giant's undying restlessness, we discover a mountainous man, lofty enough, in the poet's hyperbole, to strike the high stars, with a dwelling huge like his own hugeness.[29] This hollow within a hollow is a cannibal who feeds on human inwards and dark blood (*visceribus . . . et sanguine atro,* 622), gnawing on limbs flowing with black gore *(atro tabo,* 626). He shows his commonality with Etna by vomiting forth bloody fragments not of himself but of his victims. Yet there is a startling echo as well of the results of Aeneas' violence against Polydorus at the start of the book. Twice there we also hear the hero tell of the dark blood flowing from the wounds he was inflicting (28, 33) and of the gore that stained the earth (29).

Once again therefore we witness a pronounced change in Aeneas' attitude from that witnessed in the book's initial phase. The inflicter of torture, the render of flesh in search of knowledge, becomes not only the avoider of those who would offer similar threat but, following his father's lead, the savior of one whose life is in jeopardy. The Trojans' new protege is a Greek abandoned by Odysseus to the mercies of a devouring landscape and its kindred creatures leagued to present a common menace. It is through him that Aeneas can now at last prove unyielding to the temptations of violence and distinguish himself from its myths.

The circumstances are special. They begin with the very name Achaemenides by which Virgil poses for his reader a series of parodoxes.[30] Though Greek he is called after one of the most opulent, wide ruling dynasties of the ancient world, the Achaemenids of Persia.[31] He who by title should be rich is in fact reduced to wearing clothing held together by briars and to feeding on berries and stony cornels. The presumed exotic proves to be the primitive, squalid with unkempt beard, the man of power to be a helpless victim of bestial nature. This is Virgil's striking way to exemplify one of his favourite topics, the meaninglessness of *nomina,* the falsity of taking pride in nomenclature to herald immortality or even truth.

History both near and far also figures in Virgil's meaning. The recent past is suddenly reversed as a Greek becomes *supplex* before Trojans gradually gaining control over their own destiny. After only brief delay Anchises extends his hand in friendship, suppressing any wilder propensity for vengeance in order to exercise the very *clementia* toward the humbled proud that his words in book 6 would legislate for Roman practice.[32] A Roman of Virgil's time, dwelling further on the name Achaemenides, would have made a mental leap not only to Persia but to modern Parthia. He would have been reminded of the conciliatory tactics adopted by Augustus in dealing with Rome's former enemy.[33] Once again a paradigm that Virgil has initiated by Anchises remains in force in Augustan Rome, but whereas Anchises and Augustus, *stans celsa in puppi,* had before been models of achieved strength, Anchises now reverses the coin to exhibit an image of moderation and restraint.

The reconciliation of opposites in a name, the difference between seeming and being, that is operative in the case of Achaemenides, bears in another way on Aeneas' present situation. Achaemenides' first words of explanation introduce himself as companion of Odysseus (613-14):

'sum patria ex Ithaca, comes infelicis Vlixi,
nomine Achaemenides, . . .'

'I am from the land of Ithaca, comrade of luckless
Ulysses, by name Achaemenides, . . .'

Aeneas, rounding out the episode in his narrational voice, reconfirms both names and epithet in his concluding lines, as the Greek accepted into his company elucidates the coast of Sicily which they now skirt (690-91):

talia monstrabat relegens errata retrorsus
litora Achaemenides, comes infelicis Vlixi.

Such were the coasts that Achaemenides, comrade of
luckless Ulysses, showed us as he traced again his former
wanderings.

In the second book Aeneas had styled Odysseus *durus* and *dirus,* and, earlier in the third, *saevus.* By himself accepting the latest adjective Achaemenides had chosen for his former leader Aeneas acknowledges its truth and further admits to a change in himself. *Saevus* segregates an enemy through hatred. *Infelix* dwells on the communality of a suffering endured through years of wandering that eliminates any remaining inimical distinctions between Greek and Trojan. Aeneas is practising a verbal form of *clementia* that reaches out widely. He is fostering an insight common to contemporary Latin poetry, an insight inherent in the antinomies that the name Achaemenides suggests: that distinctions, general between rich and poor, ruler and subject, more specific between haughty Greek and abject Trojan or humble Greek and powerful Trojan, are blurred by larger levelling forces that obliterate any individual human characteristics.

The change in Aeneas' attitude to Odysseus is symptomatic of a more general alteration in his cast of mind. The activator or abetter of deadly *monstra,* who sharpens the already mortal hurt delivered to a fellow Trojan and makes war against the innocent for the pleasure of pillage, becomes the avoider of *monstra* who along with his men saves a Greek from mauling by the gigantic and irrational.[34] The initial concatenation of rending and breaking, hungers and devourings, of pollution by man, monsters and plague, is exchanged for unity of man with man to elude the monstral. The Trojans offer a gesture of reconciliation; forgiveness cleanses away past hatreds and documents a primal Roman civilizing act.

Virgil's uniqueness within his epic tradition and the alterations he makes to that tradition all converge on this act. The poet, of course, is dependent throughout the book on the general outlines of the tradition of Aeneas' wanderings. But his originality within these bounds, and the reasons behind his careful choice of allusions to the *Odyssey* and the *Argonautica,* will now be clearer. These major bows to the epic past are four in number, balanced two by two on either side of the pivotal Helenus episode which also has its Homeric counterpart in the revelations of Teiresias and especially Circe to Odysseus. They are the episodes involving Polydorus, the Harpies, Scylla and Polyphemus. The first, totally Virgil's invention, as we have seen sets the tone and establishes a pattern of symbolism for the book as a whole. It serves as touch-stone for Aeneas' conduct. The encounter with the Harpies differs from Odysseus' adventure with the cattle of the Sun because it shows Aeneas, unlike his Homeric predecessor, to be as culpably blind as his men. Virgil also transmutes a major element in the Argonauts' encounter with the Harpies as described by Apollonius Rhodius. There the Harpies grab what Phineus needs to stay alive. In the *Aeneid* it is Aeneas and his company who snatch and prepare to consume what rightfully belongs to the Harpies who only then pollute as an act of reprisal.

After the revelations of Helenus, however, allusions to Homeric precedent take a different turn. As I noted earlier, neither Scylla and Charybdis nor Polyphemus appears to have figured in the Aeneas legend as Virgil inherited it. In each instance, and unlike Odysseus, Aeneas saves his men from a devouring landscape.[35] But it is his generous action toward Achaemenides, another Virgilian invention, that completes the intellectual cycle of the book and creates a paradigm of conduct that abstracts the reader from Homer to Rome, from literary reference to the mythic and the past into the realities of behavior patterns whose ethical aptness Virgil's contemporaries would have understood. At the beginning of the book Aeneas is the searching exile, needlessly misusing his moments of power. At the end he receives someone not dissimilar to his earlier self, an outcast suppliant, prey to a setting of natural menace, into a society newly formed, or better reformed, and secure in the knowledge that the events Helenus had predicted and the religious procedures he had stipulated could be experienced and implemented without misfortune.

Two further events briefly seal the book's close, as Aeneas completes his Sicilian itinerary. The first is his stop at the island of Ortygia and apostrophe of the water nymph Arethusa. Allusion to the tale of Alpheus who made his watery way from Greece to his beloved in Sicily may have pointed reference to the voyage of Aeneas as it presses toward its goal.[36] The naming of Ortygia has an explicit purpose. Since it is equally the name for the island of Delos, which also after wandering had become firmly anchored, it recalls for the reader the second episode of the book as Aeneas hears his future prophesied by king Anius.[37] Virgil thus further documents the change from ignorance to knowledge, from insecurity to authoritative posture that occurs gradually during the intervening time and distinguishes the first half of the book from the second.

Aeneas' last words tell of the loss of his father. The book ends as it had begun, with death. A young Trojan, resettled, murdered and injured again in his tomb by Aeneas is counterbalanced by the death of an old Trojan, lost during his son's journey into enlightenment so that Aeneas now can become uniquely *pater*. But Anchises' presence in book 3, which is as much his book as his son's, offers crucial illustration of a positive evolution that compares to Aeneas' own. In the first half of the book Anchises' groping misinterpretation of Anius' oracle leads to plague on Crete and parallels Aeneas' wild ventures in the use of force. Nevertheless his subsequent clear-headed interpretation of possible peace on Italian soil through the domestication of brute energy and his magnanimity toward a helpless Greek set a standard of wisdom and humanity to be marked by Aeneas and later by Rome.

Still the brief remembrance Virgil has Aeneas give Anchises rings thinly to the reader after the Achaemenides episode which is in fact the final climax of book 3. It also serves another important rhetorical purpose. We are often told that in creating the character of Sinon, who persuades her citizens to open Troy for the wooden horse, Virgil drew upon and, the implication is, refined the earlier, tentative delineation of Achaemenides which he would have improved had he been given further opportunity to polish.[38] My own sense is that, however distinct their individual characteristics, books 2 and 3 are to be read conjointly as parts of a whole, and that the clear parallels between these two focal figures, whose adventures nearly begin and end their respective books, are Virgil's further way of carefully forming Aeneas' narrative into a unity.

This unity between the two books, like that of book 3 within itself, rests paradoxically on change. The deceiving Greek, who claims to be persecuted by Odysseus but is actually his colleague in insinuation, is replaced by the Greek who has been deceived, abandoned by a now wandering Odysseus to a potentially savage doom. The fake suppliant, a figure of destructive potential whose release means the unbinding of Troy, finds a counterpart in a true *supplex* who is saved by the Trojans only to help extricate them all from a common danger. Anchises, his vision now clear and understanding, supplants Priam who yields his thinking and his city to a cozening of lies. Finally, the destructive, occasionally suicidal violence that initiates each book and endures for most of the second, yields at their respective conclusions first, to the compliance of his father to Aeneas' will (which represents also his son's submission to Anchises), second, to an act of clemency that would seem to abhor mistreatment of a suppliant, whatever his origin.

The narrator's balance between books two and three is reinforced by the author's outer frame of introduction and conclusion. What follows easily on Dido's request (2. 1-2):

> Conticuere omnes intentique ora tenebant;
> inde toro pater Aeneas sic orsus ab alto: . . .
> All became silent and held their faces intent [on him];
> then from his lofty couch father Aeneas began thus: . . .

— when repeated at the end of the third book bears the stamp of careful formula (3. 716-18):

> Sic pater Aeneas intentis omnibus unus
> fata renarrabat divum cursusque docebat.
> conticuit tandem factoque hic fine quievit.

> Thus, with all intent [on him], father Aeneas alone told the destinies decreed by the gods and taught his wanderings. At last he became silent and here rested after he had finished.

Calculated chiasmus, as *conticuere omnes intenti . . . pater Aeneas* becomes *pater Aeneas intentis omnibus . . . conticuit,* helps the reader work forward and backward into Aeneas' unfolding story. It also serves as a reminder that Dido has been listening all this time to his dramatic tale of the interaction between ignorance and knowledge, impetuosity and gentleness. She would have heard of death's constancy in her future paramour's lot.[39] Whatever her final understanding, the transition from book 1 to book 4 seems only to continue in words the seduction of Dido initiated before Aeneas recounts his story, by the scheming of Juno and Venus.

The metaphorical flame and wound, that possess Dido as book 4 opens and are soon to become explicit in her suicide, only encapsulate what has already been adumbrated before Aeneas' words begin, in the vocabulary of love as fire and disease on which Virgil relies. Such reiteration reminds the reader that the first and fourth books of the epic are also part of a grander cycle of which Aeneas' account of his past is only the elaborate core.[40] There are suggestive parallels neatly plotted between the two framing books. I would like to conclude by noting one allusion which has special bearing on the ethical problem Aeneas will face as he attempts to practise his newly learned *clementia*. In book 1, before Aeneas reveals his presence, Ilioneus as spokesman for the ship-wrecked Trojans addresses the Carthaginian queen (1. 522-29):

> 'o regina, novam cui condere Iuppiter urbem
> iustitiaque dedit gentis frenare superbas,
> Troes te miseri, ventis maria omnia vecti,
> oramus: prohibe infandos a navibus ignis,
> parce pio generi et propius res aspice nostras.
> non nos aut ferro Libycos populare penatis
> venimus, aut raptas ad litora vertere praedas;
> non ea vis animo nec tanta superbia victis.'

> 'O queen, whom Jupiter granted to found a city and to rein in proud peoples through justice, we, pitiable Trojans, carried by the winds over all the seas, beseech you: ward off dread fire from our ships, spare a holy race and look more kindly on our situation. We have not come

either to lay waste Libyan homes with the sword or to
drive stolen booty to the shore. That violence is not in our
mind nor does such pride remain for the conquered.'

As Ilioneus sees her, Dido epitomizes an aspect of the Roman civilizing mission, reining in the proud through justice. The Trojans do not seem to offer
evidence of *superbia*. Instead, conquered, pitiable and reduced to prayer,
they present Dido with the opportunity of sparing a race that is at her
mercy.

As book 4 evolves matters reverse themselves. In Dido's eyes the Trojans
are now preparing to depart on proud ships *(ratibus superbis,* 540), and, as
her sister makes ready to serve as her surrogate in dealing with her departing
lover, she urges on her the posture of suppliant against his pride (424):

'I, soror, atque hostem supplex adfare superbum: . . . '[41]

'Go, sister, and as a suppliant address the proud foe . . .'

But reaction to Aeneas' conduct is not left solely to statement by the one
most injured and hence imputed to a character alone by her spoken words.
A few lines before Dido's command to her sister, Virgil calls Aeneas *pius*.
He then takes the reader directly into his confidence, addressing him, as he
does only rarely, in the second person (401-5):

migrantis cernas totaque ex urbe ruentis:
ac velut ingentem formicae farris acervum
cum populant hiemis memores tectoque reponunt,
it nigrum campis agmen praedamque per herbas
convectant calle angusto; . . .

You could see them streaming and in a rush from the
whole city: even as when ants, mindful of winter, lay
waste a huge heap of grain and store it in their home, a
black column makes its way over the fields and on a narrow path they carry their booty through the grass; . . .

The simile suggests that, as Virgil would now have us see it, Ilioneus'
disclaimer in book 1 was in fact unintentionally fraudulent. The Trojans
have become symbolic despoilers of the land, absconding darkly with its
booty, and Dido, literal builder of a grand domain, alters in image to a
besieged city, falling in ruins after the enemy has been allowed to enter.[42]
Such is the extraordinary subtlety of Virgil's art that whatever blame
Aeneas retains throughout the episode is largely attached by the innuendo
of metaphor, not by any direct authorial statement.

Virgil leaves questions of responsibility unanswered and readers will continue to debate the problem of guilt and blame in the actions of the two
lovers. Aeneas remains the passive hero, driven to leave Carthage by the
dictates of Jupiter who is merely implementing fate. Yet, willingly or not,
he brings misfortune with him. He is not allowed to practise the *clementia*

he had espoused at the climax of his narrative, even if he would. It is the reader who is left to ponder the tension, which Catullus had already presented brilliantly in his 64th poem, between history, its heroic makers and the suffering they experience or cause. There is a later moment at the end of the epic when Aeneas, in a not dissimilar situation, is at last in a position of responsibility and made by the poet to ponder his dilemma before acting. But this deserves separate treatment.

Brown University

NOTES

1. Among the few essays devoted specifically to the third book of the Aeneid, I have found those of R. B. Lloyd especially valuable on matters of theme and structure ('Aeneid III: A New Approach,' *AJP* 78 [1957], 133-151, and 'Aeneid III and the Aeneas Legend,' *AJP* 78 [1957], 382-400). *Cf.* also A. W. Allen, 'The Dullest Book of the *Aeneid*,' *CJ* 47 (1951-52), 119-23, who sees book 3 marking the definitive break with the past as it slowly reveals the future. The conversion of Aeneas from Trojan to Roman is also a major concern of W. H. Semple, 'A Short Study of Aeneid, Book III,' *Bulletin of the Rylands Library* 38 (1955), 225-40. M. Di Cesare, *The Altar and the City: A Reading of Vergil's Aeneid* (New York, 1974), 61-76, gives a particularly sympathetic treatment of Aeneas, 'the wanderer,' in book 3. Ways in which the reader is forced to see Aeneas in book 3 because of his role as narrator are discussed by G. Sanderlin 'Aeneas as Apprentice — Point of View in the Third *Aeneid*,' *CJ* 71 (1975-76), 53-56.

The commentary on *Aeneid* 3 by R. D. Williams (ed., P. Vergili Maronis *Aeneidos: Liber Tertius* [Oxford, 1962]) is an informative guide. In general Williams sees the book as one 'of low tension between the two intense books, II and IV' (p. 14; *cf.* p. 3). He argues that 'The theme of book III is the gradual progress toward the desired goal [i.e. Rome], with difficulties and dangers countered by divine prophecies and encouragement' (p. 18).

2. Among other topics that *Aeneid* 3 shares with the *Odyssey*, aside from the obvious plots centered on adventure-ridden wandering, is an emphasis on eating — 'That eating poem of the Odyssey' (*Tom Jones* Book 9, ch. 5) — which can betoken need, yearning, fulfillment, or a combination thereof.

3. The most detailed examination is by G. Knauer, *Die Aeneis und Homer* (Göttingen, 1964 = *Hypomnemata* 7), *passim*, especially 181-209, on the relationship of *Aeneid* 3 and *Odyssey* 12.

4. The point is made by K. Quinn, *Virgil's Aeneid: A Critical Description* (Ann Arbor, 1968), 394.

5. The importance of myrtle boughs in Greek foundation ceremonies is documented by A. Steier, P.-W. 16. 1. 1181 *s.v. myrtos.*

On the sprouting staff as marking the spot for a foundation see M. Eliade, *The Sacred and the Profane* (New York, 1959), 27. Servius (on 3. 46) refers appropriately to the sprouting cornel shaft in the legend of Romulus and Remus (re. Ovid *M.* 15. 561-64). *Cf.* also Plut. *Rom.* 20. 5ff.; Arnob. 4. 3; schol. on Ovid *M.* (p. 720 Magnus).

6. The use of *procul* in the initial line of the episode (13) is emphasized by T. Halter, *Vergil und Horaz* (Bern, 1970), 71. There are nine appearances of *procul* in *Aeneid* 3, a number equalled in other books of the *Aeneid* only by 8.

7. Aeneas' conduct here is sensitively defended by K. Reckford 'Some Trees in Virgil and Tolkein,' in *Perspectives of Roman Poetry*, ed. G. K. Galinsky (Austin, 1974), 67f.

8. On Aeneas' *impietas* here see W. R. Nethercut, 'Invasion in the *Aeneid*,' *G&R* 15 (1968), 88f.

9. To describe Aeneas' conduct Polydorus uses the word *laceras* (41): 'Why, Aeneas, do you tear at my poor corpse?' are his first words.

10. The interconnection between the stops in Thrace and Delos is discussed by W. Jens, 'Der Eingang des dritten Buches der *Aeneis*,' *Philologus* 97 (1948), 194-97.

11. At no moment in the *Aeneid* are the wanderers more helpless and lost than here. The point is made and developed in relation to the evolution of the epic by A. J. Boyle, 'The Meaning of the *Aeneid*,' *Ramus* 1 (1972), 74ff. (esp. 76).

12. In Apollonius Rhodius the name Strophades stems from the fact that the sons of Boreas there 'turned back' after pursuing the Harpies (*Arg.* 2. 296). The Harpies make their home on Crete (299). Their presence on the Strophades in the *Aeneid* is Virgil's invention.

13. As well as being a *pestis et ira deum* (3. 215), the Harpies embody *malesuada Fames,* one of the abstractions at Hell's gate, ready to work on mankind (6. 276). They are the hungry creatures who work their ill through hunger. They force Aeneas to leave his booty half-eaten (*semesam praedam,* 244) and then curse him with the desperate future need to eat his tables (*ambesas mensas,* 257).

14. 'O gods, avert such a mishap and gently save those who are *pii, '* (266) prays Anchises, quoted by his son and yet reflecting a certain authorial irony. The piety of respect for the rights of others has not much engaged the thoughts of the Trojans. There is a similar irony in Polydorus' cry to Aeneas, who is wrenching his buried body apart, *parce pias scelerare manus* (42).

The Trojan incursion into the territory of others is a prototype of one aspect of the Trojan absorption of Italy. At *Aeneid* 8. 146-47 Aeneas, in his suppliant speech to Evander, so much exaggerates the resistance he has received (. . . *gens . . . crudeli Daunia bello/insequitur*) that the reader tends to reverse matters and contemplate what violence the Trojan arrival brings that did not exist before.

15. Charles Singleton (ed., Dante Alighieri *The Divine Comedy* [Princeton, 1979], 1. 2, p. 224) commenting on *Inf.* 13. 145, speaks of 'the dominant theme of this canto, of rending, of tearing asunder by violence . . .' Dante's borrowings here from *Aeneid* 3 prove that he has caught Virgil's tone in general and in detail. For further analysis of this canto see also C. Speroni, 'The Motif of the Bleeding and Speaking Trees of Dante's Suicides,' *Italian Quarterly* 9 (1965), 44-55.

16. It is curious that the eye of Polyphemus, which Achaemenides and Odysseus' other comrades pierce with a shaft, is later considered *Argolici clipei . . . instar* (637). Odysseus' vengeance against the Cyclopes is seen in parellel terms to Trojan vengeance against Greek.

17. *Cf.* Williams (n. 1. above) on 294f. G. K. Galinsky (*Aeneas, Sicily and Rome* [Princeton, 1969], 45, 112) has pointed out the evidence in the tradition that Aeneas met Andromache at the court of Neoptolemus. Virgil's novel change of setting, with Andromache freed from her Greek captors and restored to a Trojan husband, makes her narcissistic brooding on the past the more noticeable.

On Andromache's escapism see C. Saylor, 'Toy Troy: The New Perspective of the Backward Glance,' *Vergilius* 16 (1970), 26-8 and, on the episode in general, R. E. Grimm, 'Aeneas and Andromache in Aeneid III,' *AJP* 88 (1967), 151-62.

18. Re. *Aen.* 8. 81-84. *Aen.* 3. 390-92 = *Aen.* 8. 43-5 and, with the change of *is* to *hic, Aen.* 3. 393 = *Aen.* 8. 46.

19. There is no mention of Rome itself. Though the reader learns of Rome and Romans at 1. 7 and 33 and in Jupiter's speech at 1. 234, 277 and 282, Aeneas first hears the name mentioned at 4. 234.

20. Palinurus is named at lines 202 and 513, two hundred and two lines before the end of Aeneas' narrative at 715. The pointed balance 'surrounds' the Helenus episode and marks it as a new beginning.

21. *Rubescebat:* 3. 521 and 7. 25, two out of Virgil's four uses of *rubesco.* The only other appearance of the verb in the *Aeneid* is at 8. 695 as Neptune's waters off Actium redden with blood.

22. Of the two other uses of *turritus* in Virgil, one is at 8. 693, describing the *turritis puppibus* on which the Romans attacked the followers of Antony and Cleopatra at Actium.

23. Virgil's attempts at perspective, here and elsewhere, are treated by H.-D. Reeker, *Die Landschaft in der Aeneis* (Hildesheim, 1971 = *Spudasmata* 27), 40ff. He notes the personification of the Italian landscape but does not dwell on any idiosyncracies in the description. Virgil's sense of depth and distance here is also touched upon by T. M. Andersson, *Early Epic Scenery* (Ithaca, 1976), 82.

24. Williams (n. 1. above) on 3. 543 (p. 168).

25. They are *concordes animae* at 6. 827. Virgil's only other use of *concors* is at *ecl.* 4. 47. By contrast *Discordia* and *discors* make fourteen appearances in Virgil's works, ten in the *Aeneid.*

285

On horses in relation to a triumph see, further, Williams (n. 1. above) on 3. 537; K. W. Gransden, ed., Virgil, *Aeneid:* Book 8 (Cambridge, 1976), on *Aen.* 8. 714; W. Ehlers P.-W. 2. 13. 504, *s.v. triumphus.*

26. Virgil apparently coins her epithet, and uses it, with great suitability, only here.

27. For a more detailed analysis of Virgil's description of Etna, see Reeker, (n. 23 above), 62ff., 159ff.

28. *Cf.* especially lines 39-40:

> gemitus lacrimabilis imo
> auditur tumulo et vox reddita fertur ad auris:

> A tearful groan is heard from the bottom of the mound and a voice in reply is carried to my ears.

with 576-7:

> liquefactaque saxa sub auras
> cum gemitu glomerat fundoque exaestuat imo.

> And with a groan it tosses molten rocks to the skies and boils from its lowest depth.

29. *Ingens* (619, 658)

30. The most recent treatment of the meeting with Achaemenides is by E. Römisch, 'Die Achaemenides-Episode in Vergils Aeneis,' in *Studien zum antiken Epos* (Meisenheim, 1976), 208-27. His analysis is especially penetrating on the many contrasts within the episode, for example, between the need to see the stars and the blackness of Etna (p. 210) or between man and monster (p. 222). He relates the name Achaemenides to *achos* (p. 219).

G. Highet, *The Speeches in Vergil's Aeneid* (Princeton, 1972), 28f., dismisses the episode as derivative and unimportant.

31. On the proverbiality of the wealth of the Achaemenids re. Horace *c.* 2. 12. 21, *dives Achaemenes* (*cf.* also *epode* 13. 4, *c.* 3. 1. 44). Horace uses *Persae* to mean *Parthi* at *c.* 1. 2. 22, 21. 15; 3. 5. 4.

32. Anchises' patriarchal act is, of course, a grand gesture of unity. We must, however, not lose sight of the fact that shortly before the end of his final speech to his son in book 6 Anchises singles out for mention the destructive actions of Aemilius Paulus against Greece during the Third Macedonian War. He will overwhelm Argos and Mycenae, says Anchises,

> ultus avos Troiae templa et temerata Minervae. (6. 840)

> Having avenged his Trojan forebears and Minerva's defiled temple.

In spite of the reception of Achaemenides, vengeance and *clementia* will remain opposing principles in Roman history, even in her evolving relationship with Greece. Mycenae still remains *saevae* in Ilioneus' words of greeting to Latinus (7. 222).

33. Reasons for linking Achaemenides to Parthia are detailed by A. J. McKay, 'The Achaemenides Episode: Vergil, *Aeneid* III, 588-691,' *Vergilius* 12 (1966), 31-38, *passim,* who also discusses at length Augustus' careful policy of forebearance in this instance (35ff.).

34. At line 639 Achaemenides addresses the Trojans as *o miseri,* alluding to the communality of their menace from Polyphemus and reminding the reader that Aeneas had just described him as a *forma . . . miseranda* (591). We must also recall that in the opening episode of the book Aeneas and Polydorus are differentiated when the stronger harms the weaker (41):

> 'quid miserum, Aeneas, laceras? iam parce sepulto, . . .'

> 'Why, Aeneas, do you tear at my poor corpse? Spare me now that I am buried, . . .'

Sparing comes only after intervention from the tomb.

Line 639 as a whole —

> 'sed fugite, o miseri, fugite atque ab litore funem
> rumpite.'

> 'But flee, o poor creatures, flee and rend your cables from the shore.'

— also looks back to Polydorus' double command to Aeneas (44):

'heu fuge crudelis terras, fuge litus avarum.'

'Ah, flee the cruel land, flee the greedy shore.'

Singular imperative to Aeneas, unique perpetrator of hurt, is changed at the book's end to a plural embracing all the Trojans and, ultimately, Achaemenides himself.

35. There are important differences in the treatments of Polyphemus by Homer and Virgil. These have been well discussed by J. Glenn, 'Virgil's Polyphemus,' *G&R* 19 (1972), 47-59, esp. 53ff. See also G. Thaniel, 'A Note on Aeneid 3. 623-626,' *CB* 50 (1973), 10-12; Römisch, (n. 30 above), 223, n. 18.

Resonances of the figure of Polyphemus later in the epic are also traced by J. Glenn, 'Mezentius and Polyphemus,' *AJP* 92 (1971), 129-55.

36. We also trace the movement of at least one other Greek from his homeland to Italy during the course of book 3, namely Idomeneus. At line 122 he has deserted Crete and by lines 400-1 he is besieging the Sallentine fields in southeastern Italy. Virgil there gives him the epithet Lyctius as remembrance of his Cretan origin.

37. Ortygia is named at lines 124, 143 and 154.

38. *Cf.* Williams (n. 1 above) on lines 588f. (p. 181). On the parallels between the two passages see J. W. Mackail, *The Aeneid of Virgil* (Oxford, 1930), Appendix B; W. F. Jackson Knight, 'Pairs of Passages in Virgil,' *G&R* 13 (1944), 10-14, and K. Quinn, (n. 4 above), 61 and 132f., for a sympathetic treatment of Virgil's intentions.

39. The first four books of the *Aeneid* have often been viewed by critics as a group, the first, in other words, of three major divisions in the epic. This thesis has been notably defended by V. Pöschl, *Die Dichtkunst Virgils* (Innsbruck, 1950), 279f., and G. Duckworth, 'The Aeneid as a Trilogy,' *TAPA* 88 (1957), 1-11 (re. p. 4, n. 13-15, for further bibliography). F. L. Newton in 'Recurrent Imagery in Aeneid IV,' *TAPA* 88 (1957), 33, touches briefly on imagery in book 1 that will be elaborated in the fourth book.

40. W. S. Anderson, *The Art of the Aeneid* (Englewood Cliffs, 1969), 42f., details further reasons why Dido might be moved by Aeneas' tale.

41. Dido is also *supplex* at 414 and *victam* at 434 (*cf.* 1. 529 quoted above).

42. Venus first suggests the image at 1. 673. It appears again at 1. 719 and is reiterated strongly in simile at 4. 668-71:

> resonat magnis plangoribus aether
> non aliter quam si immissis ruat hostibus omnis
> Karthago aut antiqua Tyros, flammaeque furentes
> culmina perque hominum volvantur perque deorum.

> The heaven reechoes with great wails, even as though all Carthage or ancient Tyre were collapsing before an inrushing foe, and raging fires were swirling over the dwellings of men and of gods.

The intervening simile comparing the Trojans to predator ants is a careful segment of Virgil's design.

287

AENEID VII AND THE AENEID.

I would like to deal here with the theme of metamorphosis in the *Aeneid*, specifically in the seventh book. In so doing I will touch again on a topic rightly of growing concern to Virgil scholars—the meaning of the final moments of the epic and some of the questions its hero's actions raise about Rome and about human life.

At the end of Book VI of the *Aeneid*, Aeneas and the Sibyl, under the direction of father Anchises, issue forth from the Underworld through the ivory gate of Sleep. This is the gate, the poet tells us, whence the spirits send *falsa insomnia,* treacherous, misleading nightmares, to the world above. There had been no mention of *portae* at the entrance, only a *vestibulum* and *fauces, limen* and *fores* leading into the house of Dis. The way down is easy, the Sibyl predicted, but suffering and trial await the moment of departure. That there is no apparent *labor* in Aeneas' withdrawal adds to the effect of Virgil's words and forces the reader to ponder their symbolism for the books which follow.

We can divine something of his meaning by turning back to the description of the shapes Aeneas sees on first entering Hades. They lurk, ready to make their way to the earth above, where they must spend a great deal of their time. Among other equally hideous personifications we find, at the end of the list, *Bellum,* the Furies in their iron chambers, and mad *Discordia,* her snaky hair bound with bloody fillets.

It is not long before all these vices will have full opportunity for display. At VI, 86-7 the Sibyl in her trance cries

> . . . bella, horrida bella
> et Thybrim multo spumantem sanguine cerno.

The vision soon becomes a reality. In the next book the priest who interprets the omens of the bees and Lavinia's flaming hair for Latinus agrees that she will be renowned in report and reputation (*illustrem fama fatisque*: VII, 79). The signs also portend a *magnum bellum* for the people. And Juno, addressing the unfortunate girl in her thoughts, can gloat (VII, 318-19)

> sanguine Troiano et Rutulo dotabere, virgo,
> et Bellona manet te pronuba . . .

Blood will be shed by both sides in the ensuing gory " marriage " of peoples over which the goddess of war will preside.[1]

As for the Furies one need only refer to the devastating role Allecto plays in Book VII and the anonymous *Dira* in Book XII. And *Discordia,* which Allecto boasts of " perfecting " at VII, 545, is but another name for *impius Furor* who for a brief moment is locked by Jupiter's words in the temple of Janus (I, 293-6). Juno's more realistic thrusting open of the twin gates of War (*geminae Belli portae*: VII, 607) releases an unstated Discord (and a host of warriors) whose effects can be immediately gauged.

There is another set of creatures who cluster at the entrance to Hell, on or around an aged elm. These consist, with one exception to be mentioned in a moment, of Centaurs, Scyllas, Briareus, the Lernaean Hydra, the Chimaera, Gorgons, Harpies, and Geryon. Aeneas would have attempted to kill them had not the Sibyl assured him that they were slender beings without flesh (*tenuis sine corpore vitas*) and that they floated around as spectres of empty shape (*cava sub imagine formae*). Their lives are hollow and bodiless, and what form they have is only an image. Aeneas cannot kill them by a sword-thrust which would act only against body. Their workings are more subtle. Many act on the spirit and take " physical " shape only in human natures gone sufficiently awry to serve as visible symbols for the mind's madness.

Aeneas would have been acquainted with two members of this catalogue from previous experience. In the real-unreal transitional world of Book III he knows enough of Scylla's threat to skirt the danger. Not so with the Harpies who bring out the

---

[1] At 423 Allecto, in disguise, can taunt Turnus that Latinus has denied him *quaesitas sanguine dotes*. There may be a pun in Virgil's address to Saturn as *sanguinis ultimus auctor* (49). Juno, prime cause of future bloodshed, is called *Saturnia* four times in Book VII (428, 560, 572, 622), more than in any other Book. For explicit connections between blood and war, cf. lines 541-2, 554, 595.

worst in him. He declares causeless war on their cattle (*inruimus ferro*: III, 223) and on them (III, 234-5):

> . . . sociis tunc arma capessant
> edico, et dira bellum cum gente gerendum.

Misenus, who is later killed for vying with a god, trumpets them into battle. Celaeno, *Furiarum maxima*, sums up the event with a question (247-9):

> bellum etiam pro caede boum stratisque iuvencis,
> Laomedontiadae, bellumne inferre paratis
> et patrio Harpyias insontis pellere regno?

Unnecessary slaughter of cattle leads to war against rightful inhabitants. Celaeno curses them with hunger and Aeneas misremembers her words as those of his father when the curse is fulfilled at VII, 107-34.

The same pattern begins to rework itself when Celaeno's kindred fury, Allecto, stirs up the Italian world in Book VII. Madness seizes Iulus' hounds and ambition their master, in the pursuit of Silvia's tamed stag. Italy has been for some time at peace. The inherent strength of a wild though pastoral people has been moulded to the uses of civilization and prosperous, georgic living. Aeneas brings madness with him and, in rousing opposition, renews a natural rudeness. But it is a rudeness in defense of one's own, like the Harpies' care for their land. However distasteful the external image they present, the treatment is undeserved.

In Book III the Harpy-Furies are still *Odyssey*-like personifications of emotion. The Trojans' violent action rouses direct retaliation. But Virgil takes what appears a literal myth and gradually turns it into a figment of the mind, with potency more latent. In Book VI Aeneas reacts in physical fashion to the metaphysical, naturally enough from his past experience. His attack, however, is only against the spiritual causes of anguish, somehow visible though only *imagines*. The curious fact is that Aeneas himself is one of these. He leaves the Underworld as a *falsum insomnium*. Yet *Somnia vana* stand ready at Hell's entrance, along with Grief, Suffering, and a host of other monsters, to make facile way up to torture mankind.

These other creatures will soon enter directly into Aeneas' life. Of the list quoted earlier (and with the exception of Scylla and the Harpies who appear in Book III), only one, Briareus, does not make some appearance in Book VII. Geryon is mentioned at VII, 662 as the victim of Hercules. The fury Allecto, who starts the war, is tainted with the Gorgons' poisons (*Gorgoneis infecta venenis*: 341). In the catalogue of enemies who are to confront Aeneas, Catillus and Coras are compared to Centaurs. Aventinus carries the Hydra as shield device and Turnus' crest sports a Chimaera. Briareus finds proper replacement in *saevus* Orion who appears in a simile comparing the forces of Clausus to the waves of the Libyan sea (VII, 719). These are the " monsters " whom Aeneas is to confront, and Virgil builds up their prowess accordingly.[2] But we should not forget that Latinus was ruling over cities quiet after long peace (*longa placidas in pace*: VII, 46) before Aeneas' arrival.[3] The full extent of the *falsum insomnium*, the nightmare Aeneas himself conveys and the emotions he thereby arouses, awaits final revelation only at the epic's conclusion. Aeneas is the source of Rome's heroic lineage, yet he brings torments with (and in) himself as he leaves the Underworld. The twin Gates of Sleep and the twin Gates of War have their parallels. Some of the poet's intent, however, can be determined from the opening of Book VII, to which we now must turn.

It begins on a particularly gloomy note—*tu quoque . . . Caieta.* No heroic invocation here. That occurs—if such it can be called—only after some thirty verses of intense symbolic revelation (the prayer to Erato) and then again after six hundred more lines where the goddesses of Helicon are called upon to help survey an Italy roused to war. The word *quoque* recalls that Palinurus and Misenus have recently died and given their

[2] It is curious that the four Trojan boats which take part in the race during Anchises' funeral games carry as emblems a *Pristis*, Chimaera, Centaur, and Scylla. The *Pristis* (or *Pistrix*) was a sea monster which formed part of Scylla's make-up (III, 427). The connection with future Rome is, in each instance, carefully stressed by the poet. Mythic experience switches to allegorical emblem which in future actions will become symbolic only.

[3] As late as line 285 the Trojans bring peace back from Latinus to Aeneas (*pacem . . . reportant*).

names to nearby places. Caieta is noteworthy for being the nurse of Aeneas (*Aeneia nutrix*). She cherished Aeneas as Italy, *terra alma*, nourishes those who will oppose him. We are reminded that, in spite of the ending of Book VI, Aeneas is alive as well as dead, that he is real as well as a dream and that the process of his growth continues now into maturity. But we are given a careful message also in these opening lines. Everlasting fame (*famam*) is gained only at the price of death (*moriens*). Honor (*honos*) is balanced by a tomb (*sedem*), reputation (*nomen*) keeps guard only over bones (*ossa*)—if there is any glory in that, the poet adds.[4]

The warning, to Aeneas through Caieta, is that progress demands sacrifice and that reputation is bought by death. The oracle of Faunus soon makes the same point in an ambiguous utterance whose negative implications Latinus does not seem to grasp. The newly arrived Trojans are a race, the voice says, " who by blood will bring our reputation to the stars " (*qui sanguine nostrum / nomen in astra ferant*: 98-9 = 271-2). Blood is a price as well as a cause of renown.

Anchises, at the end of Book VI, kindled in his son's mind yearning for coming glory (*incendit . . . animum famae venientis amore*: VI, 889). Virgil now warns that any search for *fama* may mislead even to the point of bringing death. The reputation of the past, he later tells us, glides on scarcely even a slender breath (*ad nos vix tenuis famae perlabitur aura*: VII, 646). For *fama* may become *Fama*, daughter of earth, a *monstrum horrendum, ingens* (IV, 181), ready to spread truth and falsehood with equal ease in Carthage. She is already loose in Italy at the moment of the Trojan's arrival (102 ff.). This time, however, the actual revolution is accomplished by still more vigorous partisans. One of them, it must be noted, is Ascanius who, in pursuing Silvia's stag, is fired with a yearning of extraordinary praise (*eximiae laudis succensus amore*: 496).

Aeneas next passes by the shores of Circe. The adventure is not superfluous but serves as precursorial symbol for the whole

[4] For a more detailed treatment of Caieta see C. P. Segal, " *Aeternum per Saecula Nomen*, the Golden Bough and the Tragedy of History: Part II," *Arion*, V (1966), pp. 56 ff.

book.[5] She is daughter of the sun but works by moonlight. She seduces by the senses. We see her groves, her proud house, her lights, and slender weaving. We listen to her songs and smell the cedar she burns. Yet we also hear the angry groans and roars of the men she has changed to animals and visualize the tension and incoherence in their beings. They rage (*saevire*) as she is wrathful (*saeva*). They have only the shapes of beasts (*formae*). Who once had the visage of humans (*hominum ex facie*) now possess the features and frames of animals (*vultus ac terga ferarum*). They are men forced to adopt the characteristics of beasts. Circe signifies the power that causes and then effects such a hideous transformation, whatever the many emotional guises each example of her craft may assume.

The groaning of the beasts recalls a moment of more intensive, elaborate horror in Book VI—Phlegethon, at whose gate Tisiphone presides, whence issue the moans of the tortured and the shrieks of whips. In Book VII the description is circumscribed:

> hinc exaudiri gemitus iraeque leonum
> vincla recusantum et sera sub nocte rudentum, . . .

The corresponding lines in Book VI introduce a lengthier roster of terrors (557-8):

> hinc exaudiri gemitus et saeva sonare
> verbera, tum stridor ferri tractaeque catenae.

"*Quae scelerum facies? . . .*" (560) Aeneas first asks the Sibyl. She responds with example after example. Nevertheless, she concludes, even with a hundred tongues and a voice of iron she could not detail all the different types of crimes (*omnes scelerum . . . formas*, 626).[6] These are the actual shapes of crime as well as its instruments. Tisiphone guards those who have

---

[5] In this respect the adventure of Circe parallels, out of many examples, the wooden horse in Book II, the *monstrum* of Polydorus in III, the panels of Daedalus in VI. Though the time is night, the breezes blow and the moon gleams with sufficient brightness for sailing. It is untrue day and travel is suspect (in Book III we have examples of breezes falling at sunset while nightfall brings the end of journeying). The moon's light is borrowed from the sun and fickle (*tremulo*). Nocturnal breezes drawing toward Circe are wrongly seductive (cf. Horace's use of *aura* at *C.*, I, 5, 11 and II, 8, 24).

[6] *Saevus* is again an adjective much in evidence (557, 572, 577).

twisted themselves by misdeeds. Circe is a symbol of the power that transforms. The road branches in Book VI and Aeneas is guided toward the Elysian Fields. In Book VII, though he appears to pass Circe by, his life takes a more realistic turn.

The intervention of Neptune apparently prohibits the pious Trojans from " suffering " such monsters, but Circe's influence penetrates the book. We hear of Picus (189-91)

> . . . equum domitor, quem capta cupidine coniunx
> aurea percussum virga versumque venenis
> fecit avem Circe sparsitque coloribus alas.

The only way that Circe's lust can keep love is to transform it into bestial form, not elevate to divinity (as Homer's Calypso proposes to Odysseus). This *cupido* demands the perverse loss of human shape and lives by diversity of superficial texture alone (her multiform animals are paralleled in the variety of colors Picus assumes here). So at line 282 Circe is styled *daedala* because, as craftsman of eccentricities, she delights in a multitude of appearances.

Though now a bird, Picus had been an *equum domitor*. The same epithet is given to two of the warriors (Lausus, 651, and Messapus, 691) in the concluding list of the marshalled Italians. Circe herself also makes two appearances in the catalogue. The grove of Angitia, we learn at 759, will weep for Umbro, the Marruvian. As Medea (or her sister—commentators differ) transplanted, she would be Circe's niece. Umbro was a priest and magician (753-5)

> vipereo generi et graviter spirantibus hydris
> spargere qui somnos cantuque manuque solebat,
> mulcebatque iras et morsus arte levabat.

But there are stronger vipers and hydras on the loose, stronger enchantments and deeper angers than he can control. He has no power against a Trojan wound. Virgil devotes to him the most poignant lines in the book, reminiscent of Orpheus weeping for Eurydice (759-60) :

> te nemus Angitiae, vitrea te Fucinus unda,
> te liquidi flevere lacus.

Finally among the followers of Turnus are those who work the *Circaeum iugum* (799). They could absorb her influence first hand.

Cedarwood figures of early Latin heroes (the Trojans would know the smell from Circe's shores) and the admonitory statue of Picus ushered Aeneas' ambassadors into the court of Latinus. They took away with them another example of the goddess' handiwork (280-3):

> absenti Aeneae currum geminosque iugalis
> semine ab aetherio spirantis naribus ignem
> illorum de gente patri quos daedala Circe
> supposita de matre nothos furata creavit.

The novelty of fire-breathing horses, Virgil's usual symbol for war, horses part divine, part mortal would have appealed to the monster-maker Circe. Aeneas would not realize the full implication of receiving such an apt gift.[7] Virgil gives us a hint when he describes the quasi-allegorical Chimaera Turnus wears on his helmet's crest as " breathing Etna's fires from its jaws " (*Aetnaeos efflantem faucibus ignis*: 786). The kinship with *spirantis naribus ignem* is inescapable.[8]

I will anticipate later, more thorough investigation of the possibilities of Circean metamorphosis by drawing attention to one detail in the description of Picus' transformation. Circe accomplishes her act by potions (*versum venenis / fecit avem Circe*: 190-1). The verb *verto* has many special places in Book VII, none more important than in the description of the fury Allecto. Like the changes that she wreaks on people (or, more exactly, the latent, devastating characteristics she draws to the

---

[7] The gift Aeneas gives Latinus, *Priami gestamen* (246), also has its irony. The fate of Priam is transferred to Latinus, each an old ruler unable to control a kingdom heading toward ruin.

[8] Though Aeneas' envoys apparently return with peace, they bring as gifts symbols of war (see commentators on *Aen.*, I, 444; III, 539 ff.), and Circe is the medium of the change.

The horses have two things in common with the portrait of Camilla at the end of the book. They are fleet of foot (*alipedes*, 277) and they are caparisoned in purple and gold (*ostro*, 277 and 814; *aurea, auro, aurum*, 278-80, *auro*, 816). It is her vanity that proves her undoing as she contemplates the accoutrements of Chloreus in Book XI, where again purple (*ostro*, 772) and gold (*auro*, 771, *aureus*, 774, *auro*, 776, *auro*, 779) are prominent (see S. G. P. Small "Vergil, Dante and Camilla," *C. J.*, LIV [1958-59], p. 298). In accepting such a gift Aeneas receives something of Camilla's superficiality and wildness as well as the possibilities of Circean metamorphosis.

surface) she is a creature of varied shapes (*tot sese vertit in ora*: 328). The words echo an ambiguity inherent in a remark Juno had just made—" I turn myself to all resources (into all things)" (*memet in omnia verto*: 309). Allecto alone is left. She has many fierce faces (*saevae facies*, 329), many façades for the beast within us.[9] Her counterpart Circe, *dea saeva*, can alter the faces of men with potent herbs. Allecto, too, makes use of subtle medicines. She is stained with poisons (*infecta venenis*, 341) when she first sets out against Amata. Her disease slips into the maddened queen with damp venom (*udo veneno*, 354). She breathes in a viper's soul (*vipeream animam*, 351) against which there is no recourse.

The Tiber's mouth at which the Trojans now land would seem at first a happy alternative to Circe's shores. Night turns into day.[10] The *vada fervida* which swirl near Circe's shores give place to *lento marmore*, a calm, sluggish sea. The similarity of the two descriptions seems to set one place off from the other. Circe's *inaccessos lucos* (11) become the *ingentem lucum* (25) which Aeneas enters happily. Her unceasing song (*adsiduo cantu*, 12) yields to the bird calls which now soothe the air (*cantu*, 34). The Tiber exerts its own form of magic charm, with deep groves and gripping voices. Indeed it could be argued

---

[9] E. Fraenkel (" Some Aspects of the Structure of Aeneid VII," *J. R. S.*, XXXV [1945], p. 5) speaks of the " private egoisms " at the root of the war.

[10] The description is usually taken as idyllic (as, most recently, E. Kraggerud, *Aeneisstudien*, p. 86: " eine Szene voll tiefer Freude ") :

> iamque rubescebat radiis mare et aethere ab alto
> Aurora in roseis fulgebat lutea bigis.

Rubesco is used three times in the *Aeneid*. The other two occasions have bearing on VII, 25. At III, 521 *rubescebat Aurora* begins the description of the first landfall in Italy (and Anchises' prediction of war). At VIII, 695 we find the sea red from blood (*arva nova Neptunia caede rubescunt*).

A similar description of dawn occurs at VI, 535-6:

> hac vice sermonum roseis Aurora quadrigis
> iam medium aetherio cursu traiecerat axem.

In Book VII Aurora gleams from a two-horse, not four-horse, chariot. The change may anticipate the *currum geminosque iugalis* (280) that Latinus sends to Aeneas. Aurora, as another daughter of the sun, carries on Circe's influence. Aeneas' steeds are also bred by Circe of heavenly descent, a bastard combination of mortal and immortal.

that it carries over into the Italian landscape the very changeability that Circe can exercise. The sea outside may be quiet,
but the Tiber itself presents a different spectacle more akin to
Circe's swollen floods than not. It swirls down with rapid
turnings (*verticibus rapidis*)—the importance of the latent
metaphor is already apparent—and breaks forth (*prorumpit*)
into the sea, as if its violence had been hemmed in or was at
last spent.[11] It is not long before we contemplate the spectacle
of all Italy gone wild after Juno breaks open War's iron gates
(*rumpit*, 622). Aeneas may not sense this (he is *laetus* at the
prospect of the stream), but Virgil gives us a careful warning
by altering the attributes attached to the river from *amoenus*
(30) to *opacus* (36). Things may be somewhat darker than
they at first seem.[12]

The irony of the address to the muse of love poetry, Erato,
when it finally comes (37) is that no love enters this world as
a result of Aeneas' arrival. Nothing is ever said of any bond of
affection between Lavinia and Aeneas whose alliance is a primary cause for the coming war.[13] Scrutiny of the uses of *amor*
in the book is revelatory. We hear first of Amata's *miro amore*
(57) for her would-be son-in-law, an emotion upon which
Allecto plays to full effect. We learn of Turnus' *amor ferri*
(461) and of the *insani Martis amore* (550) with which Allecto
fires the Italians. This causes Virgil to exclaim *huc omnis aratri
/ cessit amor* (635-6). It was *eximiae laudis amore* (496), we
remember, which causes Iulus to wound Silvia's pet.[14]

One aspect of his action deserves mention here. As he shoots
at the stag, it is *perque uterum . . . perque ilia* (499) that Iulus'
arrow flies. The shot does not kill but only emasculates the stag.
But inside the animal exterior there are near human traits. It

[11] Cf. the use of *vertex* at Hor., *C.*, II, 8, 22.
[12] This dualism in the opening lines is analyzed by K. J. Reckford,
"Latent Tragedy in *Aeneid* VII, 1-285," *A.J.P.*, LXXXII (1961), pp.
252-69. R. D. Williams ("The Purpose of the *Aeneid*," *Antichthon*, I
[1967], p. 37) calls Allecto "a personification of man's own evil
desires. . . ."
[13] See F. Todd, "Virgil's Invocation of Erato," *C.R.*, XLV (1931), pp.
46-8 and the comments of Reckford, *op. cit.*, p. 257, n. 15.
[14] The only other mention of *amor* in Book VII is at 769 (Diana's
strange affection for Hippolytus).

groans (*gemens*) and, in its grief, takes on the attitude of one in prayer (*imploranti similis*, 502). Circe's spirit alters men into beasts. In the wounded stag we may feel a more happy combination of wild and human that could stand for tamed Italy itself. It is Ascanius who is ambitious and his dogs who are maddened.

An obvious link between Turnus and the stag is only felt, not stated, in Book VII (the stag, for instance, is *forma praestanti*, 483, while Turnus, armed, is *praestanti corpore*, 783). In Book XII, however, Virgil makes a direct equation of Aeneas with a *venator canis* (no trace even of the human Iulus here!) and of Turnus with a stag (XII, 749-55).[15] At the end of Book XII Turnus is killed, but by the middle of Book VII Italy has begun to lose its manhood and the Trojans to absorb an uncontrolled vigor.

The love, then, over which Erato is called upon to preside, is perverse, not creative. Its beginnings are rooted in war, not peace, compulsion, not gentleness. If the *maior rerum ordo* to which Virgil alludes at line 44 is Rome, the remark is made with bitter stress—the rebirth of Aeneas is the " birth " of war. If it refers specifically to the catalogue of horrors that follows in the next six books, it is a begetting that leads to funerals, not lives.

The metamorphosis of peace into war begins forthwith. Though Latinus had long lived in peace two omens now predict war—the sudden advent of a cluster of bees on the palace laurel and a mysterious fire on Lavinia's head. As usual with Virgil each omen prepares us for its later reformulation.

Bees in the fourth *Georgic* are notable for their energetic industry and warlike ways. The latter quality makes itself felt here. The bees arrive with a mighty shriek (*stridore ingenti*, 65) and take such dense possession of the laurel that the sooth-sayer unhesitatingly sees them standing for a new race which will have dominion on the topmost citadel (*summa dominarier arce*, 70). This overlordship apparently brooks no compromise. And the turn of georgic occupations into martial pursuits is a motif of the Book as a whole. Worship of ploughshares and

---

[15] This point is made in an interesting article by W. R. Nethercut, " Invasion in the *Aeneid*," *G. and R.*, XV (1968), pp. 82-95.

sickle (635), the farmer's "weapons," gives place to arms of a more destructive sort. It is a *pastorale signum* (513) with which Allecto calls the countryside to war.

Camilla embodies both aspects. She carries a

> . . . pastoralem praefixa cuspide myrtum (817).[16]

This is not so much a symbol of the Italian shepherds [17] (they too were at peace before the Trojans came) as it is the final emblem of the perversion of pastoral into violent, of love misguided into war, of Venus' myrtle into a weapon of Mars. Hunting gradually changes in the *Aeneid* from an occupation necessary to produce life's staples (Book I) to the unnecessary and inflammatory search for booty (Books III and VII) to war itself, finally, as man tracks man, one predator after another.

The omen of Lavinia's burning locks is clearer still. The fire becomes metaphysical and takes many forms as the book progresses. We are told of Lavinia (75-6)

> regalisque accensa comas, accensa coronam
> insignem gemmis; . . .

We then turn to the inner world of Amata and her matrons (*furiis . . . accensas pectore*, 392). This has been Allecto's work. So also is her power, via Iulus, on the local rustics (*bello . . . animos accendit agrestis*, 482). Of still wider influence she later boasts (550):

> accendamque animos insani Martis amore . . .

Turnus' transformation is visualized in terms of water frothing as fire is set beneath a cauldron (462-6). The water itself swirls like smoke as once again elements which could well stand for pastoral and war are combined.[18] From this moment on he is

[16] Throughout the *Aeneid* Virgil reveals a fondness for metaphors from nature twisted into contexts of war. In Book VII we may note *atra . . . late / horrescit strictis seges ensibus* (525-6); *florentis aere catervas* (804).

[17] Such is the interpretation of V. Pöschl, *Die Dichtkunst Virgils*, p. 275.

[18] The relationship between this simile and VIII, 22-5 (and their respective settings) deserves further exploration. The latter simile has much in common with the description of the waters which swirl around

closely associated with fire's power, as at 577-8:

> Turnus adest medioque in crimine caedis et igni
> terrorem ingeminat.

There is a direct line from Lavinia, spreading Vulcan throughout the house (*totis Volcanum spargere tectis*, 77) to the Aetnean fires which Turnus' Chimaera sports (796). Lavinia, too, plays her part in letting slip "the dogs of war."

For further reinforcement of the omens' meaning Latinus consults the oracle of his father Faunus (82-4):

> . . . adit lucosque sub alta
> consulit Albunea, nemorum quae maxima sacro
> fonte sonat saevamque exhalat opaca mephitim.

From Circe's grove to the dark Tiber mouth to Albunea, the intensity grows. As in the case of Circe, the situation plays on the senses of hearing and smelling as well as sight. Like the Tiber's stream, this grove is *opaca*. But whereas Circe charmed by burning cedar, Faunus presents his prediction of blood and dominion from a spot that breathes fierce sulphur (*saevam mephitim*). Circe, *dea saeva*, misleads by a presentable exterior. Faunus' words issue from an Acheron which exhales a ghastly odor.

Again the words are anticipatory. Juno we soon find calling on the Underworld since loftier aids have failed her in the task of hindering the Trojans (312):

> flectere si nequeo superos, Acheronta movebo.

Her instrument, Allecto, purpose fulfilled, returns to Hell in the valley of Ampsanctus (563-71). This too has a dark grove and roaring stream (*torto vertice torrens*, 567—and we recall the Tiber, *verticibus rapidis*). There a cave lets forth the breath

Circe's land and of the goddess herself (e. g. *tremulo lumine*, VII, 9, *tremulum lumen*, VIII, 22; *luna*, VII, 9, *lunae*, VIII, 23; *solis*, VII, 11, *sole*, VIII, 23). Circe is associated with both the sun and the moon at the opening of Book VII. By VII, 526-7 the sun gleams off the shields of the newly armed rustics (*aeraque fulgent / sole lacessita et lucem sub nubila iactant*). By the start of Book VIII Turnus, his allies, and the dangers they present have become the "constellations" which trouble Aeneas' mind (*tremulum labris . . . lumen aenis / sole repercussum*: VIII, 22-3).

from fierce Dis (*saevi spiracula Ditis*)—all this the product of
Hell's bursting jaws (*rupto . . . ingens Acheronte vorago /
pestiferas aperit fauces,* 569-70). Allecto, the goddess with the
many masks for herself and others is the stench of Hell bursting
forth. Faunus' utterance initiates this particular aspect of the
evil. For whatever reason, Latinus allows the words to become
public.[19] This in turn is responsible for starting *fama* on her
way.

The next stage in the upheaval of Italy is the arrival on the
scene of Juno, *saeva Iovis coniunx,* who with her pawn puts
the power of Circe into operation. Virgil has already read us a
lesson on the futility of ambition and search for reputation, but
it is for the sake of these very goals (*honor,* 332; *fama,* 333)
that she feels the need to act. Though Jupiter's vengeful wife
might not have it so, this is the first step toward the fulfillment
of Faunus' prophecy that the future Romans will see all things
"turn" beneath their feet (*omnia sub pedibus . . . verti,* 101).
It commences, ironically, with a further display of Juno's
hatred and with her appeal to the multiform Allecto. So variable is the creature that at the moment of her attack on Turnus
she puts off her menacing face and fury's limbs (*torvam faciem
et furalia membra,* 415) to become an old priestess of Juno (*in
vultus sese transformat anilis,* 416). She assumes her true form
again when he treats her lightly (*tanta . . . se facies aperit,*
448). But her metamorphoses are only aspects of the changes
she effects in others—to release the pent up violence and irrational hatreds inherent in us all.

Among her many talents is the ability to turn brothers against
each other and overthrow homes by hatred (*odiis versare domos,*
336). She sees in the maddening of Amata the perfect example
of this (*omnem . . . domum vertisse Latini,* 407). Amata becomes a plaything, a top, in her hands, spun into action by
twists of a lash (*torto verbere,* 378). Here the way was prepared because her victim was already enraged at the coming of
the Trojans (345).[20]

[19] According to Servius in a strong comment, Latinus thereby loses
a reason *quo a se repelleret generos.*

[20] The change in Amata is echoed in the alteration from *Turni hymenaeis* (344) to *Phrygiis hymenaeis* (358). This in turn becomes the
"marriage" of Trojan and Latin at 555-6 which is closely conjoined
to the *sanguis novus* that Juno realizes must stain the warriors.

Juno boasts of Allecto's power to bring the scourge and funeral torch under roofs (*verbera tectis / funereasque inferre faces*, 336-7).[21] Both these objects serve in the metamorphosis of Turnus which is her next accomplishment. She sounds her scourges, hurls a torch at him, and fixes under his heart smoking brands (456-7):

> ...facem iuveni coniecit et atro
> lumine fumantis fixit sub pectore taedas.

The deed echoes Juno's evaluation of Aeneas as a new Paris (319-22):

> ...nec face tantum
> Cisseis praegnas ignis enixa iugalis,
> quin idem Veneri partus suus et Paris alter
> funestaeque iterum recidiva in Pergama taedae.

Juno's rage may be once more in the open, but it is the idea of Aeneas and what he stands for that Allecto "throws" at Turnus. At this fear "breaks" his sleep (*rumpit*, 458), sweat bursts forth from his body (*proruptus*, 459). Love of the sword rages in him (*saevit*) as he makes his way to Latinus, the peace violated (*polluta pace*, 467).

Allecto's next victim is Aeneas' son. She maddens his hounds and, as we have seen, he is set afire with love of praise.[22] This emotion wells up inside him, but the metaphor puts him squarely in the tradition of Amata and Turnus. The whole incident Virgil acknowledges to be that (481-2)

> . . . quae prima laborum
> causa fuit belloque animos accendit agrestis.

Iulus has appeared once before in Book VII as the unwitting interpreter of the oracle of the "tables" to be eaten. The harpy Celaeno in anger had prophesied that the Trojans would reach their destined land in such a state of hunger as to be

---

[21] She also sounds her whip against Turnus (*verbera insonuit*, 451). Tisiphone uses the same instrument at VI, 558.

[22] In one sense Iulus anticipates Allecto's efforts. We know that she is a goddess given to *iraeque insidiaeque* (326). Iulus is already at work chasing wild beasts *insidiis cursuque* (478) when Allecto arrives on the scene. *Ira* (508) aids in the result.

driven to eat their tables. On reaching Italy they are indeed compelled to eat the crusts due Ceres. Virgil's words make clear that such action is profane. Yet it fulfills Celaeno's prophecy, as Iulus announces. To this Virgil comments (117-18)

> ea vox audita laborum
> prima tulit finem . . . .

This may be the end of one phase of Aeneas' *labores*, but Iulus' action in shooting the stag, as the verbal echoes make clear, is the beginning of another. Like the attack on the Harpies' herds, this is an unnecessary onslaught against the animal world. The Trojans are not fully blameless as they now themselves present a literal cause for war.[23]

Juno puts her *extremam manum* (572-3) to her plot as if this were some special work of art that deserved a final touch (we have heard twice before of Allecto's *ars*).[24] The injured shepherds, Turnus, and Amata all stream in to force Latinus' approval for the war. He remains momentarily firm, like a cliff against which waves "bark" (*latrantibus undis*, 588) while the rocks "roar" (*saxa fremunt*, 590). The Latins, too, are "dogs," and we have heard before of both Amata and Turnus "roaring."[25] But Juno (once more *saeva*, 592) wins the day. As his resolve breaks he curses Turnus (596-7):

> . . . te, Turne, nefas, te triste manebit
> supplicium votisque deos venerabere seris.

The goddess then breaks open the iron gates of War, a task Latinus refuses, and Italy arms for battle. These are the gates, Jupiter foretold in Book I, that will be closed at the coming of Augustus (I, 293-6):

> . . . dirae ferro et compagibus artis
> claudentur Belli portae; Furor impius intus
> saeva sedens super arma et centum vinctus aenis
> post tergum nodis fremet horridus ore cruento.

[23] Of Allecto's part in the Iulus episode Servius remarks (on line 479) *studium mutavit in rabiem*. Here again the poet emphasizes the bitter uselessness of peace turned to war (536).

[24] Lines 338, 477.

[25] Lines 385, 460.

Juno's action merely gives symbolic confirmation to what we already knew, that Discordia-Furor was at large.[26]

It was one of Augustus' proudest boasts (it was incorporated in his *Res Gestae*) that the temple of Janus was closed three times during his regime whereas in all Roman history up to his time this had happened but twice before (*Res Gestae,* 13). In the same work he also gives his thoughts on war and peace (*Res Gestae,* 3):

> Bella terra et mari civilia externaque toto in orbe terrarum suscepi victorque omnibus superstitibus civibus peperci. Externas gentes quibus tuto ignosci potuit, conservare quam excidere malui.

The crucial *tuto,* "in safety," in the second sentence may be defended as sop to necessary expediency. The first statement is more open to doubt. We are dealing with times which Tacitus called a *pacem cruentam* (*Ann.,* I, 10). In the same paragraph Tacitus, while talking of Augustus, raises a moral issue which has some bearing on the end of the *Aeneid.* It is morally correct, the historian says, to give up private hatreds in favor of public needs (*privata odia publicis utilitatibus remittere*). In Tacitus' eyes Augustus was in this respect constantly delinquent. What of Virgil's Aeneas? Is his killing of Turnus an example of private hatred or of public need?

The opening of the gates of War gives Virgil the occasion for listing Aeneas' opponents.[27] The catalogue as a whole is a fascinating example of poetic artistry. I would like to dwell here only on the way Virgil describes the figure of Aeneas' arch enemy (783-92):

> ipse inter primos praestanti corpore Turnus
> vertitur arma tenens et toto vertice supra est.
> cui triplici crinita iuba galea alta Chimaeram
> sustinet Aetnaeos efflantem faucibus ignis;
> tam magis illa fremens et tristibus effera flammis
> quam magis effuso crudescunt sanguine pugnae.

[26] The "turning" of War's hinges (*cardine verso,* 621) is the final example of peace overturned by war.

[27] Virgil's prayer to the Muses is *pandite nunc Helicona.* The muses must fling open Helicon as if the mountain had gates. Juno releases *Furor* from the gates of War. It takes many shapes in the subsequent catalogue of warriors.

et levem clipeum sublatis cornibus Io
auro insignibat, iam saetis obsita, iam bos,
argumentum ingens, et custos virginis Argus,
caelataque amnem fundens pater Inachus urna.

Two pieces of his armor, crest and shield, are given the equal
stress of four lines.[28] Each summarizes and anticipates much.
The crest is topped by a Chimaera, roaring and wild, revelling
in fire and the blood of battle. He is associated with three
beasts at once, lion, dragon, and goat. The ambiguity of *vertitur*
(and to a lesser degree *vertice*), to "be turned" as well as
simply to "move," shows the power of Circe at work for the
most impressive time in Book VII. The Chimaera, the hollow
image that frightens Aeneas on his way to Hades, is loose now
as Turnus, Aeneas' dehumanized opponent.

The shield carries Io, *iam saetis / obsita, iam bos*—an even
closer connection with the *saetigeri sues* Circe creates. In the
myth itself Juno effected the transformation from human to
beast as she does here through her power to enrage. To effect
such a monstrosity is the *argumentum ingens*, as well as the engraving itself. It is a madness that derives from Juno and
Greece, not Italy, as the association with Argos which runs
through the book proves. At 286 Juno has set out *Inachiis ab
Argis* when she sights the Trojans already established on the
Latian shore. At 372 Amata, by then insane, boasts of Turnus'
ancestry as

Inachus Acrisiusque patres mediaeque Mycenae.

At VI, 89 the Sibyl styles him *alius Achilles,* a boast which he
utters himself at IX, 742. He is made to assume the ancient
Greek enmity rediscovered as well as the native Italic wildness
rearoused. Antagonism would come to Aeneas all the easier.[29]

[28] For a different, more detailed treatment of these lines see S. G. P.
Small, "The Arms of Turnus: *Aeneid* 7. 783-92," *T. A. P. A.*, XC
(1959), pp. 243-52. See also R. D. Williams, "The Function of Virgil's
Catalogue in *Aeneid* 7," *C. Q.*, n. s. XI (1961), pp. 152-3.

[29] The phrase *ipse inter primos* is used of Pyrrhus at II, 479 and of
Aeneas at XII, 579. We might expect a further echo of Greek destruc-
tiveness in our first full description of Turnus. The metamorphosis of
Aeneas into violent "Greek" is a more subtle one but crucial for our
understanding of the epic's finale.

But Virgil is more careful than to make Turnus the emblem of reason and order overthrown in favor of some Boschian grotesquerie. He associates Turnus with one more *argumentum ingens,* the belt of the dead Pallas that he dons and which contains (X, 497-8) :

> impressumque nefas: una sub nocte iugali
> caesa manus iuvenum foede thalamique cruenti.

The Danaids are also Argive, in direct line from Io. Turnus inherits their crime and elicits from Virgil a broader generality (X, 501-2) :

> nescia mens hominum fati sortisque futurae
> et servare modum, rebus sublata secundis.

This is the pattern that Nisus, Euryalus, and Camilla follow. It afflicts mankind, whether Trojan or Italian. But there is always Hypermnestra, the one Danaid who had the heroism to spare her husband and blot out a tradition of violence by the courage of restraint.

Aeneas kills Turnus at the end of the epic because he sees the belt of Pallas.[30] Turnus is even then fulfilling the curse of Latinus. As *supplex,* with knee bent, he entreats forgiveness and at the same time pays a penalty for rashness. He is symbol of a humbled race. Latinus had attached to him the guilt of a *nefas* and he now wears around his waist an *immensum nefas* that reminds his antagonist of a nearer act of violence. Aeneas kills him and offers him as sacrifice to Pallas. The verb *immolat* (XII, 949) is the same as Virgil uses to describe Aeneas' seizure of the sons of Ufens as human offering on the pyre of Pallas (X, 519).[31] Turnus is the last victim of Aeneas' *saeva dolor.*[32]

---

[30] The most recent treatment of the final scene is by R. D. Williams, *op. cit.* (n. 12 above), especially pp. 36 f. (". . . it is certain that the poem ends with our thoughts concentrated on the tragedy of Turnus, not the triumph of Rome "). A cogent expression of this new, more realistically honest evaluation of Aeneas is given by L. A. MacKay " Hero and Theme in the *Aeneid,*" *T. A. P. A.,* XCIV (1963), pp. 157-66, especially 164 ff.

[31] The sacrifice is made ready at XI, 81 ff. The only other use of *immolo* in the *Aeneid* is at X, 541.

[32] We have seen the frequent use of *saevus* in association with the

The action results, one suspects, from what Tacitus would call a *privatum odium*. Aeneas' temper is not one to wrestle more than momentarily with his father's lofty sentiments to spare the conquered and beat down the proud (*parcere subiectis et debellare superbos*). That Turnus is *superbus* (and therefore deserves defeat) we have often heard. We have not yet seen Aeneas confronted with an ancient enemy at last cowed into submission. The moment is crucial to the *Aeneid* and Rome. Virgil's words calculate a mood of wrath, not magnanimity in his hero. He is burned by rage and terrifying in his wrath (*furiis accensus et ira terribilis*, 946-7). Aeneas, as Virgil chooses to portray him, is now on equal spiritual footing with Amata (whose matrons are *furiis accensas*) and Turnus in Book VII.[33] Each succumbs to *ira* under the influence of *furor*. The difference is that in Book XII Aeneas has the help of Jupiter and the *Dira* in

enemies of Aeneas in Book VII. It is curious how often the adjective is attached to the hero himself in Book XII. Only at XII, 406 and 609 is it connected with Turnus (at 406 *saevus horror* creeps nearer the wounded Aeneas as Turnus momentarily has the upper hand; at 629 Juturna tries to persuade her brother to bring *saeva funera* to the Trojans). The instances are 107 (Aeneas is *maternis saevus in armis*), 498 (Aeneas effects *saevam nullo discrimine caedem*), 849 (Jupiter, *saevus rex*), 857 (the Dira as an arrow armed with the venom *saevi veneni*), 888 (Aeneas speaks *saevo pectore*), 890 (Aeneas and Turnus fight *saevis armis*), 945 (Aeneas recalls his *saevi doloris*). H. Benario ("The Tenth Book of the *Aeneid*," *T. A. P. A.*, XCVIII [1967], p. 35) points out that in the epic Aeneas alone (and he only at X, 878) is called *saevissime*.

It is curious, too, that Aeneas is called *heros* only until XII, 502, yet Turnus is given this designation at XII, 723 and 902. (This is not to make any specific defense of the "character" of Turnus who, at X, 443, can go so far as to wish Evander present at the death of his son.)

[33] VII, 392. Can we speak of any character "development" in Aeneas when wrath and madness are the very vices to which he succumbs in Book II (*furor iraque mentem praecipitat*: II, 316-17). That the results of each encounter are pointless seems not to have suppressed the emotion. It is scant defense of the actual killing of Turnus to say (as Kraggerud, *Aeneisstudien*, p. 23) that it, unlike a similar event in Troy, is just because done in accordance with fate. It is fate (if we can judge from Jupiter's final words—we would scarcely guess it from the context) for Juno to give up her *furor* and the two peoples to merge happily into one. Turnus' death is never once intimated to be fated, in spite of his own predictions.

humbling Turnus and yet the advantage of Anchises' schooling in necessary generosity.

The Roman, his father had warned in Book VI, pursues greater arts than bronze-casting and sculpture, rhetoric or astronomy. He moulds people to his rule and makes peace a custom. But the closing scene of the *Aeneid* is scarcely pacific. To practise one's arts on human beings and not on metal or stone requires greater control than Aeneas can muster. We would hope that the cycle of quasi-fraternal violence that runs through the last six books of the *Aeneid* might come to an end at its conclusion. Virgil is more realistic than to tell us so.[34]

One of the great points of value in the *Aeneid* is to serve as a reminder (to us certainly, to Augustus, if he was wise) of natural unrest in society which must be held in control. A certain turbulence is important in the creative individual as well as in mankind as a whole. But the forcing of individual irrationalities on society can do it fatal harm, especially when these disorders are imposed by its rulers themselves, or even offered by them as models.

The questions which linger at the end of the *Aeneid* are worth constant asking. Can, or better does, Furor remain suppressed as Rome goes about her supposed work of civilization? Can peace ever be made into a fixed tradition when any such " custom " is ever at the mercy of human caprice? By the end of Book VI, through the intellectual guidance of his father, Aeneas has become the incorporation of the dream of Rome, the embodied founder of a myth. Yet Virgil, by having him exit by the gate of *falsa insomnia*, allies him with the *Somnia vana* and other monsters, the centaurs, gorgons and chimaeras that cluster around Hell's gate. In Book VII the creatures seem to be at large in the persons of Aeneas' opponents. Aeneas does " suffer " them ultimately. He sets them free. During the course of the last books, and especially at the conclusions of Books X and XII, Aeneas undergoes a similar metamorphosis. From *pius*, faithful to his father's words, he becomes forgetful.[35] Circe, the

---

[34] Those who see in Aeneas a gradual development or perfecting of self-discipline (as, e. g., Austin on Book II, p. xvi) or *pietas* (as K. Quinn, *Vergil's Aeneid*, pp. 17 and 123) avert their thoughts from the thorough gruesomeness of the endings of Books X and XII.

[35] The word *pius* is stressed at the opening of Book VII (*pius*

308

beast-maker, and Juno, the arouser of Hell's fury, have the final say. The dream is proved false by the hero's actions. He becomes as much the representative of life's irrationality as Allecto, with her Gorgon's locks, or Turnus with a Chimaera for crest.

Daedalus, the brilliant artisan of Apollo's temple at Cumae, by overreaching is the cause of his son's death. Augustus, for all his accomplishments, will see Marcellus dead. Virgil's regular pattern leads us to expect that Aeneas will lose Pallas. By killing Turnus, however, he fails in the craftsmanship of empire, a deeper fault to suffer because self-inflicted. He is blind to Turnus as symbol of anything beyond momentary, individualistic concerns. By the middle of the sixth book Aeneas is purged of empathy with the past. Palinurus, Dido, and Deiphobus pass in final review emotions no longer relevant. Aeneas cannot even embrace his dead father who becomes a persona of the future.[36] He has become at last an original, originating being with an historical mission, the standard and emblem of a whole people. The birth of the hero is the birth of a city in Book VIII. Lavinia is only the Italian shores at last claimed and Iulus only the ancestor of a noble line. The propulsion of personal momentum now lies with Turnus and his confrères, in his love for Lavinia, in the wildness of Camilla. But the public espousal of the future, the parade of heroes watched and the glorious shield raised, cannot wholly eliminate private involvements and sufferings. In Aeneas' case these seem finally to triumph over any attempt to follow Anchises' philosophical exhibit.

In this version of the timeless conflict between moral stance and individual action, the latter wins, as is its wont. Aeneas,

Aeneas, 5; *pii Troes*, 21). In Book XII Aeneas is called *pius* only until line 311. By the end he has come a long way from the dutiful son who supported his father on lowered shoulders (*subiecta colla*, II, 721). Someone else is now *subiectus* and Aeneas, for the worse, has freed himself from any spiritual *impedimenta*. He cannot bear the weight of his father's historical and moral revelation. The "dream" is false.

[36] The words which describe the meeting (VI, 700-2) echo Eurydice's disappearance from Orpheus (*Georg.*, IV, 499-502). They are the same as *Aeneid*, II, 792-4, where Creusa leaves Aeneas. Anchises is like swift sleep, his story of future Rome is Aeneas' dream.

Virgil assures us with frequency, yearns for equity and peace. The *lacrimae rerum*, life's inherent tragedy, have left too many scars for immediate emotion to be a constant resort. As he tells Iulus before the final debacle, his son may learn of courage and suffering from him, not good fortune. There is a lofty, heroic side to Rome which Aeneas must embody. In any groping toward civilization there must also be a continuing search for honest justice and here Aeneas—and Rome—pay the price for their humanity. Aeneas is no idealized fiction, finally purged of ignoble human emotions, an automaton operated only by an unreal impetus toward impossible goals. Personal passion gains full control of reason at the moment of final crisis.

Even were the epic to end with praise of Aeneas, as it clearly does not, we would still sense that the cycle of madness would begin again. That Virgil turned down so clearly the opportunity for a fraudulent appraisal of human existence is perhaps our greatest compliment to the poet and his poem.[37]

MICHAEL C. J. PUTNAM.

BROWN UNIVERSITY.

[37] It is becoming a fashion to speak of the public and private aspects of the *Aeneid* as if they were somehow separable (their true interconnection is shown by A. Parry, "The Two Voices of Virgil's *Aeneid*," *Arion*, II [1963], pp. 66 f.). I would agree that we must not overreact against the long-standing, debilitating view of the *Aeneid* as only a glorification of Augustan Rome. But in seeking a mean line between the horror and the glory we need not at the same time partition the poet's Muse. The "private" voice may on occasion offer the most desperately "public" of utterances.

PIUS AENEAS AND THE METAMORPHOSIS OF LAUSUS

MICHAEL C. J. PUTNAM

> "I shot him dead because —
> Because he was my foe,
> Just so: my foe of course he was;
> That's clear enough; although. . . ."

Thomas Hardy "The Man He Killed" (1902)

My essay will review some aspects of the relationship between *pietas* and the use of force in the *Aeneid*. The intimate cooperation between piety and power regularly defines Rome and her founding hero. Ilioneus' sketch to Dido of his absent leader is an early example (1.544-5):

> rex erat Aeneas nobis, quo iustior alter
> nec pietate fuit, nec bello maior et armis.

> Our king was Aeneas. No other was
> more righteous in piety nor more
> powerful in war and arms.

Dido herself bitterly demonstrates this collocation in her final soliloquy, where *dextra* proves equally related to Aeneas' strength at arms and to his faithless breaking of a compact (4.597-99):

> . . . en dextra fidesque,
> quem secum patrios aiunt portare penatis,
> quem subiisse umeris confectum aetate parentem!

> . . . behold the right hand and the pledge of him
> who they say carried with him the gods of his
> fatherland, who supported on his shoulders a
> father undone with age.

The Sibyl puts the conjunction summarily to Charon, presenting her companion as (6.403):

> Troius Aeneas, pietate insignis et armis.

> Trojan Aeneas, outstanding for piety and arms.

311

Ilioneus, now introducing Aeneas to Latinus, can boast of his king's *dextram potentem* and allude again to *fides* and *arma*.[1]

But, as the epic progresses and words are replaced more regularly by deeds and definitions by exemplifications, this mating of abstract duty to gods, family and patriotic mission with the physical means towards its validation becomes a more ambiguous union, shading into the use of force for questionable goals, often for the gratification of private feelings rather than the fulfillment of idealistic, public purposes. I would like to examine in detail one striking instance of Aeneas in power drawn from the tenth book, the death-scene of Lausus, and then follow out parallel passages, ending with a brief look at Aeneas' final confrontation with Turnus.

We have learned from the seventh book of Lausus' personal beauty and of his prowess at taming horses and harrowing wild beasts,[2] but from the start we are prejudiced against his father Mezentius, the *contemptor divum* with a bent for the macabre torturing of his victims.[3] Yet in the tenth book the human, private image diverges from the public. Son remains faithful to father, and in a striking manifestation of *pietas* shields Mezentius from the onslaught of Aeneas — *genitor nati parma protectus* (10.800). The reprieve is short-lived. The titular hero soon buries his sword in the side of the youth, as he himself is centered in the language, *per medium Aeneas iuvenem* (816).[4]

At this moment, when the reader is drawn to Lausus, protecting his father and wearing a tunic woven for him by his mother, Virgil seizes the occasion for an irony pointed against Aeneas. Before he wounds Mezentius and initiates the dissolution of one of the more poignant parent-child relationships in the epic, Aeneas is given his standard epithet *pius* (783), and as he prepares to wound Lausus mortally the poet has him shout (811-12):

> "quo moriture ruis maioraque viribus audes?
> fallit te incautum pietas tua."

> "Whither do you rush, about to die, and dare
> things greater than your strength? Your piety
> deceives you in your folly."

Aeneas ironically interprets in negative terms the abstract that had always been his, symbolized in his rescue of his father and son from Troy and in his visit to Anchises in the underworld. It becomes an impediment, making Lausus vulnerable to his opponent's *saevae irae* (813), and killing him. Virgil reverses our expectations by having Aeneas grimly see himself as an incorporation of a *pietas* that destroys in a particularly vicious manner because it kills the embodiment of a *pietas* that saves. And, as at the death of Turnus which concludes the epic, Aeneas takes no responsibility. What his maddened words would have the immediate — and distant — hearer believe is that not Aeneas but *pietas*, and his antagonist's *pietas* at that, performed the deed. If Lausus had been *cautus*, the hero implies, he would not have practised *pietas* and would have escaped death.

The final *tua* (812) therefore serves a double purpose. It shows Aeneas shifting the cause for Lausus' death onto Lausus' own practise of Aeneas' virtue. But it also reveals a half-conscious awareness that he himself is blameworthy, while the reader is left wondering about the depth of Aeneas' commitment to *pietas* elsewhere. How often, we ask, does Aeneas adhere to or reject *pietas* for subjective, even self-serving, reasons?

For Aeneas to impute Lausus' defeat not to himself but to *pietas* smacks of self-deception, fabricated to ward off the full implications of his words and action. At moments of rage *pietas* and *arma* do not easily blend. In the case of Lausus' death each destroys. Aeneas' arms, working out a continued desire for vengeance, do the actual deed, but Aeneas' abstraction, as practised by Lausus and explained by Aeneas, abets the negative impulse. Meanwhile the reader's disposition changes from under-standing for Aeneas, about the sometimes violent task of establishing Rome, to compassion for his victims. Though Mezentius despises the gods, publicly abrogating an important form of *pietas*, he gains at the end a measure of our sympathy.[5] When it comes to the practise of virtue in the heat of war his son feels and displays both *amor* and *pietas*, while *pius* Aeneas performs the greatest act of *impietas* by killing first the son who protects, then his wounded father. His deeds in battle elicit our appreciation of Lausus, whose affection for Mezentius makes the latter less despicable, but our respect is undermined for Aeneas who is brutalized by an inability to respond sympathetically to his own supposedly characteristic virtue in the operations of others. In moments of rage the merely physical controls his life, to suggest more similarity with than distinction from Mezentius himself.

Then occurs one of the most beautiful and moving moments in the epic. After lines of unremitting fury,[6] culminating in the death of Lausus, we have a moment of quiet, as Aeneas contemplates the features of his victim (821-24):

> At vero ut vultum vidit morientis et ora,
> ora modis Anchisiades pallentia miris,
> ingemuit miserans graviter dextramque tetendit,
> et mentem patriae subiit pietatis imago.

> But when the son of Anchises saw the face
> and features of the dying man, the features pale
> in marvelous ways, he groaned deeply from pity
> and stretched out his right hand, and the
> picture of paternal piety entered his mind.

Epic diachronism yields to lyric depth and intensity. We enter a complex verbal world where reiteration of words, assonance and alliteration force the reader to hear sound echo in sound, and where such interweaving and repetition linguistically mimic Aeneas' own pause to look, and look again, as the poet slows action to a stop. *Vultum vidit, modis miris, morientis* and *pallentia* form unifying sound clusters, but it is the repetition of *ora* at the end of line 821 and the beginning of line 822 that especially causes the reader to follow Aeneas' own mental progress and momentarily choose contemplation over action, explanation over heedless, continued doing.[7] Line 822 adds nothing to plot, much to atmosphere. It is a golden line, brilliantly centered around *Anchisiades* which stands out, furthermore, as the longest word in lines 821-2 and the only one that lacks melodic intimacy with any of its neighbors.

As we savor this calming panel breaking the onrush of narrative, we watch, first, the metamorphosis of Lausus from living to dead, from body to spirit, from physical being to disembodied emblem. Virgil would have us think of those *simulacra modis pallentia miris* from among whom, Lucretius tells us, the ghost of Homer arose to enlighten Ennius (*DRN* 1.123). In the first *georgic* Virgil draws on the same phrase to describe those images that appeared among the disquieting portents accompanying the death of Julius Caesar. Venus, in *Aeneid* 1, tells of the apparition in dreams to Dido of her unburied husband, *ora modis attollens pallida miris* (354), raising his face pale in marvelous ways.[8] As we join Aeneas in beholding Lausus' color paling and life giving place to death, we turn from surface to substance and examine through Aeneas' eyes the change in Lausus from literal to figurative. He alters from palpable enemy, to be killed both by and even at the expense of the hero's prime virtue, to a wraith that is symbol of that virtue, *patriae pietatis imago*, the personification of piety toward one's father. As war's wildness is momentarily subdued by thought, Aeneas appears to see beyond what his previous intensity had not allowed into human motivations that should be, but have not always been, a part of his thinking during his bout of killing. Contemplation and madness, *pietas* and slaughter would seem incompatible entities.

Pause in epic thrust for a moment of lyric intensity is thus a metaphor for the differentiation between history's relentless progress — the teleology

314

of a brilliant Roman destiny personified in the conduct of its founding father — and the personal suffering this progress causes. The tale of Mezentius operates on both levels at once. Virgil imputes to Mezentius alone what seems to have been a common pattern of Etruscan behavior.[9] But by stressing the public odiousness of Mezentius' former conduct he makes more remarkable the private devotion of Lausus, faithful to his father even to the sharing of exile. Moreover, through his son's sacrifice the *contemptor divum* elicits a vivid demonstration of *pietas* which in turn forces *pius* Aeneas to become a killer of the pious. Larger abstract notions of slaying barbarous enemies to rid the world of the primitive and the bestial are constantly questioned by Virgil when focussed against the realities of human emotions, and the pause, Aeneas' and the reader's, from linear action at Lausus' death is one of the most poignant examples in the epic.

The transformation of Lausus is also the transformation of Aeneas. By imitating him, Aeneas for a moment becomes Lausus' double. The phrase *patriae pietatis imago* is equally his.[10] The Aeneas who buried his sword into the body of Lausus has become *Anchisiades*, perceiving in Lausus' saving conduct an emblem of his own behavior toward his father.[11] He no longer stands alone but becomes part of a relationship of son to father, particular son to particular father. Although he will soon proclaim, with a renewal of callousness, that Lausus' consolation is his fall "by the right hand of mighty Aeneas" (*Aeneae magni dextra* 830), that right hand is at present stretched forward in a gesture not of violence but of pity, perhaps even of supplication.[12] Pity now becomes the chief component of this late learning. Aeneas is *miserans* as he begins to speak, his initial apostrophe to Lausus is *miserande puer* (825), and he defines the youth's death as *miseram* (829).

There is another vehicle by which Aeneas not only commiserates but verbally becomes Lausus, just as he suddenly remembers his own son-ship. At the moment in the previous duel when Lausus rescues his father, Aeneas has just wounded Mezentius with his spear and, "happy (*laetus*) at the sight of Etruscan blood," has drawn his sword for the kill. This is Lausus' reaction to the sight (789-90):

> ingemuit cari graviter genitoris amore,
> ut vidit, Lausus, lacrimaeque per ora volutae. . . .

> As he looked Lausus groaned deeply from love
> of his dear father, and tears rolled down his
> face. . . .

The phrases *ingemuit graviter* and *ut vidit* recur in close proximity at the moment of Lausus' death, attached now to Aeneas, as he and we notice the youth's features, deathly pale instead of tear-stricken.[13] For Aeneas, after his mortal deed, to react in the same way as Lausus about the saving of his father, is for the poet to fuse the two characters and to have Aeneas, in the hiatus before he turns to kill Mezentius, share Lausus' emotion to the point of linguistically merging with him as well.

That the conjunction is brief does not detract from its power, but the reader is prepared by Aeneas' prior deeds in the book not only for the mood to be evanescent but to learn once again that such thoughts do not influence his actions. One previous example from book 10, which will turn our attention to earlier books of the epic, must suffice to illustrate Aeneas' inattention to *pietas* in the heat of combat. In his bloodlust after the death of Pallas he first secures eight victims to be offered alive as sacrifice on the young hero's pyre. After that he slays Magus who is a suppliant (*supplex* 523), grasping Aeneas' knees. Magus' initial words are well chosen to affect the reader, though they do not deter Aeneas who twists their tone (524-5):

> "per patrios manis et spes surgentis Iuli
> te precor, hanc animam serves gnatoque patrique . . ."

> "I beseech you by the shades of your father and
> the hope of growing Iulus, save this life for a son
> and for a father . . ."

Magus' plea is a pastiche contrived from book 6. His first line recalls Palinurus' prayer to Aeneas to lead him across the Styx (364):

> "per genitorem oro, per spes surgentis Iuli. . . ."

> "I pray you by your father, by the hope of growing Iulus. . . ."

The helmsman's request appeals to the gestures, if not the emotions, of *pietas* (370):

> "da dextram misero et tecum me tolle per undas. . . ."[14]

> "Give your right hand to me in my misery and carry
> me with you through the waves. . . ."

Before Aeneas can reply, the Sibyl forbids any intervention.

The second line of Magus' speech reaches further back in book 6 to an earlier prayer, of Aeneas to the Sibyl. His request is briefly put (108-9):

>   ". . . ire ad conspectum cari genitoris et ora
>   contingat. . . ."

>   ". . . may I be allowed to make my way to
>   the sight and face of my dear father. . . ."

And his plea follows readily (116-7):

>   ". . . gnatique patrisque
>   alma, precor, miserere. . . ."

>   ". . . kindly one, I beseech you, pity son and father. . . ."

In the press of battle he denies the power in Magus' words that he had
expected to be able to bring to bear himself, in proposing to the Sibyl his
strange, pietistic adventure. In common with Lausus he shares love of a
dear parent, but forgets its validity when passion has mastered him. In
book 6, where Aeneas is a *supplex* (115) and the tangible efforts to carry
out his mission have not brought the moral dilemma of the final books, he
is introduced by the Sybil to Charon as *tantae pietatis imago* (405). He
incorporates in himself what he will see in Lausus after he has killed him,
and rage has momentarily retreated before understanding and com-
miseration. When father and son do meet (679-702), it is again the gesturing
of hands and facial expressions which are the manifestations that, in
Anchises' words, *vicit iter durum pietas* (688). Anchises stretched forth
both palms, weeping, and Aeneas attempts in vain to clasp hands with his
father, as he too weeps. There is a shared emphasis on the features of
each, the *ora* through which both demonstrate *pietas,* by which Lausus
also showed his love for Mezentius and in which Aeneas too saw a symbol
of piety.

Pietas, therefore, reveals itself regularly by facial and verbal gestures
of supplication and affection. It is not incompatible with *arma* in a general
definition of the Roman achievement that combines force with human
understanding. Yet it remains unreconcilable with the maddened and the
irrational, especially when the weapons of war are involved. This we know
from the beginning of the epic. The first we hear of Aeneas, his sufferings in
war and conveyance of gods to Latium — *pietas* and *arma* combined —
are contrasted to the *saevae memorem Iunonis iram* (1.4-6). Immediately
thereafter the hero who appears *insignem pietate* (10) is caught between an
emotional queen of the gods (*dolens regina deum* 9) and the narrator's
amazed questioning that *tantae irae* (11) could persist among the im-
mortals.[15] The contrast remains alive throughout the book and the epic.

At lines 251-3, for example, Venus juxtaposes the anger of unnamed Juno and the *pietatis honos* that is due Aeneas for his fidelity. The contrast is summarized in the first simile of the epic. Juno has given her resentments full play and stirred up Aeolus and his winds against the Trojans. Neptune senses the confusion and rightly imputes it to *Iunonis irae* (130). Virgil compares his calming presence amid wildness untrammeled to a man *pietate gravem ac meritis* (151) who soothes a ferocious mob to whom fury lends arms (*furor arma ministrat* 150).

In the first book Aeneas is buffeted by the elemental nature of Juno and her creatures, with little power to resist. During the bitter night of Troy's fall, the subject of book 2, Aeneas can take a more active, if unproductive role. We therefore watch with interest the relationship between Aeneas' first acts of piety and his recourse to arms, and how the polarity between enlightenment of mind and dark lack of understanding often shapes this relationship. Here too *imagines* play an important role in helping Aeneas clarify the obscure, penetrate behind the facades of motivation and action, and, finally, move away from bouts of futile violence toward an acceptance of a future symbolized in the professions of *pietas*.

The first "image" in book 2 is Aeneas' dream of Hector (270-1):

> in somnis, ecce, ante oculos maestissimus Hector
> visus adesse mihi. . . .

> In dreams, behold, most pitiful Hector seemed
> to stand before my eyes. . . .

The sleeping hero cannot yet appreciate the meaning of Hector's wounds, which would be to remember his mutilation by Achilles. Hector's speech, therefore, has a twofold importance. It forces the reality of his loss on Aeneas and forewarns that his tragedy anticipates the general suffering of Troy's demise. Hector then pronounces the futility of reliance on arms and succinctly predicts to Aeneas his future, suggesting his first act of *pietas* (293-4):

> sacra suosque tibi commendat Troia penates;
> hos cape fatorum comites. . . .

> Troy commits to you her holy objects and
> her household gods; seize them as comrades
> of your fortune. . . .

The vision of Hector allows Aeneas to face the truth of both present and future. At the same time Hector's wraith, by thrusting fillets, Vesta and the everlasting fire into his hands, proclaims Aeneas as protector of Troy's gods in transition.

It is a part that wakened Aeneas is not prepared to accept. For a moment he seems aloof from the *furentibus Austris* that fan the flames and akin to a shepherd who comprehends a stream's rampage only through a distant echo.[16] Yet, forgetful of Hector's revelation and command, he plunges irrationally into arms (314):

> arma amens capio; nec sat rationis in armis. . . .

> In madness I seize arms; nor is there sufficient reason in arms. . . .

In his own words, *furor* and *ira* drive his mind headlong (316). The first "image" has proved wasted on Aeneas who takes up arms not in defense of *pietas* but under the sponsorship of the unthinking use of force that so often stands in its way.

The next revelation to Aeneas comes after the central episode of the book, the forcing of Priam's palace and the decapitation of the old king. Aeneas seems only a voyeur of this impious sequence of events as Pyrrhus kills first Polites before the eyes of his parents, then Priam himself. He makes no attempt to intervene or avenge the double murder, perhaps because he is meant to appreciate that the death of its aged leader betokens the downfall of Troy. After the appearance of Hector *armorum horror* (301) had increased to the point that it had wakened the sleeping hero. Now it surrounds him (559-63):

> At me tum primum saevus circumstetit horror.
> obstipui; subiit cari genitoris imago,
> ut regem aequaevum crudeli vulnere vidi
> vitam exhalantem, subiit deserta Creusa
> et direpta domus et parvi casus Iuli.

> But then first dreadful horror surrounded me.
> I stood amazed; the vision of my dear father
> stood before me when I saw the king, his age
> mate, breathing forth his life from a cruel wound,
> deserted Creusa came before me, my plundered
> house and the fate of little Iulus.

Yet instead of rushing thoughtlessly into war Aeneas now allows the vision to develop a deeper significance. The hero responds to the sight of *pietas* affronted by becoming possessed with *pietas* of his own. It is no wonder that the description and especially the phrase *subiit cari genitoris imago* reverberate in the remainder of the epic. Anchises appears again a *cari genitoris* as Aeneas requests the Sibyl to visit his father in Hades (6.108),[17] and the phrase *subiit imago*, as we have seen, initiates Aeneas' realization that in Lausus he had killed an emblem of *pietas,* forced to die "because of love for his dear father" (*cari genitoris amore* 10.789), and had himself became a deadly, not saving, manifestation of the same presumed virtue.

Yet, instead of implementing his new insight, Aeneas again yields to impetuosity and contemplates the killing of Helen.[18] Anger, not the spirit of filial duty, rules his thoughts (575-6):

> . . . subit ira cadentem
> ulcisci patriam et sceleratas sumere poenas.

> . . . anger overcomes me to avenge my
> fallen fatherland and to extract punish-
> ment for crimes.

As he admits, before he has a chance to turn words into deeds, *furiata mente ferebar* (2.588). He is the passive victim of insanity rather than the active pursuer of a more noble, less tangible, goal. What changes his mind is another vision (589-91):

> cum mihi se, non ante oculis tam clara, videndam
> obtulit et pura per noctem in luce refulsit
> alma parens. . . .

> when my kindly mother offered herself to my
> sight, never before so clear to my vision,
> and gleamed in pure radiance through the
> night. . . .

With the appearance of Venus both the hero's parents replace Helen as the primary objects of his thinking. Her first words demand such recollection (594-8):

> 'nate, quis indomitas tantus dolor excitat iras?
> quid furis? aut quonam nostri tibi cura recessit?
> non prius aspicies ubi fessum aetate parentem
> liqueris Anchisen, superet coniunxne Creusa
> Ascaniusque puer? . . .'

> 'My son, what great resentment arouses
> your uncontrollable anger? Why are you
> raging? Or whither has your care for

us gone? Will you not first see where
you left your father Anchises spent with
age, whether your wife Creusa and the
boy Ascanius survive? . . . .'

Useless vengeance against the past is replaced by renewed allegiance to
family ties, which means allegiance to continuity and, ultimately, acceptance of future destiny. The abstractions which polarize around this
change are standard, with one exception. The resentment, anger and rage
that press Aeneas toward the unheroic urge to kill a woman, are countered
now by an appeal to *pietas* defined specifically by the word *cura*. It is
nostri cura, "care for us," love of Venus, that should have motivated
Aeneas' deeds.

As will be the case when he is exposed to the deeper significance of
Lausus' death, Venus' potency has the other extraordinary but complementary effect of allowing Aeneas, in pondering a course of action, to
see beyond the superficial and observe larger forces at work upon human-
kind. *Tyndaridis facies invisa Lacaenae,* the (ironically) hateful features of
Helen, had, according to Venus, impelled Aeneas to an equally superficial,
negative waste of energy. Venus now dramatically unclouds her son's
vision to allow him to look beyond appearance and watch *divum inclementia*
at work. This is Virgil's only use of the abstraction in the *Aeneid*,[19] and it
gives emphasis to an occasion where Aeneas can note the force of divine
unforgiveness at work, in Juno, *saevissima* and *furens*, in Athena, equally
saeva, and in the father of the gods himself, urging on his colleagues.
Presumably Aeneas, and we, at moments where we must scrutinize the
symbolic meaning of events, would associate *inclementia* with ferocity,
and *clementia* with restraint.

The last "vision" occurs at the end of the book. Aeneas returns to
his father's house and persuades him, with the help of a series of positive
omens, to leave Troy. In the process of retreat, as Aeneas carries out his
first great act of *pietas,* shouldering his father and grasping Iulus by the
hand, Creusa is lost and Aeneas, *amens,* returns in quest. Her sudden appearance to him parallels the previous epiphanies of Hector and Venus
(772-3):

> infelix simulacrum atque ipsius umbra Creusae
> visa mihi ante oculos et nota maior imago.

> The sad ghost and shade of Creusa her-
> self appeared before my eyes and a vision
> larger than her wont.

Its potential is not dissimilar. Like Venus, Creusa chides Aeneas for his indulgence in *insano dolori* (776). Then, expanding on the example of Hector, she reveals to Aeneas the *res laetae* of the future, a kingdom and royal wife. Her last words, however, center on a love that is intimate with *pietas: nati serva communis amorem* (789). As she disappears, and Aeneas attempts to hold her, Virgil uses three lines that he will repeat exactly in book 6 as son greets father (792-4):

> ter conatus ibi collo dare bracchia circum;
> ter frustra comprensa manus effugit imago,
> par levibus ventis volucrique simillima somno.

> Three times there I attempted to throw my
> arms about her neck; three times the vision,
> embraced in vain, fled my hands, kin to
> light winds and very like a swift dream.

Each figure is a crucial *imago* in Aeneas' life, a ghost that foretells the future after a period of insecurity and search. Each exemplifies a melancholic aspect of the life of the hero, unable to embrace those dear to him, forced away from Dido for whom he does care, and allotted at the end of the epic a *coniunx* thrust on him by fate. Yet each also is a creative influence in disparate ways — Creusa, by calming his final act of *dolor* in book 2 with a look at the future, Anchises by expanding that future in a delusive vista where arms and piety, clemency and power seem to abide in harmony.

Hence in book 2 as a whole we regularly find emotionality opposed to reason, especially when directed toward long-range goals. Such moments of irrationality are often centered on immediate gratification, understandable however morally misguided. Heedless action finds its counterpoise in the words of Hector, Panthus, Venus and Creusa, and the thoughts and insights they arouse. The hero's display of aimless chauvinism that follows his dream of Hector is not defended within his narration, and his rationalization for killing Helen, argued in a soliloquy he quotes himself delivering a moment before he almost performs the deed, Aeneas himself qualifies as the product of a maddened mind (*furiata mente*).

It is inevitable that discussion of such polarities must focus on the finale of the poem as Aeneas ponders the situation of the now suppliant Turnus, and then slays him. How is Aeneas to see him, and how, as he weighs alternatives, will whatever analysis he makes of his victim sway him, as he hesitates?[20] Their differentiation (as well as commonality) is made explicit by the poet's concentration on the eyes and right hands of

each hero, preceding and following Turnus' last words. Before he speaks
we watch Turnus (12.930-1) —

> ille humilis supplex oculos dextramque precantem
> protendens. . . .

> He, a suppliant, with eyes humbled, and stretching
> forth his right hand in prayer. . . —

and after, our attention focusses on the hero in power (938-9):

> . . . stetit acer in armis
> Aeneas volvens oculos dextramque repressit. . . .

> . . . Aeneas stood fierce in arms, rolling his
> eyes, and restrained his right hand. . . .

The eyes of Turnus are humbled, of Aeneas revolving in thought, as
victoriously he plots out the possibilities before him.[21] When Turnus
states that the Ausonians have seen him, conquered, stretch forth his
hands (*victum tendere palmas* 936), he merely reinforces the contrast between his gesture of supplication and Aeneas' posture of strength, his
right hand momentarily restrained.

The gesture of supplication is one that Aeneas would have understood. He had seen his father twice use it, first, as Troy falls, in asking
Jupiter to confirm the omen of fire on Iulus' head (*palmas tetendit* 2.688),
second while greeting Aeneas in the Underworld (*palmas tetendit* 6.685),
when last he saw him. He had employed it himself to Jupiter in prayer to
save the burning ships (*tendere palmas* 5.686), and watched it in the suppliant Liger in book 10 (*tendebat palmas* 596-7).[22] The reader remembers it
from the hero's initial appearance in the epic, awed by the prospect of death
from nature and preparing to address those who die (to him) more heroically
at Troy (1.92-4):

> extemplo Aeneae solvuntur frigore membra;
> ingemit et duplicis tendens ad sidera palmas
> talia voce refert. . . .[23]

> Suddenly Aeneas' limbs were undone with
> cold; he groans and, stretching both hands
> toward the stars, speaks thus aloud. . . .

Line 92 closely resembles the description of Turnus, frightened by the Dira
sent by Jupiter to ensure his final defeat (12.867):

Illi membra novus solvit formidine torpor. . . .

A strange numbness undoes his limbs in fear. . . .

This spectacle is complemented shortly later by the prospect of Turnus incapable of movement (*gelidus concrevit frigore sanguis* 905), and imitated most clearly in the next to last line of the poem as Turnus dies (951):

. . . ast illi solvuntur frigore membra.[24]

. . . but his limbs were undone with cold.

Matters have come full circle. Aeneas, once helpless before the elements, has now become the elemental power, abetted by Jupiter and his Dira, before which Turnus must pray in supplication and which finally destroys him. But the closest parallel between the two is suggested by the previous words of Turnus (12.932-4):

". . . miseri te si qua parentis
tangere cura potest, oro (fuit et tibi talis
Anchises genitor) Dauni miserere senectae. . . ."[25]

". . . if any care of a sad father can touch you,
I beseech you (Anchises was also such a father
to you), pity the old age of Daunus. . . ."

Virgil has graphically sketched Turnus' aging and debilitation in the lines that lead up to the final duel. (Our growing sympathy for prideful Turnus now suffering humiliation is not unlike our response to savage Mezentius at the moment his vulnerability is shielded by his loving son.) Suddenly, therefore, we find his prototype not in wounded Hector but in Priam whose first, dramatic words to Achilles, as he comes to ransom his son's body, remind him of his father Peleus (*Il.* 24.486-7):

"μνῆσαι πατρὸς σοῖο, θεοῖς ἐπιείκελ' Ἀχιλλεῦ,
τηλίκου, ὥς περ ἐγών, ὀλοῷ ἐπὶ γήραος οὐδῷ. . . ."

"Achilles like to the gods, remember your
father, whose years are like mine, on the
grievous threshold of old age. . . ."

They would also serve to recall to Aeneas his own vivid display of *pietas*, searching out his father in the underworld, and, as we have observed, his preliminary position as suppliant, craving pity from the Sibyl (6.115-7):

"quin ut te supplex peterem et tua limina adirem,
idem orans mandata dabat. gnatique patrisque,
alma, precor, miserere. . . ."[26]

"Nay he also in prayer gave me commands
that as a suppliant I seek you out and approach your threshold. I pray, kindly one,
pity both son and father. . . ."

First introduced in the epic as a new Achilles, Turnus becomes now not
only Priam before Achilles but also Aeneas before the Sibyl.[27] He should
appear to his victor as a figure of Aeneas himself, as he appeals to an *imago*
Aeneas should well remember. Instead of following the pattern of book
10 where he saw Lausus as an emblem of *pietas* only after he has killed him
(and only then does he become *Anchisiades*), Aeneas has a chance to be
affected by words, ideas and memories, to pity before rather than after
a deed, even to spare, combining force with generosity, not madness. He
could show that he also has absorbed what the reader has learned from the
conclusion of book 10.

The phrase *parentis cura* and its association with two fathers,
Anchises and Daunus, should also cast Aeneas' thoughts back to the past.
The reader associates the phrase with Aeneas' love for Ascanius (1.646) and,
as Andromache reminisces, with Ascanius' for his lost mother (3.341).
Aeneas might hear again Venus' question after he has nearly killed Helen:

". . . aut quonam nostri tibi cura recessit?
non prius aspicies ubi fessum aetate parentem
liqueris Anchisen. . . . ?"

Remembrance of both parents, the *cura parentum* for which *pietas* should
provide the motivation, contrasts with the *dolor, ira* and *furor* that, in
Venus' words, Aeneas had just displayed by his desire for vengeance
against Helen. It is not, however, Turnus as image of *pietas* or even as
representative of Aeneas himself that moves the hero to act at the epic's
end. Turnus' words do in fact cause him to delay, to experience a moment
of detachment which means at least the possibility of *clementia*, of words
taking precedence over deeds. What impels Aeneas to kill is the sight of
Pallas' baldrick worn by Turnus. It serves as a *saevi monimenta doloris*
(945) which drives Aeneas mad, *furiis accensus et ira / terribilis* (946-7). It is
not *pietas*, and the moderation both Venus and Anchises see in its practise,
but *ira* that holds the hero in thrall as he embarks on his final action. The

325

clarity of broadened vision that Aeneas is allowed in book 2, when he beholds divine *inclementia* about its devastating work, and that is offered to him so brilliantly as action pauses for the double figuration of Lausus' death, is once again, and for the last time, obscured.[28]

Brown University

NOTES

[1] 7.234-5. Cf. also 6.769, 878-9; 11.291-2. The practise of *pietas* and the production of *arma* is linked in Venus' request to Vulcan (8.383): *arma rogo, genetrix nato.*

[2] 7.649-51. Only Turnus is more handsome.

[3] 7.647-8; 8.480-9.

[4] This point is made by Benario 1967.33.

[5] The reader's sympathy for Mezentius grows as the book nears its conclusion, for his self-understanding, and for his realization of how his earlier misdeeds have affected his son whose loyalty he has nonetheless retained. We hear of his *canities* (10.844) only after Lausus' death.

Leach 1971 notes well the change in Mezentius which Aeneas is unable, or unwilling, to perceive.

[6] For an examination of Aeneas' conduct earlier in the book, viewed against its Iliadic background, see Farron 1977.204-8.

[7] *Ora* is also repeated effectively at 6.495-6, as Aeneas contemplates the mutilated features of Deiphobus. Virgil uses the same verb, *subeo,* to describe Aeneas' imagining of piety at 10.824 and the carrying of his father at 2.708. Cf. also 2.560 and 4.599, quoted below.

Virgil repeats the name Lausus prominently when we first hear of him (7.649-51). *Esset* ends both lines 653 and 654; the first use is connected with *patriis imperiis*; the other has *pater* as subject. Lausus and his father Mezentius are linguistically and emotionally intertwined from the start. I cannot agree with Jones 1977.50-4 that Mezentius is "effectively isolated from his son" (53; cf. 51). The personal allegiance of Lausus, in spite of his father's conduct, remains significant.

For a sensitive treatment of 10.821-24, to which my analysis is indebted, see Johnson 1976.72-4. Professor Johnson carefully elucidates Virgil's originality by comparison with his Homeric models, especially the lamentations of Priam and Achilles at *Iliad* 24.507 ff.

[8] Cf. also the priest at the oracle of Faunus who *multa modis simulacra videt volitantia miris* (7.89).

[9] Virgil's treatment of Mezentius is analyzed by Burke 1974.202-9. His departures from tradition in dealing with Lausus and Mezentius are touched on by Heinze 1957.172 ff., 179 and 213. Mezentius' exile is a Virgilian invention which proves that, for Virgil at least, the Etruscans were capable of responding to cruelty before the arrival of Aeneas. His death at the hands of Aeneas is original with Virgil whom Ovid (*F.* 4.895 f.) follows. Tradition has him either slain later (Cato *Orig.* ff. 9-11P, noted by Servius on *Aen.* 1.267, 4.620, 6.760, and 9.742) or making peace (Livy 1.3.4; *D. H.* 1.65.5; Dio Cassius fr. 3.7 Melber [from Tzetzes on Lyc. *Alex.* 1232]). Aeneas' killing of Lausus is likewise an alteration of tradition which has him dying also in a subsequent battle against Ascanius (*D. H.* 1.65.3).

Virgil's use of tradition in moulding his characterization of Mezentius is treated by Sullivan 1969.219-25, who plots analogies with the Ajax of Homer and Sophocles, and Glenn 1971.129-55, who finds Virgil's principal model in the Polyphemus of the *Odyssey*.

[10] The phrase is similar to one used of Iulus at 9.294 (*animum patriae strinxit pietatis imago*). Though Iulus is responding to Euryalus' concern for his mother, the words more strictly refer to the *pietas* he bears his absent father, and vice versa.

[11] The power of *Anchisiades* here is discussed by Benario 1967.33. Virgil uses the patronymic on five other occasions, 5.407, 6.126 and 348, 8.521, and 10.250. In each case there are reasons to remember the father-son relationship.

[12] For the *palmas tendere* see below. The words *tendere manus* are directly associated with *amor* at 6.314.

[13] Alliteration draws the reader's attention from *cari, genitoris* and *amore* to *ora*, and prepares for the latter's repetition at 821-2.

The effect of first person narrative is particularly powerful at 10.790 ff. This witness of emotional involvement is congruent with the detailed knowledge the narrator evinces of Lausus at 10.832 (*comptos de more capillos*). This sudden specificity suggests more than the difference between death's dishevelment and life's order.

[14] Cf. also 2.721 ff. and 804. At 4.274 Mercury reminds Aeneas of *Ascanium surgentem et spes heredis Iuli*. When Aeneas acts against Magus he is no longer helpless before fate.

[15] An instance of the distinction between anger and piety, outside of book 1, occurs at 5.781-8 where the *ira* (781), *nefandis odiis* (785-6) and *furoris* (788) of Juno are contrasted by Venus with the *pietas* (783) of Aeneas.

[16] *Furentibus Austris* (1.51) helped Aeolus threaten the Trojan fleet in the epic's opening episode.

[17] The phrase *cari genitoris* is also used at 1.677 of Aeneas in relation to Ascanius-Iulus.

The parallel between 2.560 (*genitoris imago*) and 10.824 (*pietatis imago*) is noted by DiCesare 1974.174.

A *genitoris imagine* is twisted at 4.84 where Dido is misled by the image of Aeneas in the features of Ascanius, a delusion that commenced in book 1 when Cupid had adopted the same features. It is an *imago* empty of significance. An *imago* of Anchises, however, and mention of Ascanius at 4.511 ff. are the causes of Aeneas' departure from Carthage.

Aeneas accused his mother of deluding him *falsis imaginibus* (1.407-8). Throughout the epic, when *imagines* matter most, they often betoken personal lack of fulfillment, *pietas* without its final symbolic seal.

[18] The Helen episode lacks the final Virgilian polish, but *Aeneid* 2 is not whole without it. Venus' reminder to Aeneas of Anchises, Creusa, and Ascanius at 596 ff. makes little sense unless some event has intervened to make the hero forget his perception of them at 562 ff. A prior encounter with her is the logical way to explain Venus' allusion to Helen (601), the first of two creatures (the other is Paris) whom Aeneas would be prone to blame but, according to his mother, should not.

Beyond the level of plot, there are other imaginative factors that suggest the intimacy of the Helen passage with its context. Both share the polarities of seeing and non-seeing, insight and blindness. There is the common notion of fire as analogy between physical and human, exterior and interior worlds. But such themes deserve separate analysis.

[19] Virgil's only other use of *inclementia* is in relation to death (*Geo.* 3.68). By the epic's end the *inclementia* of the gods against Aeneas and Troy has become the *saevitia* of Jupiter and Aeneas against Turnus.

20 I will deal elsewhere with the importance of hesitation throughout the epic and especially in connection with the poem's final moments.

21 I follow the Oxford text of Mynors at line 930. If, with M and several later manuscripts, we read *supplexque*, then *humilis* would modify not *oculos* but *ille* and *supplex* (see Williams 1973 *ad loc.*). Dido is also seen *volvens oculos*, worrying through her course of action against Aeneas (4.363), as is Latinus, pondering acceptance of the Trojans (7.251). We are told that Aeneas *oculos volvit*, contemplating Vulcan's shield (8.618). See also 4.643 and 7.399, where madness is part of a process of decision, and cf. 1.482 and 6.469 where fixed eyes betoken decisiveness of mind.

22 Before Aeneas kills Lucagus and then Liger, his brother, he is called *pius* (10.591). Liger prays for mercy by appeal to Aeneas' parents. Aeneas' reply ends *morere at fratrem ne desere frater* (600).

23 Mezentius, when he sees the lifeless body of Lausus, *ambas / ad caelum tendit palmas* (10. 844-5), a curious gesture for a despiser of the gods.

24 Virgil uses the same line of Aeneas responding to Mercury's command for withdrawal from Carthage (4.280) and of Turnus' facing the Dira (12.868). Here too the early Aeneas maintains kinship with the later Turnus.

25 Turnus' words to Aeneas are similar to ones Latinus had addressed to Turnus at the start of the book (12.43-5). Turnus' gradual change from pride to humiliation is the book's process also.

26 There are other words common to Aeneas' speech in book 6 and to Turnus in 12, among them *genitor* (6.108) and *senectae* (114). It is apt that the Sibyl's reply first apostrophizes Aeneas as *sate sanguine divum, / Tros Anchisiade* (125-6).

27 Aeneas, at his ugliest moment of rage in book 10, is also patterned after Achilles (with *Aen.* 10.557 ff. compare *Il.* 21.125 ff.).

28 Virgil tells us something about Aeneas', and human, nature by having piety most operative in the epic when the hero is downtrodden, apprehensive of the future and without arms, least available and useful when power is assured and compassion possible without harm to his "mission." The end of the epic offers Aeneas a last, grand opportunity to unite the *pietas* of affection and the *dextra* of power. It is unfortunate, but not unexpected, that he fails. Aeneas gradually loses his power at arms in book 2 as Troy's fortune ebbs away. The regaining of weapons in book 8 and their application in books 10 and 12 show little ultimate difference from their use in book 2 where *pietas* and the associates of *furor* remain at loggerheads. It is the latter who win at the epic's end, as Aeneas' actions could be seen to negate what his mission sets out to affirm.

I would like to thank Professors Christine Perkell, Kenneth Reckford, and Charles Segal for their helpful comments.

THE VIRGILIAN ACHIEVEMENT

Michael C. J. Putnam

Scanning Virgil's three major works in the search for unity, the critic is struck by an irony in the changes of genre. As the poet advances on his career, his models grow more and more remote in time, and, it could be said, more basic in theme. The *Eclogues*, modeled often on the *Idyls* of Theocritus and clearly espousing a Callimachean credo of poetic fineness, look to a Hellenistic background. In the *Georgics*, in spite of a slender debt to Aratus and other contemporaries, Virgil turns away from Alexandria first toward the remoter Greece of Hesiod, to sing in Roman towns the song of Ascra, secondly to Roman Lucretius whose "causes of things" will serve as an enriching influence on his own agrarian gods and their world. The *Aeneid* follows the same pattern — back further in Roman time to Ennius (who had offered direct challenge to Callimachus), in Greek past Apollonius of Rhodes (to whom book 4 is but a passing bow), past an occasional glimpse at the heroes and heroines of tragedy, back to *il miglior fabbro*, Homer himself, against whose essential insights into humanity Virgil's own achievements will always be measured. It is easy to find those who deplore such a journey from Alexandria to the shores of Troy, but Virgil's spiritual diary is worthy of some scrutiny.

Manifestly there are deeper levels to this progress than those which questions of literary influence can plumb, revelatory of taste as the latter often are. There are themes common to all three works. The challenge between idealism and realism, between life as it is often dreamed and life as it ultimately is always led, is an inexorable topic. But in a survey from the pastoral poems to the end of the epic, what is perhaps most striking is the gradual elimination of spiritual distance from the actualities and importunities of existence.

Arcadian setting specifically tends to remove the *Eclogues* from immediacies. The shepherd as poet is itself an anomalous conceit. Moreover when so much space seems given over to scrutinizing poetry *per se*, verging toward an ultimately irresponsible verbalization of art's dialogue with itself, that reader is blameless who senses himself in turn the play of make-believe. Not only does Virgil at first draw us into a landscape apart, he appears to narrow his horizon still further by enforcing concentration on a poet's private vision. He orients us to those thoughts which suit or challenge his imagination. The problems of creativity are viewed from a stance of knowing uninvolvement, we could easily assume.

329

But there are deeper values and more primary concerns to the *Eclogues* than poetry in or of itself. Along with this apparent estrangement from life there is another whole area of intent in the *Eclogues* which is only now becoming critically clarified. Its presence is felt idealistically in the fourth poem where Virgil, at least in his thoughts, sings a symbolic marriage hymn for the union of Rome's consul and his own "woods," of history and paradise, time and timeless, power and poetry. *Carmina*, the efficacy of "charming" verse, are expected to induce the youthful symbol of an era without ambition's wars. Virgil would have us ponder a different golden age, beyond Saturn's facile primitivism and Jupiter's more realistic economics, to a Rome which could in fact embrace pastoralism within its moral bounds, a pastoralism involving a new Saturnian intellectual as well as social freedom.

But Virgil's contemporary Rome of the 40's and 30's B.C. is a more realistic entity and *Eclogues* 1 and 9 dispel any illusions. The position of *Eclogue* 1 is in itself a warning that any seeming escapism in the poems that follow must not be given undue significance. We may treat, if we choose, the differing positions of the two shepherds as a quasi-allegorical dialogue between happiness and suffering, freedom and slavery, and rejoice that the first also flourishes. But in the background lurks a Rome that might be, facing a Rome that does exist. One Rome possesses a divine youth who in turn fosters a dream shepherd. But the idealized pose of the shepherd Tityrus merely vivifies the immediate truth of a barbaric soldier possessing the power to exile another pastoral being. *Eclogue* 9 says in addition that the writing of poetry is impossible under conditions such as now prevail in the sylvan landscape. Their creator-poet exposes his shepherds to reality and then, in *Eclogue* 10, the last of the series, poises himself on the same threshold.

Eclogue 10 makes the transition to the *Georgics* easy. Verbally we are prepared by two phrases. The poet's love for Gallus grows hour by hour like a green alder in new spring, *vere novo*, the exact words with which the land's primaveral awakening is announced at the start of *Georgic* 1. Not only this, the poet himself will "spring up," renouncing the posture of the leisured bard for something more challenging and active:

> surgamus: solet esse gravis cantantibus umbra,
> iuniperi gravis umbra; nocent et frugibus umbrae.

It comes as a surprise to learn that shade is harmful to a singer; we have so often heard differently in the *Eclogues*. On the other hand, Virgil warns the practical farmer early on in *Georgic* 1 of the hurt shade gives crops. But it is the poet's admission of affection for the soldier-elegist Gallus that is most revealing. Earlier in the *Eclogues* Virgil, speaking for himself as poet, conjured up a dream existence or pledged a Callimachean allegiance, still within what might be called pastoral convention. Now, by acknowledging a spirited connection with the literal world of the soil and with living humanity (especially with a personage boasting of martial prestige and prowess in a very intimate poetic genre), he renounces his sylvan muse.

His closer look at reality — at nature which must be seen literally but ultimately is also symbolic — comes in the *Georgics*. The pattern of the four books is an interesting one, from the cosmological setting in which the natural world finds itself (earth and sky), to the growth of crops and trees, to the more explicit trials of animal life, and finally, to bees, partially human, partially divine, communally minded, instinctively aggressive, ignorant of love, eternal in some eyes but equally the prey of death. And then at the end we have two tales. In the first the culture-hero Aristaeus, to wrest life from death, must be initiated into the sources of existence (in a semi-divine, mythical world of water) and grasp the *miracula rerum*. The second is devoted to Orpheus, poet-lover, mesmerizer of immortal death by song but unable to control his own mortal *furor*. Finally an eight line vignette of a still more realistic life concludes the poem — Octavian thundering on the Euphrates and the slothful poet, at his leisure penning the rhythms of life.

In the *Eclogues* the natural landscape of breeze and shade tends to blur indissolubly with ideas of poetic creation and intellectual freedom. It becomes in the *Georgics* a grander, more essential metaphor for existence. Nature is unceasingly symbolized as human and made to reveal paradigms of flowering and decay, youth and old age, spontaneity and resistance, which offer formal comment on the world of man. And, as part of this more explicit intimacy with the human situation on Virgil's part, there is the same uncordial duality between idealism and realism, between the search for perfected hopes and fallible means. Though the pastoral mode has at first an escapist effect, the actualities of suffering are far from absent in the *Eclogues*. They are a constant theme in the *Georgics*, relieved, as in the *Eclogues*, only by notions which seem deliberately tenuous if momentarily ingratiating.

The first *Georgic* tells of the signs from heaven which only warn but cannot avert disaster. There are violent harvest storms against which there is no recourse. In the middle of the book man is an oarsman propelling a tiny skiff against a heavy current, in spite of the arms at his disposal, scarcely holding his own by unremitting toil in the battle against degeneration. At the end humanity is seen only as a futile charioteer who has lost control of his horses (life's brute and brutal forces) during the exactness of a race. We are reminded at the start of the book of the *gloria divini ruris*, in the end that the plough has lost its honor, that pruning forks are forged into swords, that fields are manured with blood not dung. The initial lines of the book imply that the farmer's lot is hard (he is styled ignorant, mortal, sick); the concluding intimate that it is virtually impossible.

The second *Georgic*, on the other hand, has splendidly idealistic moments — the praises of Italy, the bursting vitality of spring's coming, the concluding eulogy of morality in former rustic days (coupled with Virgil's own commentary on his inspiration). But this last has clues which undercut any false optimism. Virgil evokes a Sabine life of pre-Jupiter days, before war came and Justice left. The realities of Rome (*res Romanae* in every sense) are different and, though this rural existence elicits the poet's approval, it is of time past (*olim*). More peculiar, it is associated with Romulus and Remus, prototypes of civil war, fit exemplars for the modern Romans who, we have just learned, rejoice in a drenching with brothers' blood (*gaudent perfusi sanguine fratrum*). In this manner Etruria grew — and so does Virgil's irony! Romulus and Remus fought each other, the Romulidae fought the Sabines, the combination overcame the Etruscans, and Rome was walled. And yet Virgil would have us believe in another moment that this was the epoch of golden Saturn, before battle trumpets sounded and swords were forged. Such is the dream he has Jupiter propose in *Aeneid* 1 as the head of the gods predicts a future moment when Romulus will co-operate with Remus (*Remo cum fratre Quirinus / iura dabunt*) and *Furor* is imprisoned. But such a moment never does occur, certainly never in the *Aeneid*, and Virgil's poetic impulse tells us so throughout the *Georgics*.

The third *Georgic* has no relieving optimism, in spite of an initial urge to glorify militant Octavian. Contemplated epic quickly yields to a more direct appraisal of human life. Even love is essentially bitter and destructive. The best day for pitiable mortals is fleeting; what remains is disease, old age and hard death. The remainder of the book bears out the maxim, ending in a brutally vivid description of a plague which destroys the animal world and those humans who are unfortunate enough to come in contact with it — strange paradox for a writer of *georgica*.

The opening of the fourth *Georgic* is a welcome change. We are to be entertained by watching bees at work, by the spectacle of "light" matters — Virgil's way of telling us that the truth is far otherwise. Critics veer happily toward allegory in their view of the bees, as if they somehow embodied perfection. Yet their life, as Virgil would see it, is neither ideal nor representative, nor, for that matter, eternal. They cannot symbolize humanity (i.e. Orpheus, Aristaeus, or even us)

332

because they experience neither love nor individuality. The principal preoccupation they share with Rome is a devotion to war and, in some instances a blind (or, to put it more kindly, selfless) devotion to the "state," meaning fundamentally hard work and unswerving loyalty to those in power. They are prone to civil war which makes their passion for patriotic *pietas* the more bitter. Here fortunately they differ from Rome because their conflicts can be quelled by a handful of dust and death to the leader of lesser value. Such is the power Jupiter exerts over mankind, though from another point of view "divine" force rests in the hands of thundering Octavian (or even of Virgil, the leisured imaginer of these words) and who is to control him? The *Aeneid* responds to the unanswered question.

At the end we have Aristaeus who lost his hive for causing Eurydice's death (Virgil need only say that she was running away from him *praeceps*). Orpheus then sought vengeance by destroying his livelihood. The bees were helpless victims of Aristaeus' impetuosity just as Eurydice will soon be lost again through Orpheus' lack of control. Different levels of life come vividly, often unpredictably, into contact as the cycle of birth and death continues. There is always a divine side to existence. The bees have it in part (*partem divinae mentis*). Aristaeus can turn for help to Cyrene and Proteus, and apprehend the exalted lessons of source and variety in nature. Orpheus can charm death itself. But there is always the mortal world of emotion in all its forms. Virgil's suggestion is not only that life comes out of death, bees born from a slaughtered bullock, or even that death follows life. It is also too limiting to assert that, in spite of individual loss, the universe remains immortal. Rather he posits existence as made up of this strange mixture of tragic and comic, human and divine, of death and birth, on the one side, of poetry and power (once more), of Octavian and Virgil on the other, serving as complements and inextricably intertwined.

The birth of the bees is a case in point. It is twice described, with the tales of Aristaeus and Orpheus intervening. In the first instance they shriek, grab the air and burst forth from the carcass like a summer storm or Parthian arrows. In the second they roar swirling forth from the broken ribs, great clouds of them, and settle on a treetop from whose bending branches they hang like a cluster of grapes. There are elements of violence in each parturition but the earlier dwells on the triumph of the bees' martial instincts whereas the second envisions a more fruitful, ultimately calmer rationale. In the *Aeneid* such a cluster of bees on Latinus' laurel is one harbinger of future domination by the Trojans, seeking a dwelling place, in search of an end to their "tired affairs" (*fessis rebus: Aen.* 3. 145) just as Aristaeus turns to Proteus in like desperation (*lassis rebus: geo.* 4. 449). The resulting rebirth in the *Aeneid* is permeated with the same ambivalence as the *Georgics*, and the final outcome is even less reassuring.

For in the *Aeneid* Virgil finally comes to grips with the realities of contemporary Rome, and Rome, as its poetic masterpiece proves, can be viewed from two sides, each incorporated to a certain extent in her founding hero. Aeneas is the grand civilizer, the sturdy Roman whose art (and I rephrase Anchises' provocative words to his son in the underworld) rises above the mere technical prowess of science, craftsmanship or rhetoric to impose the custom of peace on mankind by curbing *superbia* and exhibiting *clementia* — a physical effort to implement a grand spiritual design. The Roman will create and confirm a setting for life. He will mold a society in which men can live at peace so as to have the opportunity, within an ordered framework, of being brilliant artisans in stone and words.[1]

But words are one thing, deeds another, and the struggle to bring into being an actual Rome takes us out of a realm of noble platitudes into a more realistic situation where, as in all human endeavor of a political nature, the bad triumphs along with the good. And Virgil is no naive dreamer. There is a delicate balance, which Virgil's commanding language conveys, between freedom and slavery inherent in any aspect of power politics. It is a Roman's duty to rule people by *imperium*, by the might of empire and to impose a rationale for peace. Or, as Jupiter says of Aeneas to Mercury in book 4, he should put the whole world under law. But both these preachments imply a certain bondage which under some circumstances, easily imaginable now as well as then, could make both law and peace meaningless. In partially rejecting the nineteenth century attitude about the *Aeneid* as the glorification of Augustan Rome, with Virgil merely pulling the strings at the emperor's puppet show, we are also disposing of a basic critical fallacy, namely that distinguished poetry emanates directly from the fabric of society. A poet is formed, no doubt, by the culture in which he lives, but culture is conservative. It yearns for self-preserving stability. The poet, on the other hand, comments, teaches, argues from an intellectual and emotional distance which prods society by applying the goad of quality.

If we believe this of the *Aeneid*, as I think we must, then several interesting questions arise. The hero himself is human as well as divine, sensing the grand philosophical design of a perfected society but narrowed by his own fallibility in its achievement. Must we therefore expect him to be totally "moral"? Are we justified in offering him only sympathy and understanding in moments of weakness? Is it correct — or even important — to visualize him as becoming a better, more virtuous man as the epic progresses? These are views still commonly held by the most distinguished critics, but Virgil's notions about mankind are tougher, less romantic, I suggest.[2] In the first six books of the *Aeneid*, individual suffering, the *lacrimae rerum*, is subordinate to the developing spectre of Rome, a distant image growing more distinct yet still always mental. The hero learns the future by word of mouth, and endures. In the last six books the hero executes the dream as fact. The vision has become a reality and, as always in life, truth is less easy than contemplation, to lead more dangerous than to follow.

For this reason the final three books, in which Aeneas is actually playing the role of hero-statesman with his father's moral explication of future Rome to guide him, are of special significance. At the end of book eight, as Aeneas raises to his shoulder Vulcan's blazing shield (and becomes the model of the *fama et fata nepotum*, the reputation and "fate" of his descendants), Virgil has him rejoice in the representation of events about which he was ignorant (*rerumque ignarus imagine gaudet*). This is one of those extraordinary moments in the *Aeneid*, like the bough that "delays" before the hero's touch in book 6, where the hero and his destiny meet most intensely through the poet's symbolification. In spite of the Sibyl's assurances that the bough would come easily and willingly to those fated to pluck it, it hesitates at Aeneas' touch.[3] There is nothing simplistic about Rome's mission or her founding hero. As for book 8, what is about to happen as the epic draws to its violent close is exactly this change from *imago* to *res*, from a craftsman's dream to present reality, from the aloof absorption of destiny by the mediation of ghost or engraved shield to its actual implementation. Aeneas must orient himself away from the artistry of his father's rhetoric and his step-father's bronze to live the actual *artes* Anchises preaches, his own moulding of future Roman *mores*. The appraisal is not necessarily a positive one, for Aeneas or for Rome, but it vivifies certain unending truths.

An issue of primary importance is Aeneas' *pietas*. Does, in fact can it develop through the epic's course? Is the Aeneas who kills Turnus so very different from the earlier Aeneas we see pondering the murder of Helen during Troy's dark night?[4] Virgil might have us think otherwise. This is the way Aeneas describes his own emotion at the sight of Helen (2. 575-576):

> exarsere ignes animo; subit ira cadentem
> ulcisci patriam et sceleratas sumere poenas.

At the end of 12, as he blazes with wrath (*furiis accensus et ira / terribilis*) upon seeing Pallas' belt on the humbled Turnus, his words sound strangely similar:

> '... Pallas te hoc vulnere, Pallas
> immolat et poenam scelerato ex sanguine sumit.'

I doubt that we can say of him that he grew as his responsibilities increased but rather that he stays through it all a fallible soldier given to much the same impulses even while his destiny grows more intricate.

His violent progress through book 10 after the death of Pallas is a case in point. He kills Mago, though the latter is a *supplex* and reminds him of his father and son. Over Tarquitus, whom he also does away with in an attitude of prayer (*orantis*, 10. 554), he utters the following curse (10. 557-560):

> 'istic nunc, metuende, iace. non te optima mater
> condet humi patrioque onerabit membra sepulcro:
> alitibus linquere feris, aut gurgite mersum
> unda feret piscesque impasti vulnera lambent.'

Whatever the arrogance of Turnus as he stands over the dead Pallas his gesture is somewhat more noble (10. 492-494):

> '... qualem meruit, Pallanta remitto,
> quisquis honos tumuli, quidquid solamen humandi est,
> largior...'

And Pallas had not prayed for mercy![5] Finally, like a hundred armed, hundred handed Aegaeon, Aeneas continues his gory rampage. He meets and kills Lausus. Virgil calls him *pius* before the deed (10. 783), as Lausus tries to shelter his father, and Aeneas styles himself *pius* after it is over (10. 826). At the actual moment he deals the death blow Aeneas has this to say (10. 811-812):

> 'quo moriture ruis maioraque viribus audes?
> fallit te incautum pietas tua.'...

This is quite a strange accusation for our pious hero to hurl, as his weapon passes through a tunic which Lausus' mother had knitted for him out of soft gold. When the importance of Lausus' deed actually dawns on Aeneas (son of Anchises, as Virgil now carefully calls him), it is too late (10. 824):

> et mentem patriae subiit pietatis imago.

Lausus was an emblem of *pietas* in life, but the *imago* is also now lifeless.[6]

The death of Turnus descends from this same line of conduct. Aeneas has him at his mercy. Turnus is a *supplex* and, as he says simply, Aeneas may kill him or not. Aeneas hesitates but sees the belt of Pallas at which point he furiously utters his fateful, ultimate words and kills Turnus as the epic concludes.

We have been prepared for both Turnus' defeat and his death. To those who go against his wise judgment in book 7 Latinus warns (7. 595-597):

> 'ipsi has sacrilego pendetis sanguine poenas,
> o miseri. te, Turne, nefas, te triste manebit
> supplicium, votisque deos venerabere seris.'

The words imply humiliation and late learning, not death. Aeneas himself predicts Turnus' punishment with no specific allusion to death (8. 537-538):

> 'heu quantae miseris caedes Laurentibus instant!
> quas poenas mihi, Turne, dabis!...'

But throughout book 10 we know that he is fated to die.[7] Juno, in conference with her husband can even admit this while ironically using Aeneas' own epithet (10. 617):

> 'nunc pereat Teucrisque pio det sanguine poenas.'

It is only Evander who makes it a question of personal vendetta, reasoning that Aeneas must kill Turnus in specific revenge for the slaying of Pallas. He is talking to Aeneas who, though not present, would have heard (11. 177-179):

> 'quod vitam moror invisam Pallante perempto
> dextera causa tua est, Turnum gnatoque patrique
> quam debere vides...'

It is important, then, to ponder Aeneas' hesitation before killing Turnus. If vengeance for Pallas and indeed retribution for much other suffering had been uppermost in Aeneas' mind (and there would have been no reason for him to forget, considering the emotionality of book 10), then Virgil need not have him pause. But vengeance should not be paramount and this, one suspects, is Virgil's way of telling us. Aeneas, without killing Turnus, would actually perform for the first time Rome's prototypical heroic act as defined by his father in book 6 — *parcere subiectis et debellare superbos*. Turnus has exemplified *superbia* during his career. He has now been beaten down. (That he is fated to die means nothing. It is Aeneas' reasoning that is important.) It is the function of civilizing power to spare him. And it is false reasoning, going against the whole moral thrust of the epic, to say that Aeneas is right finally to purge his future of unsophisticated opposition. This is exactly the occasion to practice *clementia*, that spirit of refraining moderation which in this case reenergizes the downtrodden and allows the defeated to become once more a part of the state instead of exacerbating old enmities by extracting the penalty of death for opposition.[8] Aeneas is momentarily swayed by the last words of Turnus' brief speech: *ulterius ne tende odiis* (12.938). Cicero defines *odium* as *ira inveterata*.[9] It would be the most appropriate as well as most impressive time to put away hatred, private against Turnus, public against all Italic opposition.

But Aeneas is moved to act differently at the sight of the belt of Pallas which Turnus wears. Virgil is specific about this symbolism. The belt is *saevi monumenta doloris*, a remembrance of Aeneas' fierce grief at Pallas' death. A tangible object draws Aeneas (and Virgil's readers) away from any lofty sphere of abstract, universal moralizing to sudden reality. Virgil has been at pains to stress the personal feelings Aeneas holds for Pallas. His physical beauty is apparent to Aeneas even in death (he is called smooth, white as snow, and compared to a soft violet or drooping hyacinth). As they travel back from Etruria to Latium Pallas behaves in a manner surprisingly akin to Dido (10.160-162):

> ...Pallasque sinistro
> adfixus lateri iam quaerit sidera, opacae
> noctis iter, iam quae passus terraque marique.

Later Aeneas himself symbolically accepts the analogy. At the moment when he is preparing the body of Pallas for the funeral cortege, he brings out twin gold and purple garments woven by Sidonian Dido (11. 72 ff.). In one of these he wraps the corpse. We never hear again of the other. Finally, it is the first person pronoun that receives double stress as Aeneas asks his terrible concluding question (12.947-948):

> ... 'tune hinc spoliis indute meorum
> eripiare mihi? ...'

Aeneas' "grief" is of an intensely personal sort, and it elicits a violent outburst of rage as we have seen (*furiis accensus et ira / terribilis*). And by using now at the end the phrase *saevus dolor* that he had of Juno at the opening of book 1, Virgil deliberately associates Aeneas not with reason but with the irrationality that permeates the epic. At the beginning of book 5, as the Trojans look back on Dido's flaming pyre, Virgil makes this comment (5.5-7):

> ...duri magno sed amore dolores
> polluto, notamque furens quid femina possit,
> triste per augurium Teucrorum pectora ducunt.

By the end of the epic, Aeneas is no longer the aloof contemplative (or even the remote cause) of such emotion but its actual symbol. Aeneas is finally, and after all, a human being.

Rage and anger have not been among Aeneas' trademarks up to now, as they have been partially of Turnus. We remember Turnus' earlier bloodlust against the Trojans —

> sed furor ardentem caedisque insana cupido
> egit in adversos... (9. 760-761) —

or his reaction to Allecto's advent —

> saevit amor ferri et scelerata insania belli,
> ira super... (7. 461-462).

But both *furor* and *ira* now guide the hand of Aeneas. We may defend his action, if we are so inclined, by appealing to *pietas*, his duty to Evander and Pallas. He himself calls Turnus' blood *scelerato*, as if the denomination of Pallas' death in battle as a *scelus* were a vindication of the slaying of a suppliant. Aeneas is last called *pius* at line 311, moments before he appeals to the opposing forces to contain their wrath and not break the treaty (*o cohibete iras!*, 12. 314). But the final adjective Virgil allots his hero in the *Aeneid* is *fervidus*.

The belt of Pallas has a symbolic value which Virgil chooses to comment upon at the moment Turnus dons it. After telling us that it has on it a *nefas*, the slaughter of the sons of Aegyptus by the Danaids, he exclaims (10. 501-502):

> nescia mens hominum fati sortisque futurae
> et servare modum rebus sublata secundis!

The wearing of the belt is a symbol not of Turnus' savagery (this in spite of the recent death of Pallas and the scene engraved upon it) but of his lack of *moderatio*. To borrow Horace's words to Augustus, Turnus' impetuosity, his animal force (*vis*), is not tempered by wise counsel.[10] It is not unwarranted to suggest (though for obvious reasons the poet cannot do so directly) that the sight of the belt has the same effect on Aeneas, as the epic draws to a close. If so, it is not his hero's continued *pietas* to which Virgil wishes to give final emphasis but his want of *temperantia* and of the very *clementia* which his father upholds in his parting words to his son.[11]

The first detailed exposure of the future Roman ideal state comes early in the first book when Jupiter seeks to reassure Venus after the

339

near disastrous storm. It is a vision of Rome under divinized Augustus, himself a conquering hero, with wars put aside (*positis bellis*, 1. 291). Romulus and Remus together will give laws and *Furor* will be enchained. In one superficial sense it would be pleasant to affirm (as major critics still do) that the end of the *Aeneid* depicts such a vision in action. Now that Aeneas has killed Turnus, the argument runs, the vista of a peaceful future opens out. The better side has won and true civilization can at last triumph over home-grown primitivism. It is a righteous violence which Aeneas displays because, though momentarily vicious, it looks toward more sophisticated ends. By a passing act of anger Aeneas will bring an enduring peace.

The trouble is that Virgil says none of this, however much some readers may wish he did. He makes not even the slightest mention of any sense of duty or any larger, moral concerns on Aeneas' part. Granted that the deeper his connection with Pallas (call it the result of *pietas*) the harder it is to forget revenge, nevertheless the killing of Turnus does not make peace customary but war. It glorifies a tradition of irrationality, not control. Virgil presents a final vignette of his hero in a blind rage (the very emotion to which he is supposedly superior). *Furor* could now be imprisoned, but instead Aeneas is *furiis accensus*. Romulus could live with Remus, for in some ways the clash between Aeneas and Turnus is civil. Aeneas is by now *indiges*, Latinized, and he and his rival are ultimately in search of the same goal, political supremacy in Italy. But fraternal peace does not happen any more easily than the possibility of putting wars aside. Violence continues to beget violence, hatreds further hate. Larger goals are easily stated, less readily achieved.

The *Aeneid*, unlike the *Iliad* and the *Odyssey*, is neither a journey into self-knowledge nor a quest for permanence amid the unstable intensity of experience. Achilles can take life or let it alone in his search for personal value in a code of heroic action. His return to humanity leaves him still terrifyingly unique, even through the eyes of a regal old man. Odysseus can encompass the richest adventures of mortal variety while at the same time knowing and then regaining an essential stability which for him surpasses even the temptation of divinity. Virgil knew, loved and absorbed each work deeply, but his epic and its hero are grounded on different intellectual bases. The *Aeneid* is a work very much in time. We know the history for which it forms the background. We are aware of the social constructs and political institutions which emanated from its action. Aeneas is the moral archetype of a civilization. He is heroic more at first because he suffers the loss of personal involvements in life. To fulfill a grander design, the noble individual gives his glory to the state instead of bravely opposing its usually shallow immediacies. Aeneas is no Antigone, nor would Virgil have him be. The self seems submerged in a social enterprise only partially of its own making.

But Aeneas is as anomalous as the Rome he exemplifies. We might expect that the final purgation of the past which Virgil portrays so brilliantly in the beginning of the sixth book would leave Aeneas free to act out his father's lofty statutes. Palinurus, Dido, Troy (through Deiphobus) and in one sense Anchises himself look to a time when the very vagueness of the hero's search for Rome and *Romanitas* laid special stress on the emotional occasions which seemed momentarily to impede the force of destiny. But it is not so easy as Rome progresses to shut out the irrational self — to claim that Rome is sheer enlightenment without the irrationality which the Greeks had long since taught was basic to *la condition humaine*. The end of the *Aeneid* proves its impossibility.

The last century has seen a revolution in the interpretation of Virgil and especially of the *Aeneid*. If in the *Eclogues* and *Georgics* we were expected to find only "entertainment," in the *Aeneid* we were supposed, with good Victorian sentimentality, to see Virgil the propagandist, chanting an Augustan panegyric. Then we had an Aeneas who, despite an occasional lapse, was little short of a Christian saint, St. George with his dragon, Turnus — an easy step. We are now learning to look at the darker side, to acknowledge the presence not only of suffering but of evil in Aeneas as well as in his presumably more primitive, impetuous antagonists. In other words along with the idealistic Rome we have a very real one as well, in which individual emotion, far from being repressed by a tight social fabric, bursts forth all the stronger. This is not to maintain that the accomplishments of historical Rome do not elicit Virgil's sympathetic praise. They do, and grandly, but the undercurrent of hatred and violence, especially martial violence, that courses through Roman history cannot be gainsaid. At the end of the *Aeneid* it holds center stage in the character of the hero himself. History is by and large a reflection of those who participate in its making and the moulder of Roman civilization exemplifies its own inherent weaknesses.

It is important to recall that there are intimations of allegory in the *Aeneid*. Virgil himself more than once subtly suggests an equation between Aeneas and Augustus. We think of Augustus *stans celsa in puppi* during the battle of Actium and Aeneas reaching his beleaguered colleagues in book 10, likewise *celsa in puppi*, holding up the blazing shield on which this very scene is triumphantly engraved. But Virgil immediately compares Aeneas to blood-red comets and Sirius bringing thirst and diseases to sick mortals. Augustus presides over an apparently peace-bringing victory and Aeneas, by momentarily bringing disease, could be said to create a productive atmosphere for the future. Or does he, and if he, prime mover and founding father, does not, can Augustus?

The *Aeneid* treats complexly the turning of myth into history and at the same time its converse, history become myth. When Anchises addresses his son in the underworld as *Romanus*, he treats him as the Roman everyman, and the philosophy which Anchises propounds offers, as we have noted, a model moral basis for living as a Roman. Aeneas' actions must therefore offer a typical paradigm of how a Roman statesman would (*not* should) act, given his social and intellectual heritage and commitment. When Anchises says to Aeneas that he should impose a custom for peace, that he should spare the suppliant and war down the haughty, he is urging his son to put into positive operation tenets mouthed by the Greeks.[12] And Cicero can even say of Julius Caesar in the *pro Marcello* (3. 8), not without a touch of flattery: "But to conquer one's *animus*, to restrain anger, to moderate one's triumphs — not only to uplift an enemy brought low, an enemy outstanding for nobility, genius or courage, but also to enhance his inherited dignity — he who does these things I do not compare with the best men but I consider him most like a god."[13]

This is one side of the coin. The other is the martial instinct and the propensity for vengeance which runs throughout Roman history. And here Augustus sets an example. On the one hand we have the grand shrine to Apollo, god of reason, enlightenment and poetry who presides over the battle of Actium, offering an instance of Horace's *vim temperatam*. On the other we find Augustus dedicating his famous temple to Mars Ultor, should he gain revenge on his enemies at the battle of Philippi. How reconcile the two? Virgil himself had difficulties, if we can judge from his treatment of Romulus and Remus in the *Aeneid*. On the shield, the Martian wolf nourishes the twins, but it is necessarily the sons of Romulus alone who make war against the Sabines. Jupiter in book 1 can first speak of Romulus founding the walls of Mars and giving his name to his race and in the next breath announce that, with the temple of Janus closed, Romulus (Quirinus) will give laws with Remus. Anchises, however, in the catalogue of book 6, singles out Romulus alone for praise.

We may apply the analogy to the end of the *Aeneid*. Sparing the suppliant is, from one point of view, sparing Remus, and sparing Remus, as *Aeneid* 1 intimates, ends civil war and renews the reign of *ius*.[14] On the other hand there is Aeneas' more immediately emotional involvement with Evander and Pallas, an unspoken *officium* based on *pietas*. The moral thrust of the epic seems to favor the former view. Witness only Anchises' anguished cry not to two brothers this time but to a future father and son-in-law: "Do not, my children, grow accustomed in your minds to such wars; do not turn the powerful strength of your father-land against her own body."

There are two further, interconnected ironies. First, this moral stance, educative influence of the living myth of Rome, contrasts with the growing Homeric individuality of the final books and especially with the final scene, which is a reversion to more realistic living (and myth-making). Secondly, it is often said that Turnus must die for reasons of a satisfactory epic plot conclusion. What a let-down for the reader, what a compromise to Aeneas' virility were he to display *clementia* to his enemy! But, as the ending finally stands, what an acknowledgment of his hero's failure for Virgil suddenly to revert to the ethics of Homeric Greece and spin off, in epic fashion, an individualist rather than a "civilized" moulder of social peace! Does (should) the Roman mission, especially in its Augustan enterprise, as seen through brilliantly imaginative eyes, sacrifice deeper concerns for an exciting scenario? One answer outrages, the other soothes, depending on how we read Augustus. War brutalizes always. Does it ever ennoble? Does Aeneas act the part of civilizer or barbarian? In Virgil's view is there ultimately that much difference between the two sides, and is not war as corrupting of Aeneas as it apparently has been of Turnus? Is not the most en-lightened politician a composite of both dreamer and realist, but when it comes to self-preservation or self-aggrandizement do not physical instincts tend to overwhelm loftier sentiments? Is the end of the *Aeneid* ambivalent or Virgil's final, bitterest moment of melancholy?

Virgil proposes for Aeneas a passionate search for Roman identity when he is in fact an outsider — Trojan instead of *indiges*, allied with Jupiter instead of Italian Saturn, an overlord fated but foreign. Aeneas has no connection with the Roman penchant for identification with ancestors, for ordering through custom and rationalizing through law. We may grant him allegiance to Latinus' rich inheritance, to Evander's primaeval ways, to Hercules' vindictive heroism, but by the end the very legality of his action is more open to question than acceptance. The emotional and intellectual ties with Pallas, *pietas* toward Arcadia, are poor balance for procreating the *persona* of Roman vengeance.[15] The paradigm is Greek, not Roman, Homeric, not Stoic. Achilles rages at the death of Patroclus, but Pallas is no surrogate for Aeneas whose final deed smacks more of self-justification than humanism. The essential Roman dream, the habituation that makes peace practicable, the suppression of individual selfhood that makes clemency viable, is not allowed to enter Aeneas' mind.

Seen archetypally, Turnus' death is the (innocent) immolation whose bloodletting is vital to any foundation. Looked at against the background of Roman historical development, the killing of Turnus announces the end of the Roman republic, of two orders balancing each other, of two consuls, of a popular tribune with veto power over aristocratic measures.[16] Tacitus speaks of the time after the battle of Actium when *omnem potentiam ad unum conferri pacis interfuit* (*Hist.* 1. 1). What replaces liberty — and this is a chief significance of Turnus' loss — is peace, but it is a narrow peace, born of violence and founded on personal impulse and the ethics of revenge.

Frank Kermode, in a recent book on *The Sense of an Ending*, speaks of the *Aeneid* (and *Genesis*) as an end-determined fiction. Unlike Odysseus' cyclic ritual, "the progress of Aeneas from the broken city of Troy to a Rome standing for empire without end, is closer to our traditional apocalyptic, and that is why his *imperium* has been incorporated into Western apocalyptic as a type of the City of God."[17] We may see with justice the *Odyssey* as a journey, literal and symbolic, of departure and return and the *Aeneid* as an open-ended voyage of expansive intellectual and political accomplishment. But perhaps, too, the *Aeneid* in a very different way is a type of *Odyssey*, a cyclical evocation of emotion which transcends the temporal propulsion of history. It is true that Troy leads to Rome, loss to fulfillment of a sort, tragedy to a type of comedy, and there is one whole level of intent — an idealistic level of fated prophecies, divine inspirations and somniac revelations — where the mastery of a perfected Rome is acclaimed. But in the poetry of action, where deed challenges word and the poet's involvement runs most deeply, mortal means obscure and corrupt apocalyptic ends. And on this level the *Aeneid* is a cycle both revelatory and humane, leading from pain and wrath on the divine level ultimately to the same emotions reconstructed by the quasi-divinized hero. The *Aeneid* is a very Roman poem not so much because it presents a vision of *imperium* functioning with civilized, and civilizing, grandeur or because it predisposes us toward a higher Stoic morality than that which a Homeric hero might contemplate (and in so doing be said to anticipate Augustine's *City* and Dante's *Paradiso*). The cycle of Roman *Aeneid*, which begins in Troy and ends with Homer, is internal and metaphysical, a cycle of madness at its conclusion appraising the primal Roman myth of two brothers who do violence to each other and of the loss of liberty that any resulting triumph or defeat portends. Peace at times means suppression, as the greatest Latin historians warn. This cycle of rage reflects Rome's past and, as Virgil would have well known, mankind's future. Eternal, boundless Rome is mortal, after all.

In spite of the "mythical" setting of the *Aeneid*, there is a gradual hardening and toughening of Virgil's version of reality as his work progresses. In the *Eclogues* the outside world is only vaguely imagined by even the shepherds who most suffer its inroads. By manufacturing miraculous vistas of the future or dwelling on poetry *per se*, it is easy enough to escape life's more inimical pressures. In the *Georgics* Virgil faces the beauties and hardships of life with the soil, but first by metaphor and then by myth extends his ambivalent insights to the world of men. At the end we are left to ask what can reconcile the leisured poet-singer with conquering Octavian. But it is the combined tales of Aristaeus and Orpheus which both summarize and forecast the outcome of the *Aeneid*. If a bard gifted with magic sufficient to tame the underworld and evoke the dead to life cannot restrain his mortal *furor*, what of those with less gifts but more power? What in fact of those like thundering Octavian whose profession by nature could all too easily lend itself to violence? In spite of the accomplishments of the *pax Augusta*, the *Aeneid* warns of the suffering and terror in the establishment and maintenance of an empire still challengingly remote in the *Eclogues*. Through the medium of myth, movement back in time ironically brings us closer to essential matters, to prospective growth and stability but also to suffering, exile, and the final exile, death. It is this realistic appraisal of Rome and of life's ultimate ambivalence — the glory but also finally the tragedy — that at the present time continues to earn for the *Aeneid* its status as a masterpiece.

Brown University

NOTES

[1] Cf. M. C. J. Putnam *"Aeneid* VII and the *Aeneid,"* *AJP* 91 (1970), 428 ff.

[2] See, e.g., K. Quinn *Virgil's Aeneid: A Critical Description* (London, 1968), 123-124; D. R. Dudley "A Plea for Aeneas," *G & R* 8 (1961), 52-60.

[3] Cf. C. P. Segal "The Hesitation of the Golden Bough: A Reexamination," *Hermes* 96 (1968), 74-79. On the gates of dreams which end book 6 see W. V. Clausen "An Interpretation of the *Aeneid,"* *HSCP* 68 (1964), 139-147, esp. 146 f.

[4] This much debated passage (*Aen.* 2. 567-588) — preserved by Servius but not in the main manuscript tradition — has been bracketed by Mynors in the new OCT. On grounds of style and tradition (how did it reach Servius if Varius and Tucca had succeeded in deleting it at Virgil's wish?), its authenticity

is arguable. For full bibliography (supplementing arguments for retention) see R. G. Austin *P. Vergili Maronis Aeneidos, Liber Secundus* (Oxford, 1964), *ad loc.* For a detailed study against retention see G. P. Goold "Servius and the Helen Episode," *HSCP* 74 (1970), 101-168.

[5] For an opposite view see. B. Otis "The Originality of the Aeneid," in *Studies in Latin Literature and its Influence: Virgil,* ed. D. R. Dudley (London, 1969), 27-66, esp. 62 ff.

[6] Virgil gives the same words to Ascanius at 9. 294, as he ponders Euryalus' devotion to his mother in the face of death.

[7] Note Jupiter's important words about fate and heroism at 10. 467-472.

[8] We may compare the posture (both real and predictive) of Aeneas as *supplex* at *Aen.* 6. 91 and 115.

[9] Cic. *Tusc.* 4. 9. 21. See also Hor. *ep.* 1. 2. 59-63.

[10] Hor. *carm.* 3. 4. 65 ff.

[11] For Hypermnestra's saving action as an example of *clementia* see Hor. *carm.* 3. 11. 46.

[12] See E. Norden *P. Vergilius Maro Aeneis Buch VI* (ed. 4, repr. Stuttgart, 1957), 334-338; H. North *Sophrosyne* (Ithaca, 1966), 297.

[13] Cf. Horace's sentiments at *carm. saec.* 49-52.

[14] See H. Wagenvoort "The Crime of Fratricide" in *Studies in Roman Literature, Culture and Religion* (Leiden, 1956), 169-183.

[15] See J. B. Van Sickle "Studies of Dialectical Methodology in the Virgilian Tradition," *MLN* 85 (1970), 884-928, esp. 926 ff.

[16] T. Mommsen "Die Remuslegende," *Hermes* 16 (1881), 1-23 (repr. in *Gesammelte Schriften* IV [Berlin, 1906], 1-21).

[17] F. Kermode *The Sense of an Ending: Studies in the Theory of Fiction* (Oxford, 1967), 5.

SUBJECT INDEX

Meleager, 231
Meliboeus, 197-99, 243-49, 252-55, 257, 259-63
Melpomene, 143-44
Memmius, 14, 252
Menalcas, 244
Menander, 219
Menoitios, 100
Mentor, 202
Mercury, x, 99, 101, 334
Messalinus, 169, 173
Messalla, 163-64, 169-70
Messapus, 294
Mezentius, 312, 315-17, 324
Milanion, 199
Milton, 46
Minerva, *see* Athena
Minos, 100
Minotaur, 52-53
Misenus, 97, 290-91
Moschus, 249
Mozart, 27, 78
Müller, L., 30
Muses, 63, 134, 139, 212, 214
Mynors, R., 30
Myrrha, 216
Myrtale, 114, 154-55

Neaera, 97
Nemesis, 75
Neobule, 96
Nepos, 14, 31, 135
Neptune, 95-96, 98, 294, 318
Nile, 15, 170, 205, 227
Nisus, 306
Numa, 40, 42

Oaxes, 249, 254
Oceanus, 8, 100
Octavian, *see* Augustus
odium, 23, 301, 304, 307, 338
Odysseus, *see* Ulysses
Orcus, 41
Orion, 249, 291
Orpheus, 219, 294, 331-33, 345
Ortalus, *see* Hortensius
Osiris, 170
otium, 253
Ovid, 32, 163-64, 168, 174, 193, 222

Pactolus, 202, 225
Paetus, 211, 213-14, 238
Palatine, 171-72, 202
Pales, 171

Palinurus, 176-77, 291, 309, 316, 341
Pallas, 229, 306, 309, 316, 336-40, 343
Pan, 171, 252
Panthus, 322
Parcae, *see* Fates
Paris, 302
Parnassus, 144-45, 148
Parthi (Parthia), 18, 204, 213
Pasiphae, 216
Patroclus, 343
Pausanias, 100
Peleus, 8, 25, 47-48, 68-73, 75, 77-78, 89, 324
Pelion, 8, 26, 68, 71
Penates, 196, 267, 270
Peneios, 25-26
Penelope, 174, 213-14
Pentheus, 231
Perret, J., 244
Persephone, 226, 230
Perseus, 227
Persius, 33
Perusia, 183-86, 188-89, 191, 195, 206-207
Pfeiffer, R., 36, 86
Phaeacia, 173, 268
Phaedrus, 250
Phaethon, 26
Philomela, 63
Phineus, 280
Pholoe, 128-32, 153-55
Phrasidamus, 248
Phrygia, 50, 73, 104
Phyllis, 97
Picus, 294-95
pietas, 25, 54, 66-67, 75-77, 216, 228-29, 231, 233, 235, 312-22, 324-25, 333, 335-36, 339, 343
Pindar, 22, 136-37, 144, 147, 149, 221
Plancus, 128
Plato, 219, 250
Plautus, 35-36, 43, 130
Pliny the Elder, 40
Pliny the Younger, 33-34
Poe, 78
Polites, 319
Pollio, 141
Pollux, 3, 10, 100, 230
Polydorus, 268-69, 271-73, 277-78, 280
Polyhymnia, 149
Polyphemus, 267-68, 277, 280
Polyxena, 27, 74-75
Pompey, 16, 277
Pontanus, 30

351

INDEX OF PASSAGES CITED

Library of Congress Cataloging in Publication Data

Putnam, Michael C.J.
  Essays on Latin lyric, elegy, and epic.

  (Princeton series of collected essays)
  "Essays . . . originally published in various scholarly journals
during the past two decades"—Pref.
  Bibliography: p.
  Includes index.
  1. Latin poetry—History and criticism—Collected works. I. Title.
PA6047.P8   871'.01'09   81-47944
ISBN 0-691-06497-0   AACR2
ISBN 0-691-01388-8 (pbk.)

Michael C.J. Putnam is Professor of Classics
at Brown University.